EDUCATION
OF A NATIVE SON

H. RICHARD DOZIER

Copyright © 2021 by H. Richard Dozier.

All rights reserved. No part of this publication may be reproduced, distributed, or transmitted in any form or by any means, including photocopying, recording, or other electronic or mechanical methods, without the prior written permission of the author, except in the case of brief quotations embodied in critical reviews and certain other noncommercial uses permitted by copyright law.

Printed in the United States of America.

Library of Congress Control Number: 2021906845

ISBN		
	Paperback	978-1-64803-610-1
	Hardback	978-1-64803-611-8
	eBook	978-1-64803-682-8

Westwood Books Publishing LLC
11416 SW Aventino Drive
Port Saint Lucie, FL 34987

www.westwoodbookspublishing.com

I dedicate this book to my children whom God has richly blessed:

Brooke Imani, Love Gnyra H. Richard II and
Twins: Armani &Jarmani Dozier

CONTENTS

Foreword ix

BOOK ONE

Chapter 1:   Old Beginnings, New Start .1
Chapter 2:   Monday Morning 13
Chapter 3:   All About Love 36
Chapter 4:   Best Made Plans 50
Chapter 5:   Family Ties 58
Chapter 6:   A Tale of Two Friendships 68
Chapter 7:   Dazes Gone By 79
Chapter 8:   New Lease On Life 83
Chapter 9:   Sunday Morning 95
Chapter 10: Take Me Back, Where I First Believed 102

BOOK TWO

Chapter 1:   The Awakening 121
Chapter 2:   Brothers Forever 133
Chapter 3:   Old Golden Rule Dazes 140
Chapter 4:   Campus Life 164
Chapter 5:   Class Is On 184

BOOK THREE

Chapter 1: Past Lives............................201
Chapter 2: Family Reunion........................210
Chapter 3: Final Curtain.........................225
Chapter 4: Rebirth...............................236
Chapter 5: Escape................................248
Chapter 6: Moving Along..........................257

BOOK FOUR

Chapter 1: Flying High...........................273
Chapter 2: Home by the Sea.......................295
Chapter 3: Too Little Too Late...................320
Chapter 4: Affairs of the Heart..................334
Chapter 5: Shipyard Shipwreck Love Affair........359
Chapter 6: Redeemed..............................369
Chapter 7: Jubilation............................387

BOOK FIVE

Chapter 1: Old Ship of Zion......................391
Chapter 2: Painful Memories......................403
Chapter 3: Healing Pain..........................406
Chapter 4: Time..................................438
Chapter 5: Innocents.............................446
Chapter 6: Return to Innocence...................453
Chapter 7: Innocent Love Revealed................462

BOOK SIX

Chapter 1: Final Days 471
Chapter 2: Redeemed 488
Chapter 3: Reunion 491
Chapter 4: Triumphant Glory 502

About the Author 527

FOREWORD

Out of the night which covers me,
Black as the Pit from pole to pole,
I thank whatever gods may be
For my unconquerable soul.

In the fell clutch of circumstance
I have not winced nor cried aloud.
Under the bludgeonings of chance
My head is bloody, but unbowed.

Beyond this place of wrath and tears
Looms but the horror of the shade.
And yet the menace of the years
Finds, and shall find, me unafraid.

It matters not how strait the gate.
How charged with
punishment the scroll.
I am the master of my fate;
I am the captain of my soul.
"Invictus" By William Ernest Henley

"Invictus" is an examination of self. Self, as defined by Webster, is "the entire person of an individual, an individual's temporary behavior or character, a person in prime condition (feel like my true ~ was revealed." Self—self-absorbed, self-appointed, self-asserting, self-contained, self-defense, self-discovery, self-denial, self-devoted, self-expression, self-made, and self-love are a few of the selves that make up one's personality. It is a complex set of characteristics that has often been under-appreciated and overexaggerated. It is filled with emotions and experiences of the past and present with preconceived notions of the future. Self—the inner spirit or voice that calls out to us. In the African tradition, it is the ancestral spirit. In other cultures, it is referred to as the guiding angel, a departed loved one, or just the conscious mind that captures one's attention. Self! It is the legacy that is set before you. It is what is to come. It is oneself!

Have you ever found yourself wandering and you did not know why? This is the self that takes you to the edge of your conscious mind. You regain control and ask yourself, "Why am I here? How did I get here? Why does it feel like I've been here before? It is all so clear, yet it is strange to me. Self—that little voice that calls out to you as the "voice of reasoning."

Author H. Richard Dozier's book, *Education of A Native Son*, is also an examination of self. Dozier examines the many facets of self as he recounts the life of Thomas Isaiah Thomas better known as "Little."

Little, the oldest of three children, is born to Ruth Mears Thomas. Ruth is a family lady, very spiritual, and determined to survive. She is married to Elijah Thomas who moved to New York to escape the horrors of Jim Crow in the south. Elisha and Esther, the younger siblings, are carefree and children at heart. They are playful, happy, and loving children who adorn their brother, Little. His family is an average American family living in the predominant Black community in the heart of New York. It is a community in which everybody knows everyone, and everyone knows everybody. It is a close-knit community where the extended family consists of the neighbor down the hall and the friend across the street. It is a community of love, extended uncles, aunts, brothers, and sisters. It is a community that cares about one another and views life in a pluralistic form. As a young high school student, Little experienced the bond of family and community involvement. He had the love and respect of his extended family as well as from his immediate family.

It was his extended family that assisted in his upbringing—knowing that they expected great things of him. For them, Little was their hopes, dreams, and aspirations for a better tomorrow. Little was the next generation to forge change in a racist society. For them, Little carried the fate of the entire Black race on his shoulders. For them, their future depended on Little's success. Success included obtaining a good education and making a difference in his community and the world. As a family unit they were there for Little and his family. They even shared meals, small conversation, and wittiness. But, ultimately, they invested their love, time, money, energy, and their respect into Little's future. But would Little be prepared or even willing to forge forward with the task set before him?

Education of A Native Son traces his lineage step-by-step from childhood to adulthood and all the many experiences along the way. But Little has a checkered past—a past that calls out to him in the middle of the night in the form of a dream. It also comes to him when he is faced with stressful situations such as racist comments. Is that his voice of reasoning or a voice from the grave? To Little, the pitch and the tone of the voice sound very familiar. Yet, Little does not recognize it. Is it just a nightmare?

Thomas Isaiah Thomas is an athletically built, tall, and thin-framed teenager. He is attractive and a talented basketball player. He is kind, gentle, and patient, and loves his family. He is devoted to his best friend, Swoosh. He is the kind of guy who would be there in your time of need. He is so diverse in his abilities that he has many career opportunities awaiting his decision upon graduation from high school. Doctor, lawyer, basketball player, coach, scientist, businessman, or teacher is among his choices. But, as talented as Little is, his temperament is sometimes irrational, and he often reacts on impulse. However, Little is a Rhode Scholar—the top student in his class among black and white students in a predominantly white high school. Unfortunately, he is constantly forced to deal with racism and racist attitudes. He is confronted with this in high school, in college at the University of New England, and even on the job.

Education of A Native Son is the author's answer to Richard Wright's classic book *Native Son*. In Wright's book, the main character, Bigger, is resurrected in this book of twisted tales and circumstances through the life of Little. Like many high school seniors who are preparing to graduate, Little becomes mentally frustrated with his uncertain future. What will he do?

Education of A Native Son is a book of emotions, self-examination, determination and the triumph of good over evil. It is reflective, funny, intense, intriguing, sad, loving, and dramatic. It is about strengths and weaknesses and love for family. It triumphs challenges and conflicts. It is about people dealing with one another. It is about being young and winning the respect of colleagues, friends, and co-workers. It's about college life and the vast difference of living on a predominantly white campus versus a predominantly black campus. It's about friendships and relationships. It's about the past and about the future. It's about pain, conflict, pride, legacy, and history. It's about *self*!

H. Richard Dozier who is a graduate of Hampton Institute (known as Hampton University today) is a native New Englander and presently resides under the topical skies of West Palm Beach, Florida—his father's hometown. He is a soft-spoken man who has given great sensitivity to the character of Little and his book *Education of A Native Son*. The trails, trials, and tribulations are very realistic. In many respects, *Education of A Native Son* is a reflection of all African Americans living during turbulent times of Jim Crow, the Civil Rights Movement, and desegregation. Each chapter is full of suspense about human life and the determination to succeed.

Eric Key
Director of Art Programs
University of Maryland Global Campus
College Park, MD
hricharddozier.com

BOOK ONE

OLD BEGINNINGS, NEW START

The sound of his feet pounding the pavement was muffled by the snow and ice covering the cold cement sidewalk and the sound of his beating heart. Exhaling, a burst of hot air spewed from between his thick, black, chapped lips and collided with the frigid night air creating streams of frost across his wind-whipped face. *Run. Got to keep running; got to get away this time. They're closing in on you—go up, go up. Climb up to the top, go to the top. Got to get away! Run faster! Run, run.*

Thump, thump, thump. With every passing second, the sound grew louder within him. The faster he ran, the faster and louder the thumping. Freezing, tired and scared, he could no longer move. "I can't run any further. Can't go anymore. I just can't." Grabbing his head, he shouted, "Stop that thumping, I can't stand it. Please, please. Please stop thumping." The more it thumped, the more his chest throbbed in pain.

Sobbing, he fell to his knees, slumping over gasping for air. In, out, in, out. Each breath mixing with the bitter, cold February night air creating a vapor of ice crystals. Streams of hot air gushing out of his mouth, he could see his breath. He was physically and audibly conscious of his heart pounding vigorously in his chest. With the drawing of each breath, his chest heaved uncontrollably with agonizing pain. No sooner had he pushed his hot breath out, he found himself sucking hard to breathe air in. Sucking wind-in, pushing air out. In, out. *Breathe in, breath out. Breathe in, breath out.* Instinctively, he put his frostbitten fingers to his mouth to free them from the ice with the forced hot air from his inner body.

The brutally raw winds continued to blow savagely through his black, waist-length, torn leather jacket. The dark blue wool scarf, which once hung around his neck, was lost several blocks back along with the feeling in his legs, arms, fingers, and toes. His teeth chattered as his body shivered violently.

The miserably cold and hostile night offer no consolation. Sidewalks, ice, and slush covered piles of snow laid like giant mountains against the unseen curbs. Exhausted, he threw his head back as his eyes frantically searched the dark winter moonlit sky. Alone, he felt the fear and emptiness.

He knew he was desperately fleeing. But from whom? What? Why? The shadowy figures chasing him, taunting him, tracking him, as if he were a wild rabid animal. The intense hatred of those in pursuit of him filled the night air. Every part of his being felt it, yet he could not escape their presence.

Now, he could hear them coming. They were not too far away. Looking up, he did not recognize the surroundings. This place was totally unfamiliar to him. He knew it was not his neighborhood. Many of the flats were boarded up and others were sparsely occupied. Some buildings were close together, while others had small alleys separating them. This was not the Harlem he knew. He did not know how long he had been running, nor how far. In unfamiliar terrain, his heart pounded harder as he continued to gasp for air. Inhale, exhale. Inhale, exhale.

Got to get away. There, go down the alley, the voice said. *You can hide in there.*

Running down the alley to the end, a ten-foot fence stood between him, the next block and capture. *There, see the door? Go in. Go in, hurry before they catch you.*

Pushing his weight against the old, weather-worn, rotting door of the tenement building, he stumbled inside as the door gave away. Quickly, he glanced down the alley, checking to see if his tormentors were still in pursuit of him. Inside the dark and cold hallway, he could feel the littered cans, bottles, and old newspapers beneath his feet. He heard rats scurrying to get out of the way of the intruder. *Go up, go up.* He climbed the stairs to the third floor and pushed open the first door he came to. Inside, it offered him no rescue from his torment or tormentors. A whirl of thoughts and feelings engulfed his mind. Something unfamiliar, a cold chill, colder than the air of the dark room blended with something warm and sticky. Blood. Whose blood? Not his. He wanted desperately to free himself of the blood. Warm blood crept and grew powerful with each passing moment. In the darkness his eyes fell upon a brick. As his fingers touched the brick, something within him screamed out in silent agony. The deep howling of the night winds beckoned him. Terror struck! He rushed back into the hallway to rid himself of the lurking shadowy feeling. Back into the hallway, he found the door to the flat facing the street on the opposite side of the building. Cautiously, summoned by a weak light coming from the window he entered. Warily, he moved in its direction. Cautiously, he peered out the window. From the glow of the lone streetlamp casting its light, the street appeared warm and safe. Momentarily transfixed by the illusion before him, he bathed in the warmth and safety of the serene and delicate offerings of the lamp.

So sweet. So sweet is the warmth.

Suddenly shattering his tranquility, the sound of horns, sirens, and screams split the silence. There was hunger in those invading sounds. Under the sound was a low and distinct tone. He heard voices, angry voices and the curses of men and cries of women. A sheet of fear blanketed him, thoughts flashed through his mind, leaving him weak and helpless. Immediately he heard another voice, different this time. An anxious, apprehensive, low, and tense voice. The voice was coming from somewhere down below.

"They're coming!"

Quick, get out of here. Go up; go up to the roof. You can hide there until they pass.

Stumbling through the dark apartment, he found himself in the hallway climbing the stairs to the roof.

The trapdoor, see it? There, the trapdoor; open it. Get out. Hide on the roof.

Pushing against it with his head, it opens. Reaching above, he feels the cold wet snow. Praying it would hold him he hoists himself upward. He could hear the sirens splitting the night silence as he closed the door behind him.

Ha-ha-ha-ha-ha. So, what, what now? Ha-ha-ha-ha-ha." Laughter, there were voices laughing at him.

"No, no, no." He could no longer hide from it; his action to escape was futile. Soon, the men with guns would come and penetrate his world. His world, where sirens, voices, cries and fear now penetrated.

"I got to get away. Where? I got to hide." His eyes frantically searched the rooftop for something; anything that would give him a clue for his next move. His fear-filled eyes fell upon the crumbling, lifeless chimney. Silently, he made a path through the deep snow toward his point of refuge. "I'll hide in it. That's what I'll do. I'll climb into it and hide until they go away."

A voice from the street shouted, "There he is. There, on the roof by the chimney."

Suddenly, the sound of a furious whisper of water, streaming like silver in the bright lights, passing him high in the air streaked above his head with a ferocious force. *Whoosh.* Like the blow of a pile driver, the water hit him in the side. His breath left him as he felt the dull pain engulfing him and quickly spreading through his body. Instinctively, he gripped the brick harder. He felt cold and his strength ebbing. With the water pounding his body and the throbbing pain, he could not hold on much longer. It seemed as if his blood crystallized like the stream of steamed air from his nostrils. The icy water, like a giant hand, clutched his body. The chill squeezed him like a circling coil of a massive boa constrictor. His arms ached. Too weak and too cold to hold on, he felt his body sliding over the edge. Down, down, down, he slid toward the edge of the building.

"Why? What did I do? Why do you want to kill me? I didn't do anything," he cried aloud, as his body continued its downward spiraling fall. All the muscles in his body contracted violently. He was caught in a spasm of reflex action. Simultaneously, as he descended through the icy cold bizarre night air, he felt his groin flushing with warmth.

Suddenly, his body stiffened as though a steel pipe was thrust through his spine. The fall ended. "It's all right, it's alright. Don't worry, it will be alright," he heard the angelic voice speaking softly into his ear. His body went limp. Someone was holding him, rocking him. Together they rocked, back and forth.

"I have you now. Everything's going to be all right."

He was safe in the arms of an angel. Together, swaying back and forth in a rocking motion, he laid cradled in the arms of his guardian angel. It was over. Slowly, he opened his tear-filled eyes. Desperately needing something, something to hold onto, something telling him if this was real or not. His eyes steadily groped around the wall. There on the wall his eyes found something. On the wall beside the bed upon which he lay, his eyes found something familiar telling him this was not a dream. Fixing his stare, his eyes began to focus on something familiar; it was a face. It was a face in a poster on the wall of his bedroom. The bedroom he shared with his eight-year-old brother, Elisha. The familiar face in the poster on the wall was of a major league baseball player. A Negro major league baseball player, Willie Mays of the New York Giants. It was something familiar to hold on to assuring him that this was reality. Everything else was the dream.

Seeing the poster gave him a secure feeling, arousing in him a pleasant memory. It was a welcomed distraction from the horror he had experienced during the nights. He recalled the day his father took him and Elisha to see Willie Mays play in Polo Stadium. It was a much, much welcomed memory.

His body continued rocking, back and forth. Instinctively, he knew the poster next to Willie Mays was of Jackie Robinson. Jackie Robinson, the first Negro to play baseball in the Major League. He played for the Brooklyn Dodgers. His mother had given them the posters, he and Elisha. She said she wanted them to know their heritage, and to be proud of their race and the accomplishments of colored people.

He realized it was his mother. It was his mother all along holding him, rocking him. Back and forth, back and forth, they rocked together. Wrapping his arms around her body, he held on to her tightly, not wanting to let go. Not wanting to let go of reality, he held on to her tightly. Locked together, they rocked back and forth.

"I am so sorry, so sorry," she cried in an emotionally charged voice, as they rocked.

He let out a slow, dull, agonizing moan. Tears in a steady deluge cascaded down his cheeks falling upon her dress. He tried to speak.

She pressed her index finger against his quivering lips. "Shhhh, shhhh, be quiet," she gingerly said, while laying him back down upon the bed. "You're safe now." Gently, she brushed his left cheek with the backside of her fingers of her half-curled hand.

He looked at the cinnamon brown-colored woman. Part of her hair was pinned back into a partially completed French roll. The other side hung below her breast partially shielding her face from his view. To see her face, slowly he raised his throbbing head off his tear-soaked pillow, which was soaked from head to toe as if someone emptied a bucket of water on him while he slept. His pillow, sheets, blanket, and mattress were dripping wet with a mixture of his sweat, tears, and urine.

For him, she was angelic. Her eyes, a soft greenish-brown, were encased in an almond shape and accented with naturally long black lashes and pencil-thin eyebrows. Her lips, soft and gentle, were a true vision of loveliness. Her face and clothes were wet.

Weak and faint, he uttered, "Momma." Holding his aching head, he tried covering his face to hide his shame. Painfully, he tried to lift his six-foot, four-inch body off the sweat-drenched, urine-soaked mattress.

"Don't move baby. Lie still."

This is real, I'm not dreaming, he concluded as he held his throbbing head while struggling to move. With great effort, slowly he spoke above a faint whisper. "I need to get up, get out of the bed. I need to get dressed, school, work. Momma, you can't be late to work this morning. I need to help you with Elisha and Esther so you're not late."

"You're sick. Sick with fever and soaking wet," she said, while gently wiping his forehead and cheeks with her blouse. Little continued struggling to lift himself off the bed. After a brief struggle, he succumbed to the bed, defeated. His mother's hand, touching him, made him feel alive and revived. Her touch was the assurance he needed to help him out of this troubled time and back into reality. Her caress ministered life to his anguished body and soul. Her mere touch sprung forth a quiet calmness that encircled his entire essence.

"Your bed and covers are dripping wet," she said sitting next to him. Hesitantly, she read the shame and embarrassment on his face. She refused to make any more verbal observations. Knowing his pain, she could feel her own emotions attempting to overtake her. In her, as she very well understood, there was a time bomb. A time bomb prepared to explode at any given moment. With all her strength, she fought back the river of tears. Her lachrymal glands threatened to burst forth. She spoke in a subdued voice. "Don't worry about school. Just wash up and change your pajamas. I'll get some clean linen and blankets for your bed."

"What about Elisha and Esther," he weakly murmured?

"Don't worry about them. I'll get your Aunt Betty to take them to school." Gently, she lifted him into her arms. Embracing him, she pressed him tight against her bosom, then kissed the top of his head. Soaked, he was unaware of her steady stream of tears mixing with his sweat.

"I want you to wash up while I'm still here, so I know you're alright." Wiping the tears and sweat from her face, she swiftly moved out of the bedroom. Closing the door behind her, she collapsed upon the wall beside the door. Looking into the kitchen, her glance fell upon the calendar hanging on the wall. Pain, pain made exclusively by the blade of a double-edge sword swiftly pierced her heart. "Friday, March 3." The barricade could no longer hold, bursting forth streamed a river of cascading tears. Her tears savagely and uncontrollably flowed down her cheeks meeting at the base of her oval shaped chin. Tears from each eye joined together to become one drop at the clef of her chin. It fell upon her already sweat, tear-stained, white blouse. Her shame, not his; it was hers and hers alone. She knew it was her shame that daunted him. It was a voice from her past. Clasping her hands on her womb, Ruth Mears Thomas pressed in as if to push out the secrecy that brought the pain.

Looking up, to the hills from which cometh her strength, silently in her pain she called upon God. Marshaling strength, she thrusted aside her feelings of guilt. Quickly, she wiped the tears from her face. In a semi-faltering strong voice, she called out to her younger son. "Elisha. Elisha, after you and Esther finish eating breakfast, I want you and your sister to go to your Aunt Betty's. She'll take you to school."

"What about Little," a small soprano voice ranged out? "Why ain't he taking us to school? Is Little going to school? I heard him crying, while I was trying to sleep last night. He kept waking me up with all his yelling. I know he had a nightmare. I told him he shouldn't be watching those scary movies."

"Little is not feeling good. He has a fever. He won't be going to school today."

Elisha protested, "Why does he always get to stay home? You don't let me stay home when I have nightmares from scary movies. You always tell me I had no business watching scary movies."

"Elisha, hush, boy, and do what I told you!"

"Yes Momma."

Little laid back down for a few minutes. His eyes traveled around the room continuing to search out familiar surroundings. Glancing across the room, he saw Elisha's bed. As usual, it was unmade. Normally, his mother would send him in to make up the bed before he left for school, but not this morning. Between the beds was a five-foot-high chest of drawers with six drawers—his chest of drawers where he neatly kept his clothes in a well-organized fashion. He kept underwear in the top drawer, socks in the second, shirts in the third drawer, pajamas in the fourth, and pants in the last two. On top of the chest of drawers is where he kept his autographed baseball from Willie Mays. He actually caught the ball. It was a home run. Willie Mays signed it.

Also, atop of the chest of drawers was an eight-and-a-half by eleven framed picture of he and Elisha; taken last Easter when he was sixteen and Elisha was six. The older, Little, had smooth dark skin, an oval-shaped face and large nostril nose, soft jet-black low-cut hair, and sparkling deep black eyes. His long eyelashes were like his mother's. An emerging mustache could barely be seen above his full, thick, dark lips. His teeth, large, bold, pearly white, he had a robust smile with deep dimples on each side that would light up the darkest of nights.

Similarities and contrasts were found in the youthful face of his young brother and himself. The jolly face of his fair skin was spotted with brown freckles across the bridge of his semi-keen nose. Topping his head was sandy brown, semi-tight, curled, fluffy hair highlighting his almond-shaped, cow-brown eyes. A wide smile stretching thinner his small lips, accentuated the permanent dimples on each round cheek. He recalled that their mother took them to a professional studio for the picture. The family picture with Momma, Pop, Little, Elisha and Esther hung on the wall in their living room.

Most importantly, attached to the picture were five small black and white photos. Discerning reality from the dream, the snapshots brought back a significant memory that evaded him. It was taken a few days before Christmas; he and Elisha went downtown Manhattan shopping.

He was extra careful, tightly holding Elisha's hand while moving among the busy crowded streets and stores filled with Christmas shoppers. Protecting his little brother, the proud big brother marched onward. In W. T. Grants, they sat at the lunch counter, ate hamburgers and French fries and drank Cokes. In Woolworth's there was a photo booth. Little read the directions to Elisha. They went in being careful to close the curtain behind them. Little adjusted the round seat. Elisha stood next to him. Elisha put the quarter in the machine and together they pushed the start button. "Smile!" Little shouted. Elisha laughed. Poof. A flash of light, one shot. Elisha put his fingers in his ears and stuck out his tongue. Poof. Again, there was another flash of light. A second shot. They changed poses. Little hugged Elisha. Poof. A flash. Third shot, Elisha hugged Little. Poof. Fourth shot. Once again changing positions, this time they hugged each other. Poof, the final flash of light and the last snapshot was taken. The machine began making winding, grinding, and whirling noises.

A very anxious Elisha, impatiently waiting for the machine to produce the pictures. "When will it be ready? Is it ready yet?" he enthusiastically quizzed his big brother.

"The machine said in about two minutes," Little replied.

"Has it been two minutes yet?"

"Not yet." To Little, it seemed like every ten seconds Elisha would ask the same question.

Bouncing around impatiently Elijah asked, "How much longer do we gotta wait?"

"About a minute and a half." At last, together they watched the pictures slowly come out of the machine and drop safely into the slot.

"Can I get them? Can I get them?"

"Okay, I'll let you get them. Pick them up by the edge. The pictures aren't dry."

Meticulously, Elisha removed the picture from the slot where they had fallen. Little instructed him to blow on them to help them dry. Elisha gently blew his breath upon the five small snapshots. Looking at the pictures, they began laughing. It was a memorable moment for both big and little brother.

The closet next to Elisha's bed was small. His good clothes, his Sunday, going-to-church clothes hung in the closet. His two suits, one black, one white, and Elisha's gray suit hung there. Now, it was all very familiar to him. Aware of where he was and who he was, he was no longer eluding his would-be captors.

Before trying to get up, Little waited for his mother to leave the room. Initially sitting up, he was dizzy. Steadying himself, he slid his size twelve feet into his slippers alongside his bed. "Ah," he sighed, as his foot slid in the slippers. The slippers were his first connection with something other than the bed, where he had laid and lost his dignity and reality. As he stood up the chest of drawers came to his aid keeping him from toppling over. He leaned against it for a few minutes. Sunlight fell into the window behind the chest of drawers. Picking up the framed picture, he smiled and weakly laughed. Wobbling, with strength coming from his customary surroundings, he took his first step. Using the wall as a crutch, he made his way out of the bedroom and down the hallway into the bathroom. Slowly, he undressed out of the wet pajamas. Wavering before climbing into the bathtub, he was uncertain about getting in. Water, streaming water; his last encounter with water was in the dream. In his dream it was cold, freezing water. The shower was steaming with hot—not cold—water. Stepping into the path of the shower, the warmth of the water felt good flowing vigorously across his body. "Gotta cleanse myself of the stickiness," he uttered.

Concerned, yet in fear and shame, Ruth secretly watched from behind the door as Little made his way to the bathroom. The sound of the shower turning on was her signal to come out of her hiding place. Scurrying around the kitchen, she cooked breakfast.

Hearing the shower stop, she shouted, "Little, I made you some eggs, grits, toast, and I poured you a glass of milk. I'll put it on the table for you. I hope you're hungry. I needed to change my clothes. I don't have time to change your linen. Besides, your mattress is soaked…" As she spoke, they both entered the kitchen. Their eyes met. Shamefully, he lowered his head. Stopping herself before finishing her sentence, she desperately wanted to spare him more pain. Aware that continuing would have caused him more pain, more shame and guilt, the shame and guilt that rightly belonged to her, not him, she looked away.

"I meant, you would probably feel much better lying down in your daddy's and my bed. After you finish breakfast, lie down in my bed. I'll stop in to check on you before I leave for work." Returning to the room while Little ate, she quietly finished dressing.

Little was hungry and was glad that she made him breakfast. The thought of being in his parent's bed was a warm, comforting feeling.

Many nights he longed to jump in the bed with them like Elisha and Esther. But he knew, at seventeen, sleeping with your parents was definitely not cool. After eating, Little wasted no time getting into the big soft, comfortable warm bed of his mother and father. Belly full, feeling warm, safe and tired, he wasted no time falling fast asleep.

MONDAY MORNING

The brisk cold March weather had no effect on Little as he slowly made his way down the street to school. His mind was still preoccupied with the events of the past few weeks. For some strange reason, unbeknownst to him, the same time of year, late January through early March, haunted him. Every year, for as far back as he could remember he was tormented at this time of year with the same thoughts, feelings, and dream. He felt a heavy black cloud overshadowing his being. This year, the cloud shrouding him was extremely dark and ominous. It was hulking, hideous, and lurking over him more so than in the years before. Somehow, he knew this diabolical cloud was coveting more than his life. During this five-week period of darkness, time dragged. Each second seemed like minutes, minutes seemed like hours, hours seemed like days, and each day seemed like weeks—weeks of eternity. By now, he was well-acquainted with the various stages. First, he felt as if he was thrown into a situation of which he was not prepared. Gradually, he began feeling fear and emptiness pervading him. A hysterical terror would seize him. He knew he was desperately fleeing. But, from what? Who and why? Even the night offered him no rescue from his daily torment. When he slept, he would toss restlessly groaning, entangled in a whirlwind of thoughts and feelings—not his own. The final night episode resembled that of a prison inmate, awaiting execution, impregnated with anguish and ambivalence. The night ended with a quiet calmness gripping his entire essence. Then, like always, the evening of March 3, without rhyme or reason, as abruptly as the darkness of the cloud overshadowed him, the cloud was no more.

Preoccupied, he could barely read the pass his homeroom teacher gave him. Taking his seat, he vaguely recalled arriving at school.

Report to: Guidance Counselor
Mrs. McGinnis, Room 12 East House
Date: March 6
Time: 11: 15 AM

It was traditional at this time of year in preparation of graduation that all high school seniors report to their guidance counselor. "Eleven fifteen, well at least this gets me out of gym class," he whispered to the student sitting next to him. "Coach Lemael ain't gonna like me missing his class. Bad enough he's mad at me for quitting the team." At eleven o'clock, Little traveled the long wide hallways to descend the stairs to the gym.

Reluctantly, Little called out to the white male standing in the room. The man, standing five feet eleven inches tall, appeared to be in his late forties, and showed early thinning signs of male pattern baldness in his sandy brown hair, wearing the traditional gym teacher's outfit.

"Coach Lemael." The man turned to face Little. His white, short-sleeved sports shirt had Physical Education Instructor STAFF written on the left side of the chest. The matching blue pants had a white stripe down the legs. He wore top-of-the-line white all leather Converse All Stars. Only the coolest of dudes in school wore Converse. Now, if you were really bad on the basketball court, you had Converse All Stars. For his seventeenth birthday, he remembered his parents got him a pair of canvas top blue Converse All Stars. Other than that, guys like him normally wore U.S. Keds sneakers. Next best sneakers were Pro Keds. The poorer kids wore PF Flyers. But, Coach Lemael had all-leather Converse All Stars. Nobody else had all-leather Converse All

Stars. Around his neck hung an official referee's whistle; he was always holding a basketball and a clipboard.

"What do you want, Thomas," he said in a genuine and friendly voice, while placing his hand on Little's shoulder. Little noticed when guys were taller than Coach Lemael, he would place his hand on their shoulder. When he talked with the shorter or female students in class, as an act of dominance and authority, Coach Lemael would put his hands on his hips or clasp his wrist behind his back and look down at them. It was Coach Lemael's way of letting you know that he was in charge. Whatever the method, it was effective with all of the students, especially with the guys and members of the basketball team.

Everyone loved, respected, and admired Coach Lemael. For many of the guys, he was more than just a coach, teacher, and role model. One thing, you didn't want to do was disappoint Coach Lemael. You'd rather have your mother slap your head in the principal's office or embarrass you in front of the class than to have Coach Lemael give you the "old son you've really disappointed me this time" speech. And for god sakes, don't get your girlfriend knocked up. It would be easier confronting her mom or dad and your parents. The fear, shame, disappointment, and pain you felt telling your parents was nothing compared to what you were going to feel after Coach Lemael found out. With Coach Lemael, there was a relationship, a special bond; he had the magic. He knew it and used it for your benefit. Most of all, he cared. Outside of his mother and father, Coach Lemael was the only other adult he considered talking to about his nightmares.

"Ah, I have a pass to see my guidance counselor at eleven fifteen."

"Thomas, let's see. Wait a minute, wait, wait, wait. Hold on one minute. First, with all your height and talent, you quit my team, then, you cut my class on Friday, and now you want to miss my class again today! Twice in a row. Thomas, you got nerves! I don't know," he replied, applying a little more pressure on Little's shoulder. "Where were you Friday?"

"I didn't cut your class Coach. I was really out of it. I had some kind of flu bug. My mom told me to stay home. Honest!"

"If I call your parents will they say you were home?" he asked tilting his head to one side at a slight downward angle. "You know I'll call them in a New York minute, Mr. Thomas. Me and your parents are like this." Coach crossed his second and third fingers. "You got some great parents, and you're a good kid Thomas. I don't want to see no hanky-panky going on, or you getting into trouble. You got a lot going on for yourself. I'd hate to see you throw it all away over something stupid.

"Oh no Coach, you know me better than that."

Coach Lemael gave Little a big smile. "Go see your counselor, but I want you dressed for class tomorrow."

"You got it Coach."

His counselor's, Mrs. McGinnis, office was located on the first floor by the main office. Two other counselors shared the common waiting area. Her door was closed. A white female student, Melissa Weinstein, entered the waiting area. She was one of the students he was paid to tutor in Algebra in the after-school enrichment program. "Hello, Melissa. How was the Algebra test?"

"It wasn't too bad. I'm sure I passed," she replied in an off-handed manner. "Are you waiting for Miss McGinnis?"

"Yeah, my appointment was scheduled for eleven fifteen; she's not in her office. What about you?" Before Melissa could reply, a short, hunched-over, white-haired, white woman of around seventy years of age—at least, to him, she looked seventy—stepped into the room. Her black sweater was draped over her shoulders. Her glasses, on a beaded chain hung around her neck, resting on her small sagging chest.

"Melissa dear," she exclaimed, "What a pleasant surprise. Are you here to see me?"

"Yes, but I don't have an appointment. I thought I could just drop in to see you for a minute."

"Sure dear, come in."

"Excuse me," Little interrupted. "Miss McGinnis, I have an appointment with you at eleven fifteen."

"I'll only be a few minutes with Miss Weinstein. Just have a seat out here in the waiting room, young man," she retorted as she ushered Melissa into her office, closing the door behind them. Little, feeling dejected, sat down in the small waiting area, looking at the fading green paint on the walls. The walls were beginning to turn yellow in spots and peeling in other places. College posters barely remained hanging by the masking tape. Old pieces of dried, yellowed scotch tape clung to the walls in some places, and there were patches indicating where other posters previously hung. Spots where tape had been removed, carrying away swatches of paint with it, dotted the walls. Little began looking at the posters. New York University, State University of New York Binghamton, Rochester Institute of Technology, Massachusetts Institute of Technology, the University of New England. On an old rickety bookcase were several college catalogs, brochures and other college related literature. He proceeded to pick up a brochure, thumbed through it, looking at the pictures, and putting it down. He repeated the actions several times with several different pamphlets and catalogs. With each brochure, pamphlet, and catalog he sensed something was wrong. Something was missing. He could not see himself, at least not in that publication, and certainly not on that campus. On the bookcase within arm's reach a bright navy blue and orange brochure on the second shelf attracted his attention. The cover was the same colors as his high school, royal blue and scarlet. The gold letters in bold font at the top of the cover read: University of New England. In smaller letters at the bottom, it read: "Educating for a Lifetime." Picking it up, he began to thumb through it. On the inside of the cover was an aerial picture of the campus. The picture indicated the campus was located on a peninsula. The caption underneath the picture read:

> The University of New England's two thousand acre-campus is located on the majestic Long Island Sound, in Algonquian Bay, Connecticut, two miles northeast of New London.

Looking at the pictures and reading the captions of the pictures struck his interest. One picture of the basketball team during a game showed three Negro players. Another photo showed a Negro student walking across the campus with a group of students. Another picture, the one that captured his attention, was of a Negro choir. The brochure indicated that the student enrollment was 6,000. *Not so bad*, he thought, *considering my high school has two thousand five hundred students.*

Miss McGinnis's door controllably creaked open. Little could partially see Melissa in the doorway. Glancing at his watch, it was ten minutes before twelve. Melissa's few minutes turned out to be thirty minutes. "And thank you for calling Case Western Reserve about my application Miss McGinnis. I'll get the financial aid information in the mail tomorrow."

"Okay, dearie. Tell your parents if they need help completing the forms to call me. I'll also be looking for some scholarship money for you. We'll get you into college and get you some scholarship money. Don't you worry, sweetie, and you can stop by any time you feel you need to. I'll see you next week. Okay?"

"Thank you, and I will." Seeing Little, Melissa stuck her head into her office. "Miss McGinnis. That student is still here waiting for you."

"Okay, thank you. Please, would you do me a favor and move the chair back in front of the desk for me, honey?"

Melissa momentarily disappeared in the office. Moving rapidly, she quickly passed Little without speaking or looking at him. He thought about how fickle she acted. When he was tutoring her, she couldn't stop talking to him about her social life and asking him questions. But, at school in the hallways and in the cafeteria, she barely acknowledged his presence. On several occasions when he passed her on the streets, she acted as if she never saw him.

"Okay, you can come in now," Miss McGinnis voice frailly rang out. Little entered her office and began to close the door. "Oh no, leave the door open and have a seat. I'll be with you in a minute." Little looked around her office as he sat down in the chair in front of her desk. Her desk was neatly organized. All papers stacked neatly and properly arranged in their place. Aware of his feelings, but not fully understanding them, instinctively Little knew he did not trust her. She made him feel uncomfortable, as if he didn't belong, like an unwelcome intruder wasting her time and invading her space. She never discussed with him his course selection nor his grades. She would pass him every day in the hall and never speak. He noticed she spoke to the other students, but not him. He doubted if she knew him. Like Melissa and several of the white teachers and students, he wondered if she knew his name or cared whether he existed or not. To them, like the other Negro students he was invisible. *Well, it just must be the way of white folks.*

"Now, what can I do for you young man?" she asked while slipping her glasses over her nose and peering at him over the top rim.

Handing her the paper he explained, "My homeroom teacher gave me this pass saying you wanted to see me."

"What is your name?"

"Thomas, Thomas Isaiah."

Taking the pass, Miss McGinnis stood up, turned around and walked the short distance to the filing cabinet. "Well, let's see. Thomas, that's T, Thomas Isaiah." Searching one drawer, she closed it and opened another. She continued to search the files opening one drawer after another until she searched all five drawers of the filing cabinet. After a brief search of the files on her desk, she exclaimed. "I can't seem to locate your records. Are you sure you're one of my students?"

"Yes, Ma'am. You signed the pass."

"What grade are you in?"

Patiently he replied, "I'm a senior."

Taking her seat, she looked at him. "Have you been here all four years or are you a recent transfer student from another school?"

He thought to himself, *What a ding bat.* "I've been here since ninth grade."

"I'll call Coach Lemael for your records. He usually takes care of all his basketball players. I'm sure a college must have recruited a big, tall boy like you by now. He probably has your records in his office.

Give me a minute. I'll give him a call." She proceeded to pick up the telephone.

Annoyed by her remarks, he responded, "I'm not on the basketball team."

Ignoring his annoyed tone, she self-righteously proclaimed, "Oooh, what a shame. Such a nice tall boy like you not on the basketball team. You probably could have gotten yourself a full athletic scholarship to college. Coaches like recruiting tall boys like yourself to play."

Little hated this more than anything else, being mistaken for a basketball player and having to explain why he was not on the basketball team. *I hate basketball and I certainly don't owe you any explanation. The only reason I played the two years I did was because everyone said I should because of my height. I hate being tall. How come every tall Negro has to play basketball? I guess she must think I love watermelon and dance too! Yea, I got rhythm!* Little grew impatient. He could not wait to get out of her office.

Clam down, calm down, the voice told him.

"Well, Mr. Thomas. What do you plan to do after you graduate from high school?"

Little was shocked. *She actually asked me a valid question.* A question he never had given much thought lately.

"Um, I haven't decided yet. I mean I haven't given it much thought."

"Don't worry, Mr. Thomas. As your guidance counselor, part of my responsibility is to help you plan your future. Since you will not be able to get into college—even if you could—you probably couldn't afford it anyway. Have you considered maybe going to trade school?"

"No, no, no. I definitely don't want to go to a trade school."

"Well, I understand." Speaking as if she were doing Little a big favor she excitingly exclaimed, "Oh, I do have something you're qualified to do. It just came in this morning. It's a job offering. It's a chauffeur job with a very wealthy and prominent family on Long Island. It's a live-in position." Whirling around in her chair while clasping her hands together in excitement she handed Little a paper with a name, address, and phone number on it. "I'll be very happy to recommend you. It's a very lovely family. Mr. Dayton is a businessman. He owns many pieces of property here in New York. You and your mother and siblings probably live in one of his tenement buildings. He's very good to you people. The wife is blind, and I believe they have a daughter who is in college."

Gazing at the paper in her hand, as if a shotgun blast ripped through his chest, Little's body slumped in the chair. "No, no, no," he screamed. His head began to spin. He fought to control the tremors and the rage that had built up inside of him. His eyes rolled back in his head. Suddenly, his mouth went dry, his smooth jet-black skin turned pale. He knew he was about to lose control of himself. He rose and started for the door gasping. "I need some air. I got to get out of here. I got to get out of here and now." Too late, he lost his battle. Turning sharply around, placing his hands on the edge of her desk, he stared directly into Miss McGinnis's eyes. With a cold sterile expression upon his face he shouted, "First, you were late for my appointment. Then, you made me wait while you saw someone who didn't have an appointment with you." He felt the uncontrollable rage in himself festering inside. His voice grew louder as he leaned over her desk, moving closer to her face. "You call two colleges for Melissa. You look for scholarship money for Melissa, and you can't even find my file. You don't even know my name. You don't know who you're talking to, and you're the one who scheduled this stupid appointment! Then all you can come up with is a job as a chauffeur. You got nerves acting like you're doing me a big favor." His hand began to ball up into a fist. He raised his fist in the air.

No, stop, don't do it, don't do it Little. If you do, you'll be in big trouble. She's not worth it. Believe me, she's not worth it.

Little was familiar with the voice. He could never do wrong without the voice interfering. Most importantly, he listened to his friend, the voice inside of his head.

He slammed his open hand on her desk sending papers and folders flying. "You incompetent, uncaring, bitter, dried-up, old, racist maid!

God. Why in god's name did I come to your office! Why are you doing this to me!? I don't need your charity, and I certainly don't want it."

Miss McGinnis face turned a bright red. Pointing her finger at Little, she shouted, "How dare you talk to me like that? After all I've done for you and your people. Get out. Get out of my office right now before I call the principal! After all I've done for you and your kind. I tried to help you. How dare you treat me like this and in my own office? You ungrateful little so and so. Get out. Get out now! I'm going to go to the principal's office and report you."

"Lady, you haven't got a clue! You call yourself a guidance counselor. You're not a counselor. You're a joke! A big joke!" Fearful of physically assaulting her, he swiftly turned around to get out of her office. Shouting as he departed, "You can go to hell for all I care!"

In the mist of the shouting, the next period bell began ringing. Students were crowding into the hall as Little exited. He had not heard the bell ringing or paid it any attention. As he passed the main office he glanced at the clock; twelve o'clock. *Must be lunchtime.* Little felt the hunger pains along with the anger and rage bottled up inside of him. Each pain had its need, and he found it difficult to choose which was the greater. Feeling angry, lost, and alone, he wanted to stay and stew in his present mood. No one would rob him of this paroxysm of rage. He decided the pain of hunger could be more immediately satisfied without disturbing his current disposition. *"Perhaps, it's just what I need to fuel my anger."*

Entering the cafeteria, he quickly noted it was filled with students, but the lunch line was not long. He got in line, "Now baby, what do you want?" Looking up; it was Miss Smith, one of his favorite cafeteria ladies. If anyone could break his mood, put a smile on his face, and make his day brighter it was her. Entrenched in his position he was determined not to let her ruin his perfectly bad mood.

"I'll have the roast beef, mashed potatoes, gravy, and corn, please."

"Honey, Miss Smith ain't gonna give you any thang till you give me a big pretty smile on that sour-looking face of yours. Come on. I know there's a smile in there somewhere. Ah ha. I sees it. It's comin'.

Dey it is, dey it is." Little could not help smiling. "I knew it was there. I saw it was comin'," she laughed putting one hand on her hip while waving the serving spoon in a circular motion with the other. They both laughed as she prepared his plate. "You're one handsome young man when you're smiling wid all those pearly white teeth. I'm going to give you an extra helping just so you can keep that big pretty smile on your face."

"Lost again! I lost again," he said shaking his head as he moved along the line to pay for his lunch. The reprieve offered by Miss Smith was short-lived as Little found a seat away from his usual crowd of friends at the end of the table where a group of white students were sitting. As he took a seat once again, his anger grew. Looking at the plate of food in front of him, with his fork he put some of the mashed potatoes into his mouth, then he cut a large piece of the roast beef and began chewing. After another scoop, the meat and potatoes disappeared into his mouth. Sluggishly, he struggled to open the small carton of milk. One gulp, and it was gone.

"Little big man, gimmie me some skin," a tall light brown skinned male said, extending his hand out in front of himself, with his palm turned face up. It was his best friend, Swoosh.

Little nonchalantly responded. "Hey Swoosh." They slowly slid hands palm side across each other. "Nothing going on here."

"Man, why you all hunched up in this corner by yourself. You is on the wrong side of the cafeteria."

"Just want to be by myself. I need to think. Something you don't know too much about."

"Hey blood, dig this. Remember that college scout at the game last week? Well, he called; offered me a full scholarship to the University of Kansas to play ball."

"For real?" Little asked, raising his left eyebrow.

Swoosh quickly sat down opposite Little. "No joke man. Check it out. I Jerald James Jefferson, Jr., better known as Swoosh, because I got the smoothest jump shot in the city, is going to college. I'm gonna play for the same college and on the same team as Wilt Chamberlain.

No doubt me and my man Wilt will be drafted into the National Basketball Association. Yea, I'm gonna be a college man. Gonna git me all the sweet honeys on campus. After that, gonna play for the pros. The big boys! Yes! Sure, sounds good to me. Now gimmie some dap, brother."

Little did not respond. "Hey man, what's your major malfunction? You gonna leave yo' main man hanging like this? You and Madear have a fight or something?"

"Sorry man, I'm out of it. I just came from McGinnis's office. First, she was late. Then, she took a white girl who arrived after me, before me, after I was waiting for her. Next, after she did call me in her office, the old fart couldn't find my records. She said, 'I'll call the coach for them.' Ask me if I was recruited by a college to play ball. Man, its' the same old story over, and over again. You know. You' tall. You' black, so you got to play basketball. Don't have any brains in your head; only way you can go to college is if you play basketball. Then that anal-retentive misfit said she'll recommend me for a job as a chauffeur."

"That's messed up bro. You're one of the smartest brothers I know. I don't know why you go see that old white bitch anyway. You know she's racist, hates black people. Don't let that card-carrying member of the KKK and Daughter of the American Revolution git to you. She was first in line to keep Marian Anderson from singing in Carnegie Hall. I bet she didn't even know your name. You know to her and the rest of them, we all look alike, eat watermelon and dance real good."

Little burst out laughing, "Man, check it out. She's gonna highly recommend me for a chauffeur job, and I don't even have a driver's license. I don't know how to drive a car, and she was going to highly recommend me for the job. My folks don't even own a car. I don't think my old man ever owned a car or anything else in his whole life. It's been so long since I rode in a car, I wouldn't know how to act." Little laughed louder. "I should have taken the job. If she hadn't thrown me out of her office, I'd go back there and take it." Little and Swoosh both, laughed loudly and wildly.

"No offense man," Swoosh said interrupting their laughter. "But if you had listened to me, your partner, your main man, and stayed on the team, like I said, you would have had boo coo colleges knocking on your door. Brother, with your height, skill, and intelligence, you'd have it made. Sports are the only way we got to make it out of this city. But no, no, not you. Not Mr. Brains. You got to study, take hard classes. You've taken Algebra one and two, Chemistry one and two, Calculus and Advanced Calculus. Then four years of Latin. You're the only soul brother I know, who ain't Catholic, that speaks Latin. Ain't a soul you can talk to but the teacher and those ofays in class."

"In case you forgot, I also speak Spanish and Italian, four years of three languages, don't forget."

"Exactly! That's exactly what I'm talking about. You took all those classes and got all those good grades. Where's it getting you? Nowhere! Ain't got not one college knocking on your door! Why? Because you Black, a tar baby, a nigger. The white man doesn't want no smart nigger. He wants a head scratchin', head bowin', and scrapin', dumb black nigger; one who could win him a national title. Man, you're the smartest guy in this school. Do you think these white people are going to let you, as black as you is, give the valedictorian speech at graduation? Hell, man your guidance counselor doesn't even know your name; never mind making you number one in the graduating class. If you want them to respect you, put a basketball or a football in your hand. On the court is where you get respect. It's the only place a brother is gonna get any half decent respect from the white man. Other than that, you're just another nigger here in their school, their city, and their country. Remember, to them, you'se a nobody."

Suddenly, quickly jumping to his feet knocking over the chair. His voice rose above the noise in the cafeteria, "Get out of my face, Swoosh. You're always so negative. I don't need you on my case."

Students turned to look at Little and Swoosh. "I got enough from that freakin' McGinnis. I don't need no static from you."

Looking around, he saw everybody looking at him. "What y'all looking at!" he shouted to the crowd as he picked up his chair. "Mind your own freakin' business."

Swoosh slowly got up out of his seat. "Man, don't take it out on me. I'm just telling it like it is."

Little put up his hand and turned his head cutting Swoosh off. "Swoosh, just leave me alone. I'm happy for ya. Okay? Right now, just leave me alone," he softly said as he sat down in the chair. Waving his hand, he motioned for Swoosh to go away.

"You got it my man. I got no beef with you. Different topic, Solomon is looking for you. She said she knows you've been intentionally avoiding her. I was on my way here when she saw me. She told me to tell you to come to her office now."

"Okay man. Sorry for snapping at you," Little said apologetically.

"Don't sweat it, you still my main man. Yea, and tell Madear and Pop I have an away game tonight in New Jersey. I probably won't get home until late tonight." Swoosh smiled and pretended to make an outside jump shot. "Hear that callin' my name? It said, Swoosh. Oooh so sweet. Wasn't that smooth and pretty?" He smiled, Little smiled back. "Don't forget Miss Solomon. I don't need her on my case, especially because of you."

"I won't. I won't."

"Now give ya brother some dap."

Little picked his tray off the table and watched as Swoosh walked to the other side of the cafeteria where the other Negro students were sitting. He and Swoosh had been friends since they were two years old when Swoosh's parents moved into the building where he lived. They were more like brothers. Swoosh's mom treated him like a son and his parents likewise. There were times they'd get into trouble and Swoosh's mom would beat him. Then she'd call his mom. He'd go home and his mom or dad would beat him again. His folks would do the same to Swoosh. Whenever Little's father got tickets to a game, a show or they'd go camping or something, Swoosh was always with them. He was always at the Thomas's for dinner, spending the night; sometimes, he would stay the entire summer. He would show up at their door, "Hey people, let me in. I'm hungry." They would sit at the table laughing. "I don't know why that boy doesn't let himself in," Mrs. Thomas would say as she gets up to open the door. "He's got a key. In fact, Swoosh lives in this flat more than he stays in his own." Swoosh was an only child. His mom was a good woman, but his father drank a lot, and he wasn't home much of the time. On several occasions, they were aware he hit Swoosh's mom. Little recalled the last time that happened was about a year ago. He remembered that night well. It was raining hard. Swoosh's mom cooked a nice big dinner. Pork chops, mashed potatoes, string beans and cornbread. His dad called and said he would be home in fifteen minutes, so they waited for him. He didn't show up. It was late, so she decided they had better start eating before the food got cold. They were at the table, almost finished eating, when his old man came through the door drunk. He started yelling and screaming about eating without him. Then he grabbed Swoosh's mom by the hair, lifting his hand to smack her in the face. That's when Swoosh yelled, "Don't hit my mother." He grabbed his father and punched him in the mouth. Blood spewed from his father's mouth as he stumbled back against the wall dazed. "Oh, so you think you a big man now. Gonna hit your own father. You think you a man now?"

He swung at Swoosh and missed. Swoosh landed a few more punches. Knocked his father to the floor and laid him out cold. When he got up, he left the house. That night was the first time Little heard Swoosh really cry. He cried from the heart. He cried because he hit his father. It hurt him really bad to do it. But he knew he had to stop his father from beating his mother. Since that night, his father never touched another drink or Swoosh's mom. Swoosh spent more time with Little's family. Somehow, Little always knew that academically Swoosh sold himself short. Too often he put basketball first. The thought of Swoosh and him not being together after this year was an uncomfortable and frightening thought. In fact, it scared him. He tried to push the thought as far from his mind as possible.

You'd better go see what Miss Solomon wants; you know she's gonna dog you. Since you're already down, can't go no lower, the voice within him insisted. Laughing out loud, he said to the student passing him, "Already lost the gig as a chauffeur. What more do I have to lose!"

Mrs. Laverne Solomon, the guidance counselor, assisted him and the other black students over the years. Her office was on the second floor in the math wing, directly above Miss McGinnis. She was the only Negro counselor. Even though she was not their assigned counselor, most of the Negro students went to her for help. She scheduled all of his classes each year. She encouraged him and the other Negro students to go to school and make something of themselves. She was tough and didn't take excuses from anyone. Everyone respected her. They'd better. Whatever Mrs. Solomon, Mr. Reid, his math instructor, and Mrs. Carnegie said, their parents believed—hook, line, and sinker. They were the only Negro professionals in the school. Students realized and parents knew that they were interested in their welfare. If one of them called your house with a negative report, you were in big, big trouble. If they recommended, rather, if they told you what course to take, you had no choice. You had better take it, like it, and pass it. Although the Negro students liked Mr. Reid, his being a Math teacher made it difficult for them. The students said they didn't know which they disliked most, Math or Mr. Reid.

Because they were afraid of them or because they didn't want to be bothered with them, the white teachers and administrators always sent the Negro students to Mrs. Solomon, Mrs. Carnegie or Mr. Reid.

"Hey, Little." It was his friend Smoothie. "Solomon is looking for you," he said as they passed each other in the hall.

"I heard, and I know Solomon hasn't been too happy with me lately. First, I gotta check out Reid's class. Haven't been to Math in a few days. I don't need Reid on my back too. Right now, I'd rather face Reid than Solomon."

"I know the story," Smoothie replied as they gave each other dap. "Did ya hear 'bout Swoosh getting recruited by Kansas?"

"Yea, he told me. Gotta go." Depressed, Little did not want to talk about Swoosh's good fortune. Continuing down the hall to class, at all cost, he wanted to avoid seeing Mrs. Solomon. He decided to go the other way to class.

Continuing his journey through the halls, Little cautiously maneuvered the corners in the hallway. Once inside the classroom, he felt safe from the deadly grasp of Mrs. Solomon. Mr. Reid had a reputation of not letting anybody out of his math class, not even to see the principal. He liked Mr. Reid, but most of all he loved Advanced Calculus. Math was one of his favorite subjects, and Mr. Reid had been his teacher since ninth grade. Feeling safe, he slid into his seat.

A shrill irritating voice ranged out over the classroom. "Thomas Isaiah Thomas. I have a feeling that you've been avoiding me for some time young man."

"Excuse me, Mr. Reid," she said directing her attention toward Mr. Reid. "Could I have Mr. Thomas in my office for a few minutes? We have some important business to discuss."

"Mrs. Solomon," Little interjected, "we have a math test today. Right, Mr. Reid?"

Mr. Reid stood up. He was about five feet three inches tall and weighted no more than one hundred-ten pounds. What Mr. Reid lacked in height, he made up in his erudite posture. His jet-black complexion and snow-white hair were a stark contrast to his dark skin. He spoke with impeccable diction. "Please do Mrs. Solomon."

"But, Mr. Reid," Little protested, "the test."

"It's okay, Mr. Thomas. You can miss this exam or make it up later if you want. You're doing excellent in my class. You have a solid A grade. Mrs. Solomon, I know you have good reason, especially if you personally came down to get him out of my class." He gave Little his distinctly sheepish look, stuck his tongue out at him, and flashed a big Cheshire cat smile. I've been waiting years for you to get caught screwing up, Mr. Little," he laughed.

Little scoffed, "Okay, so that's how it's gonna be, Mr. Reid. I thought I was your boy," as he walked out of the classroom.

Before they could get to her office Mrs. Solomon started her lecture, "Thomas, young man, why haven't you taken the SAT? I gave you the forms back in September. I told you how important it was for you to take the SAT to get into college. This is the second time you didn't show up. I don't want any more excuses, young man. I'll accept no more excuses from you. No more! This time, I'm calling your parents. Of all the students in this school, white, black, or Puerto Rican, you *are* the smartest. You're the best-prepared student this school has seen in its entire history. For the last four years, I personally hand-selected your classes and teachers. I didn't do it for my health. I did it because I know what you're academically capable of achieving. Your math skills are superior. You have an outstanding science and English background and that's not including your ability to grasp foreign languages. Academically, you are better than any student in this city and probably all of New York state! You're more intelligent and prepared to take the SAT and go to college than any student I've seen in my entire career in education. Well, I've signed you up to take it at a special session on Wednesday. This time you had better be there. I'm going to call your parents and tell them. Where is your head boy? What's wrong with you? I'm not going to let you throw your life away. You've got too much going for you. Excellent grades, a stable home, and parents that love you. You have a great future ahead of you. Don't sit there rolling your eyes at me."

Mrs. Solomon's tone turned from reprimand to pleading. "Little, you can be anything, and I mean anything you want to be. Your options are limitless. With your Math abilities, why you can be a Mathematician or Engineer; science-wise, you can be a scientist, biologist, chemist, nuclear physicist, or a medical doctor—anything you want to be. Little you have a gift, a talent. Don't throw this opportunity away. Don't you want to get out of this place? Do something with your life? Make something of yourself? Or do you want to end up like the others? Taking a low paying job, strung out on heroin, pot, cocaine, or winding up in jail or in the grave?"

Her pleading tone turned parental. "The choice is yours, and I'm not going to stand here and let you make the wrong decision. Well, what is it going to be?"

The anger in him began to manifest itself again. Here's someone else controlling his life. His mother, his father, Mrs. McGinnis, Mrs. Smith, Mrs. Perkins, Mr. Reid, and now Mrs. Solomon. He had no say in it. Despite what Mrs. Solomon said, Little knew the choice was not his to make. The choice had already been made for him. He was supposed to, no, he was expected to, follow the program as prescribed by her and endorsed by others. Her program, it was hers regardless of how he felt or what he wanted to do. He looked at her with an intense, defiant expression. *Get off my case. I'm tired of everybody on my case! Why is everybody else always telling me what to do, where to go and what I'm supposed to do when I get there? If they know what's good for my life, then let them live it. I know what I want to do. What I want to do is none of their business. So, you signed me up for all these courses. I didn't ask you to. Did I? No! You did it on your own without my consent, knowledge or input. You never asked me what I'm going to do. No one ever asked me once what do I want to do. No, you just tell me what I want to do. If you do ask me, then you say, well, I think you should do so and so. Well, if you think I should do so and so, then why did you ask me what I wanted to do in the first place? Nobody lets me do what I want to do. No. No, I've got to do what everybody else wants me to do. Well, I am sick of everybody planning my life. From now on, I am the captain of my ship. I am the master of my fate. If I decide to take a low paying job, it's my business and nobody else's. If I decided to be a bum on the street, it's my life. Why should you care lady! Get off my case! And I don't care who you call. You can call my mother, call my father, you can call the president of the United States for all I care. I'm just sick of everybody running my life.*

For sure, the only thing Little knew he had left were his own personal thoughts.

Mrs. Solomon sharply responded while pointing her finger at him. "Young man, that's the wrong attitude. Don't sit there rolling your eyes at me! I know what you're thinking, and you had better change that attitude. Yes, I am running your life, and your education is my business."

Little muttered under his breath, "Give me a break. Man can't even think around here."

You know she's right. She's only interested in what's best for you, your future welfare.

"What did you say? Don't be back talking me Mr. Thomas," she requited. "You know your mother and father taught you better than that! I don't want to call them and let them know you're sassing me back."

"Oh Jesus, not you too," he softly said.

"Don't be using the Lord's name in vain in my office!"

"Mrs. Solomon, I didn't say anything." Little frantically searched for the right words to say to get her off his back. "I've decided what college I want to attend."

Suddenly, her countenance changed. *For years I have worked hard to give him direction and a reason to move his life forward. To show him that there was more to life than what Harlem has to offer. Has he reached that point? Has my labor not been in vain?* "You have?" she asked surprisingly. "That's good. That's a step in the right direction." With anticipation, yet with hesitation, she asked, "Which one?"

"Um, um." *Oh boy.* "Which one?" *I better say the right one; one that will make her happy and get her off my back.* It was a revelation. A divine thought from heaven above. "New England! Yeah, that's the one. The University of New England, in Algonquian Bay, Connecticut."

"Why, Mr. Thomas," she exclaimed in awe, "that is an excellent school. It's a top-notch Ivy League university. Believe it or not, even though you haven't taken the SAT, the deadline date for applying is next week. You have an excellent chance of being admitted. In fact, I have an application right here somewhere on my desk." She started rumbling through the papers on her desk. "Here it is. Take it home. Start filling it out," she said, passing it to him. "I don't anticipate any major problems for you to get in. Based on your PSAT scores, I know you will score very high on the SAT; you're a National Merit Scholarship recipient. But just in case, you need to select a second and third choice school. Tell me, how did you come to select UNE? It wasn't on the list of schools we talked about. Don't get me wrong. I'm very pleased you chose it. Frankly, I just thought you would have selected something closer to home and not as large."

"Well, uh..." Little began stammering. He couldn't tell her something as frivolous as it was the school colors on the pamphlet. He only saw the school's brochure this morning in Miss McGinnis's office. He couldn't say because he saw two black students in the pamphlet. *Oh God, how trivial. Truth is I'm just telling her what she wants to hear just to get her off his back. Can't say that either.* "I want to get out of New York, and it's not too far away from home. That way, I can get back if I need to." Little looked at the application. "Gee Mrs. Solomon, this thing says it cost twenty-five dollars just to send in the application! And you want me to fill out two more! Where am I supposed to get that kind of money?"

Mrs. Solomon paid no attention to his protests. "In fact, I should have the University of New England's catalog. Their admission office usually sends the high school a couple. Yes, here it is." She said handing him the navy blue and orange catalog. He immediately recognized it, except this book was thicker and the aerial picture of the campus was on the outside cover. "Don't worry Thomas, I can get you an application fee waiver from the NAACP or the Urban League. They help young people like you get into college."

Man, what did I get myself into now? She is not going to let up on me going to this school. Why did I have to open my big mouth and say I decided to go to college? How stupid! I thought she would have let up. Instead, she's getting off on this whole scene. I should have known better. Now, I'm stuck playing her game again. Now I got to play this one out. Question is, how do I get out of it? When do I get out? Where do I get out, and how far do I go? Boy, I got to find a way out of this one. Little began studying the catalog. In the index, he found the title FEES. Page fifteen. Quickly he flipped through the pages to page fifteen. It read:

Per Year
Tuition $8,250.00
Books & Fees $1,000.00
Room & Board $3,750.00
Personal $500.00
Total $13,500.00

"Great gook-a-mook-ka, Mrs. Solomon," he shouted as he sat straight up in the chair! "This thing says it cost thirteen thousand-five hundred dollars to go to school just for one year! That's more money than my mother and father make in one year. Mrs. Solomon, I can't afford to go to this college!"

"Thomas, where have you been? With your grades, you should have no problem receiving several scholarships. It wouldn't surprise me if you get a full scholarship from the university. I have several scholarship applications that you're eligible to apply for. I have no doubt that you will get a full scholarship from UNE." Mrs. Solomon looked at him with a puzzled face. "Hasn't Miss McGinnis reviewed any of this information with you?"

"Not really. The most she did for me was to recommend me for a job as a chauffeur."

"What!"

While shrugging his shoulders, Little innocently volunteered in a sad and pity seeking voice. "Today, she called me to her office. She said, I couldn't get into college because I didn't play basketball. I said I didn't want to go to a trade school, so she offered me a job as a live-in chauffeur with some rich white family living on Long Island. When I turned the job down, on account of my not having a driver's license, she threw me out of her office. Said all the work she did for me and my people, I was ungrateful." For him to successfully gain Mrs. Solomon's sympathy and fuel her wrath toward Mrs. McGinnis, he intentionally omitted the part of the story where he leaned across her desk, started to slap her but slammed his fist on her desk instead, and called her an old, incompetent, racist maid.

"Thomas, I don't believe she said that to you! Didn't she tell you that you were ranked the number one student in the senior class? She didn't tell you that you're the class valedictorian?"

"Tell me! Mrs. Solomon, she didn't even know my name or who I was. She couldn't find my records or nothing. She started calling Coach Lemael. For some strange reason, she thought he had my records." Lowering his head as if he was ashamed, seeking her sympathy he spoke defensively and humbly. "Mrs. Solomon, I got no reason to lie to you."

Mrs. Solomon found it difficult to contain her outrage. "I don't believe it!" She said angrily. Her voice uncovered her disgust and contempt for Miss McGinnis.

He knew he had achieved his goal. He had won her over, and he gloated in it. "Believe it, 'cause she sure enough said it," he connivingly added.

"Sit here and complete as much of the application as you can. I'll help you. Then, I want you to take the application and the financial aid information home. Have your parents fill out their portion and return it to me on Thursday. You're going to go to UNE, and you'll give that valedictorian speech. I'll see to that!"

Little continue browsing over the forms. "Mrs. Solomon, I can't make heads or tails out of these forms. Now, if I can't understand them, and I have twelve years of schooling, and my parents say that I am smarter than them, then how do you expect my parents to understand them?"

ALL ABOUT LOVE

Little arrived home early. It was peaceful in the apartment. Little knew that would end when his brother and sister arrived home in an hour. He expected parents would arrive sometime after six o'clock. Little decided to lie across his bed to read the catalog. "I know if I'm going to get out of this mess with Mrs. Solomon, I have to find as many loopholes as possible. Let's see, it says the University of New England offers the following programs. The College of Architecture, College of Arts and Sciences, College of Business, College of Education, College of Engineering, College of Pure and Applied Sciences, College of Nursing. It also has graduate and professional Colleges, the College of Medicine, College of Law, and twenty-five Master of Art programs, twenty-six Master of Science programs, and fifteen Doctorate of Philosophy degrees. Wow, lots of colleges in this university."

"Okay, here we go. He began reading. "'Selecting a major. The University of New England offers one hundred-twenty-five different undergraduate majors.' What would I major in if I went to the University of New England? Mrs. Solomon said I could be anything. Anything I wanted to be. Let's see, there's chemical engineer, electrical engineer, civil engineer, computer Engineer, or a mathematician—that a lot of choices. A scientist, biologist, chemist, nuclear physicist, or a medical doctor; they all sound good to me."

"Solomon said I had a gift, a talent. I'm good at chemistry and math. I enjoy both. Think I'll check out engineering. Um, maybe I'll be an engineer like Pop. Yea, he's sort of an electrical engineer at the electric company. He always talks about the guys who are the big engineers. They all went to college and never touch a wire. They spend most of their time figuring out ways to improve the system. Not a bad idea. I like problem solving. The more complex the problem, the better I like it."

Little opened the catalog to the College of Engineering. Chemical engineer—he read the description. Electrical engineer—he read its description. Nuclear engineer—"Interesting. It says the University of New England is one of two universities in the country offering Nuclear Engineering as a major. It also works in conjunction with the shipyard in Groton, Connecticut and Newport News, Virginia. Sounds good to me! The course outline sounds challenging. I'd take Chemistry I and II, Biology I and II, and Thermal Dynamics. Nuclear Engineering combines everything I enjoy doing. That's what I'll major in." The more he read, the more interested he became in the University of New England.

"Now that I decided on a major, what else do I need to do? Guess I'll check out this section on Student Life. There are approximately thirty-seven undergraduate and twelve graduate resident halls on campus." Little read about the dining facilities, clubs, and organizations, student newspaper, fraternities, sororities, health service, football, basketball, baseball, intramural sports, the student union, and the student government. The more he read, the more he liked it. Instead of finding his loophole, he found his reason to attend. For the first time, he knew the reason why he wanted to attend the University of New England and major in nuclear engineering.

With the intentions of having as much as possible of the applications and financial aid information completed before his parents arrived home, Little turned his attention to the forms. He immediately began laboring over the information. Shortly thereafter, he heard the sound of his father's footsteps coming down the hallway. For him, the distraction was a happy one. He couldn't wait to share his revelation with his father. Little heard him put his key in the lock and pushed the door open. Enthusiastically, he turned to face the door, "Hi Pop." Standing up to greet him, Little could hardly wait to share the information with him.

A tall, brown-skinned man, slightly taller, and much huskier than himself entered the doorway. His hair was a mixture of black and silver gray. He wore a thick mustache that hid much of his thick, dark, upper lip. He was wearing a uniform. Across the pocket on the left side was the company's name and emblem, Con Edison Electric Company. Under the name was his name, Elijah Thomas. He returned Little's greeting, "Evening son. Is your mother home yet?"

"Not yet." Excited, in one breath he began letting everything out. "I had a pretty interesting day at school. I have these applications for college. Mrs. Solomon, my guidance counselor. You remember her. She gave me these forms. I've decided to go to the University of New England in Algonquian Bay, Connecticut. It's a real good college Pop. I read all about it in the catalog. I've decided to major in nuclear engineering. I'll be a nuclear engineer. The University of New England is one of two universities in the country that offer nuclear engineering as a major. There's a part of the financial aid form that you and Momma have to complete." Picking up the forms, Little passed them to his father.

"Boy, can't you wait until I get in the door good before you come giving me some papers," he shouted as he slammed his lunch box on the table. "I worked two shifts. I went in last night at eleven o'clock and worked until three o'clock today, and they want me to come in again tonight at eleven. I'm tired!" Mr. Thomas went to the sink, got a glass out of the cupboard and turned on the water. Drinking the water, he looked at Little. "I'm going to take a shower." Immediately, he turned around and left the room.

In that instance, Little's enthusiasm was quickly swept away. It was neither the response nor support from his father he had expected. Bowing his head, he slowly turned around and brushed the forms to the side. Underneath, he felt his wrath increasing. The shower turned on. Under his breath Little scoffed, "Yea, take a shower. You're in great need of a cooling off." Reluctantly, he turned his attention again to the forms and began working on them again.

After ten minutes, Little heard the shower turn off. While passing through the kitchen, his father glanced at the table where Little was working on the application. His eyes were taken captive by the navy blue and orange cover of the University of New England catalog. "Let me see the book son."

Enthusiastically, but with some reluctance, Little handed his father the college catalog. Attentively, Little watched his father's every expression as he began perusing the pages. Mr. Thomas' eyes became transfixed on something, they widened. "Thirteen thousand five hundred dollars," he exclaimed! To go to this college, it cost thirteen thousand five hundred dollars! Now where do you think we're supposed to get that kind of money? Our name is not Rockefeller. Boy, what's the rest of us supposed to do? Starve so you can go up there to Connecticut to play with your friends? How are we supposed to live? Where do you expect me and your mother, brother, and sister to live? In the streets? Boy, what you better do is find yourself a job so you can help out more around here. Money don't grow on no trees." Before Little could respond, Mr. Thomas began walking toward his bedroom. "I'm going to lay down. Call me when dinner's ready!"

Little protested, "But Pop!"

"I don't want to hear it. I've said all what I got to say, and that's that." As quickly as he came into the room, he disappeared.

"Dumping on me again," Little murmured. "He's always got to find something wrong with what I want to do. When I finally find something I want to do, somewhere where I want to go, what does he do? He's always telling me no. I knew it. I knew it all along. He'd find something wrong with it. He never wants to listen to me. He's always jumping to conclusions. He never listens to me. Nobody around here ever listens to me. Never spends any time with me. Never is interested in anything I say or do. All he does is boss me around. Tell me what to do. Clean the dishes Little. Mop the floor Little. Do your homework. Watch your brother and sister. I do everything they tell me to do. But when I ask for five minutes of his time, do I get it? No. Not now. I'm tired. I've been working all day. I'm tired. Well if you're that tired, don't work so many hours. I didn't ask you to work double shifts. Not my fault the other workers didn't show up to work. He always feels it's his job to cover for other people that don't show up for work. He listens to everybody except me. Has time for everybody else except me. Never goes anywhere. Never does anything with me."

Before he could return his attention to the applications, Little heard Elisha and Esther running down the hallway. Throwing his hands in the air he scoffed, "That's all I need right now, the two of them coming home."

Elisha and Esther began banging on the door. Quickly, Little hurried to open the door. As they entered the apartment, Little shouted softly, "Hush. Stop making all that noise. Pop's asleep, and he don't want to be disturbed." He continued yelling at them in a low voice. "All I need is for you two to wake him up with all that noise. Next thing is he'll be yelling and blaming me for the two of you making so much racket."

"Okay, we'll be quiet," Esther responded.

"You better be. Now go to your rooms and change your clothes." Little sat down at the table and began working again on the college information.

"What you doing Little?" asked Elisha.

Little made no attempt to disguise his annoyance with his younger brother. "I'm filling out an application for college."

"What you doing that for? Where's college?" asked Esther.

Elisha chimed in, "Stupid, it's where you go after you graduate from high school. And it's what college, not where's college."

"I'm not stupid. I'm gonna tell daddy you called me stupid."

"You better not wake up Pop," Little shouted. "Now both of you be quiet and go get out of your school clothes. Elisha, apologize to her right now." Elisha hesitated. "I said right now, or you'll go to your room for the rest of the evening."

"Sorry," Elisha half-heartedly replied. Esther, in rebellion, stuck her tongue out at Elisha. "Little, she licked her tongue at me."

"Both of you stop it before I get mad. Now go change your clothes and wash your hands. I'll get you some cookies and milk. If you promise to be quiet, you can watch *Captain Kangaroo* 'til Momma gets home. Okay?"

"Okay," their little voices rang out as they ran to their rooms.

"Be quiet, and don't wake up Pop or you'll be in big trouble," Little shouted softly after them.

Thirty minutes later, Little could hear his mother moving swiftly down the hallway toward the apartment. It was after six o'clock. She was later than usual. The sound of her footsteps was deeper than normal. He figured she was carrying something heavy, so he got up to open the door for her.

"Little," she sounded surprised. "I'm glad you're home. Here, take this bag of groceries please." Little immediately grabbed the bag and set it on the kitchen counter and immediately resumed his seat at the table.

Mrs. Thomas began setting her other bags on the kitchen table. "What are you doing son?" she asked peering over his shoulder?

"Filling out a college application."

"Well, right now, I need you to clear off the table. I have to hurry up and start dinner. I'm running late because I had to stop at the market to pick up a few things. Where's your brother and sister?" she asked while putting the three bags of groceries on the table next to him.

"Look out," he shouted. "You almost put the bags on my application," annoyingly he scoffed while moving the bags of groceries. "They're in the living room watching television."

"Boy, just who do you think you're talking to? I'm not one of your friends at school. You're smelling your own musk boy. Last I knew I'm still your mother!"

"I'm sorry Momma," Little said apologetically. "Ma, I need your help completing these college applications and the financial aid part."

"I'll be glad to help you son, but first I got to get dinner started and on the stove. I don't have time right now. When your father gets home ask him to help you."

"I did."

"You did? Your father's home?"

"Yes Ma."

"Why didn't you tell me? He got home early. He probably has to go in tonight again. Empty these bags and start putting away the groceries please."

Frustrated with the slow pace Little was moving, she started taking off her coat and hat. "Little, please hurry up and move those papers off the table. What did he say when you asked him to help you?"

Little let out a long sigh. Sarcastically, he replied imitating his father's voice. "'Boy, I've been working all day! I'm tired. I went in early last night, worked two shifts, and I got to go in tonight at eleven. I'm going to lay down now. Call me when dinner is ready.' Then he took a shower, then next thing I knew I heard him snoring."

"Well, your father has been doing double shifts lately. Several of the men have been out sick. I'm sure he meant no harm. We could also use the extra money. Let me see those papers."

"Ah Ma, you're always defending him. He never listens to what I have to say. When it comes to what I want, he's all the time jumping to conclusions. He never listens to me. Nobody around here ever listens to me. He never spends any time with me. He's never interested in anything I say or do. All he does is boss me around. Clean the dishes Little. Mop the floor Little. Do your homework Little. That's all I ever hear. I do everything he tells me to do. When I ask for five minutes of his time, do I get it? No. Leave me alone. I'm tired. That's all I ever hear from him. Well, if he's that tired, he ought not to work so many hours. I didn't ask him to work double shifts. It's not my fault other workers didn't come in. He always feels it's his job to cover for other people that don't show up for work. He listens to everybody, except me. He has more time for everybody except me. Acts like he loves Elisha more than me. He treats me like he's not my father, like I'm a stepchild or something."

Little's mean-spirited words pierced her heart causing her pain deep within. Enraged, Mrs. Thomas rushed across the kitchen and raised her hand stopping short of slapping his face. With a raised hand, she shouted, "Shut your mouth! That's a lie straight from the pit of hell," catching herself as she withdrew her hand.

Fearfully, Little quickly took a few steps backward. He knew he had struck a nerve. He had overstepped his boundary, pushing her to her limit, causing her rage. Her wrath scared him.

"Don't you ever, ever say that again as long as you live and breathe in this house. I better never hear you disrespect your father, ever again. You better not even think it. He's the only father you've ever known and all you'll ever have." Moving back from Little, she continued, "I don't know what's gotten into you. You better change that attitude and change it real quick. I don't ever want to hear you say anything like that ever again. You hear me?"

"Yes ma'am."

"He treats you better than Elisha and Esther. You're the oldest. He expects more of you than your younger brother and sister." Turning to the sink, she continued in her anger. "Your problem is you're spoiled—spoiled rotten. You think you have to always have your own way. Your father is always trying to please you. He's done more for you than he has for your brother and sister. Little needs shoes. Little needs pants, shirts. I saw this, and I just knew Little would like it. Oh, Ruthie honey, it won't hurt to get it for him. He's a growing boy. The minute he can't do something, or says no to you, you start acting up. You start pouting and poking your lips out a mile long clear into next week just to get your own way. You're spoiled, and he's done spoiled you rotten. I better never, ever hear you say that again."

"I'm sorry Momma. I didn't mean it."

"Let me see those papers."

Not wanting to make the same mistake with his mother as he did with his father, he handed her the financial aid scholarship application first. "Here, there are all kinds of scholarship money for college. All you have to do is fill out the forms. Mrs. Solomon said she is sure I could get enough money to go to college."

Carefully examining the forms, Mrs. Thomas began frowning. "These people want to know all of your business. Your age, how many children you have, and how much money you make. What you got in the bank. Did you file federal income taxes? Here," she said giving him back the forms. "I need to start dinner. I'll have to check them out later. Right now, I need to start dinner."

"Yes ma'am," he mumbled as he gathered his papers together and retreated into his bedroom.

It was the beginning of what seemed like an eternity to Little. In the short time frame of an hour, his mother had prepared a beef stew with carrots, potatoes and English peas in a deep gravy. The aroma of the stew simmering on the stove filled the apartment building. Smelling so good, it brought tears to the eyes and hunger pains to the belly of all within its grasp. Everyone in the building and on the block knew and loved Ruth Ann Thomas' cooking. Somebody, normally Swoosh, stopped by for dinner. The meal was accompanied with sweet golden-brown cornbread. Elisha's favorite, grape Kool-Aid, was the drink. Esther helped her mother set the table. As usual, a plate was set for their adopted son, Swoosh.

With sorrowful eyes, Little slowly ate his meal in silence. His mother and father too felt the heaviness. No one knew how to break it. Attempting to break the solemn dinner atmosphere, Mrs. Thomas asked, "Where is that Swoosh, Little? He hasn't been here for the past two nights."

Sulking, he replied, "Oh, I forgot to tell you, the school has an away game tonight."

"During this season there's no telling when we're going to see that boy. Where is the game?"

Little did not answer.

"Little!"

"Yes ma'am?"

"I asked you a question."

"Sorry, I didn't hear you," he replied in an irritated tone.

"Where is the game? And don't use that irritating tone with me."

"Yes, ma'am. Patterson, New Jersey."

From the tone of his voice, she knew he was still sulking. Using discretion, she decided not to press the issue and decided to leave him alone.

Mr. Thomas picked up on what was happening and followed suit.

Esther looked up from her plate and proudly announced with a big smile on her face. "Little's going to college. I know what college it is, Momma."

"Momma," Elisha asked, "when Little goes to college he won't live here anymore, right?"

"That's not true. Is it Momma?"

Elisha interrupted, "Girl, I told you he's got to move away, and when he's gone, I get to have a room all to myself. No Little and no more Swoosh kicking me out of my bed anymore."

Esther reached over to hit Elisha. "Naw, you don't get to have a room by yourself because Little ain't moving nowhere. Right Little?"

Elisha started to hit her back but was stopped by their mother. "You two stop fighting and finish eating your dinner. We'll cross that bridge when we come to it."

"May I go to my room?" asked Little.

"Sure, go ahead," his father responded.

The rest of the family completed their meal in total silence. The only sound heard was Elisha kicking his chair as he swung his legs back and forth. Nobody paid it any attention. After dinner, Mr. Thomas prepared to go to work. Esther helped her mother clear the table and wash the dishes. Elisha went into the living room to read a book.

Dejected and feeling all was lost, Little wanted to be left alone. Lying on his back in bed with his hands under his head, he reflected upon the day's activities. Wallowing deep in his feeling of anger and rejection, he barely heard the knock on his bedroom door.

The door slowly creaked open. It was his father. Little was determined to ignore him.

"May I come in son?"

"Yes, sir." He added, softly whispering under his breath to himself. "Free country. Besides, you pay the rent, not me. Even if I say no, you're gonna come in anyway. Why do you even brother to ask?"

Mr. Thomas walked over to Little's bed and slowly sat down.

"I'm just lying here." Having willingly succumbed to his feelings, he wanted to move as far away from his father as possible, in the tiny space of his bedroom. He shifted his body closer to the other side of the bed. Sitting up on the bed, Little positioned his pillow betwixt the headboard and the wall. He continued to retreat into the corner between the bed and the wall, as he leaned against it. He immediately drew his knees up to his chest and wrapped his arms around his bent legs. Leaning his head back, starring at the ceiling, his physical position communicated his conscience position to his father. He knew his father, whenever he was wrong always apologized and had a way of getting to him. *Here comes the old apology. You won't break this mood, not this time. Well, I don't want to hear it. I won't accept it. Not this time.*

In an attempt to draw his attention, Mr. Thomas placed his hand on Little's knee. He was never comfortable when there was distance between him and his son, especially when he caused the distance.

"Son, I want to apologize to you for losing my temper earlier this evening. It's all happening so fast and hit me all at once. Working these double shifts; I've been tired and awfully irritable. Your talking about going to college took me by surprise."

Little lowered his head and looked defiantly into his father's eyes. However, this time, there was something different. There was a difference in his voice. There was a sound, a sad sound. There was a sound of sadness in his father's voice.

"Little, I always knew that one day you would grow up and go off to college. Your mother and I have been saving for it since you were born. It seems like it was only yesterday that you were a baby, and I was holding you in my arms. Next thing I knew I was watching you take your first step." His voice began to quiver as he spoke. "Little league games and playing in the park."

Tears began to trickle down his father's cheeks. It was the first time Little saw his father cry. "I just don't know where the time went. Time has gone by so fast. I'm not ready for you to leave me son. I'm just not ready to lose you." He began shaking his head back and forth. "I'm proud of you, but I'm just not ready to let you go. I'm just not ready. It's hard for me. I wish we had more time together. Maybe, if I had spent more time with you. I don't know if you understand or not, but it's hard for me son. Real hard for me to let you go. I knew this day was coming, but not today. Please try and understand me, if I should get a little upset. It's not you or anything you've done. It just I got to get used to the idea of your leaving home. Don't get me wrong. I want you to go, and I'll do all I can to help you. It's just going to be hard for me to think of your not being here. It's going to take time until I get use to the idea."

Tears began to flow from Little's eyes as his stonehearted position began ebbing away to his father's love. For the first time, he looked and was able to see deep into his father's eyes. He saw his father's soul. Looking at him, Little saw him as never before. He saw his father for the first time. Intuitively, he thought he knew everything about the man. *I should. He's my father.* Now, for the first time, he was seeing him. Little could see for the first time, his gray hair, the lines in his face, and the weariness of a tired, worn soul. Little realized, he had never seen or understood the true man. Until now, he never had a hint of the true man. Even now, it was just a glimpse. He was much older than he looked. He remembered how his father was always talking about having worked for Con Edison for thirty-something years. How he was planning to retire in three or four years. *Retirement. That should make him around sixty-two years old. That means he was about forty-four or forty-five years old when I was born. I always knew he was older than Momma. But how much older than her? Ten years, I don't think she's fifty yet.* He was aware of that much. *How old is Momma? She can't be more than twenty years younger than him. Twenty years is the maximum.*

Suddenly, Little realized the many things that he did not know about his mother and father. He knew his father was from North Carolina. He was a good churchgoing man. Probing into his father's eyes, Little saw the great pain and loneliness he had suffered a very long time ago. In one split second, he lost everyone he loved and everything he owned was lost forever. He was a preaching, God-fearing man who tried escaping the painful memories of another life. He left North Carolina and came north. He moved to New York City and got a job with Con Edison. He couldn't bear the loneliness that surrounded him. He just wanted to die.

There was no way for Little to fully grasp or understand what he was seeing. How could he have known? It was all just now revealed to him while looking into his father's eyes. Then, he met Ruth Ann Mears. She helped him out of his self-imposed gutter and out of his pain, suffering, and misery. Because of her, he wanted to, and he did stop drinking. She got him back to attending church, back to God, but not back to preaching. Momma said that's between him and God. Momma. *Momma, no doubt, I can see it in his eyes he really loves her. He's always sweet and gentle with her. Brings her flowers and takes her to the movies. He'll give her anything. Gave her three beautiful children. He named me after his mother's father, Thomas. Thomas Isaiah. When I see him pick Momma up in his big strong arms and swing her around, she is always so happy. He makes her happy and he makes her laugh. They are so happy; we're all so happy. I love him with all my heart. I can't hate him. I can't even stay mad at him. I can't even pretend long that I'm mad at him.*

"Pop. I love you," he said sobbing. "I'm sorry about being a big jerk earlier."

Simultaneously, Elijah and Little embraced one another. There was silence as they embraced. The love of a father for his son and the love of a son for his father filled the room.

"Your mother finished clearing off the kitchen table. Why don't you get out those papers for college. Together we'll see what we can do with them. Okay?" Rising off the bed, he tenderly and lovingly kissed Little on the forehead.

Little felt his body exploding with warmth, joy, and love. He felt good about his father and his father's love for him. Most of all, Little felt good about himself. Little knew all his mother had said was true; his mother was right. His father spoiled him.

"What about work, Pop?"

"I'll call them at work and let them know I'm not coming in. Right now, you're more important. You're all that matters. Give me a minute," his father exclaimed as he left the room.

As Little took his place next to his father at the table, he felt very proud to be the son of Elijah Isaiah Thomas.

BEST MADE PLANS

"Good morning Mrs. Solomon," Little enthusiastically greeted her with a whimsical smile on his face. "May I come in?"

"Sure. I always have time for one of my favorite students. What can I do for you Mr. Valedictorian?"

Little looked around her office, nothing had changed. Nothing in the four years he had known her. Papers, college catalogs, applications, letters, and folders scattered across her desk. Neatly in one corner was a picture of her family, her husband, and two daughters. Despite all the presumed chaos, she knew exactly where everything was placed. She referred to it as her fingertip filing system.

Unlike Miss McGinnis's fading walls, Mrs. Solomon's walls and waiting area were freshly painted. Her waiting area was a nice warm soothing green, and her office was painted in the same warm green, trimmed with pink and green paint. Little knew the colors had something to do with a civic organization she was a member of. He recalled it was something about a sisterhood, a sorority—Alpha Kappa Alpha. The ivy plant and the small child's pink pail with a green shovel on the filing cabinet also had something to do with the sorority; Little vaguely understood the connection. He recalled her having said something about her pledging the sorority while she was a student at Hampton Institute, which she affectionately referred to as her "home by the sea."

Very frequently she spoke of the college in Hampton, Virginia. Virginia-Cleveland Hall, Kennedy Hall, Kelsey Hall, Wigwam, Stone

Building, Memorial Chapel, and Armstrong-Slater Hall. She said all the students at the school were Negroes. The college's concert choir was world famous and was said to have sung up the female dormitory, Virginia Hall. A man called Nathaniel Dett was the director of the choir. She also told him the Negroes in Hampton had their own Negro-owned savings and loan company. Little got an application to go there, this all-Negro College. He considered attending except Virginia seemed too far away for him. But he thought he would love to see the college and all those smart Negro students.

"Well, Mrs. Solomon you received my SAT scores."

"Yes I did," she quickly noted cutting him off, "and I am very proud of you. You scored eight hundred on the math and eight hundred on the English. You have a combined total score of sixteen hundred. It's a perfect score and the highest in the history of this school. We are all so proud of you Thomas. I know your parents must be also."

"Yes they are. Ah, Mrs. Solomon, it's May 17. I still haven't heard from the University of New England. You know their Engineering program is rated top in the country and the nuclear engineering program is one of two in the entire country. It's extremely hard to get in because it's rated number one in the country. UNE should have received my SAT scores by now. I heard from Hampton Institute, the University of Kansas, and the three state schools I applied to in New York. I even heard from colleges that I never applied to, never heard of and they gave me full scholarships. I was wondering if you would give them a call for me."

"Why sure Thomas," she chuckled. "Let me finish filing these student records." Mrs. Solomon promptly filed the folders in her hands leaving the remainder of folders on top of the filing cabinet.

She sat down at her desk and started looking for the university's number. Little handed her a piece of paper with the number on it. "Oh," she laughed, "You came prepared. Like you knew I was going to make this call."

"I sort of hoped you would."

Mrs. Solomon dialed the number. After a few rings he faintly heard the voice on the other end.

"Good morning, University of New England admissions office."

"Good morning, this is Mrs. Laverne Solomon calling from Harlem High in New York. May I speak to Dr. Rogers?"

Little strained to hear the response. He watched as Mrs. Solomon spoke. Except when she was trying to run his life, he liked listening to her high-pitched, whinny voice. Her speech was very clear, and she was careful to pronounce each syllable. He loved watching the movement of her lips as she spoke, moving up, down, twisting, and pointing as she talked. "Yes, you may be able to help me. To whom am I speaking?"

Pause.

"That's Mrs. Massini."

Pause.

Excited, Little moved to the edge of his seat. "Well, Mrs. Massini, one of my students, a Mr. Thomas Isaiah Thomas applied to the university back in March. Can you tell me if you have made a decision on his admission?"

Pause. The voice replied, but Little could not hear it.

Mrs. Solomon's head bobbed in a series of up and down movements with each question and answer. "Okay, then."

Pause. Covering the mouthpiece of the phone she looked at Little. "She is going to get your file now."

Long pause.

"He sent his application to you in March."

Pause.

"Yes, the last name is Thomas. T as in Tom, H as in hall, O as in office, M as in mother, A as in apple, and S, as in Sam."

Pause.

"The first name is also Thomas."

Pause.

"That is correct. Thomas Thomas."

Pause.

"Middle name?"

"Isaiah," Little shouted.

"Isaiah."

Pause.

"Yes, Thomas Isaiah Thomas."

Pause.

"No, I'll hold."

Long pause.

"Thomas, she is looking in another area for your application. They seem to be having some kind of difficulty locating yours, but she is sure they have it." Suddenly, as she talked with Little, she was interrupted by the woman on the phone. "Hello, yes."

Pause.

"No, he is applying to the engineering school."

Pause.

"No, he applied in late March."

Pause.

"No, it was about a week before the deadline date."

Pause.

"Yes, the SAT score was sent. The AP exams in Math, Chemistry and Latin were also sent. You should have received all of his information by now."

Long pause.

Again, she spoke to Little. She's calling over to the engineering school to see if they have your application folder." Little was about to say something when she held up her finger interrupting him. "One minute, she's back on the line."

"Yes, he was interviewed in April by Dr. Stephen Hamilton."

Pause.

"No, he's applying to the engineering program. I know Dr. Hamilton is part of the English department."

Pause.

"Okay, thank you very much Mrs. Massini. Would you transfer me over to Dr. Hamilton's office, please?"

Pause.

"Thank you." While she waited for the transfer to be completed, she glanced at Little. "The dean of admissions wasn't there. She can't seem to find your admissions folder." Turning her attention to the telephone she called into it. "Yes, I'll hold."

Pause.

"Dr. Stephen Hamilton, please."

Pause.

"Please tell him that Mrs. Laverne Solomon is calling long distance."

Pause.

"Hello, Stephen," she said flashing her big, confident, I am important smile. "Laverne Solomon. How are you?"

Little met Dr. Hamilton a few weeks earlier when he came to New York to interview him. Dr. Hamilton was a Negro. He worked at UNE in the English Department as a full professor of Literature.

Pause.

"Al and the girls are just fine. We are all doing just find. Mr. Thomas, the student of ours, I know you were very impressed with the young man."

Pause.

"We got his SAT scores in. He scored sixteen hundred, a perfect score. The highest in the history of this school," she exclaimed beaming brightly as she relayed the scores to Dr. Hamilton.

Pause.

Little could not hear his response. From her facial responses, he figured it was good, considering the information was good.

"We are all so proud of him. He is here in my office right now."

Pause.

She laughed and looked at Little. "Dr. Hamilton said to tell you hello."

Pause.

"I'm sure you would love to have him in your English department, but his heart is set on nuclear engineering."

Long pause.

"Yes, I read about the group of German professors leaving the University of Chicago. I'm sure they will be a great asset to UNE's engineering department. It will also be a great opportunity for Thomas to study under such renowned nuclear physicists. I'll be sure to tell him. He is a very bright young man; he could be whatever he wants to be. We expect great things from him."

Pause. Mrs. Solomon was silent while he spoke.

"Listen Stephen, I was calling because Thomas hasn't heard anything from the university regarding his admission status. I just spoke to a Mrs. Massini in the admissions office. She could not find his admissions folder."

Pause.

"She said she looked in the new admit file, the rejection file, and the pending file. She just couldn't find it."

Pause.

"They must have lost it. She told me he would have to apply all over again. That is preposterous!"

Pause.

"Well, maybe you could talk to them in the admissions office."

Pause.

"I thought you would. We need to get as many of our kids into college as possible, especially the bright ones like Mr. Thomas."

Pause

"Yes, he is a very rare one and an exception to the rule. Do you think someone in the engineering department could possibly have his admission's folder?"

Pause.

"Sure, you have my number. Okay, I'll wait for your call. Give my love to Doris and the children." In her normal fashion she blew him a kiss over the phone.

Little sat back in his seat, "What did he say?"

"Well, the dean of admission is out sick for the rest of the week. Apparently, the secretary, Mrs. Massini, cannot locate your admissions folder. She said even if she did find the folder, she couldn't give out that information, and no one who could give out admission information was available. But she said for you not to worry. She did say that letters were sent out last week. If yours was one you should be getting something in the mail soon."

"What was that business about my having to apply all over again for next year."

"Don't worry about that. Dr. Hamilton is going to go to the admissions office to see if he can get something out of them. He said if you were applying to the English department, he probably would have access to the information. But since it is for the engineering department, he doesn't know. He'll call me back if he is successful."

"Mrs. Solomon, you told Dr. Hamilton you would be sure to tell me about something."

"Oh yes. There was a group of German scientists that left Germany because of the war. Many of the scientists became professors at the University of Chicago in Illinois. Well, several of them have since left the University of Chicago and have joined the faculty at the University of New England. Apparently, there is a connection between the scientists, the shipyard in New Groton, and the *USS Nautilus*. I believe it will be a great opportunity for you to learn from such highly regarded nuclear scientists."

"I'm sure it will be if I get admitted; the wait is killing me. I'm not going to wait for next year to reapply," Little said sadly.

"Just a few more days, I'm sure you will get admitted. There is no need for you to worry Mr. Thomas. Here, I'll give you a pass for your class."

As Little passed down the hallway to his locker, among the noise of lockers banging closed he could hear students talking about their college selections. Melissa was amongst the loudest boasting about getting accepted to Case Western and how Miss McGinnis helped her complete the applications and apply for scholarships. Swoosh, Anthony, Marvin, Smoothie, and all his buddies on the basketball team, who were seniors, were talking about the schools recruiting them. Several, like Swoosh, had made their decision of which school they would attend. Although he was admitted to several colleges, they were not where he wanted to go.

"Hey Little," it was Smoothie. "Have you heard? I've been recruited by the University of Kansas. Man, I am psyched. Have you decided where you're going? I heard you got accepted to Kansas on a full academic scholarship. Why don't you go? That way you, me, and Swoosh can run the honeys. You're good enough to get on the team as a walk on. When it comes to basketball you got natural talent."

"I'll think about it Smoothie."

FAMILY TIES

It was late, later than usual. Little knew his mother would be concerned about his whereabouts. Glancing at his watch he saw it was after five thirty. Instinctively, he knew everyone would be at home. However, it would be about another half-hour before he arrived home. By the time he arrived home, dinner would be on the table and the family just sitting down at the table. As he walked home, he thought about going to college and what Smoothie had said. Where? He thought to himself. *University of Kansas, I got accepted there. They may not have nuclear engineering as a major, but they do offer chemical, civil, electrical, industrial, and mechanical engineering. And then Swoosh and Smoothie are going there. We can be roommates; continue to hang out, just like we always do. I can try out for the basketball team. I can be a walk on; it won't be all that bad. After all, they did offer me a full four-year academic scholarship. UK called the school several times, they're not the only college to do so. Yea, why put up with all this hassle. I need to make a decision; let these schools know what I'm going to do. I got to stop wasting my time and theirs. Like Pop always says, "A bird in the hand is better than two in the bush," and, right now, the University of New England is in the bush. I'll just go with what I have. Who knows, maybe I'll even like it there. Yep, that's what I'm gonna do. I'll tell everyone at dinner tonight that I've decided to go to the University of Kansas. I know Swoosh will be happy to hear it. Even though it is far away Mom and Pop will also be happy for me. They always said it would be good if Swoosh and I both went to the same college. We would know at least one person, each other, and that would help us to adjust. Being so far away from home, knowing someone else there is important.*

By the time Little arrived in front of his building, he had fully convinced himself to attend the University of Kansas with Swoosh and Smoothie. At the same time, he accepted the fact that he would not be admitted to the University of New England.

As Little stood gazing at the building where he lived, he could smell the pork chops frying on the stove. "Pok chops, cabbage and mashed potatoes, smothered in onions and gravy. Boy, your Momma put her foot in it this time." It was Mr. Taylor hanging out of his window. "I'm sorry to see you brang your tall lanky beehind home. I could of ate yo' plate. Is I 'vited to dinna tonight or what?"

"I'll bring you down a plate if there is anything left, Uncle Clarence," Little said smiling.

Mrs. Jones started to yell at him from her window. "You sho' nuf betta brang me sum too. Tell yo Momma to shut her windas. I can't concentrait on o'count of her food smellin' so good. She got dis whole neighborhood hongry. Boy, it's sho makin me hungry."

"Aunt Mattie! Where'd you learn such a big word, concentrate?" Little asked laughingly.

"Never you mined. Just tells yo' Momma what I say."

"Okay Aunt Mattie. I'll be sure to tell Momma."

"Hey Little," shouted Mr. Taylor. "You hear from that school up north?"

"No sir, not yet."

"What you's gonna do fo' dis fall? You ain't 'cided which college you goin' to come fall, has ya?"

"Well, I've decided to go to the University of Kansas."

"Yeah. Ain't dat da school where Swoosh goin?"

"Yes sir."

"Good, that means I gits to eat both y'alls plates when you's gone."

"Uncle Clarence is that all you can think about, your belly?"

"Yep." Mr. Taylor, Mrs. Jones and Little all laughed as he went inside.

Little opened the door to the apartment. Dinner was on the table. Everybody was about to sit down at the table to eat.

"Looks like I made it just in time for dinner."

His mother looked at him. "Yes you did son. Now go wash your hands. Why are you so late and where is Jerald?"

"I'm not exactly sure where Swoosh is. I think he said something about going to the library after tutoring. Something about a paper he had to turn in for English literature class. If I know Swoosh, he hasn't read the book yet." As he washed his hands in the bathroom he shouted, "But he should be home soon."

"That answered the question about your brother. Now, what about you? Why are you so late?"

"Me. Oh I was tutoring. Some of the students have a math test tomorrow. They asked me to stay a little later."

"You should have called to let us know."

"I'm sorry, I meant to call, but we were really busy."

"Well, hurry up son, food's getting cold. We started to eat without you."

His father laughed, "Uncle Clarence has been up here three times inviting himself to dinner. Said you and Swoosh were eating out tonight. He said you boys had hot dates with some high yellow gals from uptown."

Everyone enjoyed a good laugh at the table.

Suddenly, there was a banging on the door. "Let me in. I smell them pork chops and two of um got my name on them." Everyone recognized the voice on the other side of the door.

"It's Swoosh," shouted Esther. "It's Swoosh!"

"Boy, use your key. I am not getting up from my dinner table because your hind-parts is too lazy to reach in your hip pocket and get the key out," shouted Mrs. Thomas.

"Don't eat my pork chops, I smelled them three blocks away. Hurry up and open the door Madear."

The five voices ranged out in unison. "USE YOUR KEY."

"Y'all some cold people," Swoosh quibbled as he opened the door.

"You's sitting there treating me like I'm some hobo off the street. My name is not Clarence Taylor."

"I heards dat," ranged out a voice from below. Laughter filled the dinner table.

Quickly, Swoosh pulled out his chair and sat down. As second nature he put the basketball on his lap.

"Boy, have you taken leave of your senses? You better take that ball off my table. Get up and go wash your face and hands," scowled Mrs. Thomas. "And just where have you been?"

"The ball ain't on the table Madear. It's in my lap."

Mrs. Thomas looked sharply at Swoosh with her I don't want no nonsense look. "Move it now, and I want an answer child."

"Okay Madear," he said as he pushed the ball down the hall. "First, after practice I went to the library to do some homework. Then I played a little hoop with the fellas," he responded disappearing into the bathroom.

Swoosh emerged minutes later and began displaying his clean hands for Mrs. Thomas to inspect. "Clean enough for you Madear?" he asked as he walked over to her and kissed her on the cheek.

"Boy, go sit down."

"Hey Little," he shouted out joyfully, "Uncle Clarence just told me you said that you're going with me to school in Kansas. Alright; on time, gimmie some skin," he shouted holding out his hand for Little to slap it.

Mr. Thomas looked bewildered. "Little, you didn't tell us. When did you make that decision? Don't get me wrong, but I thought you were waiting to hear from the University of New England."

"Hey Little," interrupted Elisha breaking into the conversation.

"Not now Elisha," Mr. Thomas said cutting him off! "We're talking with your brother."

All eyes fell upon Little. He hated being put on the spot and most of all having to give an account for his actions or decisions. "Well, today I went to see Mrs. Solomon in her office. I asked her if she would call UNE to check on the status of my application." Little took a deep breath. Letting out a long sad deep lamenting sigh, he continued explaining. "Needless to say, they couldn't find my admission file. It wasn't in the accepted, rejected or pending pile. The lady in the admissions office told Mrs. Solomon that I would have to complete another application and send it in for consideration next year. Since I've been getting all kinds of mail from schools across the country, I thought about it and decided, since I was offered a full four-year academic scholarship at Kansas, I'll go there. At least this way Swoosh and I can stay together. Besides, you said it would be good if Swoosh and I went to the same college. Now, it won't be just Swoosh. It will be Swoosh, Smoothie and myself."

In an attempt to get his attention, Elisha began tugging on Little's arm, once again interrupting him. "But Little."

"Elisha, stop interrupting me. Can't you see that I am talking?" He continued. "I'll at least know two people there, Swoosh and Smoothie. They do offer engineering as a major. I decided when I was on my way home to go to the University of Kansas. That's why I didn't tell you. I mean, I got here just a few minutes ago. Besides, all of you have been so noisy, I didn't have a chance to tell you."

"Yea man," chimed in Swoosh, "We can put down on the housing form that we want to be roommates. Then, we can run that campus." Quickly, Swoosh looked at Mrs. Thomas. "I meant study together Madear. Yea, me, you, Smoothie, and Bebop," shouted out Swoosh. "Oh, I didn't tell you Bebop decided to go to UK also. He got his letter yesterday in the mail. Now, that makes three people from our high school Madear. We, New Yorkers, are going to show that country hick town who's the boss."

The dinner table was not as noisy as before. However, with the prospects of he and Little going to Kansas, Swoosh was more than his old entertaining self. In his excitement of this revelation, he had the worst-case scenario of what the family affectionately termed a bad case of "diarrhea of the mouth." For the duration of the dinner, Swoosh continued to jabber. In his normal fashion, Swoosh dominated the entire conversation on how he and Little would be together and how they were going to rule the campus.

"Excuse me Swoosh," Mr. Thomas said, "Esther did you or your brother pick up the mail?"

"I got the mail," she proudly announced. "I was standing at the door when Mr. Mailman came. First, he gave it to Elisha and Elisha let me bring it upstairs."

"Was anything in it for me," asked Little?

"How do I know? I can't read. But there was a big white envelope for you. It said Mr. Thomas Thomas. I think it's from the president of the Uniberrsarie of New England."

Little laughed, "Now how would you know it was from the president of the University of New England little Miss I can't read smarty pants?"

"Because Elisha told me."

"That's what I was trying to tell you. But you told me to be quiet," shouted Elisha.

Curiously, Little asked, "Where is it?"

Anxiously, Elisha jumped up from the table, dashed down the hall toward the bedroom. "I put it on your bed. I'll get it," he shouted. In a flash, he returned carrying a large white envelope. "See it says, Office of the President, the University of New England. Here," he said, passing the envelop to Little. "See, I tried to tell you, but everyone kept telling me to be quiet."

Five pair of eyes were fully engaged in the movement of Elisha toward Little. In anticipation, Swoosh began loathing with deep passion the envelope Elisha held in his small hand.

As if in freeze-frame slow motion, Little could see Elisha approaching with the envelope in his small hand. Elisha stopped short. However, the little hand holding the envelope continued moving toward him in a forward motion. Little's eyes were transfixed on the envelope moving toward him. With the ticking of each milli-second lasting minutes, the envelope drew closer and closer to tips of his fingers.

Fingertips, everything languished very, very slowly; all appeared to be eternal.

The envelope finally touched the tips of his fingers. Little froze. The envelope slid across his fingertips onto the palm of his hand. A hush covered the table, not a soul stirred. Little grasped the envelope firmly in his hand. Momentarily, he stared at the regular letter-size flat envelope. His heart raced. He could hear it pounding inside his chest. *This can't be good news in such a thin envelope.* Other letters of acceptance he received were in large envelopes and contained brochures, housing application and other information. Little sat staring at the envelope firmly in his grasp and prayed.

"Well open it son. Don't leave us all here waiting," clamored Mr. Thomas. "We'll all grow old waiting for you to open it."

Painfully, being extra careful not to tear the envelope's content, using precision and care, Little slipped his index finger under the flap and slid his finger along its angle. He gently prided open the envelope. With great intensity, gradually he pulled the letter from its habitation. The family sat dormant as Little unfolded and quietly read the letter to himself. With a blank expression on his face, he unceremoniously, without agitation, read the letter.

Slumping back into his chair he continued to read the letter to himself. Again and again, his eyes became clouded with tears. Then without hesitation, he sedulously read it aloud:

Office of the President

Dear Mr. Thomas:

    Congratulations on placing among the top one percent of the Achievement Program. The University of New England has a proud tradition of seeking students of outstanding academic excellence and social capabilities for its student body. The university is dedicated to excellence in all its programs.

It is with great pleasure I admit you to the University of New England this Fall as a freshmen student, and as a recipient of the Presidential Scholarship Award.

Twelve Presidential scholarships are awarded each year. As a Presidential Scholar you will receive a full four-year scholarship including tuition, books, housing and fees.

Should you decide to accept this offer, please sign and return the enclosed letter of acceptance.

I look forward to seeing you in August.

Sincerely, Edward Garvey, Ph.D.
President

For one moment, as if paralyzed no one could move or verbalize as each of them continued to process the content of the letter. There was absolute silence in the apartment. Still shocked, Little suddenly realized what he had just read. "I got accepted," he softly said. Then he shouted, "I got in. Oh, my God. Oh my God. I got accepted at the University of New England!"

Mr. Thomas still reeling in shock stared at Little. Pushing his chair back slowly, he arose from his place at the table. Little jumped up knocking over his chair. Impetuously, in one fluid motion he leaped into his father's arms. Wrapping his legs around his waist and his arms around his neck he began kissing his father on the forehead. "I got in Pop," he shouted. "I got in. I'm going to UNE."

Excited that something good just happened to their big brother, Elisha and Esther began bouncing up and down in their seat screaming. Pandemonium erupted. Mrs. Thomas, in a whirlwind fashion rushed over to Little and Mr. Thomas. Gathering around Little, they all began hugging and yelling out shouts of joy. Swoosh dawdled as he absorbed the commotion taking place around him. Not wanting to be left out of the celebration, painfully he moved over to join the family. Little hugged his mother, then Esther and Elisha. Grabbing Swoosh, Little drew him in tightly. Tightly embracing him, Little did not see Swoosh's luminous eyes had vanished. Swoosh gritted his teeth, clinched his fist, and clutched Little more tightly.

Thrilled, Little ran to the living room window and began yelling with each shout becoming a little louder than the one before. "Hey everybody, I got accepted to the University of New England. I got accepted to the University of New England. I got accepted to the University of New England."

"What dat you say boy," a voice replied? It was Mr. Taylor. "I got accepted to the University of New England."

"Ain't dat, dat big school in Kanneecut," asked Mrs. Jones?

"Yes ma'am. It's where I want to go. I got accepted. I got accepted," he joyously kept shouting out of the window.

"I here'd dat school cost a lot o' money," scoffed Mr. Taylor.

Suddenly, for the first time it dawned on Little; the presidential scholarship. "I got a four-year scholarship," he subtly whispered. He repeated it softly to himself. "I got a four-year scholarship." The whisper became louder. "I got a four-year scholarship." Louder. "I got a four-year, fully paid scholarship to the University of New England." Realizing what he was saying, he shouted vociferously out of the window, "I got a four-year *presidential* scholarship. I'm a presidential scholar! I got a four-year, all-expense-paid scholarship to the University of New England." Hysterically, Little shouted out of the window to everyone passing by.

"Boy, dat's good, I always knowed you's was smart. I's proud of you son," responded Mrs. Jones excitedly.

"I is too boy," touted Mr. Taylor, "Now what about ma pok chop?" Little turned around to face his family, "Mrs. Solomon. I got to tell Mrs. Solomon," Little shouted. "Mom, Pop, may I call Mrs. Solomon. Please? I can't wait until tomorrow. May I call her tonight?"

"Sure, I'm going to go tell your Aunt Betty," replied his mother.

Calling out to Little, Swoosh moved over to him. "My mom *is* going to be home early tonight. I promised her I'd be there." Grabbing him, Swoosh held him tightly. Breaking the embrace, he stepped slightly back.

Holding both of Little's hands between his, he gently pressed his lips against Little's exposed knuckles. In a low, melancholic voice he whispered, "I'm happy for you. You got want you really wanted. I am really happy for you." A lone tear rolled down his cheek. Quickly, he turned and walked out of the apartment.

A TALE OF TWO FRIENDSHIPS

The sun was high in the sky, the trees were sprouting leaves, and the flowers were in full bloom. It was a perfect spring day in Harlem. Dressed in a pair of tan khaki pants, a sky-blue shirt, and his favorite Converse All Star, Swoosh walked languidly down the streets and around the corners. For the last few weeks, he had not felt like his old self. Appearing unguided to passersby on the street, they looked upon his tall structure with question. Standing before a tall building, he glanced up at its upper floors with disillusion. It was a hospital he was well aquatinted with.

Aimlessly, he entered the front lobby of the hospital. Getting on the elevator, he noticed it was empty. He was glad to be the only person riding in the car. The elevator expressed him to the floor he had selected. Getting off, he trudged down the hall. Halfway down the hall he stopped at the office door of Marc Isenberg, MD., chief of neurosurgery. The door swung open before he could open it.

"Jerald Jefferson. How are you doing son?"

"Hello Dr. Gannon. I'm fine, and yourself?"

"Doing good son. You had a great season this past year. I heard you're going to the University of Kansas in the fall."

"Yes sir. I was given both a basketball and an academic scholarship."

"That's great, although I know academically, you'll do just fine."

"Thank you."

"Jerald, are you alright? Your eyes look swollen."

"Yes sir. I'm okay. It's just my allergies."

"Listen, I have a colleague from California who is a physician at the University's medical center, a Dr. Lance Griffin. Stop by my office before you leave, and I'll give him a call while you're here. He's also been following your high school record and wants you to look him up. He personally promised me that he would look after you. You know what we've talked about. He can be a big help to you."

"Sure thing Dr. Gannon. I'll stop by your office as soon as I finish." Swoosh stepped into the office. It was a large office area, dark brown panel walls with pictures. The dark-blue carpet was plush and deep. He walked over to the desk. The nameplate read: Mrs. Ruth Thomas, Administrative Assistant. With his head lowered, Swoosh passively glared at the floor.

"Jerald."

"Hi Madear."

"Are you alright?" Immediately, she stood up and walked toward him, as she spoke. "You don't look so good."

"Can I talk to you about something?"

"Sure, I can take a break now. Let me just tell Dr. Isenberg."

"I don't mean to interrupt you. It's really not all that important Madear. It can wait until later."

Mrs. Thomas saw the distressful look on his face and the apprehensive reflection in his swollen eyes. "Nonsense. No, baby, it's no problem at all," she insisted.

The door to Dr. Isenberg's office opened. A medium-height white male in his early sixties wearing a white medical coat exited. Immediately, he saw Swoosh. "Mr. Jefferson. What a pleasant surprise seeing you. Ruth hasn't stopped talking about you and Thomas," he stated as he extended his hand toward Swoosh.

Swoosh instinctively tried camouflaging his state of mind. Gathering a big smile on his face, he let out a big cheerful hello Dr. Ike. As the two shook hands, Swoosh did not engage in his customary joking with him.

Having known him for many years, Dr. Isenberg saw through Swoosh's façade. He sensed something was seriously wrong. "Ruth, I have to consult with Dr. Schmidt about a patient. I'll be out for about thirty minutes."

"Okay, Dr. Isenberg. May I use your office? Jerald wants to talk."

"Please, go right ahead. You know you're welcomed to it anytime. Take as much time as you need Ruth."

"Thank you, Dr. Isenberg."

"Anytime Ruth." Looking at Swoosh, he paused, "We're all very proud of you and Thomas. If I can do anything to help, don't hesitate to ask son. Good seeing you again. You make sure you and Thomas stop by to see me before you leave for college."

"Thank you, and I'll be sure to see you before I leave Dr. Ike." As Dr. Isenberg left, Mrs. Thomas and Swoosh went into his office. One wall of the office was moderately decorated with books. Several plaques hung on the wall along with his degrees from various universities. Swoosh always liked his office. He found it to be warm and friendly.

Swoosh stood opposite Mrs. Thomas. "Madear, I feel so bad; so dirty, and unclean. I don't know where to begin."

"It is alright baby," she said reassuringly. "Sit here and relax. Just take your time."

Like an overflowing raging river, Swoosh let it flood out, while rubbing the palm of his hands against his legs. "It's like this Madear. You know Little and me, we've been like brothers since we were babies. I just don't understand why I'm so mad at him and why I hate him so much. Don't get me wrong Madear, I'm really happy he got into the University of New England. I mean, I really want him to go there. But at the same time, I'm mad because he is going. I want him to go because that's where he wants to go. But, at the same time, I don't want him to go because then we'll be split up. We've never been split up before. I'm confused."

He paused as the tears began to well up in his eyes. "Little is my brother; you know I really love him. I really do." Mrs. Thomas found the box of tissue on Dr. Isenberg's desk and gave him a few. Swoosh did not notice she kept a few in her own hand. Quietly, she sat back and listened as he continued.

"That night at the dinner table when Elisha gave him the letter, I felt so stupid. I kept going on and on talking about how we were going to the University of Kansas together and us being roommates. I went on and on and on about us going to college together. Then Elisha came out with that letter. I don't know what got into me. I wished I had found that stupid letter and tore it up before Little got it. Everyone was so happy for him. I was too, but at the same time, I was mad at him. Madear, he's splitting us up. I hated him. These last few days and weeks I've been really miserable. Us not hanging around together like we always do. But why do I feel so betrayed by Little?" Swoosh failed at his effort to fight back the tears. Covering his face with his hands, he bowed at the waist and wept.

Mrs. Thomas leaned forward and tenderly rubbed his back with her hand. "It's alright to cry Jerald. There's no shame in crying. Let it out, baby. Just let all those pinned up feelings out."

Sitting up he continued as his body trembled. "Madear, the truth is I'm scared. I'm scared of losing my best friend and brother. Little is my only brother. I'm scared of going to Kansas all by myself. I don't know anybody, and nobody there knows me. You know of the two of us, Little is the friendlier one. He makes friends so easily. Most people I know, I know because I met them through him. You know if it hadn't been for his making me study all the time and studying with me, I probably would not have made the grades I made or graduated from high school, let alone get into college. He made me do my homework; he tutored me. He taught me all kinds of things, chess, tennis, and basketball. To be totally honest, he is the better ball player. That inside move everybody always raves about me doing, he taught it to me. How am I supposed to make it without him? If it wasn't for Little, I'd just be another dumb jock, and not a very good one at that."

Slowly, he stood up and walked to the other side of the room and faced the wall. "Madear, is it wrong for me to be mad at him? I mean, to have all these bad feelings about him. I'm so mixed up and so confused. At times, I'm happy for him, and then the next minute, I'm mad at him. Then there are times when I'm really proud of him, proud to be standing next to him, to say he's my brother. Then, out of the clear blue from nowhere, I can't stand him. I hate him. I blame him for splitting us up. How can you love and hate someone at the same time? I don't deserve his friendship or his love, and all the love you've given me."

Swoosh put his hands against the wall. Looking down, the tears began to trickle from his eyes, falling to the floor. "I don't like feeling this way. I wish we could stay in high school forever Madear. I feel so alone, so miserable. I feel so empty inside. I must be losing my mind. Am I being selfish Madear? Am I?" He pleaded for an answer to his questions. Desperately, he pleaded for an answer to end his pain.

Mrs. Thomas stood up and moved to him. Gently, she placed her hand on his shoulder. "No, you're not being selfish Jerald. What you're feeling is only natural, baby. You're feeling like you're losing a part of you. A big part; it's all part of loving someone. The two of you have been inseparable since you were three, four, five years old. The two of you were together so much people, used to think you were twins."

With a slight chuckle, she continued. "They were confused when they learned you weren't even cousins. It was a shock to the both of you when you found out that you weren't really brothers or related."

Again, in a motherly tone, she spoke. "The two of you grew up so close; you two shared everything, even your feelings. When one was sick, the other knew it. If you were sad, then Little knew something was wrong. Not only did the two of you sense each other's pain, but somehow, you also experienced it. I know this will be the first time the two of you will be apart, and it is frightening. It's only natural that you're scared. Neither of you emotionally planned for this day. There's no way you could have. Now that it's going to happen, emotionally you're having trouble handling it. Remember it's a process, and we all go through it. Don't be so hard on yourself or sell yourself short."

She took a deep breath. "You're very smart Jerald; don't let anyone tell you different. Little just helped bring out what was always inside of you. You'll find that in no time, you'll make plenty of friends and you'll be doing that silly old Swoosh shuffle. But you know what? I bet you that Little is going through the same thing."

"You really think he is Madear?"

"I know he is."

"How do you know Madear? Did he say something? He doesn't act like it."

"Jerald, you only see him parading around with his chest stuck out and all happy about going to UNE. It ain't nothing but a big act he's putting on for everybody; just like the act you've been putting on. On the outside it's an act. Just like you, it's his way of disguising his true feelings. Now that it has been a couple of days, his feelings are no different from yours. He is feeling the same things you're feeling. On the inside, he is as scared to leave as you are. He's as torn up emotionally about the two of you being at different schools, just like you."

Puzzled with her response, Swoosh turned around and leaned his back against the wall. With tear-filled eyes, he asked, "Do you really think so?"

She held her arms wide-open and gave him a warm smile. "You, if anybody should know better than any of us. You know him as well, if not better, than his daddy and me."

Rapidly, Swoosh moved into her warm embrace. "Madear, I knew I could talk to you. I knew you would understand me. Thanks for talking to me," he said kissing her on the cheek. "I better git to the library. We haven't graduated yet. I still have a constitutional law paper due."

"Okay baby. You got a key. I'll see you at home and be on time for dinner."

Swoosh chuckled as he dried his face and walked out of the office. Turning around he looked back in the office. "Madear."

"Yes Jerald."

"If you tell anyone what I said about Little being a better basketball player than me, I'll deny every word," he said chuckling.

"It will be our secret."

Passing Dr. Isenberg in the corridor, they briefly chatted about his going to Kansas for college. He remembered to stop by Dr. Gannon's office. After leaving Dr. Gannon's office, he returned to Dr. Isenberg's office. Opening the door, he heard Mrs. Thomas and Dr. Isenberg's talking. "Ruth. You're crying. What's wrong?"

"I'm alright Dr. Isenberg. It's just that Jerald shared with me his feelings about attending a different school than Thomas. He feels like he's losing a part of himself. I know how he feels. As a mother, I have the same feelings. Except, what he doesn't know is I'm losing two sons, Jerald and Thomas. Elijah and I have wrestled with this since the day those boys started their senior year. When Jerald first said he was accepted at the University of Kansas on a full-time scholarship, Elijah didn't speak to him for almost a week. He was always snapping at Jerald for little things. And Jerald, you know that boy, so carefree, he never noticed a thing. He just kept right on being himself. That boy is something else. He is amazing, and I love him so much. Then Little started with going to the University of New England. These pasts few weeks, the tension in my house has been so thick you can cut it with a knife. Elijah and I have to adjust to the fact that they're both leaving for college. Maybe it would have been easier if one went off one year and the other the next year. But both of them are leaving just a week apart. It's so hard, so very hard getting used to the idea. I love both of them it hurts. It hurts so badly inside of me. I can't help feeling like I'm losing both my sons at the same time."

That evening, the bedroom was more silent than it had been for the past several nights. Swoosh, while lying on his back, tossed his basketball in the air. "Little."

Annoyed, Little grunted a replied, "Yeah."

"I'm sorry."

"You're sorry, sorry for what? What did you do now Swoosh?" he snapped.

"It's not so much for what I did as much as it's for what I was feeling."

Little's attention was drawn away from the book he was reading. "Hah. What are you talking about?" He looked at Swoosh from the corner of his eyes. His head turned slowly in Swoosh's direction. Looking puzzled at Swoosh, he said, "Come again. What are you talking about? What are you up to Swoosh?"

Swoosh stopped tossing the ball in the air. "You know what I'm talking about Little. Man, I was mad at you for changing your mind about Kansas. In fact, I've been a big jerk and a real butt hole not talking to you. I just want you to know I'm really happy for you. You know, getting in the University of New England." Sitting up on the edge of the bed, he looked over at Little. "Man, you really wanted it, and you really deserve it. I was being selfish. I just never thought we would ever get split up."

Little sat up on the bed and looked at Swoosh. "I sort of know what you mean. I knew you were mad; I sort of played it off." Little took a deep breath and let out a long sigh. "I was afraid to show my true feelings. To be honest, I'm scared of leaving home, Mom, Pop, and you. I've been feeling bad all week. I wanted to say something to you. But I just didn't know how or what to say."

"Man," replied Swoosh, "Nobody ever told us growing up was going to be this hard. I don't know why I'm this upset over your ugly butt anyway."

"Yeah." Little laughed and threw his pillow at Swoosh. "Or this painful."

Swoosh pointed to the scar on his wrist that sealed them as blood brothers. "Brothers?"

Little looked up, gently and tenderly stroking the scar on his wrist; reaching across the room he placed his scar upon Swoosh's. "Until death us do part."

"Ya know Little, I was feeling really rotten about how I was feeling, so I went to Madear's office today to talk to her. I promised Doc Gannon I'd stop in to see him after I left her office. After speaking with Doc Gannon, I went back to Madear's office. She and Doc Ike didn't see me, but she was crying. I heard her telling Doc Ike that she and Pop are having a real tough time with our leaving home too. If you and I are feeling this bad, I can't imagine how they must be feeling. Madear told Doc Ike they're really hurting because they're losing two sons at the same time."

"I can't imagine how Mom and Pop must be really feeling. Hey Swoosh, let's go talk to them."

In the still of the quiet of the night, Little and Swoosh, dressed for bed, walked down the hallway of the apartment to their parent's bedroom. It was well past eleven-thirty. This was one of the few nights Mr. Thomas did not work a double shift. Knocking on the door, the boys waited for a response.

"Who is it?" The sleepy bass voice called out.

"Mom, Pop, it's us, me and Swoosh. Can we come in?"

"Sure boys. What's wrong?"

Little and Swoosh made their way inside the bedroom. Sitting at the foot of the bed, Swoosh started off. "Something very serious Pop. Little and I, well we were kind of talking about leaving for college."

Mr. and Mrs. Thomas sat up in the bed to listen.

"We just wanted you to know…" Swoosh stopped. "Madear and Pop, you've always been family to me. I ain't gonna lie, I'm scared about leaving. You know, going off to college and being on my own. Both, me and Little are really scared of leaving home; leaving the two of you is probably the hardest thing we've ever had to do. Leaving is hard. I kind of want to go. But then I don't want to go. But then we know we gotta go. Leaving the two of you, we believe, is the hardest thing we'll ever have to do in life."

"Boys," Mr. Thomas said interrupting Swoosh. "It's eleven-thirty. Before anybody goes anywhere, we have to go to work in the morning and you guys have to go to school. When you guys were little, before you turned thirteen and thought you were too big, you use to sleep in the bed with us all the time. You guys always said you wanted to talk. But most of the times, you were just scared." Mr. Thomas lifted up the covers. "Come on, and get in."

Without hesitating, Little and Swoosh, like two little eight-year-olds, happily climbed into the bed between their parents. As they mischievously placed themselves under the covers, years of joyous memories flooded the room. Each memory reflected on this special time and place; mostly memories of being safe in bed with Mom and Pop. This place, this time, this bed!

Mrs. Thomas once again experienced being a mother with her children safely in her arms. They were hers to love and protect. Everything was all right. Just perfect. A special ecstasy secretly overcame her. Her spine tingled with joy as her womb leaped with jubilee. That which was a separated part of her was now reunited. Her need, need to hold her sons close to her again, to love them, and to know she was loved and needed was fulfilled this night.

Little once again smelled the sweet perfumed of his mother's body upon the pillow. A fragrance he had longed for; a fragrance he would never forget. Knowing her ever-abounding love for him, he felt warm, safe, and most of all protected. No harm could come to him while he lay between his mother and father. He was their little boy—their son. Tall, gentle, and courageous like his father. Also possessing the softness, pleasantness, and craftiness of his mother, he knew he was a strong combination of both. He had the best of the best. A world—his world—it was the world they helped him build. They had provided an environment of love, comfort, strength, and support. Feeling his mother's arm draped over his body was soothing, encouraging, and warm. Between the two, he could go exploring, knowing no adversity would befall him. They were his protectors and his guardian angels. They were his parents.

The strength of Mr. Thomas's arm rested across the body of Swoosh. From his strength, Swoosh felt his nurturing, growth, and development were complete. Swoosh's sense of being was enhanced over the years by the Thomas family. It was from these strong arms all fear departed. From the guidance of Pop, he achieved heights he considered unobtainable. He experienced joys that were not measurable. Love had no limits, no boundaries. This love was not linked by blood only. For Swoosh, all was well.

Here, tonight, he knew it was all right to be a man and still be Mom and Pop's little boy. He would have it no other way. Mr. Thomas, knowing his two boys were safe within his grasp, could once again protect them, at least for tonight. He knew they were his for tonight. However, tomorrow would be another story. As for tonight, he was their protector. A lone tear fell from his eye landing upon his pillow. Reaching across the bodies of the boys, he took his wife's hand. His left hand joined to her right hand. Tonight, they were joined together in love, encompassing their sons. Tonight, peace reigned, and love was bountiful.

June 16, Thomas Isaiah Thomas and Jerald James Jefferson, Jr. graduated from Harlem High School. Elijah and Ruth Thomas were very proud of their son as he gave the valedictorian address before the crowded auditorium of parents, students, faculty, staff, and well-wishers.

DAZES GONE BY

Elijah woke up earlier than usual. He glimpsed at the alarm clock on the nightstand beside his bed. The early morning sunlight was starting to creep through the translucent shade on the window opposite the bed. "Six o'clock, and the sun is already high in the sky," he murmured to himself. The past three nights had been insufferably hot with no relief in sight. The lone fan in the window continuously hummed as it swirled the hot air around the bedroom.

The summer was promising to be a hot one, perhaps one of the hottest on record. But he knew this restless night was not due to the sultry heat. It was more due to the strong premonition he experienced during the night. It was strong and very real. It was inevitable. After this summer, he sensed things would not be the same between him and Little. Something was about to change forever. Forever changed—he wondered how, and would it be for the better or for the worst? When would it happen, today, next month, or maybe next year? He did not know, but he did know that things would change forever. Things would not be the same. He knew it was coming.

There were too many secrets, too many skeletons in the closet, and too much of the past clouding over the future. This would be the last summer they would all be intact as a family. Whatever was to take place, he felt powerless to stop. He yearned to stop it, but it was a fate not for him to determine and not his to stop. The die had been casted many, many years ago. A premonition—half-consciousness—he recalled the last time he had such a strong premonition. It was a very long time ago. A very long time ago in what he felt was another lifetime. It was in another lifetime when he had his last and disturbing premonition. *If only it all could be behind me. If it could only be behind me.*

As he laid awake thinking, his mind took him back to a place and time. To a place and time he had long since left. It was in the cool of the spring. A cool spring morning in the month of May. He was a young man of twenty-five years, living in Canaan, in Bladen County, North Carolina. Married, that coming September of that same year, he had the premonition. He and his wife Rebecca were expecting their firstborn child. Elijah and Rebecca were excited. His parents and her parents were all fascinated with the prospects of a grandson or granddaughter. They anxiously awaited the anticipated blessed event.

He was a graduate of Morehouse College, in Atlanta, Georgia where he studied business. After graduation, he entered the army to fulfill his patriotic duty and show his undying love and devotion for his country. He learned about electrical engineering in the army. Upon returning home from the army, he went to work for North Carolina Electric and Power Company. Rebecca, his wife, graduated from Spellman College, an all-women school in Atlanta, Georgia. She was a teacher at Abraham Lincoln Elementary School. It was the local school for the Negro children in Canaan.

His father, a farmer and businessman, owned a lot of land in Bladen County. Rebecca's parents also owned a lot of property. Both properties combined were the prime choice of the entire county. They had the best land in the entire county. White folks always wanted to buy it. Neither of them would ever consider selling. Papa would always say, "Son, the land is all we've got. When everything else is gone, the land will still be here. You have to leave an inheritance, a legacy to your children. Leave them the land." There was over four thousand five hundred acres between his folks and Rebecca's. Naw, they would never sell the land; neither would he. In time, he and Rebecca were going to take over the family businesses.

Elijah and Rebecca were both only children. Their parents were only children and the children of only children. They were the descendants of freeman. He and Rebecca had just built their home on the property line between both their parents. The house bordered the property between their parents, along the Cape Fear River. It was the biggest and finest home in all of Bladen County. They were the first Negroes to have a brick home with indoor plumbing and electric lights.

It was that cool spring morning, the morning of the premonition. From it, he knew his life was about to change. Change forever. And change it did.

Then it happened, the premonition. The day it happened his son, his first born, and only child was three months old. Everybody, his parents, her parents, everyone was at the house celebrating. That Sunday morning, Elijah Isaiah Thomas IV was officially baptized in Mount Zion Second Baptist Church. The same church Rebecca's father and grandfather had pastored. It was the church where he and Rebecca married. He was ordained in that church. It was the church he was expected to someday pastor.

It was getting toward late evening and all of the church folks had left the party to go home. Elijah left the house to take Sister Pearlie Mae Wiggins home. He was only gone for an hour. He lost Rebecca, his wife, little Elijah, his firstborn son, his mother, father, Grandpa Elijah, his mother's father, great grandpa Thomas, and Rebecca's parents in the fire.

County Sheriff Bo Johnston told him, "Dey musta got trapped inside. Doe musta jam. Dey couldn't git it o'pin in time. I blame da fire on a faulty lectrical wire. Fire started accidentally. Boy, y'alls lucky ya weren't in dat der house at dat time. Ya could o' died in dat tey fire jes' like da rest o' yo' kin folk."

The next morning, Elijah found the empty shotgun shell cases on the ground. The empty gas cans, horseshoe prints and the flaming cross imprint etched by fire on the ground in front of the charred house. The general store, the bakery, and the feed store owned by his mother and father nights later also mysteriously burned down. That night, and so many nights thereafter, he wished he had died. He wished he had died in that fire with his family.

Filled with grief, Elijah blamed God for their death. How could a merciful, loving God take the life of his wife, baby, in-laws, and his parents? The loneliness, he couldn't bare the loneliness and pain all knotted up inside of him. Dead inside, he just wanted to curl up in his pain and die physically.

The memories were painful. He had to escape them, so he gave up his life and all he knew. He left North Carolina and came north to New York City where he got a job with Con Edison. He left his harp in Canaan by the river. He could not sing the songs of Zion in a strange land. He gave up hope and moved north.

Running away didn't solve the problem. The painful memories soon afterwards followed him to Harlem. He started drinking. He sought to find his answer in a bottle. He spent his time drinking to forget, then drinking to pass the time away. Drinking very heavily; drinking really heavy to forget his pain. He would go to work, come home, and drink. He'd get drunk and pass out. Work, home, drink, get drunk, pass out. Every night, it was his routine. The pain and the loneliness from the void in his life was more than he wanted to bear. The loneliness, he couldn't bear the loneliness. Drinking dulled the pain, but it could not and would never erase it. Scars—the scars, too many and too deep. A long, long time ago, Elijah had a disturbing premonition.

Snapping out of his hypnotic state, strikingly perturbed, Elijah lay back down. Turning over, he stared at Ruth reposed peacefully upon the bed fast asleep. Her face, the sweetest face he ever saw. A glow illuminated around her face. To him, she had the face of an angel. The glow of her beauty through the years remained unfazed. Gently, he stroked her face with his long, thick fingers. Leaning forward, bending over her, he kissed her ruby red lips. Her ruby red lips were smoother than oil. Lying back down, he continued to gaze upon her beauty. A cold chill tingled up his spine making him shiver. That night, Elijah had a disturbing premonition.

NEW LEASE ON LIFE

It was almost eighteen years to the day when he first met Ruth Ann Mears. It was the most blessed day of his, then, non-existent life. Widowed for about sixteen years, he was living in a sparsely furnished flat in Harlem. Alone and withdrawn from the world around him, his health, life, and desire to continue living was on a declining spiral. So, lost and consumed by his misery, all seemed hopeless. He had left his harp in Canaan by the river. He could not sing the songs of Zion in a strange land. For this once-proud man, the past sixteen years his world had become work, home, the bottle, sleep, and back to work—it became his daily routine. It became all he knew. He did not care about his personal appearance, nor what he ate, when he ate, or where he ate.

His performance on the job was equally waning. Because of his drinking, personal appearance, and psychological state, he was about to lose the one thing he had left, his job with Con Edison. For him, none of it mattered. Having lost his entire family, everybody he loved, nothing mattered. *My God, my God, why hast thou forsaken me?*

Oddly enough, he remembered that day after returning home from work. There she was sitting on the stoop outside the apartment building enjoying the warm summer's night air. He was unaware that several weeks ago she had moved into the apartment across the hall from his. This evening, as he had so many times before from a lack of nourishment, fatigue, alcohol, or any combination of the three, he was too dizzy and too weak to climb the stairs of the building.

With no regards to her presence, he slumped down on the stoop beside her. To him this was his personal and private stoop. It was on this stoop that he spent much of his time and many nights. Offended at her presence, he thought that this young girl was invading his private public place. She had no right to be here. Despite his feelings of his privacy being intruded upon, he was still a gentleman, so he spoke kindly. "Hello, I'm Elijah Thomas."

"Good evening," she cheerfully replied. "I'm Ruth Ann Mears. I've seen you several times. We've passed in the hallway and walking down the street."

He looked at her with a questioning look on his face.

Reading his expression, she added, "We live across the hall from each other. I moved in a few weeks ago." She noticed he was not carrying a lunch box and his hands were trembling. "Are you alright?"

"Yeah, I'm just a little weak from working long hours." He struggled to stand up, almost falling.

Showing no concern for her own safety, she grabbed him by the arm to steady him. "No, no, don't get up. You sit here. I'm going to go to my apartment and get you a sandwich and something to drink. Now, don't you move!"

Before he could refuse her offer, she had sprinted up the steps and disappeared behind the huge wood and glass doors. A few minutes later, she emerged from the building carrying a sandwich and a tall glass of cold iced tea in her hands.

"Mr. Thomas…"

He had fallen asleep in that short time.

"Mr. Thomas…" She nudged him.

He awakened. "Oh, I must have drifted off to sleep. I didn't realize how tired I was," he said in his low, dull, drunken voice.

"I didn't have any bread, so I used a butter milk biscuit. I hope you like it," she said as she handed him the sandwich.

"Thank you, Miss, uh…"

"Mears."

"Miss Mears. This will be fine." He was extremely hungry. The thought of that buttermilk biscuit with ham on it crippled his mind. The aroma of that sweet-smelling buttermilk biscuit with ham tormented his empty stomach. He wasted no time devouring the sandwich. The buttermilk biscuit, nice and warm, melted in his mouth like butter on a hot summer's day. The ham, tender and juicy, was sweet and savory in his mouth.

"That was some sandwich," he said looking up at her wanting to smile as he drank the iced tea. "I didn't have much for lunch. No Miss Mears, the truth is…" He held his head between his hands while shielding his face. "I haven't eaten since yesterday. I may not be the best person, but I'm not a liar."

"Well, it is almost eight o'clock, passed supper time. You seem too weak to be fixing dinner for yourself. If you like, I'd be glad to make a plate for you."

He hesitated. "No, please, you've been kind enough giving me the sandwich. I don't want to put you or your family through no more trouble."

Aware of his being, she sensed his hesitation and did not want to infringe upon his dignity. "No trouble. It will be no trouble at all. I'd love the company."

The flavor of the buttermilk biscuit and ham had made his mouth water. The pain of hunger still lingered long in his belly. Feeling unsociable, and not use to having company, he wanted to say no. However, he could not resist the prospects of another taste of that sweet honey tasting ham and the hot melt in your mouth buttermilk biscuit. He relished the thought of another opportunity to encounter the flavors and smells he had not encountered in over sixteen years. He could not resist; physically and mentally he yielded to the temptation. *Just this one time, Elijah. Just this one time.*

"Just this one time—I don't mean to be no trouble to you."

Ruth smiled and helped him up the stairs to her apartment. Opening the door, she began warning him. "I'm living with Edna and Rhoda, your neighbors. Do you remember them? They told me who you were, the person living across the hall. The two of them practically know the whole history of everyone in this building and Harlem. They're retired elementary school teachers. Both of them were widowed at very young ages and they never had children or married again. They've been living together in this building and apartment for almost forty years, but then you must know all that. They just love talking about Harlem during the 1920s and 30s. They know Eubie Blake, Duke Ellington, Count Basie, Ella Fitzgerald, Billy Holiday, and they even attended Marcus Garvey rallies."

Elijah looked around the kitchen. He vaguely remembered the two elderly sisters. The cupboard was filled with several types of fine dishes. An exquisitely beautiful linen tablecloth adorned the kitchen table. Collectibles adorned the walls in various areas of the kitchen. Occasionally, years ago, when he first moved into the building he would meet and greet them in the hallway. Sometimes, he would stop by the store for them. As time progressed, their warmth, their caring, their love and persona reminded him too much of his mother and mother-in-law. It became too painful. He stopped visiting. He had not seen or thought about them in several years. The more he drank, the more he did not remember.

Things started coming back to him. The apartment was the same. Everything in it was in its proper place. However, the place appeared cleaner and brighter. Something new had been added. "I shared a few meals with them years ago. They both were very kind to me."

"Because they're blind and hard of hearing, I'm living with them now. They needed looking after. Their family felt it wasn't good for them to be alone all day and all night. I agreed to stay and look after them. Cook, clean, and help them around the apartment. I see that they make their medical appointments." Ruth continued to chatter as she prepared a plate for Elijah. "They like to eat early, around five o'clock. Then they'll read for a while and then go to bed. There's always plenty to eat and lots of leftovers." Ruth brought him a washcloth to wipe his face and hands. Then she brought him a plate of baked ham, collard greens, potatoes, and two buttermilk biscuits. After dinner, she cut him a big piece of coconut cake and brewed a fresh pot of strong coffee for Elijah to wash it down. "Now, if you don't mind, Mr. Thomas, I'm going to put away the food and wash up these few dishes while you finish your cake and coffee. I'm not rushing you off, so take your time. I must say I've enjoyed watching you eat. You got to remember, if you're going to work all day, you've got to take time out to eat. Do you buy your lunch at Con Edison's lunch cafeteria?"

Elijah looked at her, very surprised. "How did you know I worked for Con Edison?"

She giggled. "By the tag on your uniform."

She laughed. He laughed. They both laughed. For him, it was the first time he had laughed in over sixteen years. It was a strange feeling; it felt good.

"Miss Mears, it has been a pleasure eating your good cooking and being in your company. I don't know when I last ate a meal so good or laughed so hard. I really appreciate it, you're inviting me in and all."

She blushed.

For the first time he looked Ruth in the face. It was the face of an angel, a cherub in appearance and nature. She was a young woman sort of corpulent but pleasingly plump. Because of her roundness, he could not quite guess her age. He felt being the good cook that she was, she had to be older than what she appeared. Her smile was warm and friendly. It genuinely seemed to light up the room. Her dimples were deep. Her natural ruby red lips appeared very soft and voluptuous. He thought to himself, her lips look smoother than fine oil. Her long, straight, black hair was pulled back in a ponytail. When she spoke, her words dripped like honey. In her presence for the first time since that dreadful day, he forgot his pain. During his visit, he felt relaxed and reassured. He knew there was something special about her.

Looking at her lying there on the pillow, Elijah chuckled to himself. He recalled eating two big helpings of food that night. He remembered it was the first night in over ten years he did not desire to drink himself to sleep.

Whispering gently, not to wake her, he softly said, "The Lord said, when a man finds a wife, he finds a good thing. I truly found a good thing when I found you, Ruth Ann Mears Thomas. God blessed me the day you came into my life." Six months later, they would become a family.

Gazing at her, he began thinking about Little going away soon. Off to college. His visits would be for short periods. Holidays, like Thanksgiving, Christmas, spring break, and maybe an occasional weekend.

Elijah slid his hands beneath the pillow upon which his head rested. He began thinking about all the years with Ruth, Little, Elisha, and Esther. How they had gone by so quickly. *Where have the years gone? It seemed like yesterday when I was holding Little for the first time. Changing his diapers, getting his first tooth, taking his first step, saying his first word, and going off to school for the first time. It's all coming to an end, faster than I know. Times not going to stop or slow down, I've already missed too much of his growing up. The overtime is not that important; Little and Swoosh are. My relationship with them is more important than the job. The money doesn't mean that much. What is important is my family and spending as much time as possible with them. It's important, especially now. Now, before Little and Swoosh leave and are gone forever.*

Later, Elijah was aroused by the smell of bacon frying in the cast iron skillet and coffee brewing in the pot. Ruth was up doing her usual Saturday morning cooking and cleaning. When everyone was at the breakfast table eating the bacon, eggs, grits, and toast, it was that morning at the breakfast table Elijah made his big announcement, "Listen everyone. Honey, I know we haven't discussed this…" He gently placed his big powerful hand on hers. "But I've been doing some thinking, and I've made some decisions."

Ruth looked at her husband inquisitively. Everyone else paid little attention to him. "What is it Elijah?"

"First, we're going to buy a car. Then each weekend we're going to go on a family trip. And then, we're all going on a vacation." Shocked by Elijah's announcement, momentarily, the entire family was totally speechless.

"What did you say Pop?"

"Madear, I wasn't really paying attention. Pop didn't say what I thought he said. Did he, Little?"

"I must be hearing things too Swoosh. Are you feeling all right Pop? I thought I heard you say something about buying a car and going on a vacation."

"To do that Pop, it means you have to take time off of your job. That'll be the day." Little laughed slapping Swoosh five. "Hey Swoosh, you know he ain't gonna do that. New York can't survive without Elijah Isaiah Thomas."

"Yeah, Pop's Mr. Con Edison himself. Mr. El Cheapo buying a car."

"Alright boys, that's enough," Mrs. Thomas said laughing with them.

Esther inquisitively asked, "Daddy, where are we going to go on vacation?"

Mr. Thomas ignored Little and Swoosh. "Well Baby Doll, I think we'll go to visit your uncle Junebug and Aunt Madie in Washington, DC. And maybe, just maybe, we'll let Mr. Swoosh and Mr. Little tag along."

Beginning that July as Elijah had promised, they went everywhere sightseeing in the city of New York. The Bronx Zoo, the Empire State Building, they saw three Broadway plays, Hayden Planetarium, and the Museum of Natural History—as a family, they did them all. Together, they climbed up the Statute of Liberty, Bear Mountain, and spent almost every evening on the beach of Coney Island. Elijah wanted to do as much as they could do together, and they did. To everyone's delight and joy, Swoosh's father and mother accompanied them on some of the trips.

It was five o'clock Saturday morning when the family started for Washington, DC. For Elisha and Esther, it was their first time crossing the George Washington Bridge. They stayed awake long enough to get on the New Jersey side. Their new yellow Chevrolet station wagon with wood grain sides zipped along the highway. At ten o'clock, everyone was awake as they entered the city of Washington, DC.

"We should be at your uncle Junebug and aunt Madie's house in about ten minutes," Elijah said with enthusiasm.

"Good, I'm hungry," shouted Elisha.

"I gotta go to the bathroom," whimpered Esther.

"Esther," her mother corrected her. "That's I have to go. Not I gotta."

"Either way, Mommy, I need to pee."

The car turned into the driveway of a pretty brick house with a well-kept lawn. Elijah blew the horn as he approached the house, A man and a woman appeared at the front door.

"Praise the Lord! You made it safe and sound," shouted a petite, fair-skinned woman of medium height dressed in a floral print dress and wearing an apron as she was running down the driveway to the car. Not waiting for Ruth to get out of the car, she began hugging her through the open car door window. "Lord, I've been waiting for you to get here all morning. I didn't get a wink of sleep last night just waiting to see you."

The woman looked at the back seat in the car, "Oh, look at my pretty babies, my gracious they're so beautiful and so big." As Little, Esther, Elijah, and Swoosh climbed out of the car, she grabbed them until she had all four of them in her arms. She immediately began hugging and kissing each one. "You kids are so good looking. Thomas, you and Jerald have gotten so tall since I last saw the two of you. And look at you, Esther, you're so pretty just like your mamma."

"It was only two months ago at our graduation that you last saw us Aunt Madie."

"I know, but you still look like you've grown."

"What about me?" cried Elisha.

Directing her attention to the small voice, she asked, "And just who are you?"

"It's me, Elisha."

"Elisha!" she shouted, acting surprised. "No, can't be Elisha. Why Elisha, you're so big and handsome. I just didn't recognize you. Come and give your aunt Madie a big hug and a kiss."

Ruth slowly got out of the car. Madie turned to her. "Girl, you do look good, and the children—I can't get over how big they've grown," she exclaimed as they embraced.

Beaming with life, Elijah jumped out of the car.

"Elijah!" shouted Junebug, "I should have known, you said you would be here at ten o'clock and its ten o'clock sharp. Man, you're never gonna change." Junebug laughed as he hugged Elijah and patted him on the back.

He stood as tall as Elijah and was a fair-skinned man dressed very dapper. "Hey, come on into the house. I know you must be hungry. Madie has breakfast on the stove, nice and hot. Man..." he said grabbing Elijah and hugging him. "I am so glad to see you. Come on in and make yourselves at home. Don't worry about the bags, we'll get them later," he said, beckoning everyone toward the house.

"Madie," cried Ruth as they entered into the house, "the house is beautiful."

"Girl, I'll show you the house later, right now come on in and make yourself at home. I know you're tired from all that traveling."

"I gotta, I mean I have to go to the bathroom Aunt Madie," cried Esther.

"It's right over there through that door sweetheart," Madie replied, pointing Esther in the direction of the room. "Now, the rest of you come on into the family room. There's a half bath in there. You can take turns washing up while I get breakfast on the table. The rest of you just sit down and make yourselves at home."

"Madie, do you need help?" asked Ruth.

"Girl, you sit right down and rest yourself; you're in my house now," she replied as she disappeared through the door. "I just need to pull my biscuits out of the oven."

Everyone took turns filing into the bathroom. After a while, Aunt Madie called out, "Okay, you all can come into the kitchen. Breakfast is ready."

"Now Ruth and Elijah, you sit over there. Esther you can sit here. Thomas, Jerald, and Elisha you boys sit on that side of the table. Is everyone comfortable? Okay, Junebug ask the blessing of the meal please."

"Heavenly Father, we are most thankful for the food that you have provided for the nourishment of our bodies. We especially thank you for allowing Elijah, Ruth, and the children safe arrival. We ask your blessing upon this day and our conversation as we fellowship together. Amen."

"Okay everybody, let's eat," Madie shouted. Ruth picked up Esther's plate to prepare it. "Girl, you sit down and worry about yourself. I'll fix these babies' plates. It's not every day I get to be with my babies. Now you just relax girl."

"Elijah, I was so happy when you called and said you and the family were coming—man I couldn't believe my ears when you said you bought a car and you were coming for a visit."

"We couldn't believe it ourselves, Uncle Junebug, when he said he was going to buy a car," Little added.

"Looks like its spanking brand new too," Junebug added.

Elijah beamed with pride, "Sure is."

"Man, you were always full of surprises, even when we were kids. You know, I believe you haven't left New York since you moved there some thirty-four years ago."

"Now Junebug you ought to stop that; you know I was here when Junior and when Elizabeth both got married," touted Elijah. "Now this is the first time we've visited you in this house; I'll admit it has been a very long time."

"Elijah," blurted Madie, "Junebug hasn't stop talking about your coming since you called last month. He told the neighbors, the doctors at the hospital, all his patients, and the entire congregation at Mt. Olive Baptist Church. Everybody we know, knows you're coming. I declare, I don't think there's a soul in all of Washington, DC, that doesn't know you're here."

"I didn't tell the president."

"Well, he's about the only one that you didn't tell. Ruth, good thing it wasn't a secret. This man kept me up all night; then he was up at the crack of dawn. Ten o'clock wasn't coming fast enough for him."

Elijah laughed at Madie's normal stretching of the story. "Now Harold Yabor, I hope it's no inconvenience on you or Madie."

"Inconvenience," shouted Junebug. "Man, you better shut your mouth. As many times as Madie and I have been to your place in New York, I'm glad to have my brother and his family here. You know good and well that my home is your home. In fact, when you called to say you were coming, I got this whole week and next off from the hospital, so I and Madie could spend time with you. And where do you get off calling me Harold?"

"Man, you didn't have to do that. I know how busy you doctors are."

"Hey, you're my big brother, I wanted to do it. You know there isn't a thing in this world that I wouldn't do for you and your family. Besides, you haven't been to North Carolina since…" Junebug stopped short. "Since, let's just say that too many years have passed by."

The moment had turned serious, too serious for Elijah. Little noticed the twinkle in his father's eyes momentarily dimmed as his uncle Junebug mentioned North Carolina.

"Big brother," laughed Elijah, breaking the mood. "Don't make me sound so old. I'm only two months older than you."

"Well, listen," interjected Madie. "Before you two start strolling down memory lane, let's get your bags, so you can settle in. Thomas and Jerald, after you finish eating breakfast, you boys get the luggage out of the car. Ruth Ann, come on girl, I'll show you the rooms you'll be sleeping in while you're here. We have plenty of room for everybody."

The two families spent the rest of Saturday afternoon relaxing in the backyard. Elisha and Esther had fun swinging on the swing set. After dinner, tired from the long drive, everyone went to bed early.

SUNDAY MORNING

"Everybody get up. Rise and shine!" shouted Aunt Madie. "Sunday morning, breakfast is on the stove. Time to get up. Church starts at eleven o'clock, and we want to be on time."

After church, the families spent hours driving around Washington sightseeing. The children were excited to see the White House, the Washington Monument, and the Lincoln Memorial.

Madie leaned over to her husband as he was driving. "Times getting late, Junebug; we need to get back to the house. Don't forget we're expecting the pastor and some other folks to stop by the house for an old-fashioned, down-home, backyard barbecue and fish fry."

Shortly after arriving at the house, people started coming over with dishes of food. Many of the guests were Elijah's and Junebug's college and army buddies and a few of their childhood friends. While the women were in the kitchen preparing the food, the children played in the backyard. The men sat in the family room reminiscing over college days and the time they spent in the army.

Little and Swoosh perked up; suddenly, they rapidly moved across the yard to the guests that had just arrived. "Aunt Sarah," they shouted as they grabbed and hugged the walnut-colored, slim, attractive woman who had just walked into the backyard.

"How's my two favorite godsons and high school graduates? How about a hug and kiss?"

"We're doing just great, Aunt Sarah." Swoosh and Little immediately kissed and hugged her as they laughed.

"I bet I know what you boys are going to ask next; he's out front parking the car."

Little and Swoosh raced each other to the front of the house yelling. "There he is," Swoosh shouted. "Uncle Canada, Uncle Canada."

"Hey fellows," the dapper looking fair-complexioned man responded as he got out of the car.

After hugging him, Little's eyes widen. "Uncle Canada, I love it! It's a 1956 Buick Roadmaster. Hey Swoosh, check out the chrome trim. When did you get this?"

"Last week. It's just a little something to sport around town when I'm home. You like it?"

"Like it? I love it."

"Tell you what, when you finish college, it's yours."

"It's a deal, Uncle Canada."

"Where is everybody?"

"They're in the backyard, the cookout's just beginning."

"Good, I'm starved."

Little and Swoosh sat and listened attentively at the older men's war stories. They enjoyed every little detail as the men gave their own account of who did what. Frequently, the men would correct each other, letting out roars of laughter. For the first time, Little and Swoosh learned about how colored soldiers were not allowed to fight in combat. At the very end of the war, Elijah and the other colored soldiers were sent to France. Their assignment was rebuilding electrical power plants destroyed during the war throughout Europe. They listened as the older men talked about traveling throughout Europe and their many adventures. The NAACP, Thurgood Marshall's argument before the United States Supreme Court, the growing Civil Rights movement in Montgomery, Alabama, and President Dwight Eisenhower were among the many political and social topics discussed that evening. Little and Swoosh were amazed at the level of intelligence and astuteness of the men in the room. They marveled at what they heard. Most of all, never before had they ever been around so many educated men of color.

For them, it was their Uncle Canada who stood out the most. He was good friends with Dr. Ralph Bunche and Adam Clayton Powell, Jr., and worked for the United States Department of Commerce and the State Department as a negotiator. He traveled extensively around the world and was highly respected by the older men for a young man of his age. Often, he was in New York at the United Nations. They constantly praised him for his achievements. Little and Swoosh idolized him. Never before had they heard Elijah speak so intellectually, intelligently, and passionately about world events.

"Junebug."

"Yes Madie."

"Come and pay more attention to the barbecue grill baby. The food is ready, and these folks are hungry."

Spareribs, chicken, and steaks filled the hot coal brick grill. The table was filled with potato salad, coleslaw, potato chips, corn on the cob, collard greens, biscuits, cornbread, and all kinds of homemade cakes and pies. The rest of the afternoon was filled with fun, laughter, and a lot of talking.

"Hey Pop?"

What is it Little?"

"What I don't understand is all of your friends have nick names. How come you don't have a nickname?"

His father's friend Scoop answered. "Elijah is his nickname."

"But that is his name," a confused Swoosh responded.

All the men started laughing.

"Boy, you didn't know your grandfather, your daddy's daddy," responded Scoop. "See, we use to call him Snake."

"Snake?"

"Now Scoop, you better leave that thing alone," Elijah laughingly protested.

"That's right Snake. Hey Elijah, do that thing with your tongue."

"Yeah, yeah Elijah," the gathering of men jeered. "Show your boys the snake."

Elijah laughed. "Naw, come on fellas. I haven't done that in over fifty years."

"Oh come on Elijah," they said egging him on.

"Okay, okay." Elijah proceeded to move his tongue in and out of his mouth and wiggle his body like a snake. The crowd roared with laughter.

"Now you see boys why we called him Snake. Then one day, your granddaddy heard us calling him snake. Reverend Thomas had a fit; didn't like nicknames." Scoop stood up to imitate him. "I guess we were about nine or ten years old. We didn't know he was behind us with that old walking stick of his until he shouted, 'What did you call him?' I was sho' nuff scared my knees went to knocking. I looked up at him. I said, 'Snake sir.' 'What did I tell you boys about those names? I will not have you using nicknames in my house. Elijah,' he shouted, 'I've told you about that. In this house, we will use proper names.' I tell you we were scared of Reverend Thomas. Boy, if you think your daddy is tall, you should have seen his daddy. But he had a good heart. 'Your name is *Elijah*! I am not the father of a snake. Now, you boys say his name after me: Elijah.' We all said his name. Then he made all of us say our own names after one another. Now, my little brother couldn't say Elijah. He said Helijah. So, from then on, we called him Helijah instead of Elijah. You think we're saying his name, but we really aren't. His daddy never knew the difference; at least that's what we thought. I guess it was when we came home from the army, old Reverend Thomas was talking and laughing with us one night out on the porch and he said, 'You boys thought you were slick. I know you started calling him Helijah instead of Elijah.' He had us all fooled."

It was dark and very late when the last guest left. Tired from all the fun with the other children their age, Esther and Elijah were already in bed and fast asleep. Ruth and Madie had just finished putting away the last of the dishes. Ruth looked at Madie and said, "I'm going to peep in on the children, then I'm going to take my tired self and aching feet to bed."

"Girl, I know how you feel, my feet are hurting too. One thing is that we have enough food to last the rest of the week." Madie shouted into the next room. "Junebug, I'm going to bed now."

"Okay Madie. I'll be in, in a while."

"Good night. Don't you men folks be up too late," she said as she kissed Pop, Little, and Swoosh.

"Now Junebug don't keep them up all night telling your tall tales," laughed Aunt Madie.

Leaning back in his chair, Elijah said, "It was really good seeing Joe Boy again. I haven't seen him since…" Elijah's voice slowly drifted off.

"Don't be afraid to say it Elijah. Since you and Rebecca got married. You last saw him at your wedding. Now, if memory serves me right, it was at the funeral of your family."

Elijah looked down at the floor and took a deep breath. "Yeah, I guess you're right, that was the last time I saw him. You're right, it was when I buried Rebecca and my family almost forty years ago."

Little and Swoosh looked at each other in surprise. It was the first time Little heard of his father having been married before. All this time, he thought he knew the man.

"Elijah, you remember how the three of us would go fishing in the river? I know you haven't forgotten."

"I remember. Man, we spent hours down on that river fishing in our favorite spot. Talk about big perch, bass, and catfish; man, we would have fished all day and night if our parents let us."

"Those were the days. We'd go fishing all day long."

"I'd sure love to go down there now just to see the old place. I bet that old river is jumping right now with some real big fish."

Canada asked, "What's stopping you from going tomorrow Uncle Elijah?"

"What?"

"I said, what's stopping you? Why don't you, Uncle Junebug, Little, and Swoosh drive down in the morning?"

Junebug chirped in, "Yea, Elijah, you, me, Canada, Thomas, and Jerald. Just the five of us. Hey boys," he said turning toward Little and Swoosh, "when was the last time you went fishing with your daddy?"

They both answered simultaneously shouting out, "Never!"

"That's it, Uncle Elijah, you can take them fishing and you can show them where you grew up as a boy. You can show Thomas your inheritance—his inheritance."

"Yea Elijah, Canada is right. It's about time you show the boys where you grew up."

"Junebug, I don't know if I can do that. Don't get me wrong, I want to, but it's been almost forty-something years!"

"That's right Elijah, it's been almost forty years."

"Uncle Elijah, it'll be another forty years if you don't do it now.

"Time you faced it so you can put it all behind you Elijah. It's time to let it rest. Its time you started thanking God for what you have and stop moaning about what you lost."

"I know your right Junebug. I know you and Canada are right, but…"

"But nothing Elijah. Let's go?"

"Hear me out Junebug. It's too hard, I'm not ready right now, maybe next year."

"Nobody said it was going to be easy, and it won't be any easier next year. If you remember the good times, the joy, and all the love you experienced there it will make it that much sweeter.

"Hey boys, how would you like to see where me and your daddy grew up and go fishing and swimming in the same river we fished and swam in when we were your age?"

This was the first time Little had heard talk about his father's first wife. Nor had his father ever talked about his childhood days growing up. Little was more interested in seeing where their father grew up than fishing. "We would love to Uncle Junebug. I'm ready to go now; what about you Swoosh?"

"Point me to the river. What about it Pop, are we going or not?"

"Boys, if your mother and aunt say it's alright, I guess we'll be going in the morning. Junebug, I just want you to know this is all yours and Canada's doing."

"Uncle Canada are you going with us?"

"Sorry boys, but I have to meet with the president in the morning. But I'll see you guys when you come back from North Carolina. Your Aunt Sarah said we need to take you guys shopping for some school clothes. We want you both to go to college dressed in style."

"Alright, no arguments from us Uncle Canada"

Junebug looked at Canada. "Canada, you and Sarah spoil those boys too much."

"Uncle Junebug, that's what godparents are for. We're supposed to spoil them. Right boys?"

"We sure don't mind being spoiled. Do we Little?"

With a smile, Little nodded his head in the affirmative. "It's tough, but we don't want to deny Uncle Canada and Aunt Sarah of the pleasure of spoiling us."

Elijah sat leaning forward with his head between his hands. Walking over to him, Junebug placed his hand on Elijah's shoulder. "It will be good for you and the boys Elijah. You'll see."

"I just hope you're right Junebug. I just hope you're right.

TAKE ME BACK, WHERE I FIRST BELIEVED

Getting up early, the women packed the men a lunch for the trip, and food for the days they would be staying. "I make this trip home several times during the year to visit my family and to take care of business," Junebug exclaimed.

"Uncle Junebug, I thought we were going fishing. Where are the fishing poles?"

"I leave them at the house in North Carolina; that's where I stored mostly all of my fishing equipment."

It was shortly before six a.m. when they pulled out of the driveway. The morning air was cool and dry as the shiny dark blue Cadillac headed out for the highway.

"Uncle Junebug?"

"Yes Jerald."

"How long will it take us to get there?"

"The trip to Canaan, North Carolina should take about four hours."

Little and Swoosh looked out of the window as the car sped along through the city street to the highway. Junebug and Elijah were quiet as the car cruised down the highway along the Potomac River.

Swoosh read the sign on the highway. "To Richmond, Virginia. I remember reading about Richmond in my history book. Never thought

I would be passing through it. In fact, I was born in Virginia, not too far from Richmond in Goochland County."

"Is that right Jerald?"

"Yep, I don't know why my folks left the south. I know I still have some relatives there, except my father and mother's brothers and sisters live up North in New York and Connecticut. I know my grandparents are buried there and a few of my other relatives. I think they were farmers; my folks don't talk much about it, and they haven't been back since they left. I don't know why; maybe someday I'll ask them."

"Sounds a lot like the south I grew up in, lots of negroes left. But some things are best left unknown. What do you say that Elijah?"

"Huh. Sorry, I wasn't listening."

"What can I say, but welcome to the Mason Dixie boys," Junebug shouted as they crossed over into Virginia. "Your Auntie packed some breakfast in the cooler. You boys eat up. You'll learn when you travel through this part of the country there aren't too many places for Negroes to eat. When I was younger, I made this trip many times without stopping. Now that I'm older, I'll be making a rest stop. With the civil rights movement, the NAACP, and what took place in Montgomery, white folks in these parts are up in arms."

Little and Swoosh enthusiastically talked about the surrounding scenery. They found the tobacco fields in Virginia and the farmland of North Carolina huge and vast acres of land. As much as they tried, they were unsuccessful in engaging Elijah and Uncle Junebug in their conversation. While the boys chattered endlessly with nonsense, Elijah and Junebug rarely spoke to one another. When they did, it was in very low inaudible tones, scarcely above a whisper. The closer their journey brought them to Canaan, the more Elijah became silent.

It was shortly before noon when Swoosh's voice echoed out, "Hey, Uncle Junebug, Pop, the sign we just passed said Entering Balden County. Are we almost there?"

"We sure are Jerald. Be about another half hour to Canaan."

The car continued to speed along the two-lane highway, Swoosh and Little continued to chatter about the surrounding countryside.

"Sure is nice around here. I never saw so many trees, and they're full of green leaves. You never see anything like this in New York; not even in Central Park." Swoosh read aloud the sign on the road. "Canaan, North Carolina, Oldest Settlement of Negro Freeman in the United States. Hey Pop, did you see the sign?"

Elijah, lost deep in his thought, did not respond.

"Hey Pop, did you see the sign? Pop."

"Huh."

"Did you see the sign?"

"No. I'm sorry Jerald; I wasn't paying attention. What did you say?"

"Boy Pop, you've been acting spaced-out since we left Washington. The sign said Canaan, North Carolina, Oldest Settlement of Negro Freeman in the United States. Were you born here?"

"Junebug, look, I don't believe it," Elijah shouted loudly in disbelief. "The oak tree. That old oak tree is still standing. I thought by now a storm would have knocked it over, or it would have died years ago."

"Yep, still standing, just like when we were boys Elijah. The same tree Bo-not fell out of and broke his arm when we were thirteen. Remember how your daddy whipped us both good? If Bo-not hadn't broken his arm, he would have gotten one from your daddy too."

Elijah looked at Junebug and laughed. "If Bo-not hadn't broken his arm, daddy would have never found out we were climbing that old oak tree. Not unless you and that big mouth of yours told him."

"You got a point there. I did talk a lot."

"If I remember anything Junebug, you were good at squealing on everybody. All our parents had to do was just threaten to beat you, and you'd go crying and squealing. And Jerald, yes, we both were born right here in Canaan. Before we leave, I'm sure you'll know all about Canaan."

"Sure did. Saved my own hide many times for telling. I guess that was the last whipping we both ever got together."

"Yeah, but you got your fair share."

"I know I did. I even had to take a few for you."

"A few of mine, since when? You never took a whipping for me? If anything, I took a few for you!"

"Okay, you might have." They both laughed as the car turned off the main road by the big oak tree onto a blacktop road.

"Hey Uncle Junebug, before we turned off the road, the sign said Yarbor Hill Road. Is that where you grew up?"

"That's right Little. That was my daddy's place. Now, it's mine and my sister's, Theresa Yarbor Canegata. That's Canada's mother and father."

"So, he really is my cousin? How come everyone calls him Canada instead of James?"

"His father was a boxer turned actor. Leonard Lionel Canegata. He died back in 1951, I believe. In his boxing days during the 1920s, they started calling him Canada. He was a champion boxer. He won the title."

"He met my sister during one of his matches and got married in no time."

"What happened?"

"During a fight, he was hit in the head. It caused him to go blind in one eye. Then he became an actor. He was extremely talented as an actor, but he died of a heart attack in 1951 at age 44. James was named after my father, but he was a spitting image of his daddy, except lighter in complexion. People in New York called him Little Canada after his father."

"Oh, I used to always wonder why we call him Uncle Canada instead of Uncle James."

"He and his brothers and sisters always spent their summers here in Canaan." After a short ride, the car stopped in front of a huge white two-story house.

Reluctantly, Elijah painfully got out of the car. The front porch extended the width of the house. A wooden bench swing hung on the left side of the porch. Six huge columns supported the porch roof and the columns rested on the red brick foundation. Paralyzed, Elijah stood before the house glaring intensely and nervously at it. The outside was in excellent condition and was very well-kept. The lawn appeared freshly trimmed and recently mowed. From all indications as observed by the outside, the house appeared occupied.

"Boys, get the bags out of the trunk, please."

"Okay Uncle Junebug," Little replied as he watched Junebug wrap his arm around his father's shoulders and lead him up the steps onto the large front porch.

Elijah gently caressed the doorframe with his fingers. In anticipation of the long step he was about to take, he took a deep breath and tightly closed his eyes. Junebug again sensing his hesitation, led Elijah into the house. Little and Swoosh followed closely carrying the bags.

Inside, the huge foyer, the natural oak, hardwood floor gleamed endlessly with the slightest light. At the far end was a massive, but elegant, curved oak staircase that gracefully flowed to the land above. The top of the banister was large but sleek, sturdy yet refined; each spindle was finely shaped in harmony with its surroundings that echoed the angelic ambiance of the house's inner beauty. A sculptured, ornate, mirrored, coat-rack chair rested in the corner. Various pictures dating from different time periods lined the soft rose petal flowered walls. To the left, behind the pair of well-balanced French doors, was the meticulously furnished living room.

The couch, with a matching love seat, and wing back chair accenting the decorum of the room, was turn of the century handcrafted French Provincial. The royal blue cushion fabric was made of hand spun silk, trimmed with pure gold thread and dainty patterns of leaves. Solid gold tacks held the fabric in place. The matching end tables with all their delicateness supported beautifully the fine ceramic lamps with the oversize shades. The coffee table was perfect down to the last detail. The delicate white lace drapes matched the dollies that lay on the end and coffee tables.

However, it was what hung over the marble top exquisite masonry fireplace that caught Little's attention. Hanging above the mantel was a large oil painting of a middle-aged, distinguished-looking gentleman. Carefully studying the face of the man in the portrait, Little looked deeper into the eyes. His face appeared familiar. Little knew that face, he had seen it before. Suddenly, he recognized the face as the face of his little brother Elisha. It was how Elisha would look in about forty years. In the lower right corner of the picture, Little touched the date: 1621.

"You boys can use the last bedroom upstairs on the right with the twin beds. First, take off your shoes; nobody's allowed to walk on these floors with their shoes on. Then put your daddy's bag in the first room, mine go in the middle bedroom."

"Yes sir," they both responded. As Little and Swoosh entered the foyer, they saw the solid oak sliding doors to the room on the right of the stairwell were partially opened. They could not help themselves as they quickly stole a glimpse. One wall of the room was lined with shelves; books upon books filled the shelves from the floor to the ceiling. A massive rolltop desk with a black leather swivel chair held its own among the books.

After exploring the upstairs, the boys returned downstairs where they found Junebug in the kitchen. "Ah, Uncle Junebug."

"Yes Jerald."

"Where is the bathroom? I gotta go really bad."

"See that shed in the backyard?"

"Yes sir."

"Well, that's the bathroom. It's called an outhouse."

"You gotta be jokin' Uncle Junebug! I'm not going in that thing!"

"Why not? I did all the time growing up." Junebug let out a hardy laugh. "Yeah, I'm just kidding, Jerald, I'll show you where it is. First, I need to turn the water on, but if you got to go really bad, you'll have to use the outhouse."

"I can wait for the water to be turned on."

"Come on, you can help me turn it on. We just have to prime the pump."

"Pump?"

"Yeah, the pump. This is not the city. We use well water out here in the country. It's the best tasting water you'll ever drink."

"I'm sure glad I grew up in the city. Seems like a lot of work just for a glass of water."

As they were going out of the back door, Little entered the kitchen. "Uncle Junebug, where's my father?"

"He said he was going to lie down for a few minutes. Check the master bedroom. It's the bedroom at the top of the stairs in the front of the house, where I told you to put his bag."

"Thank you." Little returned upstairs, where he found his father in the large master bedroom. The bed, a massive wooden four poster bed, was set high off the floor. Elijah was lying on the bed staring at the ceiling.

Slowly, Little walked over to his father and sat down beside him. Looking into his father's eyes, he could see the uneasiness, the insecurity, and the pain; inside, he had been crying.

"Pop, do you know who lives here?"

"Right now, no one; no one has lived here for almost forty years. Funny, it hasn't changed one bit in almost forty years."

"I don't understand Pop, the house is so clean, and the lawn is well trimmed—it's so well-kept. Whose house is this?"

Elijah continued staring at the ceiling. "It's my house Little; I was born in this house; I grew up in this house." Elijah sat up on the bed and picked up a framed picture off the nightstand. "This picture," he said picking up the picture. "This is a picture of my father and mother, your grandfather and grandmother. There are so many memories in this house. I have so many memories. It's filled with memories of my mother and father. I have so many memories of growing up in this house and growing up in Canaan, North Carolina. And people, a whole lot of people. I can still smell my mother's perfume, Gardenias; it was her favorite. I gave her a bottle for her birthday. She wore it on special occasions. So many memories that are good and bad, happy and sad, many memories are here."

Tears began to roll down his cheeks as his mind strolled down memory lane. "Please, give me a few minutes son," he asked as he wiped his face. "I just need a little time to myself to contemplate."

Not fully understanding what his father was talking about, Little leaned over and embraced his father with a strong assuring hug. He whispered softly in his father's ear, "I know whatever it is Pop, we'll help you get through it. I love you Pop."

Elijah was awakened by the sound of the truck's engine. Leaving the house, he found Junebug, Little, and Swoosh in the garage tinkering with an old truck. "It's Papa's old truck. I don't believe it, it still works," Elijah exclaimed.

"Come on Elijah, let's take old Sally here for a ride. It's been a few months since I last drove her. You remember how to drive this thing, don't you?"

"Few months for the truck, forty years for me. But it's just like riding a bike. Some things you just never forget."

"Thomas, you and Jerald get the picnic basket while your daddy and I finish checking out old Sally here."

"Junebug, you really kept the place up. I know Mamma and Papa would be proud to see what you've done to the house and the yard."

"Well, I'm sorry I had to get rid of the animals. My sister generally comes over twice a week to clean the place."

The boys returned shortly carrying the basket of food. Elijah and Junebug climbed into the cab while the boys jumped into the back of the truck.

"Elijah, let's take her down to the river; we can eat there then we'll show the boys the rest of the place."

"Okay, but first we'll go the long way through town."

"Good idea. This way they can see Canaan; then they'll be able to see it from the river edge. You boys are in for a real treat."

The old truck moved along the country dirt roads, the engine purring. Finally, they turned onto the main road into Canaan. "I see old Mt. Zion is still standing, she's a pretty sight for these old eyes," Elijah interjected as they passed by the big brick church with a tall steeple. "Looks like they made a new addition on the building," Elijah exclaimed.

"Folks are coming back, and the membership is starting to thrive again. Families come from miles around just to see the place. Maybe next year, you and the family will come down for homecoming in May."

"I'd sure like that."

"Maybe, you'll bring the message."

"Now Junebug, you better leave well enough alone. Being here today is one thing; just thinking about coming back for homecoming is a stretch. Don't be rushing me like you and Canada did last night."

"Now Elijah, you got to admit, it feels good being back. Doesn't it?"

"I got to admit, it does feel good."

As they passed through the once thriving town area, Little and Swoosh saw there wasn't much left. Only old remnants of buildings remained in the vacant downtown area. Junebug tapped on the glass. "Hey boys," he said, "see the general store over there? It's the general store, and it's still owned and operated by my family." Looking forward again, he lowered his voice. "Elijah, it's not the place it was. Remember when it was so full of life? Boys, this used to be nothing but people, colored people all over the place, running the bank, the hotel and all the little shops. Elijah, remember Sister Gitlow and her dress shop, Aunt Ruby's bakery shop, and old Brother Townsend's barber shop? Times have changed."

"You're right Junebug, and so has Canaan."

After a while, they arrived at the Cape Fear River. The August air was hot, and the river edge was cool and peaceful. Elijah's roars of laughter broke the silence as he and Junebug reminisced about the many days they spent on the river. Little and Swoosh could not recall ever hearing their father laugh so hard, and so much. They watched as Elijah would throw his head back and laugh hysterically time and time again. He and Uncle Junebug shared with them many stories about the past, their childhood days, and about Canaan and its heydays. Too

Little and Swoosh, many of the stories sounded like big fish stories of the ones that got away, all the tall tales, but in all the stories they knew somewhere there was a hint of truth.

"Boys, look out over the river. All the land you see, that's my land. All the land as far as the eye can see belongs to me. It was my daddy's and his daddy before that and so on and so forth. Someday, it will all belong to you, Little, and your brother and sister. Don't worry Jerald, I haven't forgotten about you. Let me tell you about all this land and your kin folks. How we came to be here in Canaan."

With a great sense of pride, Elijah related the story to his young sons. "Now this property has been in my family for generations. Since as far back as 1590, when they settled in these parts, this whole area was settled by coloreds before slavery. The painting of the man over the fireplace, back at the house, that's my great-great-great-great-great-grandfather, Master Joshua Moses Thomas. He wasn't no slave. He came from England as an indentured servant. Joshua and your uncle Junebug's descendants sailed here with the people sent by Sir Walter Raleigh in 1587 with John White. They first landed in a place not far from here called Roanoke Island. They were supposed to start a colony in Virginia, but the captain of the ship refused to sail past Roanoke Island, so he emptied the ship of all its passengers and cargo on Roanoke Island. That was on July 22, 1587. Twenty-seven days later, John White's daughter gave birth to a baby girl. They named the child Virginia Dare. Now, Joshua and his wife both were indentured servants for the White family. Joshua's wife delivered the baby. It's believed Virginia Dare was the first English child to be born in America, except it wasn't called America then, nor was this area called North Carolina. In fact, believe it or not, this was considered Virginia. Story has it that John White went back to England for supplies. Well, not long after he left, sometime in the fall of the year, a big storm, a big hurricane came, and wiped out almost everything. They weren't prepared for such a storm; most of the buildings were still under construction and the colonists ran out of the little supplies they had left. Sickness, disease, and starvation nearly killed everyone, so the colonists set their indentured servants free. You see, indentured servants lived with the family, so the family was responsible for them. Setting them free meant they had to live on their own. They released all the colored indentured servants, said they couldn't afford to keep them, but they kept most of the white ones."

"Fortunately for them, the Croatoans lived in the area. They were a friendly tribe of Indians, and the Indians helped the colonists. The Croatoan Indians are now called the Lumbee; they still live in the area. The white settlers decided they would go with the Indians. Now, the Indians, for some reason weren't too keen about dark-skinned people—this is so even to this day. They told Joshua about a land just up the river that was fat and rich; they told them about a land that was filled with fruits and berries."

Little and Swoosh listened as Elijah, the historian, spoke with authority.

"Joshua was considered the leader of the group that led his people here to this area. It was just like the Indians told them, so they called it Canaan, because they were bound for Canaan Land. Just like in the Bible, and they've been here ever since. Yes, our people were here thirty-three years before the Mayflower ever set sail from England."

Elijah spoke with great pride as he passed on the family history to his offspring. He drew in a deep breath. "Just smell that clean fresh air. Yea, this area grew and grew; it was thriving with free colored folks, even during slavery times. I'm not ashamed to admit that some of the families owned slaves. But they didn't treat their slaves like the whites treated theirs. Naw, they didn't and don't let anybody tell you otherwise. Their slaves ate with the family. They were treated as family and were given their freedom. Many of the former slaves settled right in this area. All the businesses were owned by coloreds, the whole town was owned by coloreds."

Elijah's face beamed with pride as he continued the story. "Canaan was considered the pride and joy of the county. They called it the county seat. We even owned the electrical power plant; my daddy's bank financed the whole thing. Colored folks were rich and powerful.

White folks from miles around had to do business with us. Oh, they didn't always like it, but we were here, and they had to do business with us to live. Folks from all over the state of North Carolina, Virginia, South Carolina, Georgia, even as far away as Boston would come to Canaan to buy their clothing, furniture, livestock, and the likes. It was a known fact the best craftsmen and artisans were in Canaan. Canaan was known to have the best of everything. It was known as the land that flowed with milk and honey. Yes sir."

The sound of pride and joy rang out as he reminisced about Canaan's heydays of wealth and glory. "Colored merchants were always fair in their prices and treated all their customers with special care. All the colored children had to go to school. Free, public education started right here in Canaan, and they were expected to go to college or trade school when they finished. First, in the earlier days they were sent to England for college. When they finished, they had a good job waiting for them right here in Canaan. We had our own doctors, lawyers, bankers, accountants, and teachers. Why we even had our own representatives in the state legislator. You name it, we had it here in Canaan. We were progressive and ahead of our times. And old Mount Zion, she was a busting at the seams with folks. Every Sunday, there were about five hundred people attending regular service in Mount Zion. The fish fries, Sunday picnics after service, and homecoming gatherings. Now Papa, he could deliver a whopping good fire-filled sermon. Folks, colored and white, came from miles around just to hear him preach. And you know," he chuckled, "I wasn't so bad myself. Man, the choir, Sister Gitlow and Junebug's sister Edna. Talk about singing. When they sang, you just knew you were in heaven."

"But Pop, what happened? I mean, we didn't see much of nothing but a few old, abandoned, and burned down buildings?"

The tone of Elijah's voice slowed. "Well, son, it happened back in the early 1920s, 1922 to be exact. I'll never forget that night for as long as I live." Elijah bowed his head down as he held his silence. The nervous twitch in his eye went unnoticed by the group.

"What happened?"

Elijah turned toward the river and looked toward Canaan. His voice was heavy and darkened. "It was the night the white folks, the Klu Klux Klan, burned the whole town to the ground. It all started that Sunday evening when they burned the first house down with three generations of a family still inside. It seems like that night will never end for me." His voice was deep and his mind elsewhere as he began to relay the dark story.

Elijah moved closer to the river as he looked toward Canaan, his fingernails dug into the tree by which he stood. "Colored folks were scared to death, surely believed Armageddon had come, the end of the world. Babies crying in their mamma's arms, gunfire, nightriders were all over the place. White men wearing white robes were shooting at them. I was up on the hill. I looked over, and I could see the entire town lit up in flames. The fire was so bright, it lit up the whole southern sky for miles around. It looked like it was hell's fire. I could hear the sound of crying babies and screaming mothers, weeping, wailing, moaning. 'Rachel weepeth for her children'; her children, murdered by Herold. Weeping, wailing, moaning."

Elijah covered his ears as if he could still hear the cries of the people.

"Only thing they didn't burn down was the church, Mount Zion, God's house. It drove most of the families out of Canaan and drove me out of Canaan, and out of God's house and his arms."

Seeing his eyes were glazed over and Elijah's mood changed, Junebug struggled to change the direction of the conversation. "Elijah, Elijah, it's getting late—we had better be getting back to the house while we still have some light."

It was as if Elijah could still see the flames burning. Raising an angry fist toward heaven, Elijah cried out in a loud voice, "Oh God, where were you, God? Why?"

Junebug shouted, "Elijah!"

Swiftly, Elijah turned toward Little and Swoosh. "Promise me boys, whatever happens you won't push me away."

Somehow Swoosh was able to relate to what he said. "I promise you Pop, I will never reject you; I'll never turn you away."

Frightened, Little hesitated and moved away. Elijah grabbed his arm, stopping him. "Promise me Thomas," he shouted as he pulled him closer to him.

Little looked his father in the eyes. He saw something there that scared him even more. He struggled to get away.

"Promise me Thomas," he shouted as he tightened his grip.

"Pop," he cried.

Junebug shouted, "Elijah, you're scaring the boy."

Elijah tightened his grip.

Junebug grabbed Elijah's hand. "Elijah," he shouted. "Stop it. You're hurting him. Let him go." Elijah loosened his grip.

"That's right Elijah, it's alright."

Elijah paused for a long time; he stood staring out at Canaan.

"Elijah. We should be going now; it will be getting dark soon."

"Yeah, you're right; these roads don't have any streetlights. It gets pitch black out here. We best be going."

Junebug briskly slapped him on his back. "Do you remember how to get there from here on the old back road?"

It was as if he did not remember what had just occurred. His voice changed and the expression on his face disappeared. "Remember?" He calmly laughed. "Man, I'm not that old, I was the one that showed you the short cut. I practically made it myself."

"Yeah, and you almost busted your daddy's truck, ole Sally here, doing it." They both let out a roar of laughter as they recounted the story.

The truck chugged along the tree-lined back road trail. After a few miles of traveling, Elijah came to a sudden halt. After a few minutes of talking softly to Junebug, Elijah, and Junebug exited the truck. "Boys, wait here in the truck; your uncle Junebug and I will be back in a few minutes. There's something I gotta do."

Little and Swoosh watched as the pair walked up a small trail and disappeared behind a grove of trees. After walking several more yards, they stopped. Their voices, although they barely spoke above a whisper, could be heard echoing through the woods. "Junebug, I need your help. Wait here and pray as I continue on. I have to make the rest of this journey on my own."

"I understand Elijah. You go on whilst I pray."

Elijah continued his walk into the wooded area. About forty-five minutes passed before the pair emerged from the woods. Little noticed his father's walk was different. He walked with a much lighter step. It was as if a big weight had been lifted off his father's shoulders. His face looked more relaxed. He appeared to be two shades lighter and more rested. He appeared relieved of whatever burden that had weighed down heavily upon him for the past forty years.

Standing near the truck, Elijah motioned to Little and Swoosh. "Boys, come on with me, I want to show you something."

Still wary from his earlier encounter, Little hesitated. Elijah walked to the truck.

"Little, son, first I want to apologize to you. I need to tell you son, that I'm really sorry for what happened back there at the river. I can't explain what came over me. I'm sorry."

"It's okay Pop."

The boys jumped out of the truck and followed Elijah and Junebug through the narrow-overgrown passage. They came upon a small clearing.

In the clearing, a plot of land was sectioned off by a wrought iron fence; inside the fenced area laid two graves. The foursome entered the burial area and stood before the graves. Little read aloud the headstones.

Rebecca Anne Miller Thomas, Beloved wife of Elijah Thomas. Elijah Thomas IV, son of Elijah and Rebecca Thomas.

"Rebecca was my first wife. She died long before I moved to New York and met your mother. We had a son, Elijah Thomas IV; he was my firstborn child. He was only three months old. That over there," he said, pointing in the direction of the river, "that clearing was where our house was, our home." Further off in the distance in the direction Elijah was pointing, the boys saw the remains of a charred house.

"They died that night in the fire that burned down the house. My mother, father, grandmother, grandfather, and Rebecca's parents, they all died in the fire. I won't ever forget that Sunday night; we had just had Elijah's baptism and a big party at the house. I was gone about an hour. I had to take one of the elderly sisters home. It was the first house they burned down, some forty years ago; my entire family was in it. Then they burned down all of Canaan. Shortly after I buried them, I moved to New York, and I haven't been back since. Coming down here I realized..." Elijah took a deep breath and let out slowly. "While I buried them in the grave, I never really buried them at all. I didn't allow them to rest in peace, didn't allow myself to rest, I had no peace. I never forgave myself for not saving them from the fire, a fire I was not the cause of. Many nights I tossed, and I turned, wishing I had died in the fire with them. I foolishly blamed God and myself."

Elijah knelt down between the graves. "Today is the first time I visited here since the funeral; the day I buried them. The first time I prayed for my beloved wife and my dear son. The first time I talked to them, and I felt them in almost forty years. You know, I believe they've forgiven me for not coming here sooner. They're happy for me, happy that I've gone on with my life. Happy I got you boys. Happy I have another family."

Elijah took a deep breath and put his arm around Little. "The first time I met your mother was the first time I felt peace in sixteen years. She made me laugh that very first night I met her. I finally had some peace. Being here tonight, I can finally put it all to rest. Little, I'm sorry for hurting and scaring you the way I did earlier. Please forgive me son."

Little stood silently beside his father; he slipped his hand into his father's. "I'm glad that you've shared this with us. I'm glad that we're here with you Pop, I understand now. I promise I won't leave you Pop. I understand now, I promise. I'll never leave you."

BOOK TWO

THE AWAKENING

He was torn between where and with whom he would have his last supper, and where he would lay his head to rest for his last night. Should it be in his flat with his mother and father or the family he so loved? This decision was virtually a struggle of the heart for Swoosh. They were difficult decisions that he had to make, ones that he wished he did not have to make. But decide he must, between his parents and the family he loved so much, the Thomases. There was his mother, the woman who carried him for nine months, risking her very own life to bring him into this world. Then, there was his father. He was the man who taught him to play baseball, basketball, and provided for all of his physical needs. And then there was the Thomas's, the adopted parents who were always there for him. He could always depend on Madear and Pop. With Madear, Pop, Little, Elisha, and Esther as a family, he felt complete. He was as much a part of them as they were of him. To Madear and Pop, there was never a distinction between him and Little, Elisha, or Esther. All four of them were their children. Deciding between the two families was an extremely heavy burden upon his heart. But decide he must.

However, without a doubt in his heart he knew, whatever he decided his parents and the Thomas's would understand and honor. But to be with one would make the other unhappy. Regardless of where he spent his last night, one family would be hurt; he too would be hurting, hurting to be with his other family. *God, it's so hard. To please my parents means bringing sorrow in the home and lives of Madear* and Pop. *To make Madear and Pop happy would grieve the heart of my mother and father. How could I cause pain in for either Madear and Pop or my mother and father?* To hurt them was a thought he found difficult and could not bear it any longer.

Somewhere in his struggle between his love for his parents and for the Thomas's, in his heart he knew his rightful place. *My place is rightfully with my parents. Despite all that has happened over the years, I love them, and I need my parents. If anything, it was the one lesson Elijah Thomas taught me: family is always first.* As a family apart from their many problems, somehow, he always knew his parents loved him deeply and needed him as much as he needed them. He was a part of them, and they were a part of him, and always would be. *I am their only child.* Assured of his parent's unconditional love for him, still for him, the choice was not an easy decision to make. The thought made his headache.

The conductor called out, "122 Street."

Lost deep within his thoughts, Swoosh did not move. "Hey, Swoosh," the conductor called out. "Swoosh!" he shouted louder as he walked over to him and tapped him on the shoulder. "This your stop." Handing a small, wrapped package to Swoosh, he said, "Me and the boys enjoyed working with you this summer. Well, we just wanted you to know with today being your last, they, we got you this little going away gift."

"Awe, Gus that was really nice of you and the guys. You know you didn't have to get me anything." He began removing the wrapping paper to reveal a small box. Upon revealing the box's content, Swoosh eyes lit up; his mouth dropped opened, but no words came forth. Seeing the silver conductor's pocket watch inside moved him beyond words. A picture of a railroad train engine was engraved on the outside with the number 9875. The number of the train he worked on all summer.

"I know we didn't have to; we did it because we wanted to. Boy, this railroad won't be the same after this summer—you and all your foolishness—it just won't be the same without you. With that pocket watch you's officially a railroad man now, you's family to us."

A tall thin white male, wearing a business suit and round glasses, walked up behind Gus. "Excuse me Swoosh."

"Hey Mr. Jacobson, what's up?"

Nervously, he handed Swoosh a small package and a card. He exclaimed, "This is a little something from me and all the passengers that rode the train with you this summer. We really can't express how much we've enjoyed your being here with us this summer. You're one of the best conductors we've ever had."

Gus cleared his throat. Mr. Jacobson looked up at him and smiled. "I mean besides Gus, you're the best." They briefly laughed.

"Go ahead and open the box," a voice rang out.

Swoosh tore open the box; inside was a solid silver chain for the pocket watch. Applause ranged out from the passengers as Swoosh stood up with an awed expression on his face. "Oh God, thank you everybody. I…I…really appreciate it. I know I'm going to miss all of you. All of you have been so kind and fun to be with. I really enjoyed riding with all of you." Choking, he paused for a few seconds. "I don't know what to say."

"Now that's a first," someone shouted. Everyone roared with laughter.

"Well I do," shouted Gus. "Git off the train, we still got a schedule to keep." Gus laughed loudly, patted Swoosh on the back as he passed and waved bye. As he passed by them to exit the train, the male passengers shook his hand or patted him on his back, while older women hugged and kissed him as their expression of thanks. The younger girls took full advantage of this opportunity to do what they wanted to do all summer. Quickly, each one stole a kiss.

The engineer blew the train's whistle extra-long, looked back and shouted, "We'll be looking for ya in Kansas." Standing on the platform as the train passed, passengers looked out the window at him and waved good-bye. The four conductors hung out of the door to wave farewell to their friend and family member. Touched, Swoosh put on his usual fancy footwork, bounced his pretend basketball, made the big shot in the basket and did his Swoosh shuffle with his heart overwhelmed.

Gradually, he descended the platform with his tear-filled eyes glued to the pocket watch. Midways the platform, he sat down on the steps and opened the card. It was signed by the engineer, four conductors and over one hundred of the passengers he rode the train with each day. Swoosh knew them all. Five one hundred-dollar bills were inside the card. Overwhelmed by their kindness, slowly he made his way down the street toward home, gently caressing the engraving of the train on the watch with his fingertips.

Knowing her child's love for and devotion to the Thomases, she too, Sadie Mae Jefferson, was also torn. Like any mother, her own need was to spend this last time with her only child, Jerald James Jefferson, Jr. Having made his decision, she knew the pain and agony he was going through. She pondered over what she could do to ease his troubled heart. How could she share this last moment with him and please him? Sadie Mae painfully sought to give her son the best both families could offer.

After pondering it carefully, she thought of the only thing she could do. *I know, for Swoosh's last supper, I'll ask Ruth to prepare his favorite meal: pot roast smothered in gravy, collard greens seasoned in fatback, candied yams, baked macaroni with cheese and her famous buttermilk biscuits.*

Ruth was overjoyed by the invitation. For her, it was a privilege and honor to be a part of Swoosh's supper at home before he went away to college. Together, the mothers planned, shopped, and prepared for that evening meal.

"You know Ruth, this is jest like old times when the boys were small. You were the first friend I made when Jay, Scooter, and I first come to New York."

"I remember those days too, Sadie Mae. We'd be cooking in the kitchen and the boys would be scooting around our feet. You still call Jerald Scooter?"

"I sure do, and he hates it every time," laughed Sadie Mae. "I declare that boy still scootin' round under my feet to dis dey. They just growed up too fast for me; both them boys."

"I know what you mean girl. I'm going to miss them both. Who would have dreamed they would both be going off to colleges? But one thing for sure, I won't be missing all the mess they got into together. All that fussing and fighting they did with each other and with Esther and Elisha. They fought over basketballs, school, shoes and pants. You name it, and those boys fought over it. You couldn't tell them they weren't brothers. You remember that time we were in the kitchen baking a cake, we had just finished cleaning the kitchen and giving them both a bath." Ruth began laughing. "I don't think we stepped out of the room no more than a minute to listen to the radio."

"Lawd," chimed in Sadie Mae finishing the story, "them rascals call themselves helping us. They had flour all over the place and over themselves. We were so mad, but we couldn't help but laugh."

"Girl, I remember afterwards we tore their little butts up, but good; speaking of cake, Sadie Mae, now I know for dessert you're going to make Swoosh's favorite homemade coconut pineapple upside down cake with angel white frosting."

"You know I am. If I don't Scooter would never forgive me."

"Well, since I ain't invited to the dinner, you better save me a slice."

"I don't know, between Scooter, his daddy and Little there may not be nothin' left. The first slice will be yours, elsin you won't git any."

Both women continued to laugh and talk about old times as they prepared the meal.

They both were surprised as Mr. Jefferson arrived home earlier than usual for the evening. "Good evening ladies. Um, dinna sho' does smell good," he exclaimed as he came into the kitchen carrying a bouquet of flowers. Handing the flowers to his wife, he exclaimed, "I'll jest git out of the way, so you women folk kin finish up your cooking." Immediately, he disappeared into the bathroom.

"Lawd, now what done got into him Sadie Mae?"

"I don't know Ruth, these last few weeks he's been acting mighty peculiar. Whatever it is, I show do praise the Lawd for the change."

"Well girl, I better be getting back to my family." Turning to Sadie Mae, Ruth hugged her. Sadie Mae, thank you for inviting me to help prepare dinner for Jerald; you don't know how much it has meant to me."

"I'm so glad you were here to help. It meant a lot to me, and I know it will to Scooter more than either of us will ever know."

"Okay girl, I'll see you tomorrow and don't forget to save some cake for me."

An hour later Mr. Jefferson emerged proudly dressed in his best and only suit. He stood by his place at the dinner table. "I declare Sadie Mae, you en Madear musta been cooking the whole day." Gingerly, he helped his wife of twenty years set the table. Astonished at his behavior, Sadie Mae, Swoosh, and Little sat down for dinner. The dinner started with the blessing of the food by Mr. Jefferson. "Lawd, we just wants to thank you for this day and this meal. I really thank you Lawd for my wife and these fine boys you give us. I thank you for the land en the harvest that the land has brought forth for the nourishment of our bodies for your namesake. Amen." Carving the pot roast, he prepared each plate with exceptional care.

Only sporadic conversation about the food and brief laughter broke the silence of the evening meal. Swoosh tried, but his efforts to be his loud and flamboyant self, failed. Proudly, he showed everyone the watch and chain the conductors and the passengers of the 9875 had given him and the gift of five hundred dollars.

After the dessert was complete, it was Mr. Jefferson's words in a low, humble tone with his long southern draw that charged the air. "Yes, this was a real fine meal honey; a real fine meal for some fine boys; my boy, our boys. Why don't we go sit in the parlor for a spell? There's something I got to say to you's, something I should have said a long time ago."

Mr. Jefferson, picking up his cup of coffee moved to the front room and sat down. "Y'all come on in. Sadie Mae and Thomas, I want y'all to come in too."

Everyone curiously and cautiously entered the room. He beckoned them into the room. "Come on, sit. I wants all y'all to have a seat."

After a brief pause, Mr. Jefferson collected his thoughts. Drawing a deep breath, upon exhaling, he arose from his chair and stood behind it, gripping tightly the back of the chair for support. Slowly and calmly, he began to speak. "Son, I know I haven't been the father and example to you as I ought of been. Nor have I been the proper husband to your mother likes she deserves. U'ma shame of myself and my behavior; the drunkin' stupors and hurting your mother the way I done. I been giving y'all more reasons to hate me then to love me. But I can't change the pass, I wish I could; Lawd knows I does, but no body kin do that. I do pray y'all will forgive me. I just want you to know, that I is really proud of you son. I am proud of you son. I am proud of both you and Thomas."

Once again, silence filled the air. Nervously, he began pacing the floor. "You see, I didn't have much of the book learning, reading, writing, and the likes. But I would read as much every chance I got. I tried to learn as much as I could. My daddy never had no schooling, I got up to the eighth grade. I was the eldest of twelve children in the family. When I turn thirteen, I had to leave school to help on the farm. My daddy was a sharecropper, his daddy was a sharecropper, and ya Momma's daddy was a sharecropper too. We was all sharecroppers; back in them those days, there weren't much a colored man could do in the South where we come from."

After several deep breaths, Mr. Jefferson slowly returned to his chair and sat down. As he talked, he began wringing his hand; a thick cord of anger could be heard in his soft tone. "I hated farming. Most of all, more then anything, I hated sharecroppin'. I weren't but sixteen when I run off from home and jointed up with the army. But I told them I was eighteen, so I could join. I was sent to Fort Dix, New Jersey. There they give me a job fixing jeeps in the motor pool. I enjoyed fixing motors, and I was good with my hands like that. But even us colored soldiers had it hard during the war."

As he reminisced about his army days, a gleeful childlike expression was upon his face. Soon, the gleeful look turned to a face of hopelessness. "In four years after I got out of the army, cause I had no wheres else ta go, I went back home to the farm and started sharecropping like the rest of my family. Some of my army buddies invited me to come to New York, but I was young and scared. That was when I met your mother, she wern't but sixteen, near seventeen; I was bout twenty. We got married 'bout a year after we met. That's when I had to go to work for Mr. Jessup. Werkin his land growing tobacco, corn, and cotton like my daddy and his daddy. I hated farming, but I didn't know anything else to do 'cept fixin' motors. Back in them times, Negroes couldn't git a job working on cars. Mostly white folks that had cars. Most Negroes I knowed, if they had a car couldn't afford to pay no body to fix it anyway. They did the werk on dey cars themselves. I was planning to farm long enough to make enough money to open my own garage in Richmond, Virginia. That was my dream. Colored folks said I had high ideas and my britches was too big for Goochland county. Always say my ideas was gonna git me killed and them too."

Mr. Jefferson lowered his head as he continued to speak. His voice was low and troubled. "I want you to know, sharecropping was a terrible way of life," he said shaking his head from side to side. "Colored folks had to buy all they seed, food, clothing, and medicine from Mr. Jessup's store. We had to buy everything from Jessup's store." His voice roared with anger. "Every colored person in Fife and all of Goochland county owed that old evil man Jessup. Owed everything, owed even yo' soul to that man; colored folks swore he wern't nothing, but the ole devil himself. Every year, jest like my daddy and the other colored folks I owed the store more and more. Seems they chargin' for things we don't even buy."

A gleeful sparkle appeared in his eyes and his voice was light and cheerful. "Then you come along the next fall. I was so happy when your mama said we was gonna have a baby. I werk day and night preparing for your rival. I was so excited. I'd go to all her doctor appointments; I prayed night en day that you be healthy, big en strong. When you was born, I was so proud, proud of my first born child, my son. Yes Lawd; so proud I named you after me. Then the following year your mama delivered two dead babies before they time. She, your mamma, took real sick with a high fever. I was so scared that we was gonna lose her, you 'n her was all I had in dis world. Doctor says part of the babies after birth was still inside her, so he had to operate. After the operation, doctor said she weren't gonna have no more babies. Right then, I knowed, 'twas nothing left for us in Virginia; we had to git away."

Your mamma was always good at keeping money. We managed to save sixty dollars in a tin can we hid in the roof of the chicken coop. You musta been 'bout two years old, I reckon. I borrowed 250 dollars from Mr. Jessup, just like I did every spring. Den with the money we save, that same night, we left town. Told folks we was going to visit her mama's sick aunt down in Dinwiddie County, near McKenny. Said we be gone 'bout two or three weeks, can't gist tell folks yo business; not even your kinfolk, on o'count of they may tell ole man Jessup to collect the reward money. Your mamma and me got to Richmond and caught the first train North. Came up here and stayed with en old army buddy of mine, your uncle Busta, 'til we got our own place and we been here in New York City since."

Again, Mr. Jefferson paused for a few minutes and placed his head in his hands. After collecting himself, looking up he again spoke. "Your mamma en me we got good jobs; me with the bus company repairing buses en your mamma in the hospital's housekeeping department. We honest people, paid ole Jessup back all his money and then sent money back home to our families to help 'em out. We brought them all here to New York City. Help them git set up. Your uncles, my brothers Cornelius, Jesse, and Juice, and your aunts, Louisa Mae and Hattie, they the younger ones; we sent for them to come North. None of um had finished school, but they all got good jobs up here. Girls got jobs working in the white folks' houses on Long Island and in the

Hamptons. They didn't care too much for that, so soon afterwards they gets jobs in the hospitals doing housekeeping. And your mamma's people, they come too, 'cept they didn't care to much for New York, so they moves further up North to Bridgeport, Connecticut. They got good jobs working for a factory that makes airplanes en the girls, they kids, and husbands followed. They doing alright up there."

Taking a deep breath, he continued in a low and solemn voice. "My mamma and poppa, now that's another story; they wouldn't leave the farm for nothing. It's all they know. They was jist to old en set in they ways likes old folks sometimes be." Mr. Jefferson spoke up in a proud voice. "Some years ago, the farm went up for sale, so I bought it with the money me en your mamma saved for over ten years. Paid cash. I gave the farm to my mamma n poppa as a gift. When I buys the land, I finds out ole man Jessup he don't own it after all. White folks that lived up north in Newport, Rhode Island owned the land. They jest puts Jessup family in charge of the land for them while they live up North in they big fine house. All these years Jessup had colored folks believing that he the ones that owned the land." Mr. Jefferson got up and moved around the room; a hint of anger could be heard in his voice. "But when Pa died, I couldn't go home to the funeral on o'ccount of Mr. Jessup. Even though we sent him back all his money that ole white man was still mad at me. He say no nigga gonna trick and cheat a white man. Some colored folks mad at me too cause he was real hard on them on o'ccount of me leaving the way we did."

Mr. Jefferson's voice changed to a more subdued tone; he shifted to the next topic. "Then one day, I reckoned you was twelve, you was esplainin' something in a book to me. One of my friends say, 'I declare Jay, that boy smarter den you n I will ever be.' My folks dying, my not being welcome back home, you growin' so smart. Somewhere I couldn't take all the pressure. I felt shamed, I saw myself as a failure, less than a man. I foolishly started drinking n taking it out on your mamma. The more I drank and hit your mamma, the more shameful I felt. I jist didn't know how to stop it. The day you knocked me down, I was more shamed of myself then angry at you. I deserved it; I knowed

I wasn't mad at you. I was really mad at myself. I was shamed of myself for being such a fool, a lousy husband and father."

Mr. Jefferson looked at Swoosh. Swoosh could see the tears in his father's eyes. "But you know Jerald, I never missed not a one of your basketball games. Even the games that was out of town, me and the boys, from the bus company, we'd git together en go to all yo' school games. Every time with your first foul shot of the game before you shoot you always made a funny salute with your left hand like the ones I told you the fellas 'n me in the army would do. I always felt you was saying hello to me. Every time you make a shot, I'd hear that basket call out yo name, Swoosh. I'd sit there feeling real proud knowing you was my son. I specially loved it when the crowd would call out your name and yells swoosh when you shoots the ball in the basket. I's real proud of you, 'n shame of myself. I knowed you didn't see me, but I saw you and the Thomases. I was so glad you had the Thomases to look out for you. I was grateful to them and God fer watching over you."

Everyone could sense his uneasiness as he shifted in his chair and continued. "At your high school graduation, your uncle Buddy said to me, he said, 'Jay, I knows y'alls is proud of that boy. He ain't got to run off from home like we had to. Naw, no sharecroppin' for him. I knowed you done had it rough, not able to go see Mamma and Papa's burial, or visit they grave, or the house we growed up in. I wants you to know, you done the right thing leaving 'n never looking back. You done paid a mighty high price, but seeing Jerald git his high school depluma makes it all worth it.'"

He leaned back in his chair and appeared more relaxed. "I realized your uncle was right, knowin' you is the first in the family to finish high school. It was all worth it. It was then and there, at that very moment I decided to do right by you and your mamma. I don't want you havin' to go off to college worried about your mamma en me. Don't want you worried if I were hittin' her or the likes, or if I was falling down drunk in the streets. I wants you to do well in college. I wants you to be the first in the family to finish college. You can't do that worried 'bout me or your mamma, being so far from home. I lost myself the day I started drinkin'. I drives a wedge between me, you, and your mamma the day I first raised my hand to her."

Mr. Jefferson turned to his wife, "Sadie Mae, please forgive me; I wants you back as my wife, as the woman I married. Son, with you leaving, I don't want to lose you as my child, please forgive me. And Thomas, I behaved shamefully in front of you. Your father has been more of a father to Jerald then I been. He treated him like a son while I ignored 'n treated you and 'n my own child like strangers. I'm so glad and thank God he was there for Jerald. I wants you to forgive me too. I know you leaving in the morning, son, I jist hope um not too late."

BROTHERS FOREVER

August 23, not a breeze was stirring, and the morning air was hot and intensely humid. Little woke up earlier than usual as he glimpsed at the alarm clock on the dresser beside his bed. The sunlight had crept through the translucent shade drawn over the window by the dresser draw. "Six o'clock," he muttered. The past three nights had been brutally hot; no relief was in sight. The lone fan in the window continuously hummed as it swirled the hot air around the tiny room. Little instinctively knew his restless night was not due to the sultry heat; he knew it was because the day had arrived when Swoosh would be the first to leave their place called home for college. Yes, today was the day; a day he wished was still far off in the distant future. He also knew this day also meant the day for him to leave his mother, father, sister, and brother was swiftly approaching. Attempting to block out his thoughts, he covered his face with the pillow and silently wept.

"Blessed assurance, Jesus is mine." Swoosh was awakened by the sweet melodious sound of his mother's singing over the frying bacon. He knew it was her favorite song; it was a savoring sound he had not heard in a few years. He recalled when he was a small child, she would get up in the morning filled with joy, singing as she cooked. He would inquire, "Mamma, what you so happy about?"

She would reply, "Oh, just your daddy n me had an exceptionally good night sleep." As a small child, he did not understand the meaning of her answer. Instinctively, hearing her singing those words of praise, he knew her love for his father again exploded in her innermost part.

On this morning, despite the temperature outside, he felt refreshed and calm. Inwardly, he had a peace of heart and mind. The hot night air did not phase the exuberance and restoration he experienced the previous evening.

"Scooter, Jay, breakfast is ready. Y'all come on and eat while it's hot." The three sat down to enjoy their breakfast. As they sat down Mr. Jefferson gently laid his hand on Swoosh's shoulder. "You finish packin' son?"

"Yes sir, he quietly replied. "Little is riding with me to the station, if you don't mind. You know I don't want Mamma to be crying and carrying on at the train station. You know, making a scene and big fuss over me in front of all of them people. You know how dramatic she can be at times."

"Now I ought to turn you over ma knee 'n spank you for pokin' fun at me dat a way. I can't help it, my baby's leavin' home."

The sound of someone knocking on the door broke the emotional breakfast scene. "Hey Swoosh," said Little through the door, "the cabbie is here."

"Okay," he shouted as he got up from the table to open the door. "I got to get my bags, they're in my bedroom." Swoosh disappeared down the hallway.

"Good morning Mom and Dad."

"Good morning Little. How you feelin' son?"

"Kind of sad." As he answered, Swoosh reappeared dragging a footlocker and a huge army duffel bag.

"You boys need help?"

"No sir, we got it. Besides can't have an old man like you hurting his back."

"Old man! Boy, I carried bales of cotton heavier den both dem bags y'all carryin'," laughed Mr. Jefferson.

"Okay Pa, but I think we'll manage without you."

"Baby, you sure you got everything?" the teary-eyed Mrs. Jefferson asked.

"Yes ma'am, but just for you, I'll double check my room again," he yelled as he raced toward his bedroom. In the bedroom, Swoosh gently stroked the first-place trophy he won at school and began looking at several other mementos around about his room. Sitting down on his bed, taking extra care not to mess it, he fought back the tears. Rubbing his eyes, he bounced off the bed, picked up his basketball and ran out of the room. Quickly, he kissed his mother and shook his father's hand. "Bye mom, bye dad, see you in November for Thanksgiving. Let's go Little," he yelled as he rushed out of the door.

Swoosh and Little quietly put the footlocker in the trunk of the cab.

"Hey Swoosh, y'all didn't 'vite me to suppa last night; but that's alright." It was Aunt Mattie shouting from her apartment window. "Now boy, you be good in school 'n make us all proud of ya."

Swoosh looked up and smile. "I will Aunt Mattie."

It appeared to him as if the entire block had turned out to see him off.

Pop and Madear came out to say their good-byes just as he and Little finished putting the bag in the trunk of the cab. Mrs. Thomas leaned over, hugged and kissed him. Mr. Thomas shook his hand. Then, in a sudden swift movement, he embraced him. "Jerald, you take good care of yourself and be sure to write."

"Okay Madear. I promise I'll write."

Uncle Clarence rushed over and handed Swoosh an envelope. "Dis is a lil' somum we folk in the building collected sos ya kin hab sum travalin money and buy yo schoolbooks wid."

"Ah, y'all didn't have to do that Uncle Clarence."

"We nos. But we's so proud of ya we wanted to."

"Yea," scoffed out Mrs. Johnson from her window view; "it was his ide. Maybe now, he won't feel guilty when he stick dem corns of his unner the Thomases table whiles hes eatin yo portion of suppa." The small crowd roared with laughter. Swoosh was overcome by the love being expressed.

He knew he would miss all of them. They were his family. To keep the flood of tears from bursting forth, he began going into his old self-routine of the basketball star, dribbling the basketball, his fancy footwork and ended by pretending to make a basket. "Swoosh," he shouted to the gathering. "Like my shot, that's why they call me Swoosh," he exclaimed as he slipped into the cab after Little. "Hold it cabbie," he cried out, tapping the driver on the shoulder, "one minute, I forgot something."

Swoosh bolted out of the cab and disappeared into the building as the small crowd looked on questioning his sudden departure. Up the stairs he ran and flung open the door to his apartment. "Mom, dad," he cried grabbing his parents. He could no longer contain himself, "I love you mom, I love you dad; I always loved you. I never stopped loving you. That funny salute was my way of saying hello to you. I didn't see you, but I always believed you were there. That's why I did it. I'm going to miss you both. Oh, daddy, I forgive you and I believe you. I know you're going to take good care of mamma. I gotta go, I gotta go—the cab is waiting."

Outside the apartment Swoosh paused momentarily to dry his eyes. To prevent more tears, he ran down the hallway and outside the building. Once again outside, he waved good-bye and yelled to the crowd, "Good-bye, everybody, and thanks for everything." Again, he quickly embraced Madear and Pop. "Thank you for always being there for me. I don't want anybody to see me cry; I gotta go. I love you, Madear." Quickly, he again disappeared into the cab. Shielding his eyes, he uttered, "Go driver go. Please hurry." Swiftly the cab drove off disappearing into the early morning traffic.

Little rode in the cab with Swoosh to Penn Central Station. A sad Little watched as his brother, his best friend, Swoosh, purchased his train ticket to Lawrence, Kansas.

"Lady said the train is leaving on track number six, on the lower level at 8:15. I change trains in Philadelphia." Taking out his pocket watch, the chain firmly attached to his trousers, he looked at the time.

"That's in ten minutes," he announced to Little. "We better get down to the platform."

Solicitously mindful, he closed the pocket watch, felt the engraving and slipped it back into his hip pocket. Picking up his bags, silently the pair, carrying all of Swoosh's possessions, slowly walked to the track. Swoosh broke the silence. "Hey, bro, thanks for the footlocker. I got all of my stuff in it. Listen, you take care of yourself. I'm gonna get on that train and not look back, so give me some dap now and then get out of here. I don't want no mushy stuff; we had our fair share of that a few weeks ago."

Little and Swoosh began giving each other dap, then quickly embracing for what seemed to be an eternity. Simultaneously breaking the embrace, they backed away wiping their tear-filled eyes. Neither made an attempt to hide their tears. Rolling back his sleeve Swoosh revealed the scar on his wrist. "Brothers?"

Little exposed his scar. They pressed the scars together. "Till death us do part."

"All aboard, to points south," called out the conductor.

"Gotta go. My train is leaving. We gonna write Little," shouted Swoosh as he turned toward the train.

Little lowered his head to shield the tears.

"Little."

Little looked up at his brother.

"Here," Swoosh said tossing his basketball to Little. "I want you to keep it. Keep it in your dorm room. Whenever you need me just bounce the ball, and I'll be there. When I get drafted into the NBA, you can give it back to me then."

"I promise, I will."

Without hesitating, Swoosh jumped onto the train disappearing from Little's sight.

Little stood watching as Swoosh's train pulled out of the station and disappeared down the track. He felt a part of himself leaving on that train; today did not feel real. He felt a strange emptiness inside. Sadden, he made his way to leave the station; pausing he turned to take one last look in hopes of capturing a final glimpse of Swoosh. Unconsciously, Little walked to the subway for his ride back to Harlem. For him, the ride back to Harlem was long, lonely, and very depressing. Preoccupied, he pondered over how, in a few days, it would be his turn to leave making the ride home that more difficult.

August 28 was the day Little was to report to school. Classes were scheduled to begin the day after Labor Day. All traveling plans had to be changed. Black out. The big one finally hit New York City. His father was on duty and could not leave. Because there were only three trains to New London, Connecticut, he would have to leave for school a day early to arrive there at nine o'clock on Tuesday morning for the First Year Student Orientation. The entire event of August 23 for Swoosh was again repeated for Little. The gathering of the neighbors was completed with Mrs. Johnson in her window to see him off. A tearful old Mr. Taylor presented Little with an envelope.

"Your daddy had to go in early, but he said he would meet us at the train station," his mother assured him. "He'll be there."

"He said something about the black out and rerouting lines, so the trains would be on schedule." The Thomas family gathered inside the cab to accompany Little to Grand Central Station.

Mr. Thomas arrived as the family tearfully watched as Little purchased his ticket to New London, Connecticut. The summer proved to be one of the hottest on record for New York City. For Elijah, the summer was hot, but all too short. Time was going by faster than any of them had imagined. He had wanted to spend more time with Little and Swoosh, but the summer was not long enough. After returning from their Washington DC vacation and Canaan experience, the trio had pledged to spend as much time together as possible. However, the summer heat made it all too impossible.

Brownouts. Multiple brownouts. New York was experiencing brown outs throughout the city. The numerous power shortages kept

Elijah away from his boys. Con Edison occupied his every awakening moment and interrupted many of his night sleeps. Some days, he would leave home before the sun rose and returned home well after midnight. Financially, the overtime was a mixed blessing. But for Elijah, the money was not important. The only positive thing that Elijah could say about his employer was Con Edison and the city had thus far managed to stay one step ahead of avoiding the big one. However, a total black out was eminent. Despite all, he knew they had their memories of Canaan. It was that special time they had shared together that bonded the three of them even closer. Whenever they were together, the three of them spent their time reminiscing about their trip and listening to Elijah's big fish stories.

"I wish I didn't have to work. I was looking forward to driving you up there to school. The brownouts and now the blackout messed up everything. You take care of yourself son," he said embracing Little, then kissing him on the cheek.

"Don't worry about it Pop. I know it's not your fault; the time we did spent together was really special for me. We have our memories, some very special memories that I'll hold onto forever."

"All aboard, train to points north. First stop in Connecticut, Stamford, Bridgeport, and New Haven," called out the conductor.

"The train is leaving; I better get on board." Quickly, Little kissed and hugged his mother, Esther, and Elisha. "I love you, mom and Pop, I love you," he shouted as he ran to the train.

The four stood watching as Little boarded the train. Their hands drifted upward, waving good-bye as streams of tears flowed steadily down their cheeks.

"I love you too, Thomas," Elijah softly whispered as he watched the train disappear down the track.

Slowly, the train pulled out of the station for the five-hour-long trip to New London. To occupy his time, Little read the cards and counted the money inside the various envelopes as the tears trickled down his cheeks.

OLD GOLDEN RULE DAZES

It was four o'clock in the afternoon when Little's train stopped in New London, Connecticut. Very few people, mostly older men and Little stepped off the train. Everything being unfamiliar, he immediately began checking out his surroundings. The train station was totally unlike Grand Central Station or the train station in New Haven. Like several of the stations passed in Connecticut, this station had only one platform. The building was small and made of stone. Passing through the station, he noticed the two ticket windows with iron bars between the ticket agent and the customer. Two benches back-to-back were positioned in the middle of the building, and a few chairs were against the wall. Old pictures of New London and water scenes hung on the wall. In another area of the wall was the train schedule. Outside the quaint New England railroad station house, Little hailed a taxicab. "Can you take me to the University of New England?"

"Ya betcha," replied the driver in a deep Italian accent. "I taka mora students froma this station to the U na E in thesa last two week. Mosta tha ricga kids driva. Dey hasa dey owna car. Wherea u comma from?"

"New York City."

"Whatza matta, u no coma ta school wid da rest of va the team? All utter foodaball player coma lasta week. Uza late!" The driver proceeded to talk about the previous season's game. "U Na A gonna be ina da finals thiza year. I'ma bettin me monay ona U Na A againstza Kansaz."

Little, feeling tired and alone, felt he owed the cabby no explanation, so he ignored his remarks.

After riding for a while, Little saw the sign along the road indicating the direction to the University of New England. The driver turned left off the main street onto a road that had trees and fields on one side and the ocean on the other. After a while, Little saw the road passed through a huge boulder on each side of the road. Attached to each boulder was a New England-style stone fence. The wrought iron gate stood between the boulders at the entrance of the campus laid open for cars to pass through. Carved into each boulder written in Old English Gothic writing was:

> University of New England
> Founded 1805

Inside the gate, the road was tree-lined. A rush of anticipation quickened in Little, making him shutter. He tried hard to hide his enthusiasm from the driver as he leaned forward looking out of the window. A few minutes later, Little saw a few cottages and quaint looking buildings. As they continued, the buildings became larger and longer in scale; most of them Little could see were classroom buildings. Along the seaside of the campus, Little spotted a huge mansion.

"Thaza Dr. Garvey's hou. Heza da prezident of U Na A," the driver informed Little.

"Hey, Mr. footzabal, whera on campuz u wanna go?"

"Schaffer Hall please."

"Thatza new campuz na bestza domatoie. How coma a footzabal playa get ta live in Schaffer inteda Cromwell wheraz team stay. U niceza en tall boy. Isa u new quartzabaca people be talkin bout? Thatza it. Whatza ya know a colored quartzabaca," he shouted in surprise. The cab took several turns and arrived at a very tall building.

"Here ya go Mr. Quartzabaca; thisza Schaffer Hall."

"Thank you. How much do I owe you?"

"Thatza be fiva dolar na twenta-fiva cent."

"Okay," he said as he pulled a ten-dollar bill out of his wallet.

Little watched as the cab driver finished taking his bags out of the trunk and passed him his change. The driver called out as he started driving away, "You hava good season; I see you in the game."

Little stood looking at the building in front of him. It had eight floors and was made of golden bricks; on the top of the building was a viewing area. Next to Schaffer Hall was an identical building. Connecting the twin buildings was a two-story building, made mostly of glass. For the second time that day, a rush of enthusiasm brushed over him, making him shutter.

"Wow," he exclaimed, "I'm really in college." Schaffer Hall was imprinted on the roof over the doorway. Grabbing his two large bags, he entered in the lobby area of the dormitory. The coolness of the air conditioning felt good after being in the stuffy, hot cab. He could only imagine what it was like back home for his family in New York with only fans in the window.

He approached the check-in desk. "Excuse me, I'm Thomas Thomas. I'm assigned to this dormitory."

"Great," replied the cheerful voice from behind the desk, as the young lady looked up at him and brushed her shoulder length dark brown hair behind her ear. "My name is Stephanie," she began looking at a list of names. Puzzled, she looked at him oddly. "Here it is, Thomas Thomas. Let's see, that's room five eleven. Here's your room key; just sign your name here please," she said pointing to a space on the paper. "The elevator is not working, so you'll have to use the stairs."

For Little, she appeared very friendly. Little signed his name where she indicated. Her dark-tanned face was oval shaped, and her dark-brown button eyes sparkled as she talked. She stood about five feet, six inches tall, and Little noticed her fingers were long and slender. Her bright cheery smile stretched her lips to disappear to expose her straight white teeth. After taking the key, he started picking up his luggage.

"You can leave your bags down here in the television room; the elevator should be fixed in about an hour." Pointing to a room, she directed Little to a place where he could leave his bags. "Your bags will be safe in the television room. After you've checked out your room, if there is anything wrong let me know. I'll be up in a few minutes to go over the check-in list with you. Okay?"

"Okay," he replied as he picked up his bags and moved them into the room where Stephanie had instructed him. Little began the climb up the five flights of steps to his room. Walking down the hall he began looking for room five eleven. Finally arriving, he opened the door; buckets, mops, and cleaning fluids lined the floor of the room. There was no furniture, no bed, desk, chair or dresser to store his clothes. The room was hot and smelled of the cleaning fluids. Hot, tired, and hungry, Little made his way back to the check-in desk. "Excuse me, Stephanie."

"Yes," she replied turning around facing him.

"The room had buckets and mops in it, and there was no bed."

"Oh, I'm sorry that room was supposed to be clean. I'll call the janitor right now."

"Is there somewhere where I can lay down? I've been up since early this morning and I am tired."

"Sure, I'll just give you another room. Let me look for an open bed."

Stephanie began looking through the building roster. "Oh gosh, all of the rooms are taken. I don't want to make you wait down here, and it could take some time before the janitor finishes. I'll tell you what, I'm going to change you to room six twelve; it's the best room in the entire building, and probably on the entire campus. It's also a corner room and has a spectacular view of Long Island Sound; you'll love it. It's really first class. It has a full bathroom in it. It's normally reserved for special guests. But since nothing else is available, I guess it will be alright to put you in it. They put team members in it before; so, it should be alright."

As Little signed for the key, they heard the clanging of the elevator as it started moving.

"Just in time," Stephanie said amusingly. "Now, you can be the first person to ride it today. While you grab your luggage, I'll hold the elevator."

As the doors of the elevator began to close, Stephanie shouted something about dinner ending in an hour fifteen minutes and he would have just enough time to make his bed, take a shower and eat with his teammates.

Opening the room door, Little found it to be everything Stephanie had said and more. "Finally, I have a bed and a room all to myself. Now, it's time for me to kick back and relax." Little opened his footlocker, took out some sheets and made his bed. After making his bed, he took a shower. Lying down on his bed, he began to write his first letter home.

> Dear Mom, Pop, Elisha and Esther:
>
> The train ride here took about seven hours. I had a two-hour layover in New Haven. A nice lady from Old Saybrook traveling the route invited me to go with her to downtown New Haven.
>
> The city was not far from the train station and was very nice. I really liked the downtown green; it was very quaint. I also visited Yale University. It seemed like a very nice city; I wouldn't mind living in New Haven. Well, I finally arrived on campus shortly after 4:30 p.m. The room I was originally assigned to was not ready, so they moved me to room six twelve.

While composing the letter, before he realized it, he was fast asleep. Early the next morning Little was awakened by the warmth of the early morning August sun shining into his dormitory room window. The radiant sunbeams filled the room. He glanced at his new clock radio that Aunt Betty gave him for graduation; it was 7:33 a.m. The warm sun upon his body felt very good and reassuring to him, yet the coolness of the air conditioner protected him from the heat of the day. The sun was continuing to climb higher into the sky. Getting out of the bed, Little moved over to the window to catch the beauty of the morning sun. In total awe, he watched the sailboats with tall masks and billowing sails as they cruised along the Sound. Some of the boats were tied to the dock; they gracefully danced upon the sparkling waves while others parted the ocean waters charted for places of unknown adventures.

The sunlight bounced off the water onto the hull of the boats as they bounced with the waves. Off in the distance, he could see hundreds of dolphins darting through the waters. It was a very large school. They continued jumping in and out of the water as if they were playing a game. Some traveled alongside the boats, racing back and forth.

Little was speechless and amazed by all that he saw. Never in his life had he witnessed such a fascinating and intriguing sight. He suddenly had an overwhelming desire to capture this moment in time forever. He yearned to share this moment with someone special. Grabbing his pen and paper, he sat down to continue his letter home.

> Dear Family:
>
> It's 7:30 a.m. Tuesday morning. This is my first morning at UNE. How I wish all of you were here to share this moment of time with me. Words cannot begin to express what I have just seen this morning. Nor can I express this great feeling I have inside. I wish I could freeze time right now for me so that I might continue to feel and continue to live this moment forever.
>
> I wish I could freeze it to send to you so you may share it also. Believe me, the view from my dormitory window is not the same as the one from my bedroom window at home. I have a view of the Long Island Sound as it meets the Atlantic Ocean. As I write, I can see what must be hundreds of sailboats and yachts on the water. I see what must be hundreds of dolphins playing in the water.
>
> Last night there was complete silence. There were no sounds of sirens screaming, car horns honking, or people

traveling along the streets in the middle of the night. It was quiet. This morning, I was awakened by the warm sun shining into my dormitory window. Even though it is hot outside, the air conditioner kept me from sweating during the night and is keeping me from sweating now. It's like being in Macy's Department store.

The view from my window, oh Momma, you would really love. I want to stay here forever. This is a good place where I can live, learn, and grow. I know I'm going to love it here. The only change I would make is having all of you here with me.

With much love
Forever, your son,
Thomas Isaiah Thomas (Little)

Overwhelmed and feeling good about being in Schaffer Hall, in this room, and at the university, Little smiled. Most of all, he felt exceptionally good about himself. For the third time in his life, he felt he knew who he was and what he wanted to do in life. Life, for him, was at its fullest. He wanted to experience it with each morsel of breath, and to savor each moment. Nothing could, or would, ruin this day or this place for him.

In his euphoric state, he dressed to go to breakfast. On the elevator, he met Stephanie, and they began to chat. Together on the elevator, she insisted they have breakfast together. Little was pleasantly surprised to find out the dining hall was part of the dormitory. He noted how much larger and nicer it was than his high school cafeteria. During breakfast, Little was so excited that he began to share with her all he had experienced that morning. Stephanie listened with enthusiasm as Little kept talking. She instantly began to genuinely like him. When she had the opportunity, she told him most of the freshmen students would begin arriving later in the day, and most of them were probably from out of town and had not attended the summer orientation like himself. Those freshmen that attended the orientation session, she added, would be arriving on Wednesday. After breakfast, Little returned to his room and finished unpacking his clothes. He had made his first friend in college—Stephanie. It felt wonderful.

He carefully removed his clothes from the footlocker as he thought about his breakfast with Stephanie. He was thinking about how much he enjoyed his conversation with her. She was the first person he met on campus; he made a new friend. He learned she was a senior from Portsmouth, New Hampshire, majoring in Psychology. She was planning to become a psychologist. Thinking about their conversation, he felt she would be a good psychologist. She already had plans to attend graduate school. but she mostly talked about her finances. Little knew they would get along well; he liked her.

Suddenly, his thoughts were interrupted by the sound of the room door opening. "Hi," the chipper male voice rang out as a head peeped into the room. The owner of the voice stood about five feet eight inches tall, much shorter than himself. He sported a dark-tan complexion with sandy brown hair and dark brown eyes. He was dressed in tan khaki pants, penny loafers, and a plaid shirt, and his face was pleasant. "My name is Robert. Robert Henderson III," he said as he made his way into the room. "But people call me Bobby. You must be Thomas. I guess we're going to be roommates," he said extending his hand toward Little.

Little looked at Bobby, "Hi, Yes, I'm Thomas Thomas. My family and friends call me Little. I'm from New York City. Where are you from Bobby?"

"Landover, Maryland. Wow, what a great view of the Sound and the campus," Bobby exclaimed as he rushed passed Little to look out the window. "The girl downstairs at the check-in desk said it was the best view and room in the entire building."

Together, the pair looked out the window and talked for what appeared to be hours. They made up stories about the adventures that the sailboats encountered as they saw them cruising off into the ocean bound for distant lands and parts unknown. Staring out of the window, they saw their reflections in the window; together, they laughed. Little had a good feeling about Bobby. He felt sure that they were going to get along well as roommates.

"Where is your luggage, Bobby?"

"My parents are downstairs with it. We drove up here from Landover yesterday. We stayed in a hotel last night because they wouldn't allow me to stay here in the room. They said the dorms were only open for athletics. New freshmen had to wait until today to check in. My folks and I stayed at the hotel last night. They're downstairs with my luggage waiting on the elevator. The girl at the desk said it should be fixed in a few minutes. I wanted to see my room; the girl at the desk where I signed in told me that you were here, so I ran ahead up the stairs."

"I'll help you when they come up."

"Great. I got a lot of stuff."

After ten minutes, the boys heard voices outside the door.

"Bobby," a woman's voice called out.

"That's gotta be my mom. In here Mom and Dad." Dashing across the room, he opened the door for his parents. "Mom, Dad, come on in and see my room. It's got a great view of the Sound. Mom and Dad, this is Thomas Thomas otherwise known as Little. Little, these are my parents, Mr. and Mrs. Henderson."

Little shook Mr. and Mrs. Henderson's hands. "How do you do? Here, let me take that bag for you Mrs. Henderson."

"Oh, thank you Thomas; that's awfully kind of you," she stammered as he took the bag. "Where is your room Thomas?"

"Mom," laughed Bobby. "This is his room. We're going to be roommates. Isn't it neat?"

"Oh," she hesitantly replied. "That's nice. Ah, we better go to the car to get the rest of your luggage Bobby. Your father and I have to get back to the hotel to check out."

"Do you need help with rest of your things?" asked Little.

"Sure Little; come on," exclaimed Bobby.

"Oh no; I mean, no thank you, Thomas. There's just a few things, and we can manage the rest by ourselves," Mrs. Henderson responded quickly.

"Mom, I got a lot of stuff. We could use some help."

She spoke sharply. "I said no Robert."

As the Henderson's left the room, Little was feeling very positive about Bobby as his roommate. *Bobby's parents weren't so bad either. His mom sort of reminds me of Aunt Betty in an odd sort of way; they're both kind of bossy.* Again, he peered out the window to watch the sea of boats on the water. Suddenly, he began to laugh hysterically at the reflection in the window.

"Mom, I have no problem with it, so why should you?" cried Bobby as they entered the lobby from the elevator.

"I don't care Bobby," she snarled. "We're paying for your education, and that is final."

"But Mom!"

"I don't want to hear another word about it from you—that's final."

Mrs. Henderson approached Stephanie at the front desk. "Excuse me Miss, but there is a problem with my son's room."

Inquisitively, Stephanie inquired, "What's wrong? Six twelve is the best room in the entire building."

"Well, is it possible to change to another room?"

"I don't understand. Is there a problem with the room? Thomas, the other student in the room, didn't say anything about something being wrong. Whatever it is, I'm sure it will be fixed right away."

Mrs. Henderson leaned forward over the desk and began whispering, "There is a black boy in the room. I don't want my son living with that kind. Since six twelve is the best room in the building, you can put that black boy in another room."

Stephanie's face turned red. Slowly she backed away for Mrs. Henderson. "I'm sorry, I cannot do that," she replied as she tried to control her anger. Controlling herself, she continued, "After the first three weeks into the semester, students can change rooms if they choose. So, if your son has a problem and wants to change his room, he'll have to wait until then."

"I don't have a problem. Little seems like a nice guy."

"Shut up Robert, we didn't drive here all the way from Maryland to have you living with a thing," snarled Mrs. Henderson.

"Excuse me, but Mr. Thomas is a young man, a human being, and not a thing."

"Young lady, I don't care what you feel. I want it, no, I want that nigger out of my son's room, and I want him out now!"

Stephanie's face turned red with embarrassment. "Your language offends me. We have no other vacancies in the building. I'm only the resident assistant. I don't have the authority to change a student's room."

"Well Miss Resident Assistant, then get me someone who can. If necessary, we'll go see the president of the university. Both my husband and I are alumni. We make sizable contributions to the university on a yearly basis. We are entitled to special consideration."

Sheathing with contempt for the Hendersons, Stephanie picked up the phone. "If you like you can speak with the Dean of Student Life, Dr. Goins. His office is located in the main administration building, Brewster Hall. I'll call him to let him know you're on your way to see him."

After a while, the desk phone ranged. "Good morning, Schaffer Hall."

Pause.

"Yes Dean Goins.

Pause.

"Thomas arrived yesterday. He arrived with the other team players."

Pause.

"There are about six other team members in Schaffer. They all have roommates."

Pause.

"Yes sir. I spoke to maintenance yesterday. They said it will take a while before they get the furniture in the room."

Pause.

"They said about eleven o'clock."

Again, there was a short pause.

"Yes sir," she exclaimed as she hung up the phone. A few minutes later the Hendersons returned. To restrain herself from saying something negative to Mrs. Henderson, Stephanie held out the key to Bobby. "The Dean said I should change your room, not Mr. Thomas's, the other student, since he was in the room first. Your room is five eleven, sign here please. The room is not ready yet, the men should be moving the furniture in it. It should be ready for you to move in around eleven."

Little was still staring outside the window when the Henderson's returned to the room. "What do you know, they assigned Bobby to the wrong room," Mrs. Henderson cheerfully announced.

Little expressed his disappointment with the news. "Oh, that's too bad; hey, don't worry Bobby, we can still hang out together. You're always welcome in my room. Who knows, we may have some classes together. What room are you moving to?"

With his head bowed down, looking and feeling defeated, Bobby did not respond. He continued to look away with his head bowed down.

"Would you like me to help you with your luggage?"

"No, no, that will be perfectly alright; we can manage by ourselves," Mrs. Henderson replied as they gathered Bobby's luggage together.

Slowly, Little walked across the room to close the door behind them.

Again, turning to look out of the window he noticed Bobby had left his eye glass case. Exiting the room, the Henderson's were standing at the elevator. As the elevator doors opened Mrs. Henderson said,

"Bobby, when you get to your room, I want you to check your bags to make sure that nigger didn't steal anything."

As they turned around in the elevator, they saw the shocked and stunned Little standing in the doorway. "You left your eye glass case Bobby." Reaching out, Little handed the eye glass case to Bobby.

Mrs. Henderson, realizing Little heard her, did not hesitate to reveal her true feelings. Immediately, she began speaking as if Little was not there.

"They have special colleges for his kind. They don't have to come to our good white schools. I don't know why they want to come to ours; they don't belong here. With their low-test scores, they're ruining the reputation of the university. They're nothing but special admission charity cases; I don't care how many football or basketball games they win. They still don't belong here with us good decent white people."

"Hush Martha. God woman, he can hear you," shouted Mr. Henderson.

"Huh, it doesn't matter; he's probably accustomed to people talking to him like this any way."

A sudden pain, a pain like that of a sharp dagger struck Little deep in his chest. His eyes filled with tears, but he refused to allow the Henderson's the satisfaction of seeing him upset or cry. He felt like when he was back in Miss McGinnis's office, unwelcome, alone, and invisible. Instantaneously, his innermost parts were engulfed with anger, hatred, and rage.

His anger began festering like an infected open sore, oozing with puss deep within him. His hatred burned with a passion, like the flames of fire that destroyed Canaan. The heat of his rage within him ignited the destructive beast harboring deep inside. He felt like striking out at someone with all his strength, hitting them, hurting them.

Entering the room, he closed the door, stood against it, and began bumping his forehead against the door. So intense were his feelings they began emitting from his body filling the void of the room. He hated this place and all that it represented.

Little, totally frustrated, became out of control. His head pounded as he became engrossed in his anger. *She's right Little, you knew you didn't belong here. Not at this university. Mrs. Henderson made it clear, she is right. You, like those of your race, do not belong here nor are you welcomed at this university. Never again, never again am I going to allow anyone else at this school or any other place to humiliate me or treat me with disdain and cause me pain. I don't want to stay here; I'm not going to stay here; not a second longer than I have to. I have nothing to stay for, and most of all, no reason to stay here. No reason to be here.*

Raging with anger, Little turned toward the window. His body consumed with pain and anger. The pain! He could not stand the pain. It ached, a throbbing ache. The pain radiated from the crown of his head to the tip of his toes. He wished he could stop it by reaching inside himself and ripping it out. The pain! It was the only thing he had; it made him know that he was alive. There it was in the window; the pain, hatred, and rage filled him with guile and contempt for what he now saw in the window. He cursed that which he saw in the window. *You are so ugly, I hate you; I hate you. All you've done is cause me pain. You, you're the reason for all my pain and how I'm feeling. I can't go anywhere or do anything because of you. You even caused Pop a bunch of pain. All my life you've been a curse to me. I won't live with the pain like Pop; no not like Pop all those years. I hate you. I wish you were dead.*

Tears began replacing the twinkle that only minutes ago had sparkled in his brilliant black eyes. Slowly, he raised his giant fists and sent them crashing down upon the desk. Again, again, and again he pounded his fists against the defenseless inanimate object. Each time, his fist pounded it harder and harder.

With his insides screaming with rage, he loathed the image he saw in the sunlit window. The same image just a few minutes ago, he so joyously laughed at with Bobby. It now appeared to him ugly, dark, and despicable. The fire of Canaan blazed in his eyes and in his heart. He moved closer to the image. Raising his tightly clenched fist, he prepared to pound on the tormented scourge before him. He could not help but hate what he saw. He longed to smash it, to destroy it forever. *This is your chance, go ahead, hit it, you can do it; destroy it now. It's not wanted here; it doesn't belong here. You're not wanted here.*

No, don't do it, the voice inside his head shouted loudly.

"Shut up, shut up, shut up; you shut up, damn you, shut up," he screamed aloud. "I'm tired of you interfering in my life. Leave me alone!" Lifting his big fist up higher he struck the window, causing the pane to shake violently.

Harder, hit it harder. Send him shattering down to the ground below. I'll make them feel guilty. That's what you do. Make them feel guilty."

No, it won't make them feel guilty. Thomas, you don't want to do that. Please, you don't want to do that Thomas. Please, please, please don't do it," the voice cried out. "Enough blood has been spilled, and too many innocent people have already suffered and died.

He felt something fighting against him, trying to hold him back. "I said leave me alone," he yelled. Angrily, he ascended the desk to get closer to the image.

No, Thomas.

He felt something trying to pull him back down. "Let me go," he shouted as he pulled away from whatever it was. With his fist reeling back and forth, he prepared to strike hard at what was in the window, causing his pain. He hated it. He desired to drive it away forever. He struggled with something inside of him; it would not allow the window to break.

Stepping back, he prepared to throw his entire weight against the glass. With his body, he hit the image he saw in the window. The window cracked as his body bounced back.

No Thomas! Don't do it, the voice inside screamed and pleaded. *Think about your mother and father, Swoosh, Elisha, and Esther. Think about them. How are they going to feel? For their sake don't do this Little.*

Little continued to move backward for the momentum he needed to strike his final blow. The final blow, which would shatter the glass, sending him hurtling down to the ground below, ending it all.

I can't hold it back any longer. It must not end like this. God, oh dear God help me. It must not end like this. Remember your word, your promise. It's not supposed to end like this.

Stepping to the edge of the desk to hurdle his massive body into the image, Little prepared himself. He prepared to send it and him to crash to the ground below. At the summit of his momentum and pentacle of his anger, he stepped back and lost his balance, slipping off the edge of the desk, sending his body crashing to the floor below.

Little laid on the floor weeping in a loud voice, "Why couldn't you have left me alone? I want to die. I just want to die." He didn't care if anyone heard him. Unconsciously, he didn't know he wanted to be heard. Unconsciously, he did not know how much he wanted to be saved.

After a while, he heard the sharp rapid knocking sound on the door. Unsuccessfully fighting back tears, he wiped his swollen eyes as he picked himself off the floor. Unable to hide the pain within, in a low trembling voice of total defeat, he spoke. To disguise his tears, he slowly opened his closet door, took out his luggage, and threw it on the bed. Meticulously, he opened his drawers and began to toss his clothes in the open bag. "Come in. It's open," he shouted.

From the reflection in the glass, he saw it was Stephanie. Unsure of his knowledge of what had transpired with the Hendersons, she came up to see if Little was alright. The thickness of his intense emotions engulfed the room. Upon entering the room, she could feel the intense emotions of anger, hate, and pain.

Instantly, she knew he was aware why Bobby changed to another room. Little was caught between hiding his anger, resentment and tears, and giving his rage to her in all its fullness. Not at all feeling shameful of what he tried to do he quickly turned and faced the cracked window. Through the split reflection in the pane, Stephanie could see the tears rolling down his face.

The words that proceeded out of her mouth were evoked not from knowledge gained from textbooks, but words only as the Spirit of God would allow. Her words were spoken from the depth of her soul, and from the purity of her heart. She wrapped her arms around herself as if she were cold.

"Your pain, it fills this room, Little. I feel your pain; it's radiating all through the room. But the pain and shame you feel is not yours. I bear the shame because I bear the same white skin as the Henderson's and many other ignorant people like them. Little…" she continued as she moved closer and reached out to touch him. His body flinched as he moved away from her. "You did nothing wrong; they're wrong. They're the racists. I can't stand here and say I know how you feel, because I am not a Negro. But I do know what I'm feeling in this room is deep hurt and pain, and I know you're hurting inside because of it."

Her words coupled with his pain was more than he could handle. It was more than he desired to cope with at this time. Although he was hurting, he didn't want to stop hurting. Somehow, he found comfort in his pain. *The pain, it is my pain, the only thing I can say I possess at this time. The pain is letting me know that I am still alive. And now she wants to take what infinitesimal dignity I have left to call my own away from me.* Slowly, he turned and faced Stephanie. He could not, nor did he desire to hold it back any longer. Glaring at her in the fullness of his rage he screamed. "What do you mean? My pain, what do you mean, you feel my pain, my hurt? What do you know about my hurt? How can you? You have no idea about how I feel. How can you stand there like you're all pure and innocent and say that when you're one of the people inflicting me with the pain! All my life, you and others like you have caused me nothing but pain. From the very first moment you laid eyes on me you started inflicting the pain."

Slowly her mouth drooped open. "Please, Little. When? How?"

"Shut up. When I first walked through the front door, because I'm black and tall, you automatically assumed I was an athlete. You automatically assumed I was on the football or basketball team. Does every tall Negro you know have to play basketball? No, to you, a nigger can't be here because of his intellectual capacity."

Unaware, and not caring, his voice became louder and louder as he spoke. His fist began to curl in a ball. She could see his fist curled up as his arm slowly began to rise. Filled with shame, she stood ready to receive whatever punishment was to follow.

No Thomas, that's not the way. Don't do it Thomas; please don't. Not again, Father, please not again!

His fist slowly uncurled. "No, you assumed I'm here because of the color of my skin and a round ball. I'm just here to play a game for your personal amusement and entertainment, like every other black boy student on this campus. To you, white people, we're only good for our athletic abilities in basketball or football or singing and dancing. Shine monkey, shine; dance, nigger, dance. To you, we're just some special second-class citizens to be pitied, a charity case, something here to ease your guilty conscience. Other than that, you can't stand being around us. We're just good enough to cook your food, clean up your mess, and entertain you in your stadiums. We're all just a bunch of dark, dumb, black niggers to you!"

In a defeated, low, pain-filled tone, Little turned his back to Stephanie and stared passed the window. "Don't give me your sympathy; I don't want it. I know where I don't belong and I'm not going to stay where I'm not wanted. The one thing I know is I'm not wanted here. Both you and the cab driver were just too cowardly to say what you were really thinking. To yellow to say it point blank to my face; so you make sly comments behind my back. The Hendersons said it loud and clear, I'm not stupid. I don't need to be told twice. At least they were honest and said it to me in my face. I don't need anybody else to tell me. They're right, I don't belong here in this place; I never did, and I never will."

Through the image reflected in the window, he could see the tears rolling down her face.

No Thomas, you're wrong. Thomas, look at her and see that you're wrong about her.

He tried fighting hard against seeing the sincerity expressed in her tears. He did not want to, but he could not help hearing her tears speaking to him.

"Right now, I feel so unclean," she cried, radically shaking her head from side to side as if to rid herself of this enigma. "I feel so unclean. I never said I wasn't guilty. God as my witness knows I didn't mean any harm. I am so sorry, so truly sorry. But one thing I do know, Thomas, is that you do belong here. You belong here just as much as I do. You and all the other Negro students belong here as much as all the Bobby Hendersons and any other white student. I truly believe that. This morning at breakfast we talked, we laughed. I felt a special closeness to you. I know you felt it too. This morning at breakfast we became friends. I felt it, and I know you felt it too."

She held her hand out beckoning to him. "And now, I feel so far away, so far away from you. I don't like this feeling. Most of all, I don't like what you're feeling about yourself, or how I, the Hendersons, and people like us, made you feel. I never intended to hurt you Thomas; I didn't mean to hurt you. Please, believe me, as God as my witness, he knows I didn't mean to hurt you. I did not intend to cause you pain, especially not in the same way the Henderson's hurt you."

Stephanie began pleading with him as she moved closer and closer to him. "If you leave, it means that the Hendersons win and you lose. I lose; we all lose. Please, don't let ignorant white trash like them ruin your future, or the opportunity to change things. Their stupidity has got to go; racism has got to end. Not everyone on campus shares their views on race. By staying here, you can make some changes. We and others, who don't share their views have got to educate them about their ignorance. Leaving, you make no changes in their attitude or behavior. Don't judge us all by the Henderson's of this world. Please don't judge me by the Hendersons. If you stay, I'll help you, and I know other students, faculty, and administrators who are working to improve the relationship between the races. Give the university a chance. Please, give yourself a chance Little. One month, give it one month. Give me, the university, and yourself one month. You owe yourself that much. I'm not promising you things will be great, but give me a chance to show you how good the university really is. How it can be and how you really belong here like any other student on campus. Most of all, give me the opportunity to show you that we want you here. We need you here, Little. Please, not all of us are like the Hendersons."

Still facing the window, Little softly, but abruptly, replied, "I'm not going to promise you anything! I don't owe you, and I don't owe this university a damn thing! Can you promise me it won't happen again?"

She lowered her head and stared at the floor silently.

"Well, can you?" he shouted.

"No, I can't," she softly replied.

"I won't put myself through this again. I can't, I just can't, and I won't." Little resumed emptying the drawers as the tears continued to flow down his face.

"Then please don't leave today Little, she said as she moved toward him, gently placing her hand on his shoulder." His body jerked violently from her touch, forcing her to retreat; however, she persisted. In a pleading voice she continued. "Wait, wait until tomorrow and if you still feel like leaving, I won't try to stop you. I'll drive you to the train station myself. But, please, give yourself a little time. At least give yourself tonight to think things over. Right now, you're upset; you have every right to feel the way you're feeling. Maybe, just maybe, you'll feel a little bit better tomorrow. Please, just don't leave today."

Little turned to face her, staring her dead in her eyes. In a stern and harsh voice, he screamed, "Can you guarantee this won't happen again between now and tomorrow?"

Her head dropped. Slowly she looked up. "That's not fair Little. You know I can't give you any guarantees; you know I can't."

In a soft tone he gently replied, "Than you're asking too much of me Stephanie, and that's not fair." Turning around he again faced the cracked window.

Exhausted and emotionally drained, knowing the road ahead was going to be rough if he stayed, Stephanie slowly turned to walk out of the room in defeat. Pausing, she turned and looked back at Little. He still had his back to her. "I'll be in my room; room number four fifteen.

Please, whatever you decide, please stop by. Even if it is to say good-bye, please stop by. You can promise me that much. Can't you?"

In an extremely harsh and cruel voice he shouted, "Don't you get it girl? I don't owe you a damn thing. I don't owe you, and I won't promise you a damn thing!" Hearing the door close, Little resumed packing. Opening his footlocker to search for his train fare home, he spotted the basketball Swoosh had given him. He picked it up and clutched it tightly to his chest. Recalling what Swoosh had told him at the train station he, gave it a few hard bounces and threw the ball into the footlocker. Looking into the footlocker, he found the envelope Mr. Taylor had given him containing the money next to his bible. Slowly, he opened the envelope. The money was wrapped in a letter. Emotionally drained, collapsing on his bed, Little began reading the letter:

Dear Thomas:

I am sure this letter is a surprise to you. You know I can't read or write 'cause I never had no schooling when I grew up. I asked my grandson, Nate, to write what I say. He is in the eighth grade. He reads and writes very good just like you showed him when you was helping him with his schoolwork. He was really proud to write the letter to you when I asked him. He is a good boy and always enjoys reading to me and writing letters for me.

I just want to give you something to hold on to when times are rough and to give you a few words of encouragement. First, not all white folks are evil and not all of them mean you harm when they are trying to be helpful, friendly, and sometimes funny. I have worked as a janitor at the Columbia University for over thirty years. Not all white folks have treated me bad by calling me names and trying to make me shame of being colored, especially being as dark as I am. To some, I'll always be a boy no matter how old I am, and I'll never measure up to them according to their standards. I have met some very good white folks who were willing to help me and were genuine in their respect for me.

I suspect you will meet up with both kinds of treatment at your school, the University of New England. Don't be discouraged by the negative ones. You are the smartest person I know and you are good with the book learning. Most of all you have a very good heart. Don't let anyone tell you different. Most importantly, remember why you are there in college.

There ain't too many colored students at the school where I work. When I see them sitting in the classroom just as big, I feel real good and proud for them and myself. I tells them that from time–to-time and they tells me how hard it is for them feeling alone and unwanted. Sometimes they are treated by whites like they is not even there. They say sometimes the teacher and students act like they ain't even there in the classroom. They tells them they don't belong there and sometime the colored students say a lot of times they feel as if they do not belong there. I suspect it will be no different for you at your school or Jerald at his.

You and Jerald, now y'all both different. Both you boys is real smart. But most of all y'all is blessed by Almighty God himself. Y'all is the hope of our community and the Negro people.

Whatever you do, don't let nobody turn you round. Don't let them tell you that you don't belong at that university. You got just as much a right to be there as they do. Even more right to be there, cause the college is paying everything for you. My grandson's future and the future of the entire Negro people is upon yours and Jerald's shoulders. What Moses was to the Hebrew children, delivering them from old Pharaoh, y'all is to the Negro people. Now, I know being so young that is a big responsibility to be carrying on your shoulders and an awful weight, but I knows you can bear it with the help of the Lord God Almighty. Just remember to pray to him and he will give you the strength and show you the way. God Almighty himself got his angels watching over you and Jerald.

The money in this envelope, it ain't much, but it represents the hard work of the people, all your friends and neighbors. We are your family. They give it because they know you is going to be successful and they want to be a part of your success in some way. They give you and Jerald all they had; like the widow woman's mite, we're praying hard for you every day. We know you won't disappoint us.

I love you. Stay strong and always remember God. Put God first in your life and in all you does and say. When you can't do anything else, pray. Also remember who you are; be proud of what you are and where you come from. Be proud of your black skin and of being of the Negro race. You have already and I know you will continue to make us all proud.

As King David said in the Bible, "I will look to the hills from which cometh my help. My help, cometh from the Lord." You too must also do the same. When all else fails, pray.

God Bless You, Love Your Uncle Clarence XXX

Next to Mr. Taylor's signature were the three Xs he used to sign his name before he and Swoosh taught him how to write his name. He had practiced for several weeks to learn how to write his name. He was so proud when he did, he showed everybody. Still determined to leave; however, puzzled, torn, and tired, Little, terribly confused about what he was going to do, laid down on his bed. As Mr. Taylor had instructed him, looking upward, he prayed. While he was praying his body and mind surrendered to the tiredness he felt.

Leaving Little's room, Stephanie felt dazed and tired from the emotions she experienced. For her, what had transpired was a very traumatic experience for a girl from Portsmouth, New Hampshire. Her head pounded uncontrollably with pain. Despite the dizziness, she returned to her room using the stairs. In the stairwell, she found some peace. It was a reprieve, a place of refuge from the confines of her dormitory room. Entering her room, she was still nervous and shaken. The thoughts running through her head caused her mind to swirl around and around. Pushing aside the reality of the cracked window, she refused to believe, accept, or acknowledge the obvious. There seemed to be no end to the swirling. *It's my fault. I feel so responsible for what happened. What's going to happen to him? Thomas is going to be leaving on the next train out of New London. I've lost; the Hendersons and others like them have won. I know he's gone; he's out of here.*

"Oh, Thomas, Thomas, Thomas," she cried out. "I understand why you want to leave. I don't blame you for wanting to leave; I guess if I were in your place I would leave too. I can't blame him. I don't know what it is like to be a Negro in America. But I do know what it is like to be hurt, to feel pain." She immediately retreated to the bed. Like Little, sleep was her final refuge, her means of escape from that which troubled her so deeply.

The noonday sun was still shining brightly in the sky when Stephanie was awakened by a knock on her door. "Come in." The door did not open, but she could hear the voice on the other side.

"I'll give it one month, that's all I can promise right now. One month, after that, I'll take it one day at a time."

Surprised to hear him, she jumped up and ran to the door. After brushing her hair off her face, she opened the door and took Little's hand and hugged his neck. "That's all the time we need. Just one month, then one day at a time. Thank you Little. Thank you."

Weakly smiling, he said, "According to my watch, if we hurry, we should be able to make lunch. I'm hungry, how about it…friend?"

"Yes. I am too. After lunch, I'll give you a personal tour of the campus, friend."

CAMPUS LIFE

Little watched the upper classmen from his room window congregating in the connecting streets below. Gently, he touched the window where the crack used to be. One day, upon returning to the room from touring the campus, the window was fixed. Funny, he thought to himself. She never said anything. He did not know she had seen the crack. Glancing at the street below, he could see students moving couches, desk, dressers and other pieces of furniture into the dormitories from their automobile, trailers, and U-Haul trucks. He could hear them in the hallway barking orders, giving directions and soliciting help from others as they struggled with luggage, furniture and a sundry of items. The hallways buzzed with their amazement of the elevator being in perfect working condition. Each time someone put the elevator on hold a bell would ring. Initially, Little found the ringing amusing, but after a while he found it annoying and extremely irritating.

    The once peaceful Schaffer Hall quickly transposed into a mecca of music blasting, people screaming, and yelling as they greeted each other. Uncharacteristic of the other corner rooms, his extra-large room had two windows. One was the oversized picture window that faced the ocean; out of the other window, he could see another part of the building and the campus. Hearing the high-pitch shrieking, he opened his window to check out the hullabaloo. Looking up, he could see two floors above him the faces of two young female students hanging out of the window. They were yelling, screaming, and waving their hands at another female student who just drove up.

"Judy, ahhh, ahhh. It's Judy. Ahhh, ahhh, she's back. Wait, Judy, stay there, we'll be right down. Ahh, ahhh." After Judy saw the pair hanging out of the window, she began jumping up and down on the sidewalk, screaming wildly. Little could not help but wonder what they were really thinking. *Do they really think Judy is going to drive away after just arriving?* Amused at their behavior, he laughed. *Must be catchy*, he thought as he continued to watch the people below and heard the window-to-ground conversations continue at great length. *I wonder if it's going to be like this for me when I come back next summer.*

With students unloading their vehicles and moving back and forth into the buildings, the commotion, in an odd sort of a way, reminded him of being back at home in the streets of New York. Bicycles were everywhere. Cars of all types; sports cars, luxury cars, midsize cars; and people moving about, yelling. The excitement filled the air as well as the streets and the sidewalks of the campus—just like Harlem. The people and cars were moving everywhere, and all kinds of noises were coming from the buildings. Shouting and yelling greetings! *This is just like home; the bright hot sunshine, the music, and loud noises of people greeting one another in the streets. I like it, it's really satisfying, relaxing, amusing, and very electrifying. Just like Harlem.*

Over the past several days, Little spent most of his time with Stephanie. When she was not working, she acquainted him with the campus and the traditions that made the University of New England unique. As she took him around, he discovered the campus was larger than he had imagined. "The old campus," she explained, "is also known as Uncas after the chief of the Mohegan Indian tribe. There are approximately ten buildings in that area. Those four reddish brown brick buildings were built in the late 1600s and formed the wide-open space known as the quadrangle. These buildings were among the first built on the property. They're often referred to as the original campus. The main administrative building at the top of the quadrangle is

Massachusetts Hall; the other buildings were built in the early 1700s; Stillman, Vermont, and Connecticut halls are now used as classroom buildings."

"The president of the university, the provost and the three vice presidents—Academics Affairs, Finance, and Student Affairs along with the dean of Student Affairs, the Registrar, the director of Financial Aid, Residential Life Services, and a few other department offices are all located in Massachusetts Hall. The College of Journalism," Stephanie noted, "is recognized as the number one school of journalism in the country, and it's located in Connecticut Hall. Now, the six buildings in a gothic style comprised the white part of Uncas. Behind Massachusetts Hall are the bookstore and the Student Union Building, Niantic, and Pennacook Hall. The College of Arts and Sciences and Gollier College of Education are also on the old campus in the gothic style buildings."

One afternoon, Stephanie took him to the part of the campus called Iroquois. It was a beautiful day. At the campus bicycle shop, they rented bikes. Starting out on the section of Iroquois nearest the old campus by Fletcher Law School building and the Hillmon Law Library, they rode to the remote end of Iroquois to the area referred to as Wigwam. The ride to Wigwam was nice. Five three-floor dormitories and two large dining facilities made of red bricks were hidden in the dense wooded area. On the other end of Iroquois, closer to the city of New London, they visited the University Medical Center and the University Hospital. Melbourne Hall was the farthest building out on the Iroquois side, not far from Wigwam. Next, they rode to the section known as Quinnipiac, the area north of Uncas and bordering Iroquois. They rode by the Electrical, Chemical, Civil, Mechanical and Nuclear Engineering buildings on its north-western side. Narraganset Hall, the gymnasium, the football stadium, several tennis courts, and other athletic fields were located on the far northern part of the campus. On the eastern part, were more resident halls, marshland, and the beach. The campus was so large, and the building so far away, many of the students rode bicycles to class or used the campus shuttle. The day was long; however, Little enjoyed the tour and found the ride refreshing.

The campus was beautiful with its open field areas, trees, old buildings, quaint cottages, marshlands, and beachfront. His favorite place was the marina area right off the campus by the docks where the various boats were moored. It was in this area that he was able to see from his dormitory room window.

Earlier, during the day, Little registered for class with all the other freshmen students. For everyone except him, the registration process was exhausting. Unlike many other freshmen, he did not have to wait in the long lines.

After standing in line for an hour outside of Narraganset Hall, he received his class schedule. His tuition, housing, and student activity fees were paid. The employees working the registration desk often double checked his material and questioned his identity. "Are you sure this is your name?" the woman working the registration desk asked. She then questioned the woman sitting next to her and asked her to double check it to make sure there was no mistake.

He had no problem getting his student ID picture taken; apart from the line, and the fact the blue background made his face appear extremely dark, almost beyond recognition. The white of his eyes and his white teeth were the most prominent in the photo. He began feeling his anger and frustration increasing. Little remembered and was determined to keep his promise to Stephanie to give it one month. Therefore, he tried extra hard to ignore the facial expression on the faces, and the off-color remarks of the people involved in the registration process.

Looking at his schedule from the campus tour during the orientation process, and the tour Stephanie took him on, he determined the buildings in which he would be taking most of his classes were on the old campus, on the other side of the campus in Iroquois. Since he did not have a bicycle, he would have to use the shuttle bus service. He found the note indicating later next week he was to meet with his academic advisor and the other students in the Nuclear Engineering program. Eventually, he would meet with the presidential scholar organization.

Little could hear the voices in the hallway. "I got all my classes; this year registration was a breeze."

Another male voice responded, "Alright Ken. Way to go. I waited in the line all day. I had to get my advisor's signature, and, by the time I got it, three of the classes I wanted were closed. Now, if I want to take State and Local Governments next semester, I have to take History of the Modern World with Dr. Wochek. I dread taking him; everybody knows he can't teach."

"Yea, but he's the chairman of the history department, so you can't get around him being a history major. I heard for his class this semester he has seven books and he's requiring four twenty-five-page typed papers."

"That's just why I don't want to take him. What about you Jim? How did you make out at registration?"

"Me? Compared to you and Andrew, you guys had it easy. I'm on the waiting list for four of my six classes. I had to see Dean Baxter over in Education. He said he'd see what he could do. If I don't get two of the classes I won't be graduating this June."

"That sucks," replied Ken.

"You guys going to the clambake tonight?"

"That's all Ken and I thought about since we got on campus. You going Jim?"

"Yea. Stop by my room when you guys are ready to go."

"Okay Andrew; we'll see you later."

The voices faded as the trio continued down the hall. Little heard the room doors close and the voices disappeared. As the music continued to blast, he returned to looking out of the window to view the activity below. He was distracted by the knock on the door.

"Hey Little, may I come in? I have somebody special I want you to meet."

"Hey Stephanie; sure, come in." Little watched the boyish face, tall muscular bronze-skinned male followed Stephanie into his room. His thick, black, shoulder-length hair was tied back in a ponytail swung from side to side as he moved. His muscular arms and chest bulged through the white polo shirt he was wearing. He thrust his hand forward to capture Little's.

"I bet I know who this guy following behind you is," Little proclaimed as he stood and extended his hand to the person trailing behind Stephanie.

"I bet you do. You've been hearing a lot about him for the past few days. Little, this is my fiancé Alejandro Torres. Alejandro Torres this is Thomas Thomas, better known as Little. He's the freshman I've been telling you about."

"So, you're the new kid on the block trying to win over the heart of my fair lady," Ale said displaying a bright smile while shaking Little's hand.

Embarrassed, Little blushed.

"Ale, stop; you're embarrassing him," Stephanie said tapping Ale lightly on his chest. "Like I warned you Little, he is always joking around so don't pay him any attention."

Pulling her tightly to his side, Ale smiled at Little. "I'm sure Steff here has taken excellent care of you. She's known around here to be the mothering smothering type. But then that's why I love her," he said while pinching her cheek. "It's lunch time," Alejandro announced as he glanced at his watch. "Why don't we go down to the cafe, or, if you prefer, we could go into town for some pizza?"

"I'd love to, but I can't. I'm on duty. I have to stay on campus, but I should be off at four. Besides, I promised Little we would go with him to the Gathering, then to the clambake and bonfire on the beach."

"That's right, I almost forgot—the gathering, clambake, and bonfire are tonight. Part of the campus tradition is all freshmen students must attend the first gathering of the year. It's like an initiation as a freshman student to UNE. Steff and I met at our first gathering and we have attended every year since. You'll love it. So, it'll be your first time Little?"

"Sure will."

"That means you're a virgin!"

"Ale!" Stephanie shouted again tapping him on his chest. "You're so embarrassing."

"Come on Steff, it's tradition. You know that's what we call a freshman or transfer student attending their first gathering and clambake."

"I know, but you make it sound so, so nasty."

"I can't help it. You know how we Venezuelans are. Besides, you're the quintessential New Englander, extremely parochial and anal retentive." Ale began laughing and pinching her cheek. "I love it when you get mad. Your little nose wrinkles up and your upper lip twitches. You look so cute. Isn't she cute Little? Ah, look at that face."

Stephanie blushed, "Oh stop it Ale. You're embarrassing me in front of Little."

They all began laughing. Little had a good feeling about Alejandro, he sensed he was going to like him, and they would get along well. *But then, I thought the same thing about Bobby. One just never knows.*

"Okay you two, you're starting to get mushy just like my parents."

"You hear that, Steff; Little's calling us an old married couple. I think we've just been insulted. On that note, I think we better get going to lunch; I don't like beating up freshmen on an empty stomach." Ale laughed and threw a playful jab at Little. Little managed to dodge the blow and land a nice one on Ale. "And quick too; uh oooh, I must be getting old."

"You two old men better come on; I have to be at work in an hour."

Grabbing both Little and Ale by the arm, the trio headed for the cafeteria.

The cafeteria was crowded and noisy. Students were still greeting one another after the long summer break. "Hey Little, while Steff is at work, if you don't have anything to do, why don't you go with me to New Haven."

"Sure."

"Don't forget the gathering, clambake, and bonfire," Stephanie interjected.

"Sure, I'm coming right back. I need to pick up a few things at home, and I promised my mom I'd stop by the house sometime today."

"Okay, you guys have a good time; Little, don't let Alejandro scare you. He's really a pussy cat inside."

"You bet."

Facing Stephanie, Ale hugged her, and they kissed good-bye. "See you when we get back sweetheart. Love you."

"Love you too. Drive carefully."

Ale turned to Little, "Ready?"

"Ready."

"Then let's go. I'm parked in the back."

That evening as the trio approached the quadrangle, from the distance, Little could see a crowd of students gathering in the area facing Massachusetts Hall. Most of them he recognized as students he spent time with earlier at registration. "You see Little," stated Stephanie, "the gathering of the freshmen is an annual ritual. It's considered the rite of passage for all freshmen students. While the admissions office admitted you to the school, the gathering ceremony officially made you a member of the student body." The first person to speak was the president of the student government.

A hush went over the crowd as he climbed up the steps of Massachusetts Hall. Slowly, in a ritualistic manner, he addressed the crowd. "The University of New England was founded in 1790 by Samuel R. Jackson, a wealthy shipbuilder and businessman in Connecticut."

"Prior to the Pequot War, Algonquian Bay was a major gathering area for the American Indians living in New England. The Algonquian were a family of American languages spoken by nearly all the Indians of North Eastern America. The different tribes met here for gatherings, to settle disputes between bands, tribes, for religious ceremonies, celebrations, and various other reasons. Today, we meet here on this sacred ground to proclaim our declaration to our family."

"It is our tradition to impart, on the eve before classes begin, the history of our family to the new members of the student body. With this knowledge of the university's heritage, you will be proud to be an Algonquin. That's what we students are known as, Algonquins, after the Algonquin Nation. The school mascot is an Indian chief. History tells us that between 6,000 and 7,000 Indians lived in what we now know as Connecticut long before any European arrived. The Indians living here belonged to several tribes of the Algonquian Indian family. The Pequot, the most powerful tribe, lived in the south near the Thames River. The Mohegan, a branch of the Pequot tribe, lived near the city we now know as Norwich."

"The Connecticut colonists feared the Pequot Indians because small bands of the tribe had attacked their settlements. The Pequot saw the colonists as a threat to the Pequot way of life in the region. In 1637, Captain John Mason led a small army against the Pequot in Mystic. Mason's soldiers burned a Pequot fort, killing hundreds of Indians. That same year the colonists defeated the remaining Pequot in a fight. This would become known in history as the Pequot war."

"Our founder, Samuel R. Jackson and his family were in the ship building and shipping business. He inherited this parcel of land from his father; it was in his family since 1645. His wife was descendent of *uncas*. It was at her urging that this sacred area be set apart and used for the education of both white and Indian children. From one small building, built upon this place where we now stand, the university had its humble beginnings."

After sharing the history and founding of the school, he gave a short testimony. Other students followed after the leader, and they, too began giving their testimonies and making their proclamations. Many shared their enlightening experiences about a new revelation in their life that they had during the summer. Some announced their engagement, wedding date, or their freedom. Little found the gathering a very moving experience, and instinctively he sensed that one day he, too would ascend the steps of Massachusetts Hall to declare his being.

After the gathering ended, the trio planned to meet at seven for the annual clambake on the waterfront. Arriving early, before the crowd with blankets and a picnic basket in arms, Stephanie, Ale, and Little began hunting for the right place to sit and dig for clams. When they arrived, a number of students had already there to stake out their special place. Pockets of students were congregating in various spots along the waterfront. Others could be seen with pails and shovels digging holes along the water's edge for clams. Little watched with amusement as the small ritual of digging up clams and dropping them into the pails took place. The pair greeted their friends as they walked down the beach; plenty of hugs and kisses were being served. Each party they encountered, a conversation ensued regarding the summer events and about tonight's gathering of speakers. Stephanie and Ale made a special point to introduce Little to their friends. Finally, the trio found what they considered the perfect spot. Marking it with their belongings, they took off their shoes and went off to prospect for clams.

On this hot Labor Day night, the cool water of the Sound was soothing to the bare feet. The sensation sent chills up and down Little's spine.

"The water feels so good and the sand between my toes feels so good. I love it; I think I could get use to this," he laughed. "You guys know this will be my first time digging for clams."

"If you like this beach Little, you should go to Venezuela someday where I lived. Our house is on the beach, the sun shines all the time, the water is always warm, and all the beaches are fantastic." Loudly laughing at him as he tiptoed into the water, Ale again referred to him as a virgin. In his usual demonstrative flair, Ale picked the spot he claimed was a loaded clam bed.

"Okay, crew, this is the spot to dig for clams. Get your pail and shovel ready and prepare to dig. You'll see, this is going to be one of the greatest clam bed finds, right here in this spot." At his direction, the trio, with shovel in hand and laughing, began digging in the spot. "Nothing, there's no clams here. Okay Little, it's your turn to pick a place to dig."

Using his shovel as a divining rod, Little began racing around the beach shaking wildly like a mad man. His shovel finally slowed and pointed in the ground to the spot. "Here. We dig here," he announced. Stephanie and Ale jokingly objected to the place saying he didn't have the touch.

"No freshman has the touch for finding clams, especially a freshman from New York City," they shouted. Claiming his divinity, Little began digging. There it was—a precious sight to behold, his first clam. Excitement pulsated through Little's veins.

"I got one," he shouted as he turned around leaping into the air.

"Only one," laughed Ale. "Wow, a clambake with one clam."

"But it's one more than you found," Stephanie laughed.

"No look, look, there's got to be at least a hundred in this spot, maybe two or three, maybe a thousand."

"You're kidding," Stephanie and Ale said rushing over to look at his find. They began screaming and yelling.

Ale shouted, "It's the biggest clam bed found in years. Hey everybody, look; he's found a giant clam bed." A crowd began gathering around to examine what the rejoicing was all about.

"Great find," a voice from the crowd ranged out.

"Neato!" another said.

"Hey, he's the master clam digger," yet another voice from the crowd proclaimed.

"The master clam digger," Little laughed.

Ale shouted out, "Hey, we got a new king of the clambake." Holding up a clam he proclaimed, "To King Little, King of the clambake." The crowd enthusiastically agreed and chanted King Little, King Little, King of the clambake.

Gathering all the clams they wanted, the trio shared their treasured find with the others on the beach. Returning to the place where they left their basket and shoes, Little's face beamed with excitement as students passed by him shouting "King Little! King of the clambake!" Passing students greeted and addressed him as King Little, king of the clambake. Having fun with it, they bowed up and down before him as they congratulated him on his excellent clam bed finding.

The night air, the saltwater, Stephanie, and Ale, gave Little the warmest and fuzziest feelings that he ever felt with people outside of his immediate family. *I've never felt this way, and never thought I'd get this kind of feeling from white people.* He was king, king of the clambake. That night all honors due were paid him as scores of students passed the trio's campsite. Wood for the fire, food, hot roasted corn, as king of the clambake—as tradition would have it—that night, he was held in high esteem. As the dark night fell, campfires could be seen dotting the beach. The air was intoxicating; a hot moist breeze from the ocean blew steadily across the beach. The cracking of the wood on the bonfire added to the majesty of the night air. Around the roaring bonfire, Little was hoisted on the shoulders of the football players and paraded around. Music filled the air with students singing the school's fight song and yelling school cheers. As they settled down, lovers walked off nestled together. Friends gathered in groups were engaged in conversations; the latest tunes could be heard blasting on the radio. Little was king. Tonight, he felt he was more than king; he felt he truly belonged here. Tonight, he was an Algonquin.

At last, today is the day I've been looking forward to for quite a while; today is my first day of classes. Boy, over the last few days this campus has gone through a metamorphous, it's transformed into a totally different place from when the new students arrived. I can see that what's contributing to this metamorphosis is the upper classmen returning. The campus is alive with their greetings to each other after the long and hot summer vacation.

In the morning as he aroused from his peaceful sleep, after thanking God, he silently whispered his favorite poem, "Invictus," by William Ernest Henley:

Out of the night which covers me,
Black as the Pit from pole to pole,
I thank whatever gods may be
For my unconquerable soul.

In the fell clutch of circumstance
I have not winced nor cried aloud
Under the bludgeonings of chance
My head is bloody, but unbowed.

Beyond this place of wrath and tears
Looms but the horror of the shade,
And yet the menace of the years
Finds, and shall find, me unafraid.

It matters not how strait the gate,
How charged with punishments the scroll,
I am the master of my fate:
I am the captain of my soul.

At last, he found the peace he believed he needed to stay. Smiling, he quickly showered and got dressed. Stephanie and Ale promised to meet him in the lobby at seven-fifteen for breakfast. Pushing the elevator button, Little was still riding on an emotional high from last night's clambake and bonfire.

The elevator stopped on the fifth floor and the doors opened. "Hi, Little," a familiar voice as the person entered the elevator rang out. Little looked up; it was Bobby Henderson. "Are you going to breakfast?"

Immediately, seeing Bobby brought back the extremely painful memory of the week before. A cold chill tingled up his spine. Shrugging it off, Little had vowed to himself that nothing was going to ruin this day for him, "Hi Bobby. Yea, a man's gotta eat to stay alive."

"Can I join you for breakfast?"

"Sorry, but I'm meeting with some friends."

"Oh. Okay," he sadly replied. "I heard about you at the clambake, it must have been really great being king of the clambake."

"It was fun; I had a really good time. Were you there?"

"Just for a little while."

Little detected the sound of loneliness in Bobby's voice. He wanted to gloat, but that was not his personality. The elevator doors opened at the lobby. Bobby stepped off first. Stephanie and Ale were standing in the lobby waiting for Little by the main desk. Stephanie's heart skipped a beat upon seeing Bobby in the elevator with Little. Panicking, she gasped, "Oh no," she clutched her chest.

Concerned with her sudden outburst, Ale inquired, "What's wrong Steff?"

"The student in the elevator with Little; Little had a very bad experience with him and his parents. I told you about it; what happened the morning after he arrived on campus. I hope Little is alright." She began to get upset for fear that what had happened was about to reoccur. Tightening her grip on Alejandro's arm, she started muttering something.

"Stephanie, calm down; nothing may have happened," he scoffed as he pried away her grip on his arm.

"I'm worried about Little."

"You're getting work up over nothing. He's a big boy, I'm sure he can take care of himself."

"But Ale, you don't know...."

"No Stephanie, you don't know. Now stop it."

Little walked over to Stephanie and Ale; Bobby continued to walk toward the cafeteria. "Morning Stephanie and Ale."

"Good morning Little. Are you alright?" she inquired.

"Me? Sure. Why?"

"Nothing."

Walking into the cafeteria Ale playfully put his arm around Little, laughed and called him the clambake king. The trio found a table and proceeded to the line to get some breakfast. Walking back to their table Little spotted Bobby sitting by himself on the other side of the cafeteria. "Bobby asked if I would join him for breakfast. He's sitting over there by himself. Would you guys mind if I invited him to join us?"

"Are you sure Little?"

"Okay Mother Stephanie," growled Ale. "I told you about that; now, back off. Sure, it's no big deal."

Little crossed over the cafeteria to where Bobby was sitting. Through the corner of his eyes, he noticed several students pointing at him and remark about how he found the large clam bed last evening. Elated, he was feeling good, but for what? Was it the student's admiration or his compassion for Bobby? After a few minutes with Bobby, they returned to the table where Stephanie and Ale were sitting. "Ale, this is Bobby Henderson. Bobby this is Alejandro Torres, Stephanie's fiancé."

Ale and Stephanie greeted Bobby as he placed his tray of food on the table and sat down. Reaching across the table, he shook Ale's hand. Feeling shameful as his eyes met Stephanie's, Bobby lowered his head as he exchanged greetings with her. The foursome chatted about the gathering and the clambake while they ate. "Bobby, how do you like UNE so far?" ask Ale.

"It's alright. I guess."

"You guess? Have you met many other students?"

"Not really. There aren't that many freshmen students in Schaffer or in Schwatz Hall. There are not too many freshmen on this side of campus. Everybody I've met seems to live in Wigwam."

"Did you go to the clambake last night?"

"Only for a little while. I was by myself; I didn't stay long."

"Oh God, I think I'm going to be sick," Stephanie announced to the group.

"What's wrong Steff?" asked Ale.

"It's Cranston Crenshaw Smythe; Mr. Brainy-act himself coming over here."

"Why? What's wrong with him?"

"He is a royal pain in the butt."

Dressed impeccably, the five foot, ten inch Cranston approached the table where they were seated. "Miss Danforth, I believe you were supposed to send me a list of student mailing addresses. I want it this afternoon."

Stephanie gave him a piercing sneer, then spoke very curt. "I don't work for you, nor do I care what you want or when you want it. When I complete the list, you can get it just like all the other student groups that requested a copy."

"We'll see about that," he snapped.

"I guess we will. You live in Schwartz and I live in Schaffer. The buildings are joined by this common space and three other dorms share this eating facility and mailboxes. My position has nothing to do with yours. I'm eating my breakfast. I am not on duty, and I won't be until later. Now, leave."

"Miss Danforth, you think you're so smart. I'm sure Dean Goins is not going to find your brightness funny," he replied as he turned to walk away.

"Oooh, I'm really scared," she shouted as he left.

Little was taken by surprise by Stephanie's rudeness. "Stephanie, why were you so rude to him? I didn't think there was a person on this entire planet that you didn't like. I never would have believed that you would have said a cross word to anybody."

Ale moved back in his seat, "Stick around Little. You'll learn, she's human like everyone else, and she has a monster of a temper."

"No, that is not true Ale, and you know it," she barked. "Cranston just manages to get on my bad side. I mean he turns me off; he turns people off, a whole lot of people. He and his crew turn everybody off with their arrogant attitudes. He swears he's so smart and expects all of us to bow down and kiss his feet. Granted, he's a presidential scholar, but that doesn't give him the right to look down on other students. That whole little group of his is out of control. They feel and act as if they're better than the other students because they're PSs. So, what if only twelve are selected per year; it still gives them no right to behave the way they do. Since I've been at this school, I haven't met a PS that's worth liking; them and their holier than thou attitude just turns me off. Sad part is some of them are really nice people. But with that

Cranston around, they're hopeless causes. Dean Goins and the rest of the administration can't bow down low enough before them. They get the best of everything. Imagine, you and I gotta wait hours in lines to register for our classes, sometimes we don't get the classes we need because they're filled. PSs, their classes are pre-selected, packets put aside so the poor things, all they have to do is go all the way over to Narraganset Hall and wait with the rest of us peons to pick up their class schedule, and they complain about that! We wait to get everything. All they do is think it and they have it. Even their books are set aside for them in the bookstore. They whine and the administration jumps. They're the only group of students I know of that Dean Goins practically licks their boots to please. What really gets me burnt up are those other poor dumb students obsessed with them, like they're some gods or something. Nobody really likes them, especially since Cranston's been around. They're elitist, stuck on themselves and just downright rude. The worst part is the university supports it. They treat other students like they're garbage, use them for their amusement, and then dump them like yesterday's old newspaper. Shameful thing is nobody does or says anything. What really kills me is some of those poor slobs would do anything to hang around them. With all that intelligence you would think they would know better. It just goes to show you that intelligence does not equal good manners. The PSs haven't done one positive thing on this campus. Everything that they do is for them. No, I take that back, it's for Cranston. Personally, I don't like them, and I want nothing to do with any of them."

Finally reaching his threshold Ale ran out of patience. "Alright, alright, Stephanie," he said throwing his hands into the air. "Get off your high horse. We've been down this road before. I've heard it all before, and I don't want to hear it now."

Angry, she retaliated, "Oh come on Ale. Why are you always defending them?"

"I'm not defending them Stephanie. Why are you always getting so worked up about them?"

"Then tell me you like their little private elitist fraternity. They're sexist and racist. Name me one, just one person that's a PS you like! Then, to top things off, he's majoring in Nuclear Engineering. Those people are going to blow the world up; destroy it just like they did in World War II to Hiroshima and Nagasaki."

Turning from Ale, Stephanie looked at Little and Bobby. "Little and Bobby, give it time, and you'll see what I mean. My best advice that I can give you is to stay as far away from them. Stay as far away as you can; just stay away from them. They mean you no good. They'll just use and abuse you. Don't let them do that to you. The best thing to do is avoid them at all cost."

"That's not fair Stephanie," scoffed Ale. "Let them decide for themselves."

"I can't believe you're defending them."

"I'm not defending them Stephanie."

"See? See what I mean? They even have us fighting."

"Were not arguing because of them, Stephanie."

"Oh God, look at the time. I have a nine o'clock on the other side of campus in Stillman. If I don't leave now, I'll miss my bus. Ale, I'll see you later."

"Okay, Steff, but please try to calm down before you leave the building."

"It was good seeing you again, Bobby."

"It was nice talking to you. I have a nine o'clock also in Stillman," Bobby said standing up.

"Well, Bobby, you can ride the shuttle with me."

"Looks like it's you and me, Little. What time is your first class buddy?"

"Ten o'clock."

"Where?"

"Stillman Hall. I got English."

"Oh yea, I got a class there at ten also. I have to go off campus afterwards, so I'll be driving my car. I'll give you a ride."

"Sounds good to me."

Little and Ale watched as Stephanie and Bobby left the cafeteria. "Little, don't mind Stephanie. She gets really upset when people mistreat other people. As far as Cranston and his crew are concerned, she does have a point. The presidential scholar's do exemplify elitism on campus, and the administration hasn't made it any good for the other students when it comes to them. I hope you never have to run into them or their attitude." Ale leaned forward in his chair toward Little. "Listen, I don't mean to pry, and this may not be the right time because it is a little sensitive, but if you don't mind telling me, what actually happened between you and Bobby and his parents? I only know what Steff told me about his getting his room changed."

Feeling uncomfortable, Little shifted nervously in his chair. Looking down at his plate, he picked up his fork and began pushing the few scraps of eggs on his plate from side to side. "I don't mean any offense, but to be honest, I rather not talk about it right now. I don't have a problem telling you, but not right now, there's still a few things I need to work through. Besides, I feel so good about last night I don't want to spoil it by talking about that morning."

"It's alright," Ale said reassuringly. "I can respect that. I hope Stephanie hasn't put a damper on it." Changing the subject Ale quickly asked, "Who do you have for English?"

"I don't remember. It's on my schedule," he replied while taking it out of his shirt pocket.

"You know all this time I never asked you what you're majoring in. Don't tell me; let's see your schedule. I want to see if I can guess it from the classes you're taking."

"I don't know. After seeing Stephanie performance just now, I don't know if that's a good idea."

"What do you mean?"

Little chuckled, "When I think about it, I never asked you what you're majoring in, and Stephanie never told me. Now that I'm thinking about it, she never asked me what I was majoring in either."

"Now, that is a major miracle. She's normally all into everybody's business. Now that she's appointed herself as your personal guardian angel, especially yours."

Little laughed as he handed Ale his schedule. "If she's my guardian angel, I feel sorry for that old devil Cranston. Are you sure you want to see it?"

"Why?" he asked, raising his eyebrows as he inquisitively looked at the schedule. "Um very good, Honors English with Pascal. He's a good professor. Honors Psychology with Friedmann. Tough, but fair, but you got to watch out for her. Honors History, Hauser, never had him but word is he's trouble." Looking puzzled, Ale raised his eyebrow as he looked at Little. "This is a pretty heavy schedule Little; Qualitative Analysis for Math with Keenan." Ale giving a slight nod to his head said, "I'm truly impressed, and Nuclear Physics/Thermodynamics with Waldstriecher." Ale's face suddenly lit up as if a light bulb went off in his head. Ale looked up with sudden amazement. "Oh my God, Little, is there something you're not telling me?"

Little raised his eyebrows and looked sheepishly at Ale, "Um, would you believe I'm a presidential scholar majoring in nuclear engineering?" Laughing, he quickly asked, "So Alejandro, tell me, what's your major?"

Ale, shaking his head from side to side laughed. "Theater. Oh God, we won't tell Stephanie."

Little smiled. "At least, today, we better not."

CLASS IS ON

Classes on Thursday and Friday were short; the professors talked about the course, their expectations, and passed out the syllabi listing the dates and times when assignments were due. With each class, Little felt something was lacking, lost, and missing. But for some strange reason, he could not put his finger on it. Although he continued to search for the answer, he could not quite put a name to it. Whatever it was, he knew it wasn't there. By the end of the day, he began thinking it was just his imagination, first day of class jitters or something. He dismissed the thoughts from his mind. *No doubt it's only because the classes are practically empty. Many of the students went home with only two days of classes.*

The weekend came and went quickly. For the weekend, he found himself alone. Stephanie was on duty, and Ale had to go home. By himself with nothing to do, he decided he would use the break to get an early start on his class assignments. After reading for a few hours, he got up to stretch. Although the air conditioning felt good to him, he pushed open his room window to breathe in some fresh air. Looking out of his window to the street below, his attention was quickly drawn to the movement in the area by the bicycle rack. To his amazement, he saw something he had not seen since his arrival at the university almost two weeks ago. Reflecting upon it, he wondered why it was a strange but welcoming sight to his sore eyes. In so many ways, he was relieved to see it. Leaning out of the window he shouted out and wildly waved his arms at the figure below. "Hey, up here. Up here." He caught the attention of the student, "The name is Thomas. Thomas Thomas. What's yours?

"Michael Griffin, I live in Tunxis on the other side of campus in Wigwam."

"Wait, I'll be right down."

"Sorry, I can't stop and talk now. I'm in a rush." In a flash the student disappeared around the corner on his bicycle.

It was Monday, the beginning of the week, and the first full week of class. Already Little was running late. To catch the next shuttle bus to the old campus he had to skip breakfast. Honors History with Dr. Hauser, his first class of the day and week was in Stillman Hall. He also remembered today was the day he was supposed to meet with his academic advisor, Dr. Wassermann. Dr. Wassermann's office was in one of the new buildings on campus far from the old campus, Melbourne Hall. It was the nuclear engineering building.

Somewhat mesmerized by the environment, passing through the corridor of Stillman Hall, Little observed the large lecture rooms. In each room, as well as in the hallway, he again sensed something was amiss, but he did not know what. "Ah, room 210." He glanced at his schedule to verify the room number. Taking his seat, Little looked around the class. It was not what he had expected, especially in light of the large lecture rooms he had passed on his way. This fair-sized room had individual seats that had desks attached to the arm of the chair. A long black chalkboard stretched across the length of the wall, behind the instructor's lone podium in the designated front of the room. Lacking air conditioning, the bottom half of the four tall windows were open, allowing fresh air and the morning sunshine into the room. Students continued coming in as he took his seat.

An elderly man dressed in a brown suit, white shirt, and black bow tie entered the room and stood behind the podium. In an authoritarian manner, he instructed the students to stand up as he called their name, so he could identify them. He opened his computer-generated enrollment roster. After calling several names, he finally called out, "Mr. Thomas Thomas."

Little rose to his feet. Peering over the top of his round wire rimmed glasses, he studied Little up and down. In a questioning, condescending tone he bellowed, "Are you sure you're in the right classroom? This is Honors History; basketball players do not take nor are they assigned to my class. There are other history classes that may be more suitable for you."

Little felt all sixty-four eyes of his fellow classmates fall upon him. Being put on the spot again, at that moment, Little wished a big hole would open up so he could fall into the ground. Then he recognized what it was, instinctively he knew what had eluded him earlier in the hallway and last week in class. He was the only black student in the class, perhaps even in the entire building. "Yes, I am registered for this class."

"Check your schedule."

"You called my name. If it's on your class roster, then I am in the right class."

"Let me see your schedule." Little took out his schedule, walked to the front of the room and handed it to Dr. Hauser. Hauser closely scrutinized the schedule then passed it back to Little. "Okay, you can go back to your seat," he said waving his hand at the wrist as if to dismiss Little from his sight.

In a defiant voice, he loudly announced, "And I'm not a basketball player."

"Well, I certainly hope you will be able to keep up with the class. I do not grade on a curve or give special treatment to anyone for any reason."

Humiliated, Little sat back down with ambivalent feelings about Professor Hauser, the class, and himself.

"I haven't and will certainly not ask you for any special treatment," Little shouted back. As Professor Hauser began speaking, Little found it extremely difficult to concentrate on his lecture.

The movement of the students in the class let Little know the lecture was over. He felt relieved as he exited the room. *I'm glad that's over; just wish I didn't have to go back.* Checking his schedule, he noted, *my next class is Honors Psychology at nine o'clock with Dr. Friedmann in Vermont Hall. That gives me ten minutes to get there. No problem, Vermont Hall is just across the quadrangle opposite Stillman.* Shrugging off what had happened in History, he made his way out of the building. *I'm not going to allow Hauser to affect my impression of the next instructor or class. Besides, a psychology professor would not hold stereotypical views and be as narrow minded as Hauser.*

His honors psychology class turned out to be twice as large as his honors history class, with about sixty-five students. Professor Friedmann asked everyone to stand up and give their name, major, and year. He discovered that he was the only freshman student; the others were mostly sophomores, juniors, and a few seniors. Again, he noticed his face was the only black face in the classroom. To Little, Dr. Friedmann seemed fair; he liked her approach to the subject. Looking at his schedule, he noted that his last class of the day was Thermodynamics. Class began at one o'clock in Melbourne Hall.

My Thermodynamics class with Waldstriecher is in four hours on the other side of the campus. That means I have three hours; that gives me enough time to get lunch at my dormitory complex and then it's off to Melbourne Hall. After that I have a meeting with my academic advisor. That's right, he remembered. *Mrs. Solomon said Professor Waldstriecher was one of the German professors that left the University of Chicago and he was considered a leader in the field of nuclear physics. Looking around the classroom there were only twelve students. But again, I'm the only student of my race in the entire class.*

Despite the heavy German accent, Little thought Waldstriecher was great. The chapter he read during the weekend prepared him for the lecture. He even answered a few questions. From his reaction, he could tell Dr. Waldstriecher was impressed with his knowledge of the material. "Young man, you have a good grasp of the material. That's very good. Most students find this difficult to understand. You seem to have no problem."

After class, Little met with Dr. Wassermann, his academic advisor in the same building. Wassermann, stunned by his appearance, acted as if he did not remember scheduling the meeting. It was a very short and non-productive academic session. *That meeting was really a waste of my time. He just put me off; just like Melissa and Mrs. McGinnis acted as if I wasn't there. I could tell he was afraid to be in the office with me. Maybe, Waldstriecher would consider advising me.*

Starting to feel depressed, Little waited for the shuttle to go back to Schaffer Hall. He observed the other students pairing off talking. The bus stopped at Tunxis Hall; *this might be a good time to go in and meet the student I saw from my room window this weekend. I think his name was Michael, Michael Griffin.* Getting directions from the desk, Little made his way up the stairwell to the third floor to Michael's room. Knocking on the door, Little heard the smooth baritone voice echo, "Come in. It's open."

"Michael Griffin?" he asked as he pushed the door open.

"That's me," replied the person seated at the desk.

"Hi, I'm Thomas Thomas. I was the one who called to you from the window in Schaffer Hall this weekend."

"Oh yea," Michael said turning around to face the person coming into his room. "Sorry I couldn't stop that day. I was expecting a call from home; I had to rush back to the dorm. I stopped by your room a few times after that, but you never seem to be in. Come on in and have a seat," he said motioning to Little as he stood up extending his hand toward Little.

Little closely examined Michael; they stood about the same height except Michael's body frame was physically more muscular, making him appear slightly shorter than himself. His long, round-shaped fair complexioned face was dotted with a few dark brown freckles across the bridge of his wide nose, and he also had a few on his cheeks. His naturally arched eyebrows were accented by his deep-set hazel eyes. The straight jet-black hair in its combed back position gleamed with natural waves rippling over his head. His dark lips, when parted, displayed an array of huge white teeth with a gap between the two front teeth. He slightly resembled someone Little knew.

"This weekend, I spent a lot of time in the library studying."

"Good place to be, especially if you want to stay in school. Hey, have a seat." Little sat in the chair as Michael sat on the bed.

"Thomas?" he asked questioningly.

"Yep, that's right, Thomas. Thomas Isaiah Thomas, and don't ask. It's a long story that I don't quite understand myself," Little responded laughing. "Just call me Little."

"Okay Little. Where are you from?"

"New York City, I live in Harlem. What about yourself?"

"I was born in California, lived in Philadelphia, and my folks moved to Lawrence, Kansas about five years ago.

"Hey, my brother Swoosh, well he's really my best friend, but I call him my brother, he goes to the University of Kansas. He was recruited for their basketball team."

"Oh yea; that's a good school. What year is he in?"

"He's a freshman like me."

"My father is a MD there. He teaches in the university's medical center. Dad is a big basketball fan. He knows all the players and invites them over to the house. He especially tries to look out for the black players. Not too many black students there."

"Not too many here neither. You're the first and only black student I've seen since I've been here."

Michael laughed and ran his fingers across his head. "Most of the black students live here in Wigwam. There's about, I'd say around thirty-five of us on campus."

"Thirty-five! How come you're the only one I've seen since I've been here? All the students in my classes and in my dorm are white; with the exception of some international students."

"Like I said, most of us live on this side of campus, out here in Wigwam. And don't kid yourself, there are so few of us here that you'll probably never see any of us in any in your classes. If two of us were in the same class, it would be a miracle. And then, there may be some in your class, and you just don't know it."

"What do you mean?"

"Passing. Got a few of us passing."

"Passing what?"

"Little, where have you been! Passing; passing as white."

"You're kidding!"

"Two of them are living in Schaffer with you."

"How do you know that?"

"Little, there is a whole lot that you're gonna learn between now and the time you die." Michael leaned forward and assumed the position of a wise old man. "I mean, the books are one type of education, but life and living are another type of education. Tell me, how did you get into Schaffer?"

"I don't know," Little said shrugging his shoulders. "I received my housing assignment in the mail like everyone else, I guess. Why?"

"The area you live in is called Massasoit. Massasoit was chief of the Wampanoga Indian tribe. Chief Massasoit helped the first European settlers when they arrived here. Just like the name implies, royalty, special treatment. If your family is wealthy, powerful, congressmen, or a big alumni donor, you get assigned to Massasoit. Mostly all freshmen are assigned out here in Iroquois, the badlands, the jungle, far from the main campus."

"What do you mean?"

"You don't get it; the Iroquois Nation is not from New England like the other tribes. In fact, the Iroquois Indians chased the Pequot out of Upper State New York. Now, I ask you again, how did you manage to get into the newest resident hall on campus? And from what

I saw you're in the most prime room on the entire campus? That room is usually reserved for very important visitors to the campus."

Little tossed his hands in the air and shrugged his shoulders. "I don't know; guess I'm just lucky. Stephanie Danforth, the RA, she assigned me to the room because the building was filled, and the room I was originally assigned to had brooms, mops, and all kinds of cleaning fluids in it."

"That reminds me," tooted Michael, "I forgot the most elite of the elite: the presidential scholars. They're the elitist group on campus. Now, they get to live in Massasoit; more specifically, Schaffer or Schwartz Hall."

Little laughed, "Didn't you know? I'm a PS."

"Sure, and I'm Snow White. Get real, a Black PS? That will be the day."

Both boys laughed hysterically. "So, you know Stephanie Danforth."

"Yep, she was the first person I met when I arrived on campus."

"Yea, she's good people."

"You know her too."

"She's engaged to my cousin."

Little eyebrows raised in surprised, "Your cousin! Who? You mean Alejandro?"

"Ah um. Alejandro Torres. He's my cousin."

"But he's Venezuelan."

"Yea, and he's also my cousin. My mother and his mother are sisters; identical twins, Cynthia and Charlotte." Michael took out his wallet to show Little a picture of his mother and aunt. In another picture, he and Ale were standing in front of their mothers. "Both of us were born in California, lived in Philadelphia, and raised in Connecticut."

"But..."

"No butts about it. I told you about black folks on this campus passing for white."

Surprised, Little slumped in the chair from the of the news. Again, he felt betrayed by someone he had come to trust. "I don't believe it. He took me to his house in New Haven, pretended to be my friend, showing me around campus and everything." *Deceived again, I must be a fool. It must be written all over my forehead.*

"Now don't get bent out of shape Little. His father is Venezuelan and his mother, my aunt, is Black. Technically, he was not lying to you, and he lived in Venezuela for about fifteen years. He doesn't deny being black or being my cousin. Now, he doesn't go around bragging about it either; being on this campus I don't blame him. In fact, he's the one that convinced me to come to the UNE. My parents thought it was a great idea; I don't regret it. He's not only my cousin, he's my best friend."

Little folded his hands together as if he were praying; resting his chin on his fingertips.

Michael could see he was disturbed by something. "What is it man? What's bothering you?

"Michael, how do you deal with being the only black person in your class?"

"I know what you're feeling, man. I won't lie to you, it's tough." Before he could finish, his room door swung open.

"Hey Michael," a voice rang out as the door swung open. "Little, what are you doing here?" the voice shouted in surprise. "I didn't know you knew my cousin."

"Hey Ale," he said as he turned to face him. "Michael just told me you guys were cousins. I saw him this weekend from my dorm room window. He told me his name and dorm, so after my last class, I thought I'd stop by to meet him. We really just met about ten minutes ago."

"Remember I told you I wanted to introduce you to my cousin. In fact, I was just coming over to ask Michael to meet us for dinner, but I'm glad you guys already met."

"Ale, you mean to tell me this is the king of the clambake? The one you told me about?"

"Yep, sure is. That's him."

Michael laughed. "Mr. presidential scholar over here, sitting in my room?"

"Little," shouted Ale, "I understand me, but you've known Stephanie for over two weeks and you haven't told her you're a presidential scholar, and after only ten minutes you let my cousin know."

Michael froze. Shocked, he stared at Little. "Wait a minute, you were kidding about being a PS, weren't you? I thought you were just joking."

Looking inquisitively Ale asked, "Michael, you really didn't know?"

"I swear Ale, I thought he was kidding; he said it so jokingly. I asked him how he got into Schaffer Hall. You know only alumni, the wealthy, and those with special privileges like PSs get into Schaffer. I thought he was kidding when he said he was a PS."

"See Ale," Little protested, but laughing, "You let the cat out of the bag."

"I never thought I would have a PS in my room. Never mind my room, I never thought I'd ever see a black PS. Unbelievable! So, Mr. Presidential Scholar, what are you majoring in? No, wait! Don't tell me. You're majoring in nuclear engineering?"

"That's right, nuclear engineering. So, Michael, what are you majoring in?" Little replied laughingly.

Michael was still stunned as he weakly answered, "Journalism, I wanna be a television broadcaster. Wait, wait, wait. Right now, this is too much for me to deal with. I need some air. Let's get out of here. Let's go get some pizza or something."

Ale laughed at his cousin's dilemma. "Okay, I'm parked in the lot out back; first I need to stop by Stephanie's. She goes on duty in a little while."

Michael looked at Little. "I don't believe it, king of the clambake, a black presidential scholar, and nuclear engineering major. You are definitely a first!"

As the trio entered Stephanie's room, she was preparing to get into the shower before going to work. "You guys are going out for pizza? Sorry I can't join you, but I gotta work. I have desk duty tonight until ten. Have a good time."

Leaving the room Little was the first in line. Laughing to himself he turned to Stephanie. "Hey Stephanie."

"Yes Little."

"Ale, Michael, and I decided this would be the best time to tell you this before you find it out."

"Find out what? Oh no Little, please don't tell me you're planning on leaving school."

Little hung his head and pretended to be saddened. "No. I'm afraid it's something worse than that. In fact, after I tell you you'll probably wish you'd never met me," he said laughing. Ale and Michael joined in the laughter.

"What? What's so funny? What are you guys up to? What do you have up your dirty little sleeve? Let me in on the joke. fellas."

"Do you know what my major is?"

"No I don't. In fact, I was intending to ask you the other day when we were at breakfast, but Cranston, that arrogant PS of a pea brain temporarily distracted me. I have the list he was asking for over there. It lists everyone in the building. I confess I was going to look up your major while I was on duty tonight, but since you're here you can tell me. Oh, and I also realized I was wrong about Bobby. We rode the bus and we had lunch together. We had a good talk, but that's another topic."

You're rambling again Steff," scoffed Ale.

"I am, aren't I? Anyway, what is your major?"

"Well, remember what you said about Cranston and the PSs?"

"Yes."

"Well, I'm majoring in nuclear engineering, and I'm also a presidential scholar."

"Funny. Very funny guys."

"Like Santa, you better check your list," replied Ale handing her the folder containing the list.

Opening it, she found the list of president scholars. She read aloud Little's name and his major. Her mouth dropped open as she looked up at the trio, "Oh my God, no. This can't be true, it can't be true!" she screamed at the three men as they ran out of the room into the stairwell laughing.

The ride to the Pizza Palace was filled with laughter and jokes about Stephanie. Michael and Ale expressed how much they wished they could see Cranston's face when he meets Little for the first time. With Little getting a perfect score on the SAT, it meant that he scored twenty-five points higher than Cranston, making him the first PS to hold that honor of distinction.

At the Pizza Palace, the conversation was light-hearted. "Michael?"

Michael continued eating his pizza as he answered Little with his eyes by looking up.

"I asked you earlier. How do you and the others deal with being the only black students in your classes?"

"Well Little, it's not easy. I go to class knowing I am the only black student in the class. I get along with the white students, but I know many times I'm isolated from a lot of things going on in class and on the campus. I guess having Ale here helped me a lot. I have him to talk to, along with some of the other black students. Most of the time I talk with the other black students and with Dr. Hamilton; he's a professor in the English department. When I get frustrated, and it's really easy to get frustrated around here, but I talk to them. The most important thing man is you just can't let it get you down. And if it does, you can't let it keep you down or you'll go crazy."

"I know Dr. Hamilton. I met him when I was in high school. He interviewed me."

"He is really a good man. We black students are getting together to form a Black Student Union because we're not treated the same. There's a lot of resistance to it by the students and the administration. They don't understand that our needs are not always the same as the white students, and they definitely are not always meeting our needs. White students can get their hair cut on campus. There's neither a black barber nor a hairdresser for our women on campus. We end up going to New Haven most of the time. When it comes to entertainment, it's always some white band, lecturer, or group. Whites sit in every classroom on the campus; they sit on every committee, and all clubs and organization on this campus. We don't begin to scratch the surface; there aren't enough of us here."

"This morning in my history class, Dr. Hauser stuck me out. He called me to the front of the class, checked my schedule to see if I was supposed to be in his class and then he told me not to expect any special treatment. I felt humiliated. Then, my faculty advisor was surprised I was black, so he didn't say anything relevant. He acted as if he was afraid to be alone with me in his office! After I left his office, I was really feeling bad and out of it; that's when I decided to stop by your room when the bus stopped at Tunxis."

Michael put down his pizza and looked at Little. "I know. I had some bad things happen to me. I was called nigger and had it written on my room door. I complained; nobody did anything. And the other black students, similar things have happened to them."

Little pushed back from the table, "The strange thing is, when I first went to class, I knew something wasn't right. I felt something was missing; I just couldn't put my finger on it. It wasn't until Hauser pulled that stunt in his class that I noticed I was the only black student in class. I don't know how I overlooked something as obvious as that, but I didn't see it."

"That's not uncommon Little. It's a type of denial. You didn't see it because you didn't want to see it. Everybody wants to feel accepted; to be a part of the student body. So psychologically you block out the most obvious thing that would make you different and stand out from the rest."

"Hey Little," interjected Ale, "nobody wants to be the odd man. I get some of the same treatment. My father is Venezuelan, and my mother is Black. Michael's mother and my mother are twins. I've been called half-breed, Nigzuelan, and all sorts of names. I can't begin to tell you the number of threats I've received for being with Stephanie. You just can't let it get you down."

"Then why do you guys and other black students come back here?"

"Little," Michael responded, "it's like I said, you just can't let it get you down."

Little shook his head. "It's not so easy. The first day I was here... Bobby," Little stumbled nervously on his words as he began to recount the event.

"Not Bobby, but his mother. I know the reason she had him moved out of the room was because I'm black. When he was moving out, his mother told me point blank to my face that they had schools for niggers, and I don't belong here. She said all kinds of wild racist stuff. She talked about me while I was standing there, like I was invisible. I just can't, I don't know how much more I can take. I felt so bad."

"I know, man; it hurts. We can relate to that, Little, we've been there," replied Michael. "Tell us, why did you come to UNE? Didn't you know anything about the school?"

Little chuckled to himself. "Well, that's a story in itself. I saw several college brochures in one of the guidance counselor's office at my high school. None of them had any black students in them, but the UNE brochure had a black student in it. Hey, it was you Michael that I saw in the brochure. That's why I thought I knew you from somewhere."

"And a good picture of me, if I must say so myself. They have four different shots at that."

"They weren't too bad. But then, I saw an all-black choir. I thought it was great, an all-black choir. I know it's a poor reason to select a college, but when I saw those black students, I saw myself here. Then they did have my major and all, but it was mostly because of the pictures in the brochures."

Ale responded. "That was the Hampton Institute concert choir. It was the one positive thing we got the administration to do."

"You mean those students aren't students here?"

Michael chimed in, "Hey, people have selected colleges for a lot worse. But then your choice wasn't bad; you're a presidential scholar. I don't think you did too badly for yourself. A full, everything-paid-for, four-year scholarship. You know, it puts you in a great place to help us get the university to understand our need for a Black Student Union. PSs get everything they ask for."

"Didn't you see me in that brochure?" Ale asked.

"Now that I think about it, were you the one with the group of black guys dressed in black suits? Michael was in the photo also."

"Yep, that was me."

"What group was that?"

"Our fraternity, Alpha Phi Alpha."

"I didn't see your fraternity house on campus with the other houses on fraternity and sorority row."

"Those are the white fraternities and sororities; they don't accept Blacks. And there are not enough black men on campus to have a chapter here. We pledge with the chapter at Yale."

"This is all new to me, fraternities and sororities, pledging and rushing. I never heard about black fraternities."

"We're having an interest meeting next week. I'm inviting you to it." Ale paused momentarily. "Listen Little, I don't want you to feel that we're using you. I was your friend before I knew you were a PS, and I'll continue to be your friend if you choose not to help us."

"Hey, get use to it Little," Michael chimed in. "As a PS a whole lot of people will be trying to use you. So you might as well understand and get used to it now."

"I sort of understand what you're saying just from the few things I've experienced already. Tell me more about this Black Student Union."

PAST LIVES

Swirls of snow flurries danced along the city streets at the beckoning of the chilling December wind. The sky above was filled with dark black clouds threatening to empty its contents upon the earth below. The wind continued to howl as it pushed passers-by along the city streets. The fierce raging wind rattled the wooden frame windows of the Thomases' apartment.

Despite the bitter cold weather outside, Ruth's voice could hear above the clanging noise of the radiator pipes as the steam made its way from the boiler in the basement to the radiators in the apartment. As she continued to prepare the evening meal for her family, echoing the rooms and hallways was the sweet angelic sound of her singing. Everyone knew it was her singing that warmed the air throughout the building and not the heat from the furnace. The sound of her contralto voice, mixing with the irresistible aroma of her culinary delights made all within range forget about their troubles, cares, and the raging cold outside.

What a friend we have in Jesus, all our sins and griefs to bear! What a privilege to carry everything to God in prayer! O what peace we often forfeit, O what needless pain we bear, all because we do not carry Everything to God in prayer! Have we trials and temptations? Is there trouble anywhere? We should never be discouraged. Take it to the Lord in prayer. Can we find a friend so faithful, Who will all our sorrows share? Jesus knows our every weakness. Take it to the Lord in prayer.

Are we weak and heavy laden, Cumbered with a load of care? Precious Savior, still our refuge. Take it to the Lord in prayer. Do thy friends despise, forsake thee? Take it to the Lord in prayer. In His arms He'll take and shield thee. Thou wilt find a solace there.

With only twelve days before Christmas, her heart was overjoyed. The excitement of the Yule Tide season was reflected in the decorations in the apartment and the frost covered windows. Affectionately, her thoughts turned toward Little. *My baby's coming home from college next weekend for the Christmas and New Year holidays. He'll be home in time for Christmas. When he gets home, the first thing we'll do on Saturday is the annual family trip to the tree farm on Long Island. Esther and Elisha always look forward to the hayride and selecting the family Christmas tree.*

In her normal meticulous fashion, Ruth had carefully prepared the usual place in the living room where the tree would stand. Positioned in the same place each year by the front window, she was extra careful in preparing the area this year. Last evening Elijah had taken the decorations out of storage as she had requested. When their eyes saw them, Elisha and Esther danced with excitement at the sight of the tree lights, bulbs, and the Christmas stockings.

Esther was enthused with the approaching of Christmas this year. Last evening, she asked her father if she could put the angel on top of the tree. He said, "Sure thing Baby Doll." The idea of her putting the angel atop the tree this year made her that much more excited.

Ruth's heart raced as she moved into Little's bedroom. It was quiet. Inside her chest, she could feel her heart beating with excitement and joy. *Oh, I had been looking forward to his coming home from college this past summer, but he didn't. They offered him a job on the campus, working in the lab. I missed him dearly. The last time I saw my baby was in April when Elijah, the children, and I visited him during parent's weekend at the university.* Oh, how happy and elated he was introducing us to his friends, his fraternity brothers, and showing us all around the campus. We got to meet all of his friends, Stephanie, Alejandro, Michael, and Bobby. Also, Dr. Hamilton, the professor who Little admired so much. All the people he wrote about in his letters—we got to meet them all.

It was Dr. Hamilton, however, that she was most thankful to.

Yes, it was Dr. Hamilton who helped Little adjust to the campus environment and deal with being a black student on a white campus. I'm so glad Little and the few other Negro students have someone they can talk to. He's able to relate to their problems and concerns. I'm so glad they have someone to encourage and assist them. Besides each other, Dr. Hamilton is all they have. Last year, when he was home for Christmas, his friends were all he talked about.

Ruth enjoyed listening to Little as he talked on for hours about school. The Christmas vacation of his first year in college was the last time they had spent quality time together. *A time she remembered and cherished.* She chuckled within as she reflected: *During parent's weekend, everyone we met spoke so very highly of Little. Elijah and I are so proud of him. That man Dr. Waldstriecher, his thermodynamics professor kept following behind us the entire weekend. Man kept praising Little and complimenting us on what a brilliant and fine boy we raised. He couldn't tell us the same thing enough times. Over and over again, he told us that Little had a promising future as a nuclear physicist, and that one day he expected that Little would be very renowned in the field of nuclear engineering.*

"Mr. and Mrs. Thomas, I am honored to be your son's professor, to have him in my class, and to have him employed in my lab doing work on my research project. He is brilliant! He resolved an equation my colleagues and I had been working on for several months. I asked, 'How did you do that?' He said, 'When you see letters, you put them together to form words. Then you put the words together to form sentences. Well, when I see numbers and symbols, I put them together to form equations, and the equations together to form formulas.' One day, his name will be listed among the great people in the field. He has the makings of a Rhodes Scholar, Oxford Fellow, and Nobel Prize recipient. Above all, he is a fine gentleman. You both should be very proud," Dr. Waldstriecher exclaimed.

Dear to her heart were the words Dr. Garvey, president of the university, said about Little at the dinner for the parents of the presidential scholars.

"Today, we have among us one of the most promising young minds in America and possibly all the world. As a freshman, he has demonstrated his outstanding intellectual capabilities in his chosen field of nuclear engineering. Without a doubt he will be a Rhodes Scholar, a member of Phi Beta Kappa, and one day we anticipate a Nobel Prize recipient. Most notably, he is a gentleman, respected by the faculty, the administration, and his peers. He is a socially and academically, a well-grounded individual. I understand he is the king of the clambake. Mr. Thomas, through his endeavors, helped us to recognize the social pressures Negro students face on white campuses. Today, on our campus we are the first university in the nation to establish a Black Student Union. We also pledge to aggressively recruit Negro students. Without a doubt, he is a credit to the University of New England and to his race."

Here they were, Elijah and Ruth Thomas. They were the only Negro parents among all those white parents. They were seated next to the president at the head table. *It was my son the president was holding in high esteem and praising above the entire student body.*

It was also during parents' weekend that Little showed them the special governmental research project he was working on with Dr. Waldstriecher. Ruth was impressed and overwhelmed with the nuclear reactor and the research project laboratory. It was at the reactor where Little first broke the news to her.

"Momma," he said, "To work on this project in this lab is a once in a lifetime opportunity. But to continue my work on the project means I have to stay here for the summer. So, I won't be home for the summer. I'll be working in the lab on the project."

Her heart cringed when she heard those words: I won't be home this summer. He was so excited about the project; she did not have the heart to say no. But in her heart of hearts, she wanted her son to be home with her. Working with dangerous radioactive material and going on a nuclear reactor submarine at the shipyard in Groton, Connecticut. To her, it was all so new, sudden, and frightening. She was concerned for his safety; she was concerned about missing him.

"Momma," he pleaded. "This is a once in a lifetime opportunity. It's my destiny."

She looked into his eyes. He was so excited. How could she or his father deny him this once in a lifetime opportunity, especially for someone so young, gifted, and talented. After what everyone was saying about him, someone so young, so promising, and so determined. How could she hold him from his destiny?

Elijah told her that she had to let him go. "Now Ruth, you have to let him go honey. I know it's going to be hard, but we've got to let him go."

In her heart, she knew her husband was right. Letting go was hard. After all, although he is my firstborn, he is still my baby. But she knew one day she had to let him go, but not today. "Maybe tomorrow, maybe tomorrow, I'll let him go."

Staring around the room, she slid her hand into the pocket of her apron. Feeling inside, she retrieved the letter she received from him in the mail earlier that week. She read it again for the third time today.

Dear Mom and Dad,

I'm sorry I haven't written in a while, but I've been very busy with my studies and with the work in the physics lab. Final exams are next week, so I have to prepare for them.

The plan for the nuclear reactor that I've been working on is going to be completed in a few days. Dr. Waldstriecher and I have been working on it night and day. It's been so exciting working on it with Dr. Waldstriecher. The plan is to start building the reactor in January at the Newport

News Drydock and Shipbuilding Company in Newport News, Virginia.

Dr. Waldstriecher asked if I would like to go to Newport News to continue work on the project. I would receive college credit for the work. But I declined the offer. However, it was awfully tempting. I didn't realize how much confidence he had in me. I felt honored that he asked.

Dr. Hamilton and Michael send their regards. If it wasn't for their help, I don't know how I would have survived this semester. It has been a tough semester for me. I'm glad it will be ending very soon, and I will be home for the winter vacation. Believe me, I need the break, and I'm looking forward to it and spending the time with you, Pop, Elisha, and Esther.

Tell everyone I said hello, and I'll see them in two weeks. Make sure you tell Aunt Betty I have her Vermont Maple syrup. I love and I miss all of you.

With Love, forever your son,
Little

If anything, Ruth enjoyed receiving letters from her son. They were always the highlight of her day. Many times, she would repeatedly read the letters over and over. When she missed him, to be comforted, she had only to pick up one of his letters and read it. The entire Thomas household looked forward to Little's letters as well as letters from Swoosh. For Ruth, the next best thing to seeing her son was receiving a letter from him. As often as she could, she spent time writing to him. As the feeling of melancholy began to lift from her, she returned to the kitchen to resume her preparation of the evening meal and to her singing.

As her voice ranged out over the clanging of the pipes, she scarcely heard the knocking on the door. Wiping her flour-covered hands on her apron, she rushed to the door. "Who is it?"

"Western Union. I have a telegram for a Ruth Mears Thomas," the voice on the other side of the door replied.

Perplexed, anxiety swept over her as she hurriedly opened the door, "A telegram? That's me."

"Sign here please."

Apprehensively, she signed her name. With the telegram firmly grasped in her hand, she closed the door and searched for a chair. Instantaneously, the luster, joy, and song that she had only moments ago experienced evaded her.

Slowly, she sat down and laid the envelope on the table. "Telegram for me," she whispered. "A telegram, and right before Christmas. This can't be good." Ruth sat staring at the telegram. The first thought that came to her mind was of her firstborn child. "Oh God, it must be about my Little. I know it's from the university. He's the only member of the household that's not here. Something terrible done happened to my baby. I just know something terrible done happened." Her mind was befuddled with various thoughts of the lab blowing up and radiation leaking out of their containers. Clouding her thoughts and flashing through her mind were visions of the Japanese people the atomic bomb was dropped on during World War II. Mothers, fathers, children, and little babies; their flesh burned by radiation. They were left to die in the streets of Nagasaki and Hiroshima. Mentally, she saw her son lying helplessly on the floor of the lab with his frail body burned by radiation. His skin burned off exposing his bones. He may be dead or worse, he could be hospitalized enduring excruciating pain, unable to die.

"It's that nuclear project he's working on. I knew it was dangerous, all those radioactive chemicals, all that radiation," she said remorsefully shaking her head from side to side. In a low whimpering voice, she called out to her son. "Little, oh my precious Little. Please, be alright." Picking up the envelope, she pressed it hard against her breast. "Oh Lord, something terrible done happened to my baby," she cried. Her almond shaped eyes began filling with tears.

Slowly, she stood up and slipped the telegram into her apron pocket as she made her way into her bedroom where she collapsed upon her bed face down and wept. After a few minutes, she found herself sitting on the bed. Rocking back and forth, she cried, "Oh Lord, please don't let anything bad happen to my baby. Please Lord, please," she wailed.

Slothfully, she removed the telegram from her apron pocket where she had safely placed it. Clutching it to her bosom, she continued to rock back and forth. Fearfully, she slipped her finger under the flap of the envelope and removed its contents. Using her apron, she slowly wiped the tears from her eyes. She began reading the content of the telegram.

> Mother dying, come home.
> Want to see you and family. Jerome

Going limp, Ruth fell slump upon her bed. *Twenty years. It has been almost twenty years since I left home. Twenty years since I last saw my mother.* Tears flowed from her almond-shaped eyes as memories began to visit her. Memories of a place, mixed memories of a time she had long forgotten. Leaving home was not her choice. It was a decision made for her by the circumstances and by her mother. It had been years since she had thought about what happened. It all started in February of that year with the death of her sister, Bessie. Bessie was her mother's favorite child. She knew she could not live at home anymore. Her mother made it very plain and clear. She could not stay. So, during the night she left and moved to New York. The memory was a painful one. *For the past twenty years Mamma's refused to speak to me. All the letters and cards I sent her, they were either unanswered or returned unopened. Now, after all these years, my mother wants to see me. Her mother's dying wish. Even though she rejected me, in spite of all that's transpired, I still love my mother.*

Many times, she longed to see her mother, to hear her voice and feel her touch. Many nights she cried herself to sleep, wishing her mother would ask her to come home. After many years, the pain had dulled and finally vanished. The memories no longer haunted her. *Now, why now? After all these years, just when I've finally gotten over the pain, she wants me to come home. After all these years, I've accepted never seeing them again.*

Ruth paused. She feared what the future held. Anguished by her thoughts, she knew returning to Chicago meant an even greater cross for her to bear. What she had hidden for so long would finally be revealed. Sin. Her sin, the sin she had committed in the dark would now bear forth into the light. No longer in the darkness, but it would be for all to see. Shame—her shame. Could she risk it? *No, my mother is dying. My mother wants to see me, and I want to see my mother. I want to see her so badly. I need to see her. I want to tell her I love her, and I've forgiven her. Now she's dying. It is her dying wish. How can I not go home? I have to go home. I must go home. Maybe, just maybe, she's finally forgiven me at last. After all these years, maybe she has finally forgiven me.*

"Oh, dear God, maybe after all these years she's finally forgiven me."

FAMILY REUNION

The Thomas family prepared for the long twelve-hour drive from New York to Chicago. First, Elijah had to drive to Algonquian Bay, Connecticut, to get Little.

Little was packing his suitcase when Michael stopped by, catching him off guard. With the revelation of a part of his mother's past, a confused Little was extremely preoccupied. Even though they had known each other for only a year and a half, Michael sensed the awkwardness of Little's state of mind.

"Are you okay?"

"My mother's mother is dying."

"You mean your grandmother?"

"I guess so. My folks are picking me up this morning."

"I know. They're downstairs now."

"They are?"

"I saw them outside. I told your father I'd let you know they were here. Are you alright?"

Little paused from his packing and looked up at his friend. "Michael, I didn't know my mother's mother was still alive and she has a brother. I didn't even know she was from Chicago. She always talked about graduating from the same high school I went to. I thought she was from New York, and my Aunt Betty was her sister. I don't know and…" Throwing up his hands, he sat on his bed. "I just don't know anything. Right now, there's so much that I just don't know."

"I'm sure there's an explanation for it all. You know that things happen in families Little."

"No Michael, you don't know my mother. That's not like her! She loves her family. She's always saying that family is the most important. She always said when everybody else fails you, your family will be there for you. And now I'm finding out she had forsaken her own mother and brother." He paused as he bit his lip to control his anger. "Not just anybody, but her mother and brother? Why? Something is not right! It's just not right! I can feel it. No good is going to come of this trip Michael. I can feel it in my bones! No good is going to come of this. What an idiot, what an idiot I am."

Little stood up and began throwing his clothes into his bag. "First, my father, and now my mother. I thought I knew them. But they're strangers. All these years, I've been living with complete strangers. I really never knew my parents. What a stupid fool!"

Michael rushed over to him. Grabbing his hands, he stopped Little from throwing his pants down in the suitcase. "Little, right now you're upset. Look man, all of this is coming at you at once; you just finished with finals. You've had a tough semester with classes and the project. Look, I know you're rushing. I'll tell you what. So, you don't have to worry about it I'll put your stuff in storage for the break. I won't be leaving for Kansas until Sunday. I'll take care of your stuff and signing you out. You have my address and phone number. If you need anything, give me a call. Okay?"

"Sure."

"Promise?"

"I promise. Here's the key. Thanks Michael, I really appreciate this." Picking up his suitcase, Little somberly walked out of the room leaving Michael behind.

Seeing his son exiting the building, Elijah wasted no time getting out of the car. He opened the back of the station wagon for Little to put his luggage inside. Little's eyes met his mother's as she too got out of the car. He could see she had been crying. Void of feeling, he kissed her on the cheek as he always did. She quickly turned away to avoid any further eye contact or questions he might ask.

"Your legs are longer than mine, so you take the front seat Little," she said as she opened the rear car door and slid inside with Elisha and Esther.

The mirthless atmosphere in the car made the ride to Chicago long and uneasy. On several occasions, Elijah tried to make small talk while he and Little took turns driving during the night. No one was in the mood.

It was two-thirty in the morning, Chicago time, when they arrived at the outskirts of the city. Everyone, except Elijah and Little were asleep. There was a certain peacefulness inside and outside of the car; light snow had begun to fall on top of the already snow-covered streets.

"Ruth. Ruth, honey, wake up baby. We're in Chicago. I need the directions to your brother's house."

Exhausted from the ride and from weeping silently, Ruth yawned as she awakened from her light sleep. "I have the directions here in my purse. Give me a minute." Opening her purse, she pulled out a piece of paper. "Jerome said he lives on the southeast side of the city in Hyde Park on Woodlawn Avenue. I believe it's the exit after this one." Looking at the sign she was sure it was the exit. Elijah turned off the expressway at the South Parkway exit. "Take a right at the light. The directions say to go north on South Parkway to 47th Street; make a right on 47th. Continue down 47th past Drexel Boulevard. Go three blocks to Woodlawn and make a left onto Woodlawn. After passing 46th Street, start looking for the house on your left."

Elijah followed the directions as Ruth helped identify the various streets. "There's the house, the one with the lighted reindeer on the lawn." Elijah turned into the driveway. "Wake up children; we're here." After a little prodding, Elisha and Esther aroused from their sleep. As they got out of the car and gathered at the front door, the snow began falling heavily.

Ruth rang the bell as the snow began covering the ground, with the family of five standing at the front door. The icy Chicago wind blew swirls of snow around them as they stood at the door shivering. Esther and Elisha whined about the cold wind and the snow. The door opened; they were quickly ushered inside the house by a tall husky man wearing a red silk bathrobe.

"Jerome? Jerome is it really you?"

"It's me Bunny."

"Oh my God, Jerome, it's really you," she cried as she fell into his arms.

"Come on in out of the snow. Leave your bags here in the foyer and come on into the living room where it's warm," he said as he led them into the room.

Elijah and Little put the bags down and guided the sleepy Elisha and Esther through the foyer and into the living room.

"Jerome, it's so good to see you," she said hugging him tightly. Tightly, he embraced her. Wiping the tears from her eyes, she looked at her family.

"Jerome, let me introduce you to my family. This is my husband Elijah, and these are our children Thomas, Elisha, and Esther. Children, this is my brother, Jerome. He's your uncle, Uncle Jerome." The two men shook hands and exchanged greetings.

"Elijah," Jerome said extending his hand to him. "Good to meet you. I see you've taken good care of my baby sister. Elijah politely smiled as they shook hands. Turning to Little he exclaimed, "My, Thomas, you're a pretty tall fellow just like your daddy here," he said flashing a big smile while shaking Little's hand. "And look at these two little sleepy heads. You have a beautiful family Bunny." I can't believe it. It's really you," he said cradling her in his arms. "I can't believe it. It's been almost twenty-six years since I last saw you."

"Pepper," a female voice called out as a woman appeared in the room.

"Is that them?"

"Lanet, did we wake you baby?"

"Oh don't worry about it. I could hardly sleep anyway."

"Lanet, this is my sister Ruth, her husband Elijah and their children, Thomas, Elisha and Esther. This is my wife, Lanet."

"Hello," she said as she hugged Ruth and Elijah. "You all must be tired. You've been driving all day and half the night to get here." Upon seeing Esther and Elisha, she exclaimed, "Look at these precious little ones. Ruth let's get these babies to bed. They're still sleepy. I'll show you your rooms upstairs. Pepper," she said motioning to her husband. "Take their coats and then bring their bags upstairs honey. Ruth, you and the children come with me so we can get these babies to bed. We'll have plenty of time to talk later this morning when the sun is up."

"I'm not really tired. I slept in the car most of the way. I just need to lie down for a little while," Ruth responded. Little, carry your sister upstairs for me please."

"Yes ma'am."

"Here, let me have your coats," Jerome said reaching for Elijah and Little's coats. "How was the drive Elijah?"

Elijah looked at his brother-in-law as he took off his coat. "Little drove most of the way. I imagine he's more tired than me. Your directions were fine. We had no trouble getting off the freeway and finding your place. Right now, I could use a shower and a strong hot cup of coffee."

"Okay. Let me show you to your room while the girls put the little ones to bed. There's a bathroom in your room, and Lanet left you some clean bath cloths and towels on the bed. If you need anything, just call me. While you shower and rest up, I'll put a pot of coffee on and make something for breakfast. When you finish, come on down to the kitchen. We should have breakfast ready around seven-thirty if that's not too early for you."

"That's fine. We normally get up around six in the morning."

Lanet was up early preparing breakfast. Jerome, Elijah, and Ruth sat at the kitchen table talking as they ate. "Bunny, how old are your children?"

"Well, there's Thomas; he's the oldest. He turned twenty last month. Elisha is twelve, and Esther is ten."

"Girl, you look good for a woman who's had three babies. That Thomas, he's a tall and handsome young man. What does he do?"

"Little? That's what we call Thomas. He's in college."

"Good. What school does he go to?"

"The University of New England."

"In Algonquian Bay, Connecticut?"

"Yes, that's the one."

"Say what," exclaimed Jerome. "Excellent school. UNE is an Ivy League school, one of the top schools in the country. Two of the guys that work in my office graduated from there. What is he majoring in?"

"Nuclear engineering," answered Elijah. "He's a presidential scholar and has a full four-year scholarship. He made straight As every semester."

"A four-point grade average. Boy must be super smart like his uncle Jerome. Or does he get his brains from you Elijah?"

"Now Pepper honey, what do you mean smart like you? Man, that's got to be wishful thinking on your part. Pepper always tells people he graduated magna cum laude, but he really graduated thank you laude," Lanet playfully bellowed. "I know you're both proud of him."

Elijah gently squeezed Ruth's hand as he spoke. "We are Lanet. Little has made Ruth and me very proud. No man could ask for a finer son."

"They're some very good-looking children Bunny."

"Thank you. What about you? Do you have any children filling up this big house?" Ruth asked.

"I don't know about filling up this house, but we somehow managed to have two. Now Pepper, that man wanted a bunch, six; I didn't want any. I was too busy being a career woman. But we compromised. I told him I'd give him one child, a son. I always felt every man should have a son. He said he wanted a daughter as beautiful as me. Now that was so sweet and very tempting. We tried for years to have a baby, but nothing happened.

Then eleven years ago after we had given up, I had twins. Boy and a girl. Honey, would you get the picture in the living room to show them for me please?" Jerome left the room and returned with the picture of the children and handed it to Ruth. "Named the boy after his daddy, Jerome Anthony Mears, Jr., and our daughter, her name is Jasmine Alisha."

"They are beautiful. She looks just like you Lanet."

"Thank you. But having my first baby at thirty-eight was no picnic. Then, I turned around and had twins. I wouldn't recommend it girl," she laughed.

Jerome looked at his wife. "Oh baby, it wasn't bad. We had a good pregnancy. I'll admit we had a rough time with the delivery; we were in labor twelve hours."

Lanet grabbed his hand, "What do you mean we? Man, I don't know where you get off with this we stuff. I don't recall you carrying around those babies in your belly for nine months. I don't recall your belly getting big or you having one labor pain. Girl, your brother and this we stuff. Makes me laugh each time he says it."

"Where are they now?"

"They're still upstairs asleep. They were so excited about their aunt, uncle, and cousins coming from New York. They stayed up half the night waiting for you. Every time a floorboard squeaked, or the wind blew, they'd wake up and come running into the room. 'Are they here Mommy? Is that them? Daddy, when are they going to get here? Don't forget to wake us up when they get here.' Lord, all day and all night long. Now, they're so tired they can't wake up."

"Originally, we had planned to visit Lanet's parents in Los Angeles for Christmas. But then, Momma seemed to turn for the worse, so we changed our plans."

"What's wrong with Momma?"

"I can't say. She was experiencing a shortness of breath, so we took her to the doctor's office. Doctor said her heart isn't as strong as it used to be, but he said she could live another ten, twenty years with proper care.

Physically, she's always been a strong woman. We were talking about going to California for Christmas, when all of a sudden, she got sick.

Lanet got up to pour herself another cup of coffee. "They weren't all that interested in spending Christmas in Los Angeles with my parents anyway. They'd rather be here with their cousins and in the snow. Anyone want another cup of coffee? Oh Pepper, I think I hear the phone ringing. We really needs to get that thing fixed." Jerome started getting up out of his seat.

"No baby, stay there. I'll get it. I just hope it's not the hospital calling me."

Ruth looked at her brother. She knew and understood their mother had manipulated them. Quickly, she changed the direction of the conversation. "I can't get over how you haven't changed one bit. Let me see if I remember. I believe you left home when I was what, about eleven, twelve years old?"

"That's about right. But I do have a few gray hairs now. All because of that wife of mine," he laughed. "I do remember I turned eighteen that May. I graduated from high school in June and left for California the next day. I went to the University of California-Berkeley. But then Bunny, I can't get over how much you've grown up. You were just a little girl in pigtails the last time I saw you."

"Now Pepper, you know I never wore pigtails. Tell me, how did you and Lanet meet? Was it at Berkeley?"

"Actually, we met in the hospital. She was a medical student. I was her first patient."

"Ooh, I hope it wasn't anything serious."

"No, just a case of appendicitis."

Lanet returned to the room responding to the statement. "And believe me, he has been my patient for the last eighteen years." Smiling,

Lanet continued, "We had a whirlwind of a romance. We got married nine months later. Then Pepper told me we were coming to Chicago for a short visit. Stayed so long we ran out of money, so I had to start looking for a job. I ended up getting a job at the University of Illinois Hospital. Been here since, and that was what, fifteen-sixteen years ago?"

"What do you do at the hospital?"

"Now? I'm chief of surgery at the hospital. Pepper's a CPA. He has one of the largest accounting firms in the city."

Glancing down at her empty plate, Ruth's appearance reflected her changing mood. "Pepper, do you know where Kenny is? He was almost thirteen years old when I left home."

"Sure. He lives here in the Chicago area in Cicero. Would you believe our little baby brother is married and has five kids!"

"When I came back to Chicago sixteen years ago, Kenny was a teenager. He's mostly the reason why I moved back here. He was a good kid, but you know Mamma. She neglected him. So about two years after you left, he came out to California to spend the summer with Lanet and me. We wanted him to stay and go to school. But he loved Mamma and didn't want to leave her here in Chicago by herself. To this day, I can't understand it. Regardless of how bad she treated him, he loved her that much more. Things weren't going well between him and Mamma, but he still wasn't going to leave her. You know how teenage boys can be. If you leave them alone long enough, they'll eventually find something to get into. He got into some trouble. I believe he was reaching out for help. Thank God he had sense enough to call me. Since he still didn't want to leave Mamma, Lanet said we had to move Chicago."

Jerome stood up and walked over to his wife. Putting his arms around her, he affectionately kissed her on her forehead. "I won't forget, she said, 'if the mountain won't come to Mohammed, then Mohammed will have to go to the mountain.' She's an amazing woman. I thank God each and every day for her. Next thing I know, she had a position at the University of Illinois Hospital. Two months later we moved here, and Kenny came to live with us. We supported him through college, marriage, and five babies."

Lanet said in her joking fashion, "They're over each other's houses at least two to three times a week. Our children are around the same age. I get sick of them. I wish they would stay home sometimes. He and his wife both teach at the university."

"What can I say, he's my little brother, and I love him dearly."

"We love them dearly," Lanet added, squeezing her husband's hand. "Excuse me, we love them dearly. He knows you're coming. He wants to see you."

"I feel so bad, we were really close. I was always watching over him, helping him with his schoolwork. I practically raised him till I left home. He was so young. I couldn't explain why I was leaving, and I didn't have a chance to say good-bye to him. I know it was hard for him. My leaving him without saying anything and leaving him alone with Mamma."

"He told me. He said after Bessie's death, everything at home changed for both of you. Bunny, it was no secret, we all know that Bessie was Mamma's favorite. In Mamma's eyes, the sun rose and set with that girl. When it came to Bessie, to Mamma she could do no wrong, and we could do nothing right. I was sorry I couldn't make it back for her funeral. At the time I was in graduate school and I couldn't afford it. Believe me, I have no regrets."

Very perceptive, Lanet noticed a tensed atmosphere was developing as the conversation continued.

"That was him on the phone. He, Shera, and the children are coming over this morning. They should be here in about an hour."

Using this as her cue, she seized the moment to make the atmosphere more relaxed. "Bunny, the man worships the ground his big brother walks on. I declare, the man won't fart without first consulting his big brother." Everyone roared with laughter from Lanet's remark. "And now that he's all grown up, don't call him Kenny anymore. Naw girl, he wants to be called Kenneth."

Jerome laughed. "Woman you are so disgusting, I don't know what I'm going to do with or without you. Come give me a kiss."

Knowing her technique worked, she leaned over and kissed Jerome. "Now Honey, you're telling me Mr. Holy Ghost himself is going to miss church this morning? Bunny, that man must really want to see you. They don't miss church for nothing and nobody. To my knowledge, this is a first. If he died on Saturday, he'd rise on Sunday mornin' just to make service."

"That's the truth," Jerome added.

"Although the one thing I can say about Kenneth and Shera—and, Pepper, you know I'm telling the truth—they have a powerfully strong relationship with God. If I ever get sick before you send for the doctors, call them. They are some praying people. They have that faith that can move mountains and raise the dead."

"That is true. And he thanks you for that Bunny. He said you use to take him to church all the time. If it hadn't been for his faith in God, he doesn't know how he would have made it this far or alone with Mamma. In fact, now he'll tell you he wasn't alone. He said God was always there with him. If anything, he loves you for it; for introducing him to his Lord and Savior, Jesus Christ. Even after you left, he said Mamma made him go to church, even though she herself never went."

Lanet nodded her head in approval. "They attend a Pentecostal church. They call themselves 'Spirit-filled.' But the people are genuine in their walk with God. I've never heard a ministry quite like it. It's sort of a Billy Graham, Oral Roberts type. They believe in reading the Bible, praying, speaking in tongues, and healing. Kenneth said if it's in the Bible and God promised it, he's going to get it. He wants everything God has to give. The man is like King David, a man truly after God's own heart. And you know I believe he has it. I'm a doctor, and I've seen times when Kenneth, or Shera, or someone from that church would come to the hospital and pray for patients that have given up hope, and they recovered. As a doctor, there's so much that I can do. After that, it's all in the hands of the good Lord. I've learned that much from Kenneth and Shera."

Ruth lowered her head. "I'll tell you I don't know whom I'm more afraid of to see, Kenny or Mamma. For a long time after I left, I wrote both of them. But Kenny never wrote back and all the letters I sent Mamma they were returned unopened. So many years have passed. There's just so much in the past to deal with. I still don't know if my coming back here was the right thing to do."

Pepper placed both his hands on hers. "Bunny, she's a sixty-eight-year-old woman who feels her time on this earth is not long. She knows she done wrong. I chose to believe she wants to make peace with her children before she dies. Mamma specifically asked me to find you. She said she needed to see you and your family before she died. She said there was something she had to do. Something she should have done a long time ago. She had your address from the letters you sent to Kenneth. He never wrote you back because Mamma never gave him your letters. He never knew about your letters until last week when she gave them to me. She kept every last one of the letters you sent him. That's why he didn't write. He honestly didn't know."

"Did he say he was mad at me for leaving?"

"Sure, at first he was angry with you when you left. You protected him from Mamma, fed, and clothed him. For all practical purposes, you were more of a mother than a sister to him. He looked up to you. When you left, his whole world fell apart. Bunny, he was what, eight or nine years old?

He didn't know or quite understand why you left. He said he couldn't make heads or tails out of what was going on. He knows that now; he understands why you left. Believe me he forgave you a long time ago. He prayed and never gave up hoping that the two of you would be together again someday. And praise God, today his prayers have been answered."

"Do you know why I left, Jerome?"

"Mamma and Kenneth told me only bits and pieces."

The ringing telephone extension in the room where he was sleeping aroused Little from his deep slumber. It was after ten o'clock. Looking around, for the first time he saw the bedroom where he had fallen asleep. Looking toward the window, he saw the snow had stopped, but he could hear the whistling of the wind as it howled outside. Gathering his thoughts, he remembered meeting his mother's brother, his Uncle Jerome, for the first time earlier that morning. At the foot of the bed, he found a bathrobe and a pair of slippers. Slipping on the robe and slippers, he made his way down the stairs to the kitchen. Standing in the doorway, he overheard his mother and uncle talking. "Good morning everyone," Little said, interrupting his mother as he entered the kitchen.

A sudden hush followed a deep silence in the room. As customary, each morning when he was home, he kissed his mother and father. He knew he had interrupted whatever they were talking about them and they chose not to say anything in front of him. But deep inside he knew it all had to do with their being there.

Lanet let out a big greeting. "Good morning. Oooh Bunny, he is a handsome child. If I weren't married to his uncle and a few years younger, he'd be in trouble. Come here baby," she said motioning to him as she stood up. "I'm your aunt Lanet. Come over here and give me a big one of those that you just gave your mother and father." She smiled as she held her arms open.

Little looked at his aunt, she stood about five feet eight inches tall. Slender, she had a well proportion body for a woman her age. Her bronze-colored skin was striking against her green eyes. She was humorous. Right away, he knew he was going to like her. Laughing, Little hugged and kissed his aunt for the first time.

"And you're a good-looking woman. If I was a few years older and you weren't my mother's brother's wife, I might have taken you up on the offer."

Blushing, Lanet was taken by surprise with Little's quick-witted response. "Oooh, and a sense of humor."

"Ah ha! See? There. You walked right into that, Lanet," Jerome said laughing.

Lanet laughed as she pretended to adjust her hair. "You're just jealous old man because a handsome young man finds me attractive. Come on, Thomas, and have a seat. Are you hungry?"

"Yes, ma'am. I haven't had a thing to eat since yesterday."

"Well," she responded. "Tall, dark, handsome, and manners too boot. Y'all ought to feed this boy. Here baby sit down right here," she said pulling out a chair from the table "and let your auntie Lanet fix you a plate. We have bacon, sausage, scrambled eggs, toast, cheese grits, orange juice, and coffee. Do you drink coffee? If not, we have milk, tea, anything you want. Just tell your auntie."

"Okay, I'd like some bacon, scrambled eggs, toast, cheese grits, orange juice, and coffee please."

"He's got a healthy appetite too. I likes that in a man."

The remainder of the breakfast conversation centered on the University of New England. While his aunt and uncle asked many questions of him, all his questions went unasked. After a while Elisha, Esther, Jerome, and Jasmine were all at the table eating breakfast.

After breakfast the grown-ups moved their conversation into in the living room as the children came down the stairs. They talked by the warm fire Jerome had started. Little was on his way down the stairs from getting dressed when the doorbell rang. Jerome opened the door. Little observed as Jerome hugged the man, woman, and their children. Five small children immediately ran past Little on the stairwell and quickly disappeared down the hall. The man and woman removed their coats.

Trembling, his mother appeared in the foyer. His father stood behind her with his hands resting on her shoulders as if he was trying to steady her. She and the strange man in the doorway eyes searched out one another. They stood staring at each for the longest time in disbelief. Slowly, they walked toward each other.

Thin framed, he stood about five inches taller than her. Ruth lifted her hands up and placed them on his cheeks. She began feeling his face as if she were a blind woman as his hands slowly caressed her face. Seeing them face-to-face, Little was amazed at how much they resembled each other, yet he still wasn't sure who he was. She softly whispered his name, "Kenny. Is that really you?"

He nodded in affirmation and replied, "It's me Bunny, your baby brother."

"Oh God, it is really you Kenny." With tears flowing, Ruth and her youngest brother embraced, holding each other tightly and crying. Together they stood in the foyer embracing each other tightly and crying for five minutes. It was an emotionally-charged moment; Jerome, Lanet, Elijah, and Shera surrounded Kenneth and Ruth and wept as well. Not knowing who the man was or what was transpiring, Little was emotionally overcome as he stood on the staircase carefully watching them, wondering.

FINAL CURTAIN

The previous evening had been filled with the many introductions that come along with meeting relatives for the first time. In the course of one day, Little found out his mother was born and raised in Chicago. Her mother was still alive, and his mother had two brothers, Jerome and Kenneth. From what he gathered, Bessie, their oldest sister, was killed by her boyfriend the same year he was born. Although they talked and laughed about her, Little detected there was something else about her death they shied away from talking about. Sunday evening arrived. Together the three siblings visited their mother. Despite the joyous, emotionally-filled reunions and all the talk, Little was confused. He now had more questions and still no answers.

The evening in some sense reminded him of the scene at his aunt Madie and uncle Junebug house in Washington, DC. The women, three sisters-in-law were in the kitchen preparing the evening meal. The men lounged in the living room being waited on and talking politics and the likes.

Ruth noted the three were related only through marriage, yet they had so much in common. "Bunny, you are blessed this day," Shera informed her sister-in-law. "You know, normally Dr. Mears here doesn't cook every day. Don't get me wrong, she's a great cook. But she knows her way around the operating room better than she does her own kitchen. That's why she has a cook and maid service."

"Girl, you ought to stop that! No Ruth, it's just that being a surgeon and chief of surgery, I can afford someone else to clean my house and cook my meals. Between my hospital work schedule, that man, those two kids, and this big house, I just don't have the time. Whenever I have off, I always cook for the family. And I feed Miss Shera and her crew all the time."

"I know you didn't say that."

"What about you Shera? What do you do?" Ruth asked.

"No Bunny. Let me tell you about Miss Thang sitting next to you and what she does."

"Girl, you better hush your mouth."

"You see what she's wearing?"

Laughing, Shera stood up and twirled around. "And you know I look good in it."

"Yea girl, you know you can work those clothes. But Miss Shera here, she doesn't shop for her clothes like regular people. Oh no, not her. She doesn't wear no store off the rack bought clothes. She's too good to pick her clothes off the rack, like us. You know what I mean? Naw Bunny, she has all her clothes tailor made by Madame Vera T. LaSalle, and the children clothes too."

"Ooh girl, we know about Madame LaSalle in New York. You can't buy her designs in a department store. You can't get them, not even in some of the finest department stores. You can only find her collection in the most exclusive and expensive women shops, and then she only has one of a kind. No two outfits are alike."

"That's it girl! That's where Miss Shera gets all her clothes and her children's. She goes to her shop in Gary, Indiana to have them exclusively made. And she's on first name basis with Madame LaSalle."

"Now I can't help it if my baby likes me to look good, and you know because of my fine shape, I can't buy off no rack."

"Girl, you ought to stop that." Playfully, she hit Lanet with the dishtowel. "Bunny, you asked what I do? I learn bad habits from her."

"Okay everybody," Lanet shouted. "Dinner is ready. We can finish this conversation around the dinner table."

The family of sixteen, seven adults and nine children, managed to sit at the formal dining room table. "Kenneth, please ask the blessing of the meal."

"It's my pleasure big brother. Thank you for asking me."

"Heavenly Father, thank you for answering our prayer of being a family again. I ask your blessing upon my brother and his family and my dear sister, who was lost, and upon her husband and children. Thank you for bringing her home again and for giving them a safe journey over the highways. We know it was a blessing as only you can provide. Now, bless this meal we are about to receive, for the nourishment of our bodies, and bless the hands that prepared it. In the name of our Lord and Savior, Jesus Christ. Amen."

"Bunny, you asked earlier what I did? I teach nursing at the university."

"That's wonderful. How did you meet my little brother?"

"Kenneth and I met in church."

"Where else," interjected Lanet laughing. "She saw this fine-looking brother. Heard his baritone voice in the choir, and she just could not sit still. She just had to meet him."

"Lanet, you're so bad. This is my story so let me tell it." Leaning over the table she whispered, "She's right. He was so fine, I just couldn't resist him, and you know you still are baby," she said kissing him.

"I know I am," he replied. A wave of laughter swept through the table.

"Anyway, I had just completed nursing school and Kenneth was in his last year in college. He was majoring in architecture. He proposed to me after one month, and, nine months later, we were married."

"What's with you, Pepper and Kenny? Both of you married after nine months."

"Hey, can't help it. We Mears men know what we like. When we find it, we get it," Kenneth said as he and Jerome slapped five. "And, Bunny, the name is Kenneth."

Shera shouted, "Now, man, please don't start that again. As I was saying, we were married about a year when I got pregnant with Kenneth, Jr. Two years later I got pregnant with the twins, Richard and Raymond. Three months after the twins were born, I kept getting sick. I went to specialist after specialist to find out what was wrong. I believe in faith healing, but there is nothing wrong with going to the doctor."

"Alright girl preach on! Speak the truth!"

"Now, God gave us doctors, so we might as well use them. Besides, the doctor can tell you what's wrong. Then you can pray for exactly what ails you. After a month of going to different specialists, they couldn't find anything wrong. Then, this really old doctor, her name was I believe Doctor Lanet Mears looked at me and said, 'Chile, you're pregnant.' I laughed, because I just knew I wasn't. But guess what? At the time, I was working as a surgical nurse. I had to stop that because it was getting to be too much, the pregnancy, three kids, and a husband. Then, we found out I was having another set of twins. Kenneth said I should go get my masters' degree in nursing. By that time, he was on the faculty and staff at the university. Then the twins, Hope and Faith were born. So, while I was home pregnant, home with five children under four years old, I got my master's degree and a PhD in nursing. I wanted to spend time with the children, and I also wanted to work. A position opened up on the faculty in the nursing department at the university. While I was at home, I had some of my articles published in some medical journals, and I helped author one of the nursing textbooks. The university was more than happy to have me in their employment. I applied and got the job. So now both of us have the summers and winters off to spend with the kids."

"That is really so nice. It's so strange we have so much in common. Nine months after Elijah and I met we got married, and I work in a hospital as a secretary to the chief of neurosurgery." Ruth, Lanet, and

Shera all found it interesting. Only through the bonds of marriage they were related. Yet, they had so much in common.

It was early afternoon. As the car traveled along the south side of Chicago on Indiana Avenue, Little began squirming from uneasiness. Today was the day when he would finally meet his grandmother. Little sensed he had been here before. Crossing over 47th and South Parkway, he could see the Royal Theater. At 47th and Indiana, Ernie's Kitchen Shack was still there. Finally, around Fiftieth Street, the two cars stopped in front of the apartment building, 3721 Indiana Avenue.

The nine crowded into the apartment building's small foyer. Jerome used his key. Ruth remarked how at one time they had to press the bell and wait to be buzzed in. Together, they went up the steps to the second floor. After twenty years, Ruth found herself with her brothers back in the apartment where they grew up. The one difference this time was she was a married woman with her own family, her husband, and three children. *Lord, this is something I always dreamed about. I never thought it would come true.*

Inside the apartment, Little looked around; it was dimly lit.

Ruth gasped as she remarked, "This is the same furniture from twenty years ago when I lived here."

Kenneth watched as Ruth brushed her hand against the chair. "I offered to let her live with us, but she refused. I even tried to buy her new furniture. She told me this was her apartment where she paid the rent, and these were her belongings that she paid for. Said she didn't want anything from no one. So, to make her happy, I paid the increase in her rent and never told her. She hasn't changed. The old girl is as stubborn as ever."

Little was puzzled by his mother's shrinking, submissive, yet overly, anxious behavior. She became super sensitive. Slowly, Little sat down on the couch.

"Git off of that," she screamed. She cringed and yelled at him when he sat down on the couch. He was startled. Never before had she ever reacted to him in such a manner. He did not understand her sudden unexplained behavior. He sensed something wasn't right. From the very beginning of the trip until the time he walked into the apartment, Little had a strange feeling. It was as if a dark shadow was cast over him and his mother. Jumping off the couch he wanted desperately to get out of the apartment.

"Mamma," she called to her mother gently as the group entered the bedroom. "We're back. I brought my children to see you like I promised yesterday." The elderly woman looked up from her bed and smiled pleasantly at her daughter. Ruth called each of them into the room. "Mamma, this is my daughter, Esther. She's ten years old." Esther, who was standing in front of Ruth, moved to the bed to see her grandmother.

The elderly woman smiled and gestured for Esther to sit down next to her. A frightened Esther obediently sat down on the bed.

She spoke quietly, "Such a pretty little girl, a pretty little girl with long braids. Let grandma give you a kiss." She lifted her hand and placed it around the back of Esther's head and pulled the small child's head down and kissed her on the forehead. "She's a pretty girl, Ruth Ann, a pretty girl."

Ruth was pleased with her mother's blessing of her daughter, Esther. Smiling, she pulled Elisha in front of her. "And Mamma, this is my son Elisha, he's twelve."

Elisha looked at his grandmother. Smiling he said, "Hello grandma." She politely smiled and grabbed his hand to hold it. Again, the elderly Mears patted the bed gesturing for him to sit next to her. "What a good lookin' boy you is and polite too." Stroking his head, she commented, "And all that pretty curly hair on your head."

"Thank you grandma," Elisha said, beaming with joy. "You look just like my mother."

Hearing it brought a smile to her face, "I do?" she chuckled. "Let grandma give you a kiss." She cupped her hand around the back of his neck pulling him down as she raised herself slightly off her bed. She kissed him on his forehead. "Such a sweet young man."

Before getting up, Elisha bent over and kissed his grandmother on her cheek. Tears formed in her eyes as he kissed her. She looked over to Ruth and again gave her approval. "They are both real fine children Ruth Ann, and he's a real fine boy jist likes my Kenny."

Ruth looked adoringly at her children as she wiped the tears from her eyes and grabbed Elijah by the hand. She lamented, "Oh Mamma, I wish I had brought them sooner to see you and they could have gotten to know you. I just wish there was more time. And now, Mamma, this is my eldest son, Thomas. He's twenty years old. He's a sophomore in college."

Little pushed passed his uncle Kenneth to move in sight of his grandmother. He looked at the elderly woman lying on the bed before him. Her brown skin appeared dry and scaly. Other than the tears adding a sparkle, her eyes appeared dull and lifeless. Her former kind-looking, round face was now thin and wrinkled. Her freshly braided shoulder length silver hair lacked the luster and shine of its true beauty. She appeared gentle, but not as weak as he imagined. Little was moved with compassion as she beckoned him to move closer to her. She patted the bed, gesturing for him to sit like she did his younger siblings. Obliging, uneasily he sat next to her on the bed, as did his younger brother and sister. In his mind, he wondered what the root of the uneasiness was that he felt inside. He wondered if it was because she was dying, or for some other unforeseen reason.

Ruth was pleasantly surprised and yet very pleased. Her mother had accepted him. She had accepted all her children.

Little sat on the bed patiently watching as the elderly woman on the bed drew deep breathes and stared up at him. Lifting her hands, she cupped them around his face as her long bony fingers slid across his cheeks. Little found her touch hard. He found it was difficult to read the expression on her face. Her sunken lips were no longer supported by the false teeth she once wore. They moved as if she tried to speak. He leaned forward as her hands moved to his neck and drew his face closer. Tears ran down her cheeks and fell to her pillow as his face drew closer to hers.

Ruth, Jerome, and Kenneth stood crying tears of joy and became overwhelmed as they saw their mother's acceptance of Ruth's firstborn child.

Moved by her actions, and feeling guilty for his unfounded uneasy feelings, Little thought about of Isaac and Esau in the Bible, and how important it was to receive the blessing. He was the oldest, the firstborn. It was only proper, and he knew it would please his mother very much that he, too, should be blessed by her. Like his siblings before him, Little leaned forward to receive his blessing and birthright from his dying grandmother. So close, Little noticed the sweet expression on her face change and her smile fade as the hatred within her revealed itself.

Without warning from her puckered lips, a thick wad of warm excrement spewed from the old woman's mouth hitting him squarely in his face. Simultaneously, catching him and everyone else off guard, her long brittle fingers wrapped around his throat and began choking him.

Traumatized and shocked by her action, Little began gasping for air as her clasping fingers tightened their grip around his neck. His ensuing action was instinctive as he fought to free himself from that which was cutting off his air supply. In defense, automatically his hands wrapped around her wrist and began trying to rip them from around his neck. She was strong, stronger than anyone had suspected. Desperately, he struggled trying to pry her hands from around his neck to free himself, but to no avail. He struggled gasping for air to once again fill his lungs. He could feel himself not breathing as the last bit of air in his body was exhausted. Feverishly, he tried to loosen her grip, but found himself too weak to pry away her deadly grip.

Momentarily dumbfounded, dazed and stunned, no one could move as they looked on in disbelief. Suddenly, breaking the silence Ruth screamed in utter horror breaking the moment. "No! Mamma, no! Stop Mamma, oh God no Mamma please stop! You're killing him. You're killing him! Oh God, she's killing him." Pandemonium broke out in the room as the unsuspecting family stood shocked by the elderly woman.

Little's bulging eyes gaped into her face. A bewildered Little muttered, "Why? What did I do?" Looking at her, he saw the contempt and a deeply rooted hatred for him in her face. "But why? Why do you hate me? What did I do?"

She rose up to push her victim onto the floor as she held her deadly grip. On top of him she screamed, "You bastard, you should of never been born. Your daddy killed my Bessie. I'm gonna kill you. Gonna kill you like he killed my Bessie. Gonna take you to hell with me to see your daddy."

Jerome, Kenneth, and Elijah were perplexed and astonished by her strength as they unsuccessfully tried to pull her off him. Hearing the reverberating snap, no one expected the awesome power of her desire to manifest such physical strength. It was hopeless, her adrenaline, driven by her deeply propagated passion of hate, superseded the trio's strength. Accomplishing that which for years she had vowed, she wailed, "You demon child from hell. Now, go to your damn daddy."

Little heard her words just before something snapped in his body. Then everything suddenly turned black. His body went limp. Little's lifeless body lay on the floor as she grabbed her chest and screamed. Her body trembled from convulsions. Only through her physical agonizing pain did the bond of her grip loosened, freeing her lifeless victim.

Amid the blackness, Little found himself standing in an upper corner of the room watching everything transpire.

Getting themselves up, the men lifted her body off Little's and placed her on the bed. Eyes wide opened and rolled back in his head, a breathless Little laid on the floor pale, motionless and lifeless. A small trail of blood flowed from his partially parted lips. From the upper left side corner of the room, Little observed Doctor Lanet Mears as she knelt beside his body. Instinctively, she signaled for someone to bring her doctor's bag. Immediately, surgical nurse Shera Mears assisted in the effort to revive him. Placing two fingers on his neck, she checked for his pulse. Touching the neck, she felt his crushed larynx. Opening the bag, she took out a stethoscope and placed it on his chest to listen for a heartbeat. Swiftly, she struck his chest with her fist. Dr. Mears using all her medical knowledge, training and years of experience, began the arduous task of resuscitating the patient. Placing her mouth to his, she blew air into his mouth to force air into his lungs. His crushed larynx was obstructing his bronchi.

From her years of medical training and experience, she knew it was impossible to get air into his lungs. She had to bypass the larynx. She had to perform an emergency tracheotomy. Watching her, Nurse Mears instinctively searched the medical bag for a scalpel and tubing. Together, the sister-in-law medical team worked swiftly. Dr. Mears made a small incision in his neck to the bronchi and inserted the tube and began blowing into it. His chest inflated with air. As a doctor, she was aware of the elapsed time with no oxygen to Little's brain. If she did manage to revive him, chances are he would be brain damaged. On the other hand, with the broken neck, he may be paralyzed for the rest of his life. Reviving him was hopeless, a no win-situation, but Aunt Lanet had to keep trying.

Ruth stood over her son screaming in horror; Esther joined in. "Jerome," Lanet screamed. "Get Ruth and the children out of here, now." Again, she pressed on his chest and blew breath into his lungs via the tube. "Come on, Thomas, breathe. Come on, breathe, breathe." Aunt Lanet worked intensely to bring life back into the lifeless body of her nephew. For the next twenty minutes, she tried to the point of exhaustion. Shera grabbed her hands forcing her to stop. Methodically, she removed the tube from his throat. A tearful Shera handed her the needle and thread to suture the incision. She had completed her task; medically she did all she knew how.

Trembling, Lanet looking up at Elijah, with tearful eyes, shook her head. Bending over his body, she closed his eyes and wept. Continuing to weep, she rose to her feet and fell into the arms of her husband. In all her years as a doctor, she had lost patients before, but never had she cried over the loss of a patient as she did this time. Little was special to her. He was not a patient. Little was her nephew. The nephew whom she had just met, and she loved instantly. Collapsing in her husband's arms, she buried her head in his chest and cried. Elijah, trembling with grief left the room to search out his wife. He found Ruth in the adjacent room.

From the look on his face, he did not have to speak a work. "Oh no God. My son, my son. No. No. No." Ruth cried out in pain and agony for her now deceased child.

Stoically, Dr. Mears directed her attention to the elderly Mears. Using her stethoscope, she checked for a heartbeat in the elderly woman. She could hear her heart beating faintly and erratically. Before she could do anything, the elderly woman let out a distinctive, guttural utterance as she drew her last breath. Gingerly, Dr. Mears reached over closing the eyes of the late Annie Mears.

From his perch in the upper left corner of the room, Little continued to look. Suddenly, he found himself at the opening of a long dark tunnel. A bright light was shining at the opposite end. The warm ray of the alluring light was enticing him to come. The light was beautiful and glorious. He could not resist the alluring light's beckoning call. Without hesitation, he began the journey of walking through the tunnel toward the light. In the light he experienced a comfort, warmth, and peace like never before. In the light, he heard a voice calling his name. It was a peaceful, calm, and serene voice. The voice was calling him to come home to be at rest.

REBIRTH

The train started out slowly from the station, at a snail-like pace; it chugged along its way until it was out of the city's limit. Gradually, it began picking up speed, moving swiftly through the countryside setting. The night before a heavy snow had fallen. The morning sun beamed brightly off the fresh snow, covering the earth, making the surroundings appear like a white sheet of glass. The trees, barren of their leaves, exposed the small communities and the vast farmland alongside the tracks. Off in the distance, smoke could be seen rising from the occasional farmhouse they passed. Old wooden barns, worn by the years of changing seasons, covered in snow, dotted the landscape.

Cows stood in the fields grazing on bales of hay. White-tail deer, their brown bodies sometimes blending in with the barren trees, stood out in the snow as they raced alongside the speeding train. There was an assured tranquility and a relaxing peace reflected in the appearance of the hot sunrays meeting the cold white snow-covered ground.

Night had fallen. Little woke up unsure of where he was and still confused about what had happened. Was this the journey he had taken? Is this his bright light at the end of the long dark tunnel? Before entering the tunnel, he remembered watching his aunt Lanet using all her medical knowledge to bring him back. But it was his choice not hers. He loved how the bright light felt. It was the place where he chose to journey. Little longed to remain there in the illuminating warm light but now, he found himself on the train. The train bound for glory; the Gloryland Train.

He watched his grief-stricken mother and father standing over his lifeless body. It mourned his heart as he had observed them weeping, but not enough to make him want to return.

His mother was hysterical with grief as his uncles picked his lifeless body up and laid it on the bed in the room. He watched as his aunt Lanet gave his mother a sedative and pronounced he and his mother's mother dead. Finally, he watched as everyone, except his aunt Shera and uncle Kenny, stricken with grief leave the room.

His aunt Shera and uncle Kenny knelt beside his lifeless body. They placed their hands on his body and began to pray. Together, united as one, agreeing in prayer, they laid hands on him and called upon God to restore his spirit. They were not loud, nor did they fall on the floor weeping and wailing. Nor was their prayer long.

"Father God, we know what has happened is not of you. This is the work of the adversary. But we know you are Lord, and you are God. We ask you now Father God, to restore your spirit of life into your servant Thomas. Lord, you were with him in the beginning and we know he is with you now. We are your humble servants Lord, your children. In your word you said when two or three are gathered in my name, you would be in the midst. We are touching and agreeing Lord, on the return of your breath of life into our dear nephew. In the name of Jesus, your Son and our Savior, we ask you Father God. Amen."

Then they spoke to him. "Thomas, in the name of our Lord and Savior, Jesus Christ we command you to rise."

Still, he heard yet another voice calling out to God, pleading for his life.

Oh God, it's not supposed to end like this. It's not supposed to end like this, Lord.

They were quiet and ended their prayer by asking in the name of Jesus. Their prayer was so sweet, kind and loving. Little was moved. As he basked in the bright light, he heard a voice coming from the light say, "It's not yet your time Thomas. Go back." He felt a powerful force; it began drawing him back through the tunnel. Having already spent an eternity in the light, he pleaded with the voice to let him stay. He did not want to leave this place. His lifeless body began to convulse spasmodically as his lungs fought for oxygen. He started coughing uncontrollably. Each breath became precious as he continued to gasp for more air to come back into his lungs. Like in his nightmare, his body sucked in more air, than it let out. More air in, little air out, more in, little out. The rhythm continued until his breathing became easier. He was back. God had heard and answered their prayer.

Ruth slowly aroused from her state of shock as the sedative wore off. Elijah moved closer to her as she laid on the couch in the living room. Jerome, Lanet, Kenny, and Shera stood near her, patiently waiting for her to stir.

Awakened, Little kept hearing a ringing sound in his ear; it was the phone extension in the room. He wished someone would answer the phone, but it kept ringing. Finally, it stopped only to start again. Reluctantly, he picked up the bedroom extension. It was the hospital calling for Dr. Mears. He could not speak above a whisper. The caller identified himself as Dr. Gaither. He said to tell Dr. Mears the autopsy was complete, and the hospital was releasing her mother-in-law's body to the funeral home. His neck and throat burned with pain. It felt as if they were on fire. Wobbling to the bathroom, looking in the mirror, he saw the bandage covering his throat below his Adam's apple. Something deep within told him it wasn't just another bad dream. Staggering out the room, feeling weak, he rested on the foyer steps outside the living room before delivering the message. From where he sat, Little could hear his mother talking.

"I knew I shouldn't have come back here to Chicago. I was hoping, hoping she would have forgiven me by now. I should have known she wouldn't have changed."

"Bunny, it's alright," Jerome tried assuring her.

"No Jerome, it's not alright. You chose to believe she had a change of heart. I wanted so badly to believe you. You were wrong, and I was wrong for believing you. It's not all right. Everybody needs to stop saying it's all right. I've been carrying this thing around in me for more than twenty years. It has haunted me since the day it happened, and my son has suffered and almost died because of it. I was barely seventeen years old.

Yesterday…yesterday, it almost killed my son. Everyone thinks they know what happened. Everyone thinks they know why I left. Everyone thinks they know how I felt and why I didn't come back. Nobody knows. I'm sorry, but not even you Elijah. I never told anybody the whole truth. Not you; not even Betty. I want you to hear my side."

"You don't have to do this to yourself Bunny."

She continued weeping. "No, I have to."

"No, you don't."

"No, don't you understand I need to get it all out. I got to get the truth out. I've been carrying it around with me for too long, almost twenty-one years, and now it almost killed my child. It's time I got it out of me once and for all. Little has suffered because of it and almost died because of it."

Elijah cradled her in his arms. "It's alright to tell us baby, it's alright." Many nights, he was awakened by her reliving that evening in her sleep. She would cry out in pain, sometimes fighting him off as if he were her attacker. But she didn't know he knew what took place. The next morning, she woke up not remembering. He wanted more than anything for her nightmare to end. He knew the pain, the pain of carrying something around for so long. He knew the story. His ended, and he wanted hers to end too.

Pausing, as Ruth took a deep breath before speaking, curiously, Little slipped into the living room unnoticed. "It happened about two weeks before Bessie was killed by Bigger. He just got the job as a chauffeur with the Dalton family. That's the family of the white girl Bigger killed before he killed Bessie. Bigger and Bessie were going to go out and celebrate his getting the job. They asked me if I wanted to go along with them. Since times were so hard, and most colored people living in the black belt on the south side of Chicago were on relief, getting a job was a big cause to celebrate. He landed a good job. The Daltons' was a rich white family living not far from here in Hyde Park. Mr. Dalton and his wife were always giving money to all kinds of charities, and especially to colored people. During Biggers' trial, we found out that Mr. Dalton owned most of the slum buildings where all of us colored people lived along Indiana Avenue on the south side."

Ruth's mind began to wander back as she recalled the events. "I wasn't one for going to night clubs and drinking like Bessie, but I liked Bigger. He was nicer to me than he was to Bessie. I think Mamma and Bessie both knew it. She kept asking me to go, and back then, Mamma couldn't get enough of Bigger. Mamma loved him, and she kept telling me I ought to go. She said Bigger was nice enough to invite me, and I could at least be sociable and go. Finally, Mamma told me I had to go. So, like a dummy, I eventually gave in and went with them to the club."

Ruth again paused. "When we got to the club, Bessie kept pressuring me to have something to drink. I never had anything to drink before, and I never have had anything since, not even so much as a glass of wine. I didn't really want to drink, but Bigger bought me a drink called Long Island Tea. He kept saying it really didn't have alcohol in it, it wasn't that strong, and it was a drink for a lady. Bessie told me I had to drink it, so finally I drank it just to please Bigger and Bessie. I kept sipping on it till it was all gone. It was nice, but I didn't care that much for it. After it was all gone, I wasn't feeling too good. I was dizzy and feeling lightheaded. Bessie and her wild self drank so much until she got drunk as usual. Bigger said he'd help me get her back home.

To be honest, I don't remember how we got there or how long I had been home. It was late when we got home. I guess Mamma and Kenny must have already been asleep in bed. I thought Bigger was gone when I started getting undressed. Then, he came into the room. I don't know where he came from. He must have been standing on the other side of the door. I heard the door open, and when I turned around, there he was, standing in the room. I thought I was dreaming again. I had a schoolgirl crush on him."

Ruth eyes appeared glazed over as her mind transposed from the present to that night almost twenty-one years earlier. She began reliving the past. Lanet, recognizing her sister-in-law was on the verge of a mental breakdown, opted to give her a sedative.

Ruth protested as Lanet tried to prick her arm with the hypodermic needle. "No, please, I need to talk. I need to get it out," she cried.

"It's only a mild sedative, Ruth. You won't go to sleep. It will help you relax as you talk."

Reluctantly, Ruth consented. "Remember, I told him he had to leave, so I covered myself with a sheet and walked him to the door. First, he said he just wanted a kiss good night. Said he wanted a sort of a congratulations kiss for getting the job. I shouldn't have let him kiss me. It was stupid. I knew what I was doing, but then I didn't. It was like I wasn't in full control of myself. Like I was only dreaming like the other times. I guess I was still lightheaded from the drink. But then, I was no baby. I was seventeen, about to turn eighteen in May. It was the first time I was ever kissed by a boy. I was attracted to him. Every girl I knew was. He was a good-looking man, five feet nine with flawlessly smooth, jet-black skin. His facial lines were sharp with strong-boxed cheekbones. His eyes, black as coal, set deep in his head, teeth, big and white like pearls. Everybody knew he was one good-looking man."

The sedative began to take effect. Divorced from her body, Ruth was no longer herself. She slipped into what appeared to be a hypnotic state. As if she was an observer of the action-taking place, she began giving an account of what happened that night. "She liked him and desperately wanted him to take her into his powerful, muscular, black arms and kiss her with his thick dark lips. He did, and something exploded inside of her as his tongue slid into her mouth and gently stroked her palate. Their tongues locked. It was all so new; she had never been kissed before. She didn't want the feeling she got from the kiss to end. It was so passionate and felt so good. She became like putty in his rock-hard but gentle grasp. He commenced kissing her on the neck and simultaneously caressing her breasts with his hands. Her breasts had never been touched by a man or stimulated like that before. The nipples stood firm and erect in his hand as he played with them between his fingertips. She didn't want him to stop as her body yearned for more.

"The sheet she was using to cover her naked body slipped to the floor as she wrapped her arms around his neck. Her body began to gently quiver as he held her tightly. His shirt was open. That was when she felt his bold, broad chest for the first time, his washboard abdominal felt virtuous against her tiny waist. Never before had she experienced such an erotic sensation. He began kissing her breasts, then gently weighing them in the palm of his hand. Wrapping his long, slender fingers around them he began sucking on her fully erected nipple. The movement of his tongue on her nipple was driving her out of her mind.

"Losing all her senses, she began panting heavily and nibbling on his ear. She couldn't help herself from wrapping her legs around his waist. She didn't want him to stop doing what he was doing; it felt so good. Holding her, he guided her trembling body to the couch and laid her softly upon it. While meticulously kissing her inner thighs forcing her to spread her legs wider, his tongue gently stroked the inside of her vagina, tantalizing her clitoris. Warm nectar flowed from inside her. He said it was sweet honey in his mouth and was making his nature rise. Together, they lay naked, before she knew he was on top of her. The sweat from their hot naked bodies mingled together and fell gently upon the couch. She felt his strong back muscles as he softly pressed his nature against her. Panting heavily, she held onto his buttocks. Excited, he moaned with pleasure from the pain derived from her fingernails digging into his back. His nature became even harder. He begged her to dig harder, he loved the pain.

"Their hot bodies together covered with sweat, sweet sweat mingling together between their hot bodies. Sliding her hand over his smooth firm buttocks, she moved her hand between them. She touched his manhood. It stiffened in her hand. His erected manhood was long, thick, and hard. She felt it pulsating in her hand. He groaned in ecstasy as her slender fingers held his manhood. Wrapping her fingers around it, it grew harder and throbbed with pain. He couldn't control himself. Her eyes widened when he pushed himself inside of her."

Suddenly, Ruth's voice became very agitated. No longer divorced from the situation, she shouted, "That's when I realized what was happening. It wasn't a dream. It was really happening."

Coming out of her trance-like state, Ruth shouted, "'Oh no, Bigger, stop; please stop. I begged you to please stop. I never did it before. I'm still a virgin.' He didn't listen to me. He wouldn't stop. I cried, 'Please Bigger, oh please stop Bigger; don't do this to me, please.' I started crying, and I pleaded with him to stop, but he kept thrusting himself inside me."

"It's alright Ruth. It's alright. You don't have to say anymore," Lanet said consoling her.

She continued weeping. "No, I have to."

"No, we understand. It wasn't your fault."

"No, don't you understand I need to get it all out? I got to get the truth out. I've been carrying it around with me for too long. It's time I got it out of me once and for all. Little has suffered because of it and almost died because of it."

Divorcing herself from the scene, she testified to what he did. "He put his hand over my mouth and told me to be quiet before I woke everybody up. I was so scared. I didn't want to wake up the family, then again, I was afraid not to. I began beating him on his chest and tried squeezing my legs closed. The pain made him only desire me more. He grabbed my hands and pinned them over my head against the arm of the couch. With one hand, he held my arms there. With his wet body between mine, he forced my legs open as he wildly kissed and sucked on my breast.

"I was completely exposed and vulnerable to his manhood. I cried and begged him to stop. He pushed himself inside of me again. Oh the pain, the pain. I began crying. Savagely, like a ferocious beast, he continued to thrust his long, thick nature in me over and over again. Each time he penetrated me deeper and deeper. He was groaning wildly with pure delight. I wanted to scream, but I was afraid of the consequences of waking up the family. What would they say? What would they do? Afterwards, I felt him repeatedly and forcefully exploding inside of me. His juice, his seed was flowing inside of me. I could feel his seeds gushing inside of my womb. Like an erupting volcano, his body jerked uncontrollably. With each thrust of his body, he held on to me tightly. He screamed wildly with excruciating pleasure as he climaxed, as his seed burst forth in me.

"He conquered me, delighted himself in my budding womanhood and innocence. His heavy body laid limp and helpless on top of me. I was afraid to move. I remembered his muscles twitching with delight, him whimpering like a newborn puppy. Breathing heavily on my breast, exhausted with pleasure, he lay upon me for the next ten minutes softly whimpering how much he loved me, as I softly cried." After a while, I felt his nature soften and it slid out of me. It was over. I knew it was over." She softly whimpered.

Weeping, Elijah held his wife tighter as he comforted her, rocking back and forth. "It's alright, baby, you're safe now. Nobody will ever hurt you like that again, nobody, you're safe now."

Ruth slowly collected her thoughts. "Oh, God, I felt lost, confused and so filthy. I felt so violated, dirty and no good. I stayed on that couch all night and cried. What happened was my fault; it was my fault. I brought it on myself. I knew what I was doing. It was my fault.

"Next morning when Mamma got up and saw me lying there on the couch, she saw the blood and knew what had happened. I was scared to say anything to her. But I needed to tell somebody, so I told her. I told Mamma. She slapped me and called me a dirty little tramp, a strumpet, whore, and all other kinds of dirty names. She said I betrayed Bessie, my own sister because I slept with her boyfriend. She said it was my fault, that I seduced Bigger. Said she noticed that I had been trying to steal Bigger away from Bessie, and that I'd been lusting after him for a long time. She said I asked for it. Bessie, she knew too. That morning she laughed at me and said, 'Now you spoiled, Miss Sanctified.' No more Miss Pure and Holy and Miss Innocent. She called me a tramp. I didn't want to believe it. To think my own mother and sister were in on it. I cried and cried for days."

Ruth began to calm down. "It was about late March, after Bigger died in the electric chair when I found out I was pregnant. I didn't know what I was going to do. I was so scared. I couldn't say anything to Mamma. I was seventeen and pregnant by the man who killed my sister. I told Betty. She said I could still go to school and graduate from high school in June because I wasn't showing.

"I remember the morning I was washing up when Mamma came in the room. She saw my belly was getting big, and she knew I hadn't had my period. She asked me if I'd got myself knocked up. I started crying. She asked me whose baby was it. I told her Bigger was the only man that had me. She went crazy. Said she wanted me to get rid of it right away. Said she wasn't going to have that murdering nigger's bastard baby in her house. She went to see Miss Sophie. When she came back, she told me I was to see Miss Sophie the next day. I was so scared I didn't know what to do. One thing I did know, I didn't want Miss Sophie digging in my insides killing my baby. I never saw her like Mamma told me. A week later Mamma found out I didn't see Miss Sophie.

"I was in the kitchen cooking dinner. It was right before Kenny came home, when she came in the house and grabbed me by my hair and started beating me with the broom. She told me I had better go see Miss Sophie. I cried and said I couldn't do that. Told her I wasn't going to kill what was growing inside of me. It wasn't the baby's fault what his daddy did. I said I would give it up for adoption. She started screaming and beating me again. I fell on the floor, and she kicked me in my face and in my stomach. Said she was going to stomp the black murdering bastard's baby out of my belly. She said his baby didn't deserve coming into this world, and she was going to kill it. Kill it like he killed her Bessie. If Kenny hadn't come in she would have. He stopped her from killing me and my baby. She said for me to never set foot into her house again. Not until I got rid of the vile vermin inside of me. I said I wasn't going to kill my baby. She vowed, before she died she would kill it with her bare hands. I knew she would. So that same night, when she went out, I grabbed a few of my clothes and ran away to Betty's.

"Betty took me to see Mr. Boris Max, the lawyer that defended Bigger. That night, he called his friend and arranged for me to go to New York City. He said he would get my school records, so I could finish high school there. He said I couldn't contact anybody in my family until things calmed down. He said a lot of people were mad about Bigger. I couldn't even call you in California, Jerome. Cause if anybody found out they may come to New York after me and the baby. He said I should wait at least two years before I write anyone, even him.

"Things were really bad in Chicago with Bigger killing that rich white girl. White people were going crazy. After the trial, because of the death threats, Bigger's mother, his brother, Buddy, and his sister, Vera, had to leave Chicago. White folks were after revenge. They wanted blood, and they didn't care whose blood they spilled. When Bigger was on the run, the police turned loose mobs of white men in our area. They broke down colored folk's doors, searching from house to house for Bigger. Most colored folks were scared and mad at Bigger for what he'd done. They killed one poor girl's two-year-old baby because someone said it was Bigger's child. I was scared of what they might do to me if they found out I was carrying his baby. I was scared Mamma was gonna tell them I was carrying his baby if I didn't get rid of it. *The Tribune* had all kinds of stories every day. That March, when he was electrocuted, white folks were dancing in the street.

"I knew Mr. Max was right. So that night I took the train and moved to New York. It was safer there for me and my baby. Betty didn't want me going to New York by myself, so she said she would go with me. His friend met us at the train station in New York. He had arranged for me to get a live-in position caring for two elderly sisters in Harlem, and Betty got herself a job in the hospital's housekeeping department.

"When the baby was born, I named him Thomas Isaiah Mears. I gave him part of his daddy's name. I didn't hate Bigger, nor did I hate Mamma or Bessie for what they'd done. I hated what he did and what they did to me, but I didn't hate or blame them, and it wasn't the baby's fault. That same summer when I moved to New York, I met

Elijah. He lived in the same building just across the hall from the two sisters I was taking caring of. He was so kind and gentle. We fell in love before Thomas was born. He was with me the whole time, caring for me and for another man's baby. Elijah wanted to marry me before the baby was born. I wasn't sure if it was the right thing to do. Two months after Little was born, we married. That was six months after we met. He officially adopted Thomas and gave him his name. That's why his name is Thomas Isaiah Thomas. Elijah's middle name is Isaiah.

"Oh, Elijah, you've been good to us. I'm so sorry, I'm so sorry I never told you before. I'm so sorry, so sorry. You've been so good to me and so good to us. I'm so sorry. Please forgive me."

ESCAPE

The train continued along the track at a high speed. There was a rhythm to the sound of the wheels as the train rolled along the tracks. "Ticket please," the conductor called out as he walked along the isle checking the passenger's ticket. "Ticket please." Absorbed in his thoughts, Little did not hear him. "Excuse me son, I need to see your ticket." Looking up, Little passed the conductor his ticket. Taking it back, he returned to looking out of the window. Glancing at his watch, he noticed it was eleven-thirty. Turning again to the window, he watched as his warm breath met the cold window creating a frost. Playfully, he blew on the window enlarging the patch of frost. In the window he saw his refection. Carefully, he opened the collar of his shirt to reveal the bandage covering the incision in his neck. Touching his throat, he softly caressed it. Sore, it throbbed with pain. *Funeral service at the church should almost be over by now. Service was scheduled to begin at nine-thirty this morning, same time the train was leaving the station. The family left the house at eight o'clock. I had just enough time to make it to the station to catch this nine-thirty express.*

It was a small family gathering at the church with a few friends and well-wishers in attendance. As customary, everyone was dressed in black. The men in black suits and the women wore black dresses with black gloves and hats. The minister tried to comfort the family by preaching the elderly Mears, whom he did not know, into heaven. The snow the night before blanketed the graveyard, making their path to the burial site difficult. The earth was cold and hard beneath their feet.

Frost streamed from the mouths of the attendees. The graveside service was very short as the minister said the final words, "Ashes to ashes, dust to dust. Into thy hands, we command her spirit, oh Lord."

All the children and the grandchildren filed past the coffin placing a flower on top of it. The guests followed. It was over. The procession of cars rolled onto Woodlawn Avenue to Jerome and Lanet's house. The guests, coworkers from the hospital, firm and university came in to show their respect to the Mears family and partake in the abundance of food that many had provided for the family of the deceased.

Little suspected no one would miss him until well after the guest had left. This was one funeral he definitely did not want to attend. The family had agreed, physically and mentally, attending was not in his best interest. Healthwise, exposure to the icy cold weather would not be good for him. However, there was a greater underlying reason. He knew the one person that did not want him to attend was the deceased. *Just to spite her, maybe I should have gone, made her turnover in her coffin. It would serve her right.*

When the family left the house to attend the service, he gathered his few belongings and left ten minutes after them. He figured perhaps, somewhere around one or two o'clock someone should find the letter he left for his parents on the pillow in the bedroom where he had been sleeping. Either way, he knew by the time they discovered he was gone, he would be miles and miles away.

Arriving home from the cemetery, Jerome, concerned about his nephew, decided to look in on him. He saw the envelope pinned to the pillow. Without hesitating, he found Elijah. "Elijah, I need you to help me with something in the den." In the den, he immediately handed him the letter. "Little is not here. I found this envelope on his pillow."

Slowly, Elijah opened the envelope, took out the letter and began reading. Reading the first paragraph, fear engulfed him, causing his body to go limp. Grabbing a hold of the chair as he knees buckled, he murmured, "Oh Lord. Lord. Hell's fire is a burnin' in Canaan. Not this time. I gotta save my child from the flames. Jerome, this time I gotta save my family from the fire. I can't die like I did before. I have to save myself," he said in a low voice as he turned his back to Jerome.

"Elijah, what wrong? What do you mean?"

"Little is gone. He didn't say where," he replied passing the letter to Jerome. Jerome read the letter. "Jerome, I don't know how much more Ruth can take. Now, now that Little has run away, I'm scared it's going to drive her over the edge. It's going kill her."

Jerome placed his hand on Elijah's shoulder. "Elijah, he hasn't run away. He said in the letter he needed to get away to think. He wants to give himself some time to think. He's confused and needs to sort things out in his head."

Elijah resumed his composure. "Be best to wait until the guests leave before sharing the letter with Ruth. I think it will be good if Kenneth and Shera be here when I tell her Little is gone."

"I agree. It's going to be difficult keeping Ruth from wanting to check on him. But whatever you do, don't say he's run away."

"I know. I'll try my best to keep her occupied." Not wanting to upset Ruth, Elijah stayed close to her side mainly to keep her occupied, as he said he would. Several times, she insisted upon going upstairs to check in on Little. "Ruth baby, he's resting. Let the boy rest. He needs the rest," he insisted. Finally, when the last guests left, the three couples retired into the living room.

"Don't worry about cleaning up, Ruth," Lanet stated. "I've hired a service to come in the morning." Sitting down next to her husband, she kicked off her shoes and leaned against him. "It was nice of Loretta and Ben to take all the children to their place. I know the children always have fun on their farm."

"Ruth."

"Yes Elijah."

Everyone gathered around sitting close to each other.

"What's wrong Elijah? Something is wrong! What's wrong?"

"Nothing is wrong. I just need to tell you something. It's about Little, honey."

Ruth sat up straight on the couch. "What about Little?"

"He's gone," he said passing the letter to her.

"Gone? Gone where?"

"Baby, he left us a letter."

Ruth jumped to her feet. "What do you mean he's gone? Gone where Elijah?"

"Here baby," he took her by the hand. "Sit down please. I mean he's left. Here, he left us a letter explaining everything."

Ruth took the letter. "Oh God, what else? What else is going to happen?" She looked at the letter in her hand. All his letters she had kept and cherished, reading them over and over again. But this letter, not this one. "No, no, I can't read this. Not now Elijah! Not now! Why, oh why did I ever come back here to Chicago?" she cried shaking her head and trembling. "Here Elijah, you read it," she gasped as she passed the letter back to him.

Elijah slowly unfolded the letter and read it aloud.

Dear Family,

By the time you find this letter, I will have been gone for several hours. I left right after you left for the funeral services.

First, I want to apologize for leaving the way I did. I hope you will understand, if you do, then you're better than me because I can't really say I understand everything myself. However, I do know I can't stay with you any longer. You would have tried to stop me if you had known I was planning to leave. I would have respected your wishes and placed them above my own need. Therefore, I decided not to tell anyone. If I left over your objection, it would be disrespecting you. In all my life, that is something I've never done intentionally. But, the way I feel, I would have had to leave. If I didn't, I would have died inside.

Secondly, please do not worry about me. I will tell you where I am and contact you when I arrived at where I am going. I know the pain you have endured, and I don't want to cause you any more pain than what you have already suffered. If at times my letter seems harsh or cold, I mean no disrespect. I am only expressing what I'm feeling inside. It is not my intention to blame or hurt either of you. Most of all, rest assured, I have no intentions of hurting myself. I would never give your mother that satisfaction.

You're probably wondering what is going on in my head. I don't know what's going on in my own head. The truth is, I am confused, and I won't lie—I am scared. I don't know who I am or what I am. In the last few days, so much has happened to me. There was so much that I didn't understand, much of which I now know. All of which is why I feel my whole life has been a lie. I will try to explain.

Mother, when you called to tell me your mother was dying, I had many questions. I never knew your mother was alive. Nor did I know you were from Chicago. You led me to believe you lived all your life in New York. You lied to me. I realize that now you're a stranger. I don't really know anything about you. I have a lot of questions. I was angry because there was no time to ask the questions I had, nor was there anyone to ask. Knowing what I know now, you probably would not have answered them. I think I didn't ask the questions because I was also afraid of the answers. I didn't know what would become of us as a family. Tragically, look at what has happened.

After the initial shock about your mother and Chicago, I then found out that you had two brothers and a dead sister. In all my twenty years, you never spoke of your mother, brothers, or sister.

You raised me to believe Grandma Edna was your mother, Mimi Rhoda was my great aunt, Aunt Betty your only sister, and you grew up in New York. Now, I find out Grandma Edna, Mimi Rhoda, and Aunt Betty are no more my blood relatives…

As Elijah's eyes fell upon the rest of the sentence, he paused. A lump developed in his throat. He knew he had to be strong for his wife, but is own spirit was wounded. Buried deep in his subconscious mind was the truth. That which he had always known but had forgotten or just refused to acknowledge was now thrust into the open for him to face. It was a painfully reminder of the truth. He could see the flame leaping from the letter reaching out to engulf him. Grievously, he passed his hand over his head and bit into his lower lip. His voice faltered as he tried to read aloud the words. A tear dropped on the letter, landing next to the stain left by Little's tears. Quivering lips and trembling hand, he tried to read but his voice continued to crack.

Jerome, seeing his brother-in-law struggle, moved next to him, placed a reassuring hand upon his shoulder and he gently tried to remove the letter from Elijah's massive trembling hand.

A grieving Elijah reluctantly gave up the letter with a brief struggle. Looking up at Jerome, Elijah gave him a nod of approval to read the letter. Gingerly, Jerome read as a brokenhearted Elijah listened.

> Now, I find out Grandma Edna, Mimi Rhoda, and Aunt Betty are no more my blood relatives than Elijah is my father. The man whom I was raised to believe was my father.
>
> Hearing this, Ruth gasped loudly as she buried her face in her hands.
>
> That's right. I learned the truth after your mother tried to kill me. Elijah is not my father. I know, now, I heard the entire story that night from your lips. My fathers' name is Bigger Thomas. He was from Mississippi, arrived in Chicago five years before he died. I am the son of Bigger Thomas. That's right, the man who killed your sister Bessie, a rich white girl, and the same man that raped you. I heard the entire story. I can't imagine you're having to live with the knowledge of being raped. I know it was painful for you to have kept such a secret for almost twenty-one years.

Especially when I, the result of that rape, was there to remind you of it each and every day for the past twenty years, and now for the rest of your and my natural life. A truth we will all take to our graves. I believe it was painful for you to tell it. I just want you to know it was equally painful and devastating for me to learn of it. Especially in the manner I did. Yes, I now know I am the son of a two-time murdering rapist. It scares me, and I wonder what evil lurks inside of me.

When we first arrived in Chicago, I felt I had been there before. I recognized many of the streets and buildings. I now know why. I have been there every February, for as far back as I can remember. That's right, the reoccurring nightmare I had each year. It wasn't about me. It was about him, Bigger Thomas, who is a very big part of me. Year after year, I suffered from those nightmares and you, if anybody, knew how those nightmares tormented me year after year. Moreover, you and you alone had the power to make them stop. You chose not to. How could you have let me suffer all these years over and over again? I want to know why you didn't stop them. You know how I suffered, and I wondered why. I didn't do anything. If you truly loved me, you would not have allowed me to suffer like that. For that, I can hate you.

I have two wonderful aunts and uncles. You also intentionally deprived me from knowing them and them from knowing me. Aunt Lanet and Uncle Jerome, Aunt Shera, and Uncle Kenneth, considering what I've done, I pray you do not think unkindly of me. You don't know how much it means to me to know I have real aunts, uncles, and cousins. I really wish I could have spent more time with you. Perhaps, one day in the future, we will. I really want to get to know you better and for you to know me. I truly believe you're wonderful people. Maybe, you can tell me what kind of mother would set her own daughter up to be raped? And to think, her sister was in on it. How sick! A woman so consumed with hatred that, twenty years later, she would try to kill her own daughter's child for the second time. I don't understand, and it scares me. Having sprung from the loins of a vile, savage animal scares me. I can only wonder what's in me. Knowing what I know, I wish she had kicked me out of your belly. I pray that there is more of you in me than the evil that was in her and Bigger. Fortunately, I can say some good has come out of this mess. Elisha and Esther will grow up knowing you and their cousins. And again, God answered your prayers.

Elijah, thank you for adopting me, caring, and loving me for all these years. I want to believe you tried to do the right thing. Despite my hurt and pain, you are the only father I have known for the past twenty years. I hope I will someday again consider you my father. I pray you understand my confusion and my anger. You've always been there for me, but you are not totally innocent. You also knew. You could have told me the truth, but you chose not to. Forgive me, but I now feel I was only a substitute for the son you lost in the fire. I pray I'm wrong, but considering all that I now know, I can't help the way I feel. If you can, please tell me why I feel the way I do? But then, I'm not your son. You're a kind, decent, and gentle man, not the lying, murdering, rapist that sired me. But that's who I am. I'm the son of Bigger Thomas. Funny, I even have his name. I wonder what else.

This all could have been avoided if you had only raised me with the truth. The scar around my neck no doubt will someday heal, and I'll get my voice back. Who knows, the scar may even disappear. If it does not, like I am to your mother, it will serve as a reminder of what a pathetic, dysfunctional, lying family I have. What hurts the most is not the physical scar. What this has done to me psychologically and emotionally will never heal. I have both of you to thank for that. Please, don't think I hate you. How could I when I'm just now realizing I really don't know you? You're not who I thought you were or who you said you were. Nor am I the person I was raised believing I am. Right now, I feel so despicable, so dirty and unworthy. I don't know who I am or what I am. I need to find out. For me to find out, I can't be around any of you.

Please say good-bye to Elisha and Esther. Isn't it funny, when it comes to leaving without saying good-bye to family, I guess in this regard we're both alike, Mother. Tell them I love them. I will talk to them as soon as my voice comes back. Also, hurting the ones we love seems to be another trait we share. Do me just one favor, tell them the truth. Don't let them grow up living a lie like you let me. If you don't tell them, I promise you I will.

I can't help but wonder if there is something else you're hiding from me. I need to get away to think, and too clear my mind and too find myself. Again, don't worry about me. To show you I'm not a complete monster like Bigger, on my behalf and for your peace of mind, in a few days I'll have someone call you for me to let you know I'm safe. Whatever you do, don't try to find me. Just like Mr. Max helped you disappear; I must now perform the same vanishing act.

Sincerely,
Thomas the Bastard

Ruth sat in shock and disbelief. Once joy had filled her heart; just days ago she relished receiving letters from her firstborn child. Now, only sorrow filled her heart, her heart was torn with grief.

Shaking uncontrollably while thrusting her face into her hands, she cried. "Elijah, oh Elijah, what have I done? What have I done? Please, somebody tell me what have I done? Oh God, will I ever see my son again? Oh dear God, will I ever see our son again?" Looking at her husband, she buried her face in his chest and wept.

Just a short time ago, Elijah had a disturbing premonition.

MOVING ALONG

The train continued speeding along the tracks, occasionally stopping at a station in cities along the route. Physically, Little tried to get comfortable, but the more he tried, the less comfortable he became psychologically. Wound up, his mind would not let him rest, the pain would not let him sleep. Seeing his face reflected in the train window made him think back to his first day at UNE and Mrs. Henderson. For him, UNE had been nothing but a menagerie of psychological pain. Racial attacks, the word nigger scribbled on his dormitory room door. Students refusing to sit at the same table with him, as if he had leprosy, or maybe they were afraid his color would rub off. How insensitive—wanting to feel his hair as if he were an oddity. Constantly being asked how tall he was and if he played basketball. To him the presidential scholar group was a big joke. It was an exclusive, a "whites only" organization. He did not fit their bill. Initially, he made himself available to them until he got tired of being rejected. It was only because he was a PS that the university took notice of what was happening to the black students on campus. Cranston was shocked and tried to have his scholarship revoked. The only good thing that happened was the president revoked Cranston's scholarship after finding out he was the one that wrote the word nigger on his door. King of the Clambake. It was only an exercise in futility. He didn't belong. Why did he stay? The comment he hated most was being told, "I don't think of you as a Negro" and "you're not like the rest of them."

He not only had to endure ignorant treatment from the students, but also from the faculty and administrators. First, there was the incident in Hauser's class. Later, it turned out Fiedmann, his psychology professor, was racist. She accused him of cheating on her test. He thought about her comment. "I never had a student like you make an A on my test before." Last semester, a teacher accused him of plagiarism. The professor even had the audacity to ask him in front of the class if he knew the definition of a word. He thought about Dr. Garvey at the presidential scholar dinner during parent weekend. He said, "Thomas is a credit to his race." *A credit to his race, what the hell was that supposed to mean?* "All the Negro students should be as proud of him as his parents and as we are at the university." The man had no clue he was insulting him. To Little, his comments were just lies. Every time they needed a face for a magazine, television or newspaper, it was a white face. He was constantly overlooked when it came to publications. But when they wanted to get government funds or to impress someone with the caliber of students, when they needed a Negro student to speak at the NAACP banquet or for race relations, that's when they called him. The school was using him. They knew it and so did he. Sometimes, he had to question Waldstriecher's behavior. But he soon learned Waldstriecher didn't care about anything but his nuclear project.

Little despised the university, and he harbored a deep feeling of contempt for many of the students and administrators. Since Stephanie and Alejandro graduated, things changed. Had it not been for Michael, his Alpha Phi Alpha Fraternity brothers, and Dr. Hamilton, he would have left after his first year. They were the only people willing and able to help him. When he complained about the treatment of Negro students on campus, it fell on deaf ears. Racewise, there were many problems at the university, and they either didn't know it, refused to acknowledge it, or said he was being too sensitive.

However, above all for Little, it was from the loneliness that he suffered most. *While other students pair off or find someone special, I have no one. Female companionship is missing in my life. There's an expectation by whites that all black students are compatible. Just like every white person does not like every white person they come in contact with, not every black person likes every black person they meet. Not all black students like the same music or share the same opinion. The few black students enrolled at the university are expected to get along. While some did, others didn't. On the surface, they all get along, they have a common enemy. I know it is all superficial. It's all a facade.* Little's mind kept ticking and ticking and ticking until his head hurt. Inside, he cried, he wished he could shut it off.

Five hours passed. The conductor announced the train was entering the St. Louis, Missouri station. Glancing at his watch, he thought, *By now, they should have read the letter.*

His stomach growled since the train pulled out of Peoria, Illinois two hours ago. The growling only reminded him that he had not eaten breakfast or lunch. Because he was still in shock, he had not eaten anything since the night before. Even then, his aunt Lanet had to force him to eat the little bit of soup he had.

The train finally slowed as it entered the station. The conductor announced they were arriving at track number fifteen. Little knew he would have to change trains in St. Louis. Listening as the conductor called out the different train connections, and the track they would be departing from, he heard him call out, "Kansas City, Kansas." That was his train. "Track number seven, departing at two forty-five." It was two twenty-five. That gave him twenty minutes to find track seven. His stomach again growled from hunger. As he stood up, he felt weak and faint. Exiting the train, he decided he'd better grab something to eat before finding the track. Seeing a concession stand, he got a hot dog and a soda. Finding track seven, boarding the train, he found the nearest seat. Seated, he started eating his first meal of the day. Swallowing made his throat palpitate with excruciating pain. Was it the pain from hunger or the pain from swallowing? He had to make a choice. Throwing away the hot dog, he had to be content with drinking the soda.

The trip to Kansas City, Kansas, was three and a-half hours long. In Kansas City, he had to take a local to Lawrence, Kansas. There, he'll call Michael from the station. As he thought about his plan, he remembered no one was aware of where he was going. Not even Michael was aware of his coming. He decided when he arrived in Kansas City he would call Michael to make sure it was alright for him to come for a visit. He didn't think it would be a problem, after all, Michael did extend the invitation. He had met Michael's parents on several occasions. They seemed to like him and told him he was always welcome at their home.

They also knew Swoosh. Mrs. Griffin told him Swoosh was over their house all the time. She said Swoosh spoke of him so much that she felt as if she already knew him. "All Swoosh talks about is his brother Little, and Michael also speaks very highly of you." But then, he thought, *how do I explain to them out of the clear blue my just showing up at their doorstep?* The last thing he wanted to do was think about his problems. First there was UNE, then his family, and now this. *Too late to turn back; you've come a long way, and you're almost there.*

Little dismissed the thoughts from his mind. As the train started out of the station with something in his belly, he surrendered to the weariness of his body.

"Kansas City, Kansas," the conductor called out, "Son, isn't this your stop? To go to Lawrence, Kansas, you have to change trains here." Little gathered his bag, exited the train, and went into the station. He had a half-hour wait for the train to Lawrence. Then it would be at half hour ride before he arrived there.

He could not speak at all. Aggravated from the food and soda, his throat was extremely swollen, and throbbed with pain. His injury and the cold weather made his throat hurt more. The swelling made his breathing difficult. Using a pad and pencil, he asked a lady to make the call to Michael's house for him. She was very kind and helped him out. She explained to Michael that his friend had a terrible case of laryngitis and asked her to call. Michael said he would be waiting for Little at the station in Lawrence.

It was a pleasant surprise for Little. Swoosh was at the station with Michael. Seeing Swoosh, he felt he was looking at the only true family member he had in this world. Tears came to his eyes as they hugged each other. He struggled to speak. He wanted to speak to his friend and brother.

"Little," Swoosh said encouraging him not to talk. He joked. "All the time I wished you would say something to me, and now I don't want you to speak. This has got to be a switch."

"Yeah man, don't talk," Michael added. "I don't know if you remember, but my dad is a doctor. I'll ask him to look at your throat when we get to the house. Okay?"

"Hey bro, what's this Michael told me about your grandmother? I thought Grandma Edna was Madear's mother."

Unable to talk, Little shrugged his shoulders and shook his head. Using his hands, he motioned to Swoosh.

Swoosh laughed. "What is this? Charade? Ah, we're using hand signals now. Okay, okay go ahead."

Swoosh and Michael tried to interpret as Little continued to make hand gestures. Cupping his hands together at the wrist, he formed a 'Y'.

"Let's see, Y."

Little nodded his head in the affirmative as he pointed to his eye.

"Okay, eye."

He shook his head yes and pulled his hair.

"Head."

Little shook his head no.

"No not head, hair. Why I. Yeah. I got it." Swoosh said bouncing up and down with excitement. "Why am I hair? Here. Oh. Why am I here? I'm playing in an exhibition game on December 21."

The trio continued playing their game until they arrived at Michael's house.

After greetings were over, Mrs. Griffin persuaded Little to take a few sips of some Campbell's Tomato soup for nourishment. He found the soup was not nearly as painful as the hot dog. He was hungry and managed to scoff down two bowls.

"Okay Little," Dr. Griffin said holding a small flashlight and tongue depressor. "Now that you've finished eating, let me take a look at your throat. Now, open wide."

Little opened his mouth while Dr. Griffin examined his throat. Little was hesitant and flinched before allowing him to remove the bandage covering the stitches. Again, he flinched as Dr. Griffin touched the stitches. Curiously, Dr. Griffin examined them. "Little, did you have an accident? Were you hit in the throat?" Little nodded in affirmation. Continuing to examine his neck, Mr. Griffin noticed the laceration. "The incision is healing nicely. Right now, all I can do is give you something for the pain. It will take some time for the swelling to go down."

Mrs. Griffin touched Little lightly on the shoulder. "Little, do you need to call your parents to let them know you're here?"

Little had not thought about it. *I really don't want them to know where I am.* To avoid a confrontation and himself some embarrassment Little nodded yes. Picking up the pen and paper on the table, he wrote down his uncle Jerome's number. Along with their telephone number in his note he wrote, parents at my uncle's house in Chicago. Tell them I arrived safely. Don't tell them about throat swelling; don't want to worry them. Thank you.

"Hello, this is Lance Griffin in Lawrence, Kansas. I'm trying to contact a Mr. or Mrs. Elijah Thomas."

Pause.

"A visitor must have answered the phone."

"Yes, this is Lance Griffin, Michael Griffin's father. I believe my son attends the University of New England with your son Thomas."

Pause.

"I know Little is not there, that's why I'm calling you. He's here in Kansas at our home. He has laryngitis, so he asked me to call you to let you know he arrived safely.

Pause.

"Yes, he is all right. I'm a doctor, I hope you don't mind—I checked his throat. The sutures in his neck are healing as expected."

Pause.

"Okay, let me give you my number." Dr. Griffin called out his phone number. "Would you like to speak to him?"

Pause.

"He just won't be able to answer you. I think the cold air caused it to hurt a little. Little, telephone," he said handing the phone to him. "Your father wants to speak to you."

Reluctantly, Little took the phone from Dr. Griffin and listened.

Elijah instructed his wife. "Whatever you do, when you talk to Little don't ask him when he is coming back. Just let him know you're glad that he is safe and that he called and that you love him. Okay? Whatever you do, don't cry."

"I'll try."

For everyone in the Mears's household, waiting for Little's phone call had appeared to be an eternity. Ruth cried with joy just to know her son was all right. Although they had not met his parents, Ruth and Elijah had met Michael at the university. Talking with Dr. Griffin, they felt assured he was at a safe place.

"Was that Little calling?" asked Jerome.

Elijah replied, "That was him. He's staying at a friend of his from college; Michael Griffin, in Lawrence, Kansas. We just spoke with his father, Lance Griffin. Little used to speak about him a lot."

Lanet, who had been listening to the conversation, perked up her ears.

"Lance Griffin. Do you know if he's a doctor?"

"He is. He said he looked at Little's throat. Apparently, the cold weather made it swell. He said he gave him something to help with the pain. He said the sutures are okay."

"We know him. We worked together and we belong to the same medical association. We know him and his wife Cynthia very well. We know Lance and his family. I forgot that his son Michael, attends UNE. When I was an intern, Lance was my supervisor. He was the one that assigned Jerome to me as a patient. He's responsible for Jerome and me getting married. I'm surprised he didn't recognize the telephone number. Ruth and Elijah, I think it's extremely important that we let Little know we know the Griffins. If you don't mind, I'll give him a call."

"Why? I don't feel that's necessary," Ruth protested.

"The truth; it's the truth. If Little finds out accidentally then he'll feel we are hiding the truth from him. He may also feel the Griffins betrayed him. If that happens, there's no telling where he might run off to or what he might do."

Elijah looked intently at his wife. "Lanet and Jerome, we know you're right. Right now, Little is so mixed up and confused honey. He feels his mother and me are against him. He's feeling so hurt and alone. I know, I've been there, and so have you Ruth. There's no need to add more fuel to the fire already burning inside of him; especially when we can prevent it. Call Dr. Griffin and talk to him. See what he thinks would be the best way to handle it."

With everyone's blessing Lanet called. "Hello Lance."

Pause.

"Yes, it's me Lanet."

Pause

"Oh, we're just fine. Jerome's mother died, and we buried her today."

Pause.

"I'm sorry we didn't let you know. It was just a small family service."

Pause.

"Thank you, I know you and Cynthia would have. I'll be sure to let Jerome know. Listen, this is really not a social call. Little, Thomas, is our nephew. He's Jerome's sister's child, Ruth Thomas. He just called here a few minutes ago from your house."

Pause

"That's right. I thought you would have recognized the number."

Pause.

"No, no please, don't get him just yet. I want to talk to you first. There was a small problem here. You see, Little overheard some extremely disturbing news; that's why he left and showed up at your place."

Pause.

"I prefer not to say right now. I won't tell you unless Little says it's alright to discuss it with you."

Pause.

"Yes, it has a lot to do with the lacerations around his neck and the bruised larynx. I did the tracheotomy."

Pause.

"No, it's nothing like that. His parents are good people; they would never intentionally harm any of their children. But it is serious. He needs to talk, get it out. Believe me I hope he does feel comfortable enough to talk with you. He really needs to and should talk to somebody."

Pause.

"Swoosh. No, I haven't met him. But while he was here, he mentioned his name several times." Lanet looked over at Ruth and Elijah. "Lance said Little's best friend Swoosh is there. He'll be playing in a basketball tournament and is supposed to leave the day before Christmas."

Ruth sighed. "That's good. Little and Swoosh are very close. They're like brothers."

"His parents are glad Swoosh is with him. Maybe he'll talk to him. I'm glad Swoosh is there too. Lance, let me talk to Little now."

Pause.

"Hello, Little, it's me, your aunt Lanet. I know because of your throat you can't answer me back, so just listen. Tap on the receiver once for no and twice for yes. Okay?"

Little tapped twice.

"First, baby, we are not mad or upset with you. We're glad you called and you're safe. We do understand why you felt it necessary to leave. I'm calling because we want you to know Dr. Griffin and his family—they're friends of ours. We first met them when I was in medical school. We felt it was very important that we let you know that. Okay?"

Two taps.

"Lance is an excellent doctor. I trust him explicitly. He'll know how to treat your neck and throat. Let him treat you. Okay, baby?"

Two taps.

"We know you may want to talk to someone. You've been through a lot these last few days. Only if you say it is okay to get things started, I'll talk to Lance about what happened with your grandmother and mother. He'll understand why it was important for you to get away for a while and help you put things in their proper perspective."

Very long pause. She could hear him sniffing.

"Little, I won't say anything if you say no. It's up to you baby."

After another long pause, she heard one tap.

"Okay. Trust me, I won't say anything. If at any time you should change your mind, just let me know. Okay?"

Two taps.

"We love you Little, and your parents love you too. If you need anything, just pick up the phone. I don't care where you are or what time of day or night it is. Okay?"

Two taps. Pause.

"Let me talk to Lance."

Pause.

"Lance, he doesn't want me to say anything to you right now. Please, keep us posted on his condition. I know you and Cynthia will be there for him. His parents and I appreciate it very much."

Pause.

"I'll talk to you later. We're glad he's there with you. Thanks again Lance."

Little's throat still swollen, made it difficult for him to breathe. A concerned Dr. Griffin decided to monitor him through the night. Because Michael liked his room on the cool side, Mrs. Griffin suggested Little and Swoosh sleep together in the guest room. Swoosh joked saying it would be like old times, him taking care of his little brother, Little.

Little emerged from the bathroom and sat on the edge of the bed. Swoosh entered the room and immediately saw the bandage on his throat. Looking closer, he saw the lacerations around his neck.

"Little, what happened to your neck?"

Little motioned for Swoosh to leave him alone as he rolled back the covers and slid into the bed.

"Are you alright?"

Little nodded his head in the affirmative and slid the covers over his head. Before laying his head on the pillow, he sniffed it for her smell.

Tired, both boys fell asleep. Shortly thereafter, Little awakened finding it difficult to breathe. Agitated and disturbed, he gasped for air as he laid in the bed, thinking. In his mind, he kept repeating twenty-one years.

Twenty-one years, she carried it for twenty-one years. The thought of his carrying what happened another day began to haunt him. Little began weeping as he sat up in bed and held his pounding head. The more he wept, the more difficult his breathing became. His erratic breathing and restlessness woke up Swoosh.

"What's wrong Little?"

Gasping for air, Little struggled to breathe, but it was not his swollen throat that was most painful. What hurt most was what was eating away at him inside. He motioned for Swoosh to leave him alone as he fell back on the bed and continued to gasp for air.

Swoosh sat up in the bed and began to shake him. "Oh God, Little! Little, what's wrong?"

Again, he motioned for Swoosh to leave him alone.

"I'll go get Dr. Griffin."

Little shook his head no. Wanting to stop the pain inside, Little motioned for Swoosh to get the pad and pencil. Taking the pad, he scribbled, Elijah, not my father, Madear raped. Dr. Griffin call Aunt Lanet.

After writing the note, he fell back on the bed and began desperately gasping for air.

Fear swept Swoosh as he read the note. "Little, what are you saying?" Staring at Little, Swoosh felt helpless on both accounts. Scared by his gasping for air and the content of the note. Swoosh started screaming. Racing to the door, he opened it and yelled down the hall. "Oh God, Doc Lance, Doc Lance help me. Somebody help me."

Struggling for air, Little collapsed on the bed. His eyes turned back into his head and his body began twitching.

Frightened and panicking, Swoosh sat on the bed and held Little in his arms and began rocking him back and forth. "Don't die, Little, don't die. Please don't die," he cried as he held Little in his arms. "Doc Lance, Doc Lance, help me. Somebody please, help me."

"What's going on?" Michael asked as he rushed the room. Seeing Little's twitching body, he immediately began yelling down the hall, "Dad, Dad, come quick! It's Little. Something's wrong with Little, he's having a seizure!"

"What's wrong?" Dr. Griffin shouted as he rushed into the room followed by Mrs. Griffin.

"He can't breathe Doc Lance. Little can't breathe. He's dying, help my brother, he's dying," Swoosh cried. "Don't die Little, oh please don't let him die."

"Michael, quick get my bag by the front door." Immediately, he checked Little's pulse. Then he put his hand on Swoosh's shoulder. "He's going to be all right Jerald. Don't worry, he's going to be all right."

Tearfully Swoosh cried, "Oh please don't let him die Doc. Lance. Please don't let my brother die," he continued to cry as he cradled Little in his arms.

"Don't worry Jerald, I'm not going to let anything happen to him. He'll be all right." Michael returned with his bag. Opening it, he took out a vile of medication and a needle. "Okay I need you to hold him still for me, Jerald."

Swoosh stopped rocking and held Little tightly.

"That's right; hold him still. Good, just like that. I need to give him this injection." Using the needle, Dr. Griffin administered some medication into Little's arm. "Thomas, this is going to help you breathe easier, and it will stop the seizures. Okay? You'll feel it in a few minutes. Try to relax, son, and breathe slowly."

Little looked up at Dr. Griffin acknowledging he understood. After a few minutes, his breathing began stabilizing.

Swoosh showed Dr. Griffin the pad, "Look what he wrote Doc Lance. I don't know what he means. What does it mean? He said for you to call his aunt. Why does he want you to call his aunt?"

Swoosh continued to cradle Little in his arms rocking back and forth with his head resting atop of Little's. Breathing easier, exhausted and feeling secure, they slowly drifted off to sleep.

BOOK FOUR

FLYING HIGH

A cold chilling wind whipped through the nation's heartland. The midmorning was overcast with heavy black thunder clouds filling the sky; a heavy snow threatened to fall deeply upon the earth below. It had snowed for the past three days; a blanket of white laid beyond the horizon as far as the eye could see. Pathways through the snow, from the houses and driveways to the street, marked the landscape.

The only visible things at ground level were stretches of black tar pavement. To this end, the streets were plowed. It was now possible for the breadwinner of the household to make it safely to work, for the school buses to pick up children, and for the general traffickers to travel about town. The Griffins and Little made their way down the streets to begin the second part of what would become his long journey home.

Arriving at their destination, they found the airport terminal was crowded with mostly businessmen and college students traveling back to school after the long holidays. Most of the travelers, weary and worn, were scrambling around nervously. Sighs, moans, and groans could be heard echoing each time an announcement was made regarding another flight cancellation or delay. Checking his bags at the terminal, Little listened for the announcer to announce the gate from which he was scheduled to depart. He was one of the fortunate ones. Upon hearing the announcement of his departing flight, he was accompanied by Dr. and Mrs. Griffin to the gate. He walked over and stood in line.

Kissing him good-bye Mrs. Griffin asked, "Thomas, are you sure you have everything?"

"I seem to be leaving with more than I had when I arrived a few weeks ago. I want to thank you for everything, opening up your home, your hearts, and listening to my problems. I don't know what I might have done if you hadn't been there for me."

Dr. Griffin placed his hand on Little's shoulder. "Son, you don't have to thank us. We were more than happy to have been there for you. And you know everything is going to be alright. Just remember to always trust and believe in God. Don't forget, if you need anything, I don't care how big or small, don't hesitate to call us. Okay?"

"Yes sir, I promise I will." The announcement came over the loudspeaker calling for the final boarding of flight 732 to Lambert, St. Louis International Airport and Chicago's O'Hara Airport. Little hugged Dr. and Mrs. Griffin. "I love you both," he exclaimed as he dashed out of the exit.

"You have a good flight and call us when you arrive," shouted Mrs. Griffin as she waved good-bye."

"I will, and thanks again for everything." Little was a little bit nervous as he walked through the gate to the airplane. As he began climbing the stairs to board the plane, he could see Dr. and Mrs. Griffin in the window waving. He waved back and quickly disappeared onto the plane.

Seated on the plane, Little leaned back and took a deep breath. *Oh God, what am I doing? Whatever it is, I have no idea, I just hope I'm doing the right thing. God only knows, because I sure don't.* He had never flown on an airplane before. Many times before, he watched airplanes flying overhead. Often when he and Swoosh did not have anything to do, they would go to La Guardia Airport and watch the planes take off and land. Sometimes, they would pretend that they were on one of the flights, flying off somewhere to a distant land. Putting together big business deals, or just vacationing. This was a day he had always looked forward to and dreamed of, his first time flying above the clouds into the sky.

He chuckled to himself as he recalled the time he and Swoosh slipped onto the airfield and boarded an empty Boeing 727. They sat in the cockpit and pretended to fly the plane. The journey started when they flew over the Statue of Liberty, then on to London, and on to France to see the Eiffel Tower. Next, they were off to Northern Africa to visit Egypt. Egypt was their favorite place as they zoomed over the pyramids and the Sphinx. They found the Congo breathless, and the wild animals of Africa fascinating. It was in the Congo where they stayed for a few days to go on a safari deep into the heart of the jungle. Before they knew it, time had slipped away, and night had fallen. His mother was worried. When they got home, she was so mad at both of them for being away without telling her where they were. He chuckled as he remembered that they didn't fear her as much as his dad. To their surprise, he didn't give them a beating. Instead, they got a two-week punishment, but, for them those few hours in the cockpit were worth every moment they spent on punishment.

Observing his surroundings, it was no different from the plane he and Swoosh had flown. He listened intently as the stewardess performed her duties. "We have been cleared for takeoff and will be taxing down the runway in a few minutes. The captain has turned on the no smoking signs, and the seat belt signs. Make sure your tray and seat are in the upright position. Once we are in the air, and the captain has turned off the seat belt sign, we will begin serving a snack. Our first scheduled stop is Lambert Airport in St. Louis, Missouri. Passengers making connecting flights to New York, Washington, DC, and other points east, may deplane at that time. Those traveling on with us to Chicago may remain on the plane. The plane will be at the terminal for a half-hour. They are experiencing inclement weather east of the Mississippi. There is a large storm system causing several flight delays and cancellations. The captain will keep you informed regarding any connecting flights. Thank you and enjoy your flight."

The plane started taxing down the runway. The slow movement at first felt like a car; it was the roaring sound of the loud engines that let him know it was not. Initially, the sound of the DC-9 jet engines roared in his ears. The plane's speed increased more and more as it moved along the runway in order to lift off the ground. The force of the plane's movement forward pushed Little back in his seat. Finally, he felt the plane lift into the air. A loud thump sounded throughout the cabin, and Little wondered what happened. However, the plane continued to gain altitude.

Looking out of the window, he watched as it climbed higher and higher into the sky. Everything on the ground became smaller and smaller as the plane climbed higher. The pressure of the cabin caused his ears to start popping. Looking out of the window, he watched as the plane flew into the clouds. As it continued to climb higher into the sky, he felt the plane turn to the left. No longer was he able to see the snow-covered ground below. His view was of the dark clouds hovering in the sky above. The white earth below him disappeared as the plane flew into the clouds. Again, the stewardess addressed the passengers. "The captain has turned off the seat belt and no smoking sign. However, we encourage you to remain in your seat with your seat belt fastened."

After a while, the captain spoke over the loudspeaker. "Ladies and gentlemen, this is Captain Francisco. Thank you for flying with us today. We will be cruising at two hundred fifty miles per hour, at an altitude of twenty-five thousand feet. We are experiencing a lot of air turbulence. Visibility is low; we should be arriving at Lambert Field in St. Louis, Missouri in one and a half hour. There have been several cancellations for all points east. I'll give you an update on those flights. So, for now, sit back and try to relax."

The elderly woman sitting next to Little was very friendly. During the entire flight, she talked to him about her husband, children, and five grandchildren. By the time the plane landed in St. Louis, Little knew the names of her four children, the spouses of her two married children, and their children. He felt he knew her entire family history. *Boy, does this woman talk; does she ever shut up? I know everything about her and her family, and she barely knows my name. Not that I want her to, but you would think she would be a little considerate.* She and her husband worked for the city of Chicago, her husband and the mayor of Chicago were first cousins. *There is nothing that I don't know about this sixty-one-year-old secretary. One thing, she loves her children, and her entire life is wrapped up in them. All she talks about is her love as a mother for her children and how she sacrifices everything for them.* She continually said that, without her children, she didn't know what she would do. *If I didn't know better, I'd swear that Mrs. Griffin arranged the seating on the plane and seated her next to me.* But he was polite. He smiled, looked at her pictures and tried to make pleasant conversation.

The captain turned on the seat belt and no smoking signs as he announced their approach and decent into St. Louis International Airport. There was a loud dragging sound. He felt the plane slow as its nose tilted forward. His stomach tickled and his ears popped as the plane descended through the clouds. On the window, he could see droplets of rain streaking across, as the plane descended through the clouds. The kindly woman seated next to him gave him some gum. She said it would help with the popping of his ears. The plane made the final approach to the runway and touched down on the ground. Not knowing what to expect, he tensed up as the plane roared in slowing down. Deplaning, he bade Mrs. Daley good-bye.

Moving through the terminal, he looked for the monitor indicating the time and gate where his flight was scheduled to depart. Crossing the terminal, he located the gate of his next flight. The schedule indicated his flight was delayed for an hour. With time to spare, Little explored the airport. Delta, United, and Eastern shared the same terminal. Other small airlines were also in the airport along with several international airlines. Shortly after he completed his tour of the airport, he heard, the announcement his flight was beginning to board at gate twelve. Boarding the plane was nothing different from the first time except Dr. and Mrs. Griffin were not there. He missed having someone at the airport to see him off. Finding his seat, he noticed there was a vacant seat between him and the other passenger, a white male businessman, who was not very friendly. *Well, at least he won't talk me to death like Mrs. Daley.* The stewardess and captain made the same announcements as before; having heard it only a short time ago, he felt he knew the routine, so he barely paid it attention.

This time, his flight would be three hours, and the stewardess would be serving lunch during the flight. Once in the air the captain turned off the seat belt and no smoking sign. Little loosened his seat belt, leaned his seat back, and closed his eyes.

With no one to disturb him, Little used this quiet opportunity to reflect on the past weeks he spent with the Griffins. During the whole time he was there, Mrs. Griffin smothered him with love and kindness. She treated him as if he were her own son. Swoosh decided to stay until the tenth of January, making Christmas and New Years that much more special for him. For Little, of all the Christmas gifts Swoosh ever gave him, his staying was the best Christmas gift ever.

Dr. Griffin, Mrs. Griffin, and Michael made sure he and Swoosh had a very good Christmas. Reminiscing, he thought about his reason for his unannounced and sudden departure from Chicago, his traveling to Lawrence, Kansas, and what happened his first night at the Griffins. After having listened to his aunt Lanet on the phone, things drastically changed. He recalled late in the middle of the night waking up choking. *I couldn't breathe. I was so scared that I was going to die. I was dreaming I was back in her apartment and she was choking me all over again. I just had to let it out. Tell somebody. I was so scared; it seemed so real. I woke up screaming and gagging for air. I won't forget how the next day, all day, I felt so guilty and ashamed of myself, and dirty. Everyone knew my secret about Ruth, Bigger, Elijah, and Ruth's mother.*

The next day when he, Dr. Griffin, Mrs. Griffin, Swoosh, and Michael sat down to talk, from shame he found it extremely difficult to look them in the eye. It was the shame, the shame of being the product of a violent act, a rape, not even a love child—less than a love child. *To know and then to tell somebody, especially strangers I was not the result of love between my mother and father. To say that I was the result of a rape was so hard and embarrassing. I was so scared Swoosh would turn away from me in shame. But he didn't.*

Little saw himself as a mistake, a terrible mistake. As something that should not have happened; he was never meant to be. He was that which was never meant to be, the result of a criminal act, the result of a pregnancy that should not have occurred. A baby created not out of love or want, lesser than a teen pregnancy, but from a violent criminal act. *I am the baby that should not have been conceived, that's what I am. I am a bastard.*

Not being able to speak, to communicate what he was feeling inside, frustrated him more and only compounded his problem. Dr. Griffin told him that he had no reason to be embarrassed or ashamed. He was not responsible for the actions of his father and grandmother. Most importantly, he was okay. That's what really mattered the most. Despite all everyone said to comfort him, he could not help how he felt inside.

Eventually, his voice came back; it took more than a week for him to speak clearly enough for anyone to understand him. At first, it was very difficult for him to express his feelings, but eventually he began talking to Dr. Griffin about the whole episode with his mother's mother and how worthless, dirty, shameful and disgusting he felt inside. Sometimes during the night, to relieve his pain, he would share various things with Swoosh. Swoosh knew the most about everything. He felt better after sharing it with Swoosh. When it weighed upon him so heavily until it disturbed his sleep, he would share it with Dr. Griffin. Although he found exposing himself extremely difficult, sometimes he'd share it with Michael and Mrs. Griffin. Dr. Griffin told him that it was good; it was good therapy and helped in the healing process.

Yet, it was Mrs. Griffin who was the sweetest, yet the hardest on him. It was often as if she could read his very thoughts—his deepest secrets were revealed to her. Many times, as she spoke revealing his true feelings, he felt naked before her. She was relentless in her pursuit and would press him to make commitments to call his mother and father.

Holding his promise to his sister and brother, he called Elisha and Esther the day after Christmas. His voice wasn't the greatest, but he did want to speak with them as he promised. In his letter, he promised that as soon as he was able to speak, he would call them. He wanted to keep his word. Of all those he missed the most, it was Elisha and Esther. Most of all, he dreaded hurting them by leaving the way he did. With all the craziness after meeting their grandmother for the first time, he knew they didn't know or could not fully understand what happened. *And if they do know what happened, I wonder how it's affecting them. After all these years, how could I tell them that they're only my half brother and sister? How could I tell them that we have the same mother, but not the same father? How could I tell them that my father raped their mother and not have them hate me? Will they see me like I see myself?*

How could he relate something to them that he himself did not completely understand? How could he tell them that his father brutally raped their mother with the blessings of her mother and sister? *How could they understand that? How could they, when I myself didn't?* He did not want to accept it; it was forced upon him. Like it or not, it was the truth, and he had to live with it.

Only after being pressured by Mrs. Griffin, did he briefly speak to his parents. He argued, after being betrayed and deceived, he wasn't ready to talk to them.

Getting straight to the point, she was more direct and said, "What you mean is, you're not ready to forgive them."

Little wanted to challenge what she said. How could he when buried deep in his heart he knew she was right. *Not only am I not ready, I don't want to forgive them! Why should I forgive them? How could I forgive them?*

"Thomas, the longer you wait to forgive them, the harder it will be in the future to take that step. Time heals wounds; wounds heal faster with medicine. Forgiveness is a potent medicine. Don't wait until it's too late."

The time between his returning to New York or school wasn't long enough; the wound was deep, too deep, and there wasn't enough time for therapy. Little talked with Swoosh about the University of Kansas, how things were there socially and racially. For the first time in a while, Little began acknowledging his true feelings about UNE. Over the past several days, he had been building up to reveal his thoughts to Swoosh and Michael about not going back to college. Confronting his own thoughts was one thing, sharing them with Swoosh and Michael was entirely different.

After pondering it for a while, that night as the three sat in Michael's room talking about nothing, in the middle of the conversation Little blurted it out, "I've decided not to go back to college."

Swoosh and Michael looked at him.

"What did you say?" Swoosh asked.

"I've decided not to go back to school."

"Do you mean, back to school, or back to UNE?" Michael asked.

"I'm not sure which, maybe both. I don't know."

"Hold it Little," Swoosh responded, jumping to his feet. "What do you mean you don't know? I think you're taking this whole thing just a little bit too far. Now, I understand what happened to you was a shock. I'll admit you've had it rough these past few weeks. I'll grant you that much, but that's no reason for you to drop out of college. I think." Swoosh bit his lip. "No, I know you're overreacting to this whole situation."

Little stood nose-to-nose with Swoosh. "Swoosh, this is tough enough. I don't need you acting like you're my father."

"Little, I'll give you all the sympathy you want. But I'm not gonna support you doing something stupid."

"You misguided misfit. I didn't ask for nor do I want your sympathy!"

"You stupid jerk. What you want is a pity party. I'll give you a pity party." Shouting aloud, Swoosh announced as he raised his arms above his head and waved his hands motioning the crowd, "Hey everybody. Let's feel sorry for Thomas Isaiah Thomas. We're having a pity party over here for Thomas. Let's hear it everybody."

"Shut up Swoosh!"

"Hey, hey. Swoosh, Little, this is getting us nowhere. Come on guys, calm down, sit down, and keep your voices down. You don't want to get my folks coming in here. That's the last thing you want."

Temporarily calming Little and Swoosh down, Michael looked Little in the eye. "Come on Little, what's going on? What do you mean you're not going back to school?"

"It's just what I said Michael. It's not about Chicago or them. I've been thinking about this for a long, long time. There's nothing there for me."

"What do you mean nothing there for you? I don't believe you. What about your work on the project? That's something! Think about all the things you accomplished at the university."

"Like what?"

As Michael spoke, he became agitated and loud. "Remember when Stephanie found out you were a presidential scholar? She challenged you to make the organization more than a bunch of arrogant snobs. You did by starting the Christmas child program. It was a huge success, and it's the best program ever at the university. Practically alone, you solicited the aid of the fraternities and sororities, and collected toys for over one hundred families the first year. This past year, again you outdid yourself. You expanded the program so every dormitory floor and student organization participated.

Each sponsored a child and some more than one. Because of you, over 500 poor families in the New London area had a wonderful Christmas this past year. Tricycles, bicycles, board games, dolls, doll houses, dresses, tea sets, footballs, basketballs, bats, trucks. The kids got everything they asked for, needed, and more. Coats, gloves, underwear, shirts, pants, blouses, slips, bras, sweaters, shoes; you name it, they got it. There were all kinds of clothes and toys. It's the largest and most successful program at the university presented by students. We tried for years to get a Black Student Union. Because of you, it will be a reality."

Michael continued, "Then you got the PSs into tutoring children in the local schools and undertaking civic projects. Little, in one year, you changed that campus so much. Who else managed to gain a favorable ear of President Garvey. Because of you, we have an upcoming meeting to talk to him about hiring black faculty, staff, and actively recruiting more black students. Before, he would have never ever considered such a meeting, but you changed all that. Look, you got elected to the student government; the first black student in the school's history to be elected to the student government. The way things are going, you'll be the first black inducted into the honors society, Phi Beta Kappa. You're the first black nuclear engineering student. You're the most sought after and well-respected student, black or white, on that entire campus, and in the city. Little, you're more popular than the mayor. The faculty, staff, and students look up to you. All the black students are counting on you."

Little scratched his head and held it as if it ached. "That's it Michael, that's just it! The first. I'm always the first. All the black students are counting on me. The white students, faculty, and staff all rely on me. It's a heavy weight upon my shoulders I never asked for. What makes me the spokesperson for the black race? I never applied or asked for the job. Everybody seeks me out to help them, but who's there for me when I need comfort?" Little's voice trembled with emotions. "I mean, yes you're my friend, but I, I, I'm still...Look, with the PSs, I can't tell you how many times one of them told me 'I never think of you as a Negro' or 'you're not like them.' They don't see my color—to them I'm invisible. If they can't see my color, as black as I am, then to them I don't exist. In their minds, if I am to exist, then I have to deny my race; I am not going to pretend to be something or somebody just to please them. I'm passing, and I'm not trying to, only because they refuse to see my blackness. All of the black students, their parents are doctors and lawyers, professional people. Mine are working class people."

Little stood and leaned against the dresser. "You know why I picked UNE to attend? I never told you Swoosh. I saw some black students on the brochure. There was an all-black choir. I thought there were more black students on the campus. Some black females." He looked at Michael. "Even if I was attracted to white females, I couldn't date one. Look how they acted toward Stephanie and your cousin Alejandro. It was tolerable because his father is a rich, white-looking Venezuelan. Remember when I told you about the time Megan and

I went to the movies together? We were just friends going to a movie after a hard day of working on a program. Look what happened. We got all kinds of stares. Someone sent me a letter saying, 'nigger stay away from our white women.' Then there was the time Caroline gave me a ride to the subbase. I was told to 'stick to my own kind.' I can't tell you the number of times I was told to go back to Africa where I came from. I'm sick of it. I can't take it anymore. I'm not made up of the same stuff you are, Michael; that's just that. No matter how you look at it I, I, I'm still..." Embarrassed, Little turned his head away, facing the dresser. Looking back at Michael and Swoosh, he finally blurted it out. "Lonely! There I said it. I'm still lonely. I want a girlfriend just like everybody else, like any normal, college, adolescent male. Someone I can talk and laugh with, share things with, to be in love with, and to feel loved. I'm no different from any other guy. Besides, with all that I've gone through at UNE and Chicago, I just can't deal with it."

Swoosh moved closer to his blood brother in a threatening fashion. "Can't or just don't want to Little? Which one is it Little? Tell us, which one is it Little?"

"What do you mean, can't or won't?"

"Hey, I know it's difficult. You're acting like you're the only one going through things. I'm going through similar things at UK. It's no different being on the basketball team; students and administration only see me as a basketball player. No one believed my grades. They expected me to be on academic probation, not the honor roll." An angry tone could be heard in Swoosh's voice as he spoke. "I'm majoring in premed, everybody laughed because I said I want to be a medical doctor. Coach told me, 'major in physical education, I can help you get tutors for your classes.' Does he tell that to his white players? Probably not! They're majoring in accounting, premed, predentistry, political science, and vet medicine.

"They got tutors for their classes, but because I'm black, they think I can't handle the academics and basketball." As he spoke, he continued to get louder and louder as his anger increased. "No matter where you go, the treatment is not the same for black as it is for white students. You're no different. What makes you think you're so special that you should be exempt?" Momentarily, Swoosh looked up at the ceiling as if he were searching for what to say. "So, should I throw away my entire education and future because of their ignorance? I don't think so, Little. I thought you were a whole lot smarter than that."

Swoosh turned around to sit down on the bed. Suddenly, no longer trying to control his temper, he turned and charged at Little, shouting. "Just think, I use to look up to you, I'm in college because of you. Now, you're the one talking about quitting. What did you think it was going to be easy, stupid? You know what you are? A joke. You're a big joke, Little. No, you're a punk, a little punk, a wimp, and a big joke."

Again, they stood nose-to-nose shouting at each other.

"Who are you calling a punk? I'll show you just how much of a punk I am!" Little pushed Swoosh. "Get off my back Swoosh. I don't need you…You got your buddies with you. That's all you talked about and wrote about in your letters. You, Smoothie, and Bebop.

"Guys, guys, hold it down before you wake up my parents."

Suddenly, the room door swung open. "Hey, hey, hey! What's all the shouting about?" Dr. Griffin yelled as he entered the room.

Swoosh and Little were standing toe-to-toe, ready to get physical. As his father entered the room, Michael quickly grabbed Swoosh by the arm to keep him away from Little.

"I hear you boys on the other side of the house. What is going on in here?"

All three boys stood silent as Michael stood between the two.

"Well, I'm waiting for an answer."

Swoosh pointed at Little.

"Shut up Swoosh," Little screamed as he slapped Swoosh's finger way.

Swoosh shouted back at Little. "No, I'm not going to shut up." Directing his attention to Dr. Griffin, he yelled, "This fool here wants to drop out of college.

Little yelled back in defense. "That's not what I said Swoosh, and you know it. Stop. You stop twisting everything I say around. You know you're lying. If you got a problem with it, then butt out of my business."

"You're stupid if you think I'm gonna stand by and let you throw your life away."

Dr. Griffin stepped into the room, raising his voice. "Boys, stop right now.

"It's my life; so just shut up Swoosh! You talk too much. Just shut up and mind your business!"

"No, I'm not going to shut up. You're so bad, make me shut up. You act as if you're the only one with troubles. I told you, I have my share of troubles too. Now, you're only adding to them."

"It's not about you Swoosh, or your troubles. Why does it always have to be about you? I didn't ask you to idolize me. That's your problem, not mine. Get out, just get out. You're getting on my nerves."

"Then why don't you be honest about it and tell the truth! Only reason you're quitting school is to hurt Madear and Pop. You're just trying to get back at them. That's why you're quitting, and why you've been doing all this boohooing."

Swoosh struck a nerve in Little; Little felt it. "I said shut up Swoosh. You leave Ruth and Elijah out of this."

Swoosh brushed passed Michael and stepped over too Little, pointing his finger in his face. "No, I won't shut up. It's just as much about them as it is about your grandmother. Be honest, you know that's what this is all about. And just where do you get off calling them Ruth and Elijah? They're still your mother and father!"

Little fought desperately to change the direction Swoosh was heading. "Shut up and get your finger out of my face or I'll break it off! I'll call them whatever I want."

Suddenly, Swoosh pushed Little, making him fall on the bed. "Who's gonna make me shut up? Not you, you wimp!" Little jumped up off the bed and charged at Swoosh. Michael quickly stepped in between Swoosh and Little to hold Little back from Swoosh, but it was too late as Little hit Swoosh.

A tearful Swoosh screamed, "This is about Madear and Pop. What you need to do is get over it and stop trying to hurt them. They didn't do anything to you. If anything, they're guilty of is trying to protect you from being hurt. But how do you repay them? Well, I'm not going to stand by and let you hurt them."

Little covered his ears with his hands, "I'm not going to listen to you."

Again, Dr. Griffin shouted for them to stop. Swoosh grabbed Little's hands and struggled with him to pull them away from his ears as he continued to shout. "You're going to listen to me. Don't try and skirt the real issue. You're going to hear what I've got to say. I don't like what you're doing to Madear and Pop, bad mouthing them and treating them like they're some kind of monsters. You're hurting them and I'm not going to let you hurt them anymore. You're spoiled and ungrateful, that's what you are, spoiled and ungrateful. You just remember you're not hurting them as much as you're hurting yourself. It's your future you're trying to throw away."

"Shut up Swoosh. I said shut up. You don't know what you're talking about."

Locked together, the two began to struggle with each other. Angry with both of them, but angrier with Little, Michael attempted to break them up forcefully. His bias was obvious as he directed his force against Little. Suddenly, the three of them fell upon the bed. The wooden slacks supporting the box spring and mattress gave away sending the bed crashing to the floor.

A surprised Dr. Griffin stood over them shouting.

Mrs. Griffin appeared into the room carrying a bucket filled with a mixture of slushy wet snow and ice. Calling out, she warned her husband, "Stand back, Lance." Without hesitating or warning, she poured the mixture over the three boys.

Hastily, the boys screamed and separated as the freezing mixture hit them, soaking their clothes and the broken bed.

Shaking her head, she stood looking at the boys, "Now, that ought to cool you off. Now, I'm going back to bed. You boys had better settle this tonight without waking me up again, or I'm coming in next time, and it won't be pretty. And, Thomas, I don't want to repeat myself. Don't you ever again, and I don't want to hear you ever again, refer to your parents by their first name. In this house, you will show them respect. Do I make myself perfectly clear?"

The three stood shivering in their wet pajamas.

"What has gotten into the three of you?" Dr. Griffin shouted as he stepped in front of the trio, forcing them back down on the wet bed. "I want to know what is going on in here. Look at this room. You broke the bed and knocked everything on the floor. Have you boys taken leave of your senses? When I left you boys a half-hour ago, you were talking and laughing. Next thing I hear, you're at each other's throats. Michael you're the oldest one here, I expected better of you. How could you have let this turn into a fight?"

Michael stood speechless, looking at his father.

"I want some answers," he shouted.

"I didn't do anything, Dad. I was trying to break it up. Why are you blaming me? I…"

"That's enough of your backtalk, young man, I don't want to hear it, Michael. All three of you change out of those wet clothes now, then, I want you in the kitchen. Hurry up!"

Quickly changing their clothes, the trio went into the kitchen and sat down at the kitchen table. Dr. Griffin poured each one a cup of hot chocolate. As he took his seat, he spoke. "Okay Michael, start talking."

Michael sighed as he looked at Little, Swoosh, and his father while he sat stroking his nose.

"Stop stalling. I'm waiting for an explanation."

"We were talking, when Little said he didn't want to go back to school. We, Swoosh and I, well we sort of got mad with Little's saying he wasn't going back to school. We sort of lost our tempers, and I guess it got out of hand."

"You guess!" Dr. Griffin turned to Little, "Okay Thomas, talk to me. What's wrong? Why don't you want to go back to college?"

Little's reminiscing about that night was interrupted by the captain's voice over the intercom. "Ladies and gentlemen, we are running into some air turbulence. Please, take your seat and fasten your seat belt."

The plane began to bump up and down and rock from side to side. With each bump, loud gasps from the passengers could be heard. The captain again addressed the passengers. "Ladies and gentlemen, due to the storm, Washington's Dulles National Airport and all airports from Richmond, Virginia, to Logan International Airport in Boston, Massachusetts, have been closed. Our flight has been rerouted to the next available airport, Patrick Henry Airport in Newport News, Virginia. Please, keep your seat belts fastened and remain in your seat. To avoid heavy turbulence, the plane will be climbing another five hundred feet. Our estimated time of arrival is in forty-five minutes. I will keep you updated of any changes."

I was supposed to meet Uncle Canada at the airport. We were supposed to talk. Now the plane won't be landing in Washington. I don't have any way of contacting him, and I don't know how I'm supposed to get to DC. Everything is so screwed up. Little reflected on the phone conversation he had with his uncle at the Griffin's.

The woman seated in the plane's cabin on the opposite side of Little was nervously crying. Her husband, taking her by the hand, tried to comfort her. Immediately, she started yelling, "Don't touch me, just leave me alone. It's your fault I'm up here. I told you I didn't want to fly."

Whining and sobbing was all around him as passengers expressed their fear of crashing and possibly dying. With a smirk on his face, Little remained calm; for him this was nothing. *Hey lady, what are you scared about? This is nothing. I've been a lot closer to death than this. I'm not scared because it's not my time; I've cheated death before, and I will again. Don't worry, as long as I'm on this plane, nothing is going to happen. Well, at least not to me.*

In Little's arrogant state of mind, he settled back into his seat. Chuckling to himself, he reflected on the fight between he and Swoosh.

It was one of many they've had over the years. Each one had its own merit, some more serious, while others, over something very frivolous as an ice cream cone. Either way, they've always ended up the same way. It would end later that night with both of them laughing about the fight and pressing their wrist together, marking them as brothers forever. They could never stay mad at each other for very long. Most of the time, their anger lasted only a few minutes to a few hours, at best it lasted one day.

Little recalled the last time they were mad at each other was after he got accepted at UNE. That time, they barely spoke to each other for almost two weeks. It was the most miserable time in his entire life. Every little thing they would say or do for each other, no matter how kind or generous, would irritate them. Once, Swoosh tried to break the ice. He was getting up from the kitchen table to get himself some Kool Aid. He asked Little if he wanted some. He poured himself some while he was up. They both were sitting at the kitchen table. Out of the clear blue, he told Swoosh he wasn't helpless. "If I wanted some, I'd get it myself."

After Swoosh put the Kool Aid back into the refrigerator, he got up, got the Kool Aid out of the refrigerator, and poured himself a glass.

Then, there was the time he tried to make up to Swoosh by buying him his favorite ice cream. When he gave it to him, despite it being Swoosh's favorite, he threw the ice cream in the trash and said, "I have my own money. I can afford to buy my own ice cream."

Smiling, he thought about the time when they were six years old, and they had their first real physical fight. It was over a pencil, a stupid pencil. They got a good spanking from their mothers. Then they were told that they could not see each other for the rest of the day. They both felt that was an unfair punishment, separating them, and saying they could not play together for the rest of the day. As their mothers dragged them off in different directions, he remembered they cried after each. From that time on, to punish them, they would be sent into different rooms. Being separated from each other for any length of time, no matter how long or short, was the punishment they hated the most. No matter how often they fought, they always ended the same way with the touching of the wrists. That night at bedtime, they would laugh about the fight and other things. Little knew this fight was no different.

That night, they talked it over chocolate chip cookies and hot cups of Ovaltine. Dr. Griffin was wise, and his wisdom was clearly pronounced as they talked. He told them he understood what Little was going through. He explained that he himself experienced a similar dilemma when he was in college. For him, growing up in the mid-west was a lonely life. There were only two Negro families in the town where they lived. His father retired from the Air force, and those two families were related. As a military child, he traveled around the world with his family; never staying in one place long enough to make friends. He was fourteen when his father retired as a colonel from the Air Force.

He commented on how he was envious of Little and Swoosh's relationship. He never had a friend to be that close. He called them life-long friends, brothers forever, and a rare treasure. He said that when he went off to college in California where in spite of the odds, he persisted. Finally, he went to medical school at Yale. That was where he met Cynthia, his wife. If it had not been for her, he said he might have left medical school. He said, throughout the years, she has been his best and only friend. He also helped Swoosh understand what Little was experiencing. He reminded Swoosh that unlike Little, he had basketball and his teammates to help him through his difficult periods.

Swoosh thought about it and realized in addition to basketball and his teammates, he also had the Griffins. Swoosh acknowledged that he had Dr. Gannon to thank for that. It was Dr. Gannon who, over the years, proved to be a very good friend of Madear, the Griffins as well as Little's aunt Lanet and uncle Jerome.

Looking at Little, Dr. Griffin said for him to take his time and not to make any hasty decisions; he still had a few weeks to think about what he wanted to do, and to take the time to explore his various options. Dr. Griffin said that questioning what Little wanted to do was all right, and he did not have to make a decision right away. In the meantime, Dr. Griffin cautioned Little not to close any open doors. One of those doors was his course registration at UNE. "Little, call your aunt and uncle and any other relatives you have to get their input. Remember, you don't have to do what they say; you just want their suggestions. Swoosh and I talk a lot; is there someone at UNE that you talk to?"

Perking up, Michael said, "Dr. Hamilton. He's a good person to talk to, Little."

"He's right Little," replied Dr. Griffin. "I've heard Michael and Alejandro speak of him many times. I also had an opportunity to meet him. If you're comfortable with him, give him a call. Maybe, he could offer some suggestions that you haven't thought of. You don't have to explain everything to him, just things about school."

"Hey, Little,' Swoosh interjected, "there's Uncle Junebug in Washington, DC. He's Pop's closest and dearest friend. He and Pop are like Little and me. Little, you can give him a call."

All these years I've been calling them Uncle Junebug and Aunt Madie. They probably knew Elijah wasn't my father, and they just pretended. I feel so stupid and so unclean. How could I have been such a dummy?

"Shut up Swoosh."

Everyone including Little was surprised by his response. The thought of calling his uncle Junebug and aunt Madie took him off guard and made him feel uncomfortable. "I didn't mean that. I'm sorry, Swoosh; honest, I'm sorry."

A wounded Swoosh replied, "Don't worry about it." But his spirit to help Little was greater than his bruised feelings. Enthusiastically, he sprang back, "I know. You can call and talk to Uncle Canada. I know he can help Little."

"Hey, yeah. You're right about him, Swoosh. I'll do that. I'll call Uncle Canada. Thanks for the idea, I'll do that."

That night they continued their conversation at length into the morning hours. "Well, if anything resulted from this whole thing, guys, it is that I know that I have some decisions to make." The trio looked at the soaked and broken bed in Michael's room. They decided to sleep in the guest room together. As the three laid in the big bed, Little looked over at Swoosh. Holding up his hand, he said, "Brothers?"

Swoosh immediately pressed his wrist against Little's. "Until death us do part. Now, go to sleep, worm head."

As the days went by, Little wanted to know his options and began desperately searching them out. *What would I do if I don't go back to UNE? Where would I go? Not to New York, I'm not going to their house. The University of Kansas is another choice. Naw, don't want to hear Swoosh's mouth. What would I do? I don't know, I just don't know right now.* As he talked with Dr. Griffin, Swoosh and Michael the more apparent everything became. His unhappiness with UNE, his disassociation with his parents, and his feelings of loneliness only made him more confused. Dr. Griffin continued to probe his mind and asked him to think about his objectives. Was it to run away from reality? Or was it to seek a new direction in life? He knew he wanted to continue in school, or did he? The only real thing he knew he was sure of was that he had to get away.

Little found that Mrs. Griffin was more direct. Being home with her during the day, he felt she was brutally honest. She forced him to face the truth. She liked to describe her approach as client-centered. Both of them encouraged him to explore all of his options, including the benefits and consequences of each. With their help, he explored the consequences and benefits of his options. They reinforced the notion that he must do what was right for him, regardless of what others thought or said. Notwithstanding their sound advice, he knew they wanted him to continue his education.

His aunt Lanet and uncle Jerome were more direct. They felt that leaving school now was not to his benefit. His aunt Shera and uncle Kenneth talked about their experiences. Fear and anger kept him from seeking out his Uncle Junebug and Aunt Madie. *Perhaps, Uncle Junebug would offer me an opportunity to work in the hospital with him. But to call him means talking about it. Do they already know? They probably do.*

Then, knowing Uncle Junebug and Aunt Madie, the first thing they would do is get Elijah and Ruth involved. I ain't gonna have that. That idea only made him angrier. The hardest part of it all was he had only two weeks left to decide what he was going to do.

For days, he had hesitated to call Dr. Hamilton and his Uncle Canada. He was concerned; he knew how passionate Dr. Hamilton is about black students staying in school. *And Uncle Canada has always been very supportive of me and Swoosh in school. No, I can't disappoint him and Aunt Sarah.* He felt ashamed and did not want to disappoint them by telling them of his dilemma, nor did he want to explain what happened in Chicago. Finally, breaking down, he called. As things turned out, Dr. Hamilton was most helpful. They talked about the nuclear project. With his connections, he could arrange for him to receive academic credit for work on the project and arrange a place for him to stay in Hampton, Virginia. He would also see if it would be possible for Little to take classes at the local university, Hampton Institute.

Little remembered Hampton is the-all black university Mrs. Solomon, his Uncle Canada, and Aunt Sarah attended. *If Dr. Hamilton can pull it off in the next few days, then that's what I'll do. Well, if it doesn't work out, at least, I explored the possibility.* Dr. Hamilton said if he had contacted him earlier, he knew he could have definitely arranged something. However, since it was a week before school was to begin, he could not give him any guarantees, but he promised he would do what he could. With this comforting thought in mind, he put it all to rest. He was relieved; now, if he had to, he could go back to UNE.

As usual, his uncle Canada was most supportive and extremely helpful by putting it all together. He promised to help all he could and said that he would keep it a secret. It was his advice and guidance that Little decided to follow. *I don't know why I didn't think about him before. I'm sure glad Swoosh made the suggestion.*

HOME BY THE SEA

The pilot announced the plane's arrival outside of Patrick Henry Airport in Newport News, Virginia; however, the plane was placed in a holding pattern until it was cleared to land. The plane continued circling the airport for another twenty minutes before landing. Little thought about how Mrs. Griffin encouraged him to call his parents to discuss his plans. He did not feel it necessary to talk to them. When she found out he had not called them, she reprimanded him and made it unconditional. He had to call his parents when he arrived. At the airport, she looked at him. "Thomas. Look at me Thomas." Little turned and looked at her. "I want you to promise me that you will call and talk to your parents the first week you're there; alright?"

"I promise I'll call them." *Sure, I'll call and speak to Elisha and Esther.*

"No, I said promise me you will call and speak to your parents. That means your mother and father, not your little sister and brother."

Doggone it, she read my mind again. Looks like I'm not going to get out of this one. Reluctantly, he promised. "Okay, I promise. I'll call and talk to my parents within the first week." *Each time I've spoken with them our conversation was superficial. So why do I even bother.* Emotionally, he was not ready to talk to them about what happened in Chicago, nor did he wish to share his life with them. *I don't care to talk to them about what happened in Chicago, or about my future. My plans don't involve them.* He knew if their relationship was to go anywhere, they had to talk about it. It was an obstacle that he was not ready to overcome or willing to let go. *I don't really care what happens between us.*

He felt the pain and agony of it all was his only source of something to hold on to. His feelings let him know that he was still alive, and this was not a cruel nightmare. *All these years, nobody cared about me or my feelings. So why should I try and patch things up between us? Besides, they have each other; they really don't care anyway.* The pain was still too deep, and the wound was still fresh and wide open.

"Ladies and gentlemen," said the pilot, "we have been cleared for landing. We will be making our final approach to Patrick Henry Airport in a few minutes. Please remain seated. We will be experiencing a lot of air turbulence on our descent as we pass through the storm clouds."

As the plane descended, Little looked out of the window. The plane began to be bumped around by the air. Passengers could be heard letting out sounds of fright with each rocking of the plane. Looking out of the window as the plane was passing through the storm clouds, he could see the mixture of rain, snow, and hail as they hit the window. Descending through the dark clouds, he finally saw the snow-covered ground below. The plane touched down on the ground and skidded to a stop on the snow and icy-covered runway. Throughout the plane's cabin, he could hear passengers sighing with relief.

The terminal was warm and crowded with weary travelers. Passengers from other diverted flights could be seen sleeping and lounging in chairs and on the floor. Others paced up and down the terminal praying for a flight out of the tiny airport. From the crowd, Little thought he heard someone calling out his name.

"Little. Little Thomas. Over here." A middle-aged woman stood in the crowd waving her hand at him.

Curiously, he approached the woman calling out to him. "Hello. Am I supposed to know you?"

"I don't know," she jokingly laughed. "Are you supposed to know me?"

"I was expecting a man. A Dr. Charles Haden."

In a snappy laughing tone, she replied, "Now really Mr. Thomas. Do I look like a man to you?"

"Well, how do you know who I am?"

Wittingly she replied, "Boy, you sure do have a lot of questions, but I have all the right answers. Tell me, how many Negroes did you see get off that plane!" Laughing she asked, "Just how many of us's did you see riding in that plane with you?"

Little and the woman laughed as he looked around the crowded airport. "You got me there."

"I guess I do."

"Well, you know who I am, but I still don't know who you are. My mother told me never to go anywhere with strangers."

"I guess I better introduce myself or you'll be sleeping in the airport tonight with the rest of these people." She looked at Little puzzled, "Who am I? Oh, I know. I'm Jean Picott. I may be old, but I ain't senile yet. I do remember who I am, and you might be surprised to know I do know where I live. Dr. Haden couldn't get his car started, so he asked me to pick you up at the airport."

Little was intrigued with Mrs. Picott. He could see she was friendly and had a sense of humor. He loved her high pitch nasal tone voice. "I was supposed to arrive at Norfolk Airport from Washington, DC. How did you know my plane was landing in Newport News?"

She chuckled. "Boy, give me some credit! I wasn't born yesterday, and I haven't lived over forty years to not learn anything. You're not the only genius around here, you know. But if you must know, when I saw it was snowing, I called to the Norfolk airport to make sure that your flight wasn't canceled. I wasn't going to go out in this mess for nothing. They told me Norfolk airport was closing down and all flights were rerouted to Newport News. When I called the airport, they said that your plane was scheduled to land at four-thirty. It was snowing so bad, I was sure your plane wasn't going to land. Now, do you have any more questions before we get your bags and go to the car? Before you ask, yes, they gave me a driver's license out of pity, and I can't drive a lick in snow!"

"You know something, Mrs. Picott?"

"Boy, what now?"

"I like you. You're too much," he said hugging her and laughing.

Mrs. Picott rolled her eyes. "I don't believe this," she laughed. "Stop it. People may think I know you, or worse, they may think were related."

Little shouted, "Aunt Jean, I'm so glad to see you."

"Oh Lawd, now you're embarrassing me," she said laughing. "You're a nut if I ever saw one."

The duo went to the baggage claim area to get his bags. The airport was crowded with stranded passengers. The monitors displayed all incoming and departing flights were canceled for the remainder of the day. Over the intercom a voice announced, "All incoming and departing flights have been canceled and the airport is officially closed due to the weather."

Little's was the last flight to land. "I guess I landed just in time."

"I guess you did."

"Lucky me."

Together, Mrs. Picott and Little trudged through the snow to the car.

The wind was blowing fiercely around them. "Phew, this is going to be some blizzard. It usually only snows here once, maybe twice a year. Out of three hundred and sixty-five days a year, you had to pick today to fly in!"

"Yep. Aren't you lucky?"

"I should be. So, you're the boy genius from the University of New England that everybody here has been raving about! What makes you classified as a genius?"

"I don't know about boy genius, but I did attend the University of New England."

"Dr. Haden bragged all about you. He and Dr. Stephen Hamilton, that's all they've been talking about all week."

"You know Dr. Hamilton?"

"Of course, he used to teach at Hampton before he went to the University of New England. I know the whole family, his wife and their four children. He is an extremely bright man. When Hampton lost him, they lost an excellent teacher. They lost a teacher who really cared for his students and a good role model. But Hampton's loss was the University of New England's gain."

"Well, I'm glad he was at UNE for me."

"I'm sure you were. So tell me, how does a Negro get to be named Thomas Thomas?"

It was a question he was asked all his life, and he had no idea until seven weeks ago. Little had not anticipated being asked the question. He felt a sharp pain in his chest. "I don't think you really want to know. It's a long story."

She laughed. "Look here Little, let me tell you something. Just in case you haven't noticed, with all this snow and as slow as I'm going, right now all we got is time. Besides, I want to know what kind of mother would give her child two last names. Or is it two first names? Whichever one it is I bet your father named you. It's just like a man."

I really did not want to get into this. For whatever reason, I feel comfortable with her; I think I can trust her. "My father died when I was a baby, my mother remarried and my father, I mean my stepfather, adopted me. His last name is Thomas."

"As tall as you are, why do they call you Little?"

Little tried mimicking her. "Um. Boy, you sure do have a lot of questions, but I have all the right answers."

"Well!" she laughed. "I guess I should have seen that one coming."

Little laughed with her, "My father, I mean stepfather said, when I was born he said I was a little something. He kept telling my mother I was so little. My mother used to call me her little man. Then he started calling me Little, and everybody has called me Little since then."

"Well you're certainly not little anymore. How tall are you?"

"And I haven't been little for many years. I'm six four."

"So, I hear you will be working at the shipyard in their engineering department."

"Yes ma'am. I worked on the design of a nuclear reactor with Dr. Waldstriecher at UNE. I'm helping in the construction and installation process."

"Wow! That is wonderful. How old are you?"

"Twenty."

"You could have fooled me with all those brains. I'm sure your parents are really proud of you."

"Yeah, I guess they are."

"I'm going to warn you about the shipyard. Those crackers there don't like Negroes, especially smart ones. Most Negroes work in the yard building the ships. There aren't any that I know of in the engineering department; you'll be the first."

Not again.

"What do you mean not again?"

"Don't tell me you read minds?"

She laughed, "Boy, you'd be surprised at what I can do."

"Well, being first is nothing new to me. I'm the firstborn, first this and first that."

"The shipyard is nothing like you've ever experienced before. I don't think they know you're a Negro. They're in for one heck of a surprise!"

"Why would you say they're in for a surprise?"

"How many Negroes go to the University of New England, and how many of them are majoring in nuclear engineering? Then, on top of that you're rated the number one student on the campus, and maybe in the entire country. It's a white school; it's only natural that everybody thinks you're white. Except us folks at Hampton. We know the truth."

"Yeah, I see what you mean." *Looks like instead of running away from it, I've run right into the thick of it. I hope she's wrong.* Somehow, he knew she wasn't.

"If you were looking at running away from white folks and being the first, you're in a heap of trouble. Okay Mr. Little, the campus isn't far from here. I'd take you to my house, except Mrs. White is expecting you at Holly Tree Inn."

"Exactly where and what is Holly Tree Inn? I thought I was staying on the campus."

"Holly Tree Inn is on the campus. It's like the campus hotel, but I think they may be putting you up in the Trustee House, which is very nice. Most folks like Holly Tree Inn better. You just have to watch out for Mrs. White. She runs the place with an iron fist, but she really cares for the students. She has a good heart, and she's the best cook."

"Oh, so I can get something to eat there also?"

"Sure. Most of the time the faculty and administration eat there for lunch and sometimes dinner. Right now, it should really be nice. The school is in intercession, so there are a few students on the campus staying in the inn. With this snow, the fireplace should really feel good today."

"It sounds nice."

"You can say it's quaint, very quaint. Landwise, Hampton is a big campus, but there aren't too many buildings on it. The school owns a lot property in the surrounding area. Most of it used to be farmland."

"What do you teach?"

"I'm not on the faculty. But I probably see more students and teach students more about life than most of the professors. I run the campus greenhouse. Everybody, some time or another, comes through the greenhouse. I'd show you around campus, but not today with all this snow. It's not a good idea, especially since we will barely make it to the campus. Besides, I don't want to get stuck and have you to push the car with all those brains. You might hurt yourself. I must say, the campus is beautiful when it snows. Now, my favorite time is the Spring when the Azaleas, Rhododendrons, and the Magnolia trees are in bloom. Now, that's when the campus is gorgeous and picturesque."

The car traveled along until they arrived at the campus. A brick wall on both sides of the entrance with a wrought iron gate marked the front of the campus. It reminded him of UNE's entrance. The car stopped in front of a white quaint-looking inn. The building was a very charming-looking cottage-type inn with a screened-in front porch. The wind blew so strong that it almost knocked them both down as they got out of the car. Scrambling, they held on to each other as they carried his bags into the inn. Several students and faculty were gathered together in the living room of the inn, keeping warm by the fireplace.

A very light skinned black woman dressed in a white uniform greeted them. Had not Mrs. Picott told him he would have thought she was a white woman. "Jean, y'all come on in out of the cold and close the door. Don't be lettin' that snow and cold in here. I'm tryin' to heat this building, not the world. Let God heat the outdoors, that's his job, not mine," she grunted with a big smile. Eagerly, Mrs. Picott and the woman hugged as they greeted each other. "Now, you must be Thomas Thomas. I'm Mrs. White. I'm in charge of the place. I understand you will be staying with us for a spell."

"Yes ma'am."

"I have the key to your room." Promptly, she gave him the key as she shook his hand. "It's room two hundred. Grace, show Mr. Thomas here to his room. Roland and Marcus, take his bags for him. Come on; Y'all students hurry up. You move so slow. Ya'll movin' like a bunch of old folks. I'll tell ya Jean, I never seen such a slow bunch of students before like these," she pleasantly scoffed at them.

Mrs. Picott laughed and joined in on the fun. "Just as lazy as they can be, especially that old Marcus. Mrs. White, I bet you don't get a dime's worth of work out of him.

"I tell you, he ain't worth a plug nickel, Jean."

"You cats are always on my case," protested Marcus

"Boy, I done told you time and time again, I ain't no animal," scoffed Mrs. White. "Now Mr. Thomas, you have just enough time to change out of those clothes. I spect you' been travelin' in them all day. Baby, I got to close this kitchen in a half hour. So, if you want some dinner, you need to hurry."

Grace smiled at Little. "Now, Mrs. White, I don't know why you're rushing him. You're not going anywhere in this snow."

"Now, chile, I done told you to stay out of grown folk business. How you know I'm not going out in the snow? For all you know, I could have a pair of skis in the kitchen under the stove, or my reindeer and sleigh could be parked out back." The group laughed as Mrs. White made all kind of gestures.

"Jean, how is it out there?"

Grace leaned over and whispered to Little. "Don't worry, her bark is worse than her bite."

"I heard that Grace. I may be old, but I'm not blind and even though I paid for them, I still have my teeth. I'll show you just how hard I can bite if you don't hurry up and show him to his room. Mr. Thomas, after you finish, come on back down and join us. Then I'll introduce you to everybody."

"What's on the menu, Mrs. White?"

"Never mind what's on the menu. Question is, are you hongry or not? That's all you got to worry about. No baby, I'm just teasing. After a while, you'll learn Mrs. White likes to talk bad. Ain't that right Marcus?"

"If you say so, Mrs. White."

"If you want to keep on eatin' here, you'll agree with me."

"I love your cooking. Yes, you're right."

"Despite his callin' everybody cats, that Marcus has got good senses.

Now baby, Mrs. White has stewed beef with cornbread and mashed potatoes. Now don't forget, kitchen closes in a half an hour. Now, are you hongry? I realize you've been riding on a plane all day. If you are and you think you're going to be a little bit longer, I'll put a plate aside for you."

"Sounds good to me. I would sure appreciate that Mrs. White."

"Smells really good too Mrs. White, I didn't hear you say anything about how good it smells!" she jested.

Little shook his head and chuckled. "You and Mrs. Picott are too much. It smells good too."

"Why thank you Mr. Thomas. I do appreciate that very much."

The room was large and spacious, but not as large and scenic as his room at UNE. Facing the front of the building, he had a very nice view of the lawns and other structures in the vicinity. It was warm and cozy. Little looked at his watch. Gently, he stroked it as he fondly remembered receiving the watch this Christmas as a gift from his Aunt Lanet and Uncle Jerome. His aunt Shera and uncle Kenneth had given him a Bible for Christmas. Pants, shirts, and a suit from his parents were included in the Christmas package they sent him in Kansas. As usual, they included gifts for Swoosh as well. It was six-thirty; he started out at ten o'clock this morning. What was supposed to be a three-hour flight, turned into seven hours. What should have been a thirty-minute drive from the airport, turned into an hour and thirty minutes. Quickly, Little changed his clothes and washed up. Hungry after the long flight, he made it down just in time to eat.

"Little, I have to be going home now," Mrs. Picott informed him. "They say the worst of the storm is about to come. My husband, Randy is waiting for me at home, so I better go home now to take care of him. I'm sure the students will help you. Dr. Haden said he'll be here tomorrow to see you. Mrs. White, thank you for dinner. It was very good and thanks for the plate for Randy. I know he'll appreciate it."

"Okay Jean, you drive carefully. And don't worry, we'll take good care of Mr. Thomas here."

Little walked over and hugged her. "Thank you, Mrs. Picott. Drive carefully."

The clock radio sounded. Little rolled over and looked out of the window. The radio announcer said, "The winter blizzard has finally come to an end. Folks, it is one for the record book and I hope that it will not be broken for another twenty years. By that time, I should have saved enough money to retire in sunny Florida. Five and a half feet of snow has fallen in the last eighteen hours and has paralyzed everything in Hampton, Newport News, Norfolk, and the surrounding area. Now this is something."

The announcer placed a special emphasis on his next statement. "Even the shipyard has closed down because of the storm. This is a first in its history. It will be several hours before the streets are plowed. You know we are not use to this much snow, so the governor has declared a state of emergency, and has requested snowplows from as far north as New Jersey to help out. The governor is requesting that you remain in your house and not get out on the roads until the plows have had a chance to clean the streets."

Little watched as the final few snowflakes continued to fall, helping to create the winter wonderland outside of his window. The brilliant sun reflected off the snow-covered ground, making the day even brighter.

The announcer continued, "The sky is clear of clouds, so you'd better wear your sunshades when outdoors. The bright white snow can cause snow blindness. So be careful folks."

All was quiet and peaceful. Glancing at his clock radio, it was seven thirty-five. *What a good night sleep I had. I haven't slept like that in several weeks. Guess I won't be going to work today.*

Outside of his room door he could hear the commotion in the hallway. Among the laughter and other noises, someone knocked on his door. "One minute," he shouted as he grabbed his robe to open the door. It was Grace.

"Good morning Thomas. Did you sleep well?"

"Good morning Grace."

"A couple of us stopped by your room last night after you left. We knocked, but you must have been asleep."

"I must have really been tired from all the traveling. I haven't slept like that in weeks."

"Mrs. White cooked breakfast and you can't refuse her oatmeal, especially on a cold morning like this or you're liable to get hit with one of her cooking spoons. She says, 'A good hot bowl of oatmeal on a cold day is good for the constitution.' The woman thinks she's everybody mother; in fact, my mother is not as bad as she is. So, if you want to live, you'd better come down for breakfast."

"You mean Mrs. White made it here this morning in all that snow?"

"Not actually, she stayed here last night. But even if she did go home, she would have made it right back here this morning to cook for us. I told you she thinks were her children and treats us just like it. Yesterday, I said she wasn't going anywhere. Last night, she kept waiting for the storm to stop, but it only got worse. After you left, it really snowed heavily."

Little laughed, "I guess her reindeer decided to fly away with the sleigh without her."

"Yeah, and her skies must be in her closet at home." He and Grace laughed.

"I was listening to the radio this morning and the weatherman said that over five and a half feet of snow fell overnight. Two feet fell in just one hour. Have you looked outside?"

"Yea, I was looking out of the window when you knocked on the door. It is awesome."

"The campus is beautiful, especially the chapel. Tell you what, after breakfast I'll give you a personal guided tour of the campus."

"Sounds good to me; you sure Mother White is going to let us outdoors?"

"Good point. I see you learn fast.

From behind Grace, a head appeared in the door.

"Hey dude," said Marcus, one of the students he met last night. "We're getting ready to go down to get some of Mrs. White's famous oatmeal. Then afterwards, we're going to go outside and play in the snow. You want to join us?"

"Sure, I heard on the radio that the shipyard is closed down because of the storm. I don't have to go to work. Let me get dressed, then I'll join you for breakfast. I hope I got something warm enough to put on."

"Just throw on any old thing."

"I would, but I figured I was coming South. So, I didn't come quite prepare for all this snow. I'll see you downstairs."

"If you don't, you can borrow something of mine. We look about the same size."

"Hey, thanks Marcus."

Grace looked pleased as Little accepted their invitation. "Okay, but hurry up. Mrs. White is determined to feed us and get out of here."

After breakfast, the male students volunteered to help the maintenance department. Arming themselves with coats, gloves, boots, and shovels, they set about digging out the campus streets and sidewalks. When the work was completed, it was time for fun. Together, they built a snow family. A father, mother holding a newborn snow baby in her arms, three brothers, two sisters, and a few relatives covered the lawn across from Holly Tree Inn. The students gathered large blocks of snow together for Claude, the art major, to create several large and small snow sculptures that they would work on for the next several days. With the aid of everyone, on the circle in front of Odgen Hall, he sculpted an eagle perched on a branch. At the entrance of the campus, he sculpted two six-foot high horses. In front of Huntington Hall, the library, he created a school of fish reading. The sculpture on the lawn by the campus chapel was of two swans and a few geese swimming on a pond.

Grace, Little's self-appointed personal tour guide, relayed the history of the campus as they helped with the sculptures. "Booker T. Washington, the founder of Tuskegee Institute in Tuskegee, Alabama, is one of Hampton's most famous alumni. That building over there," she said pointing to Armstrong-Slater Hall, "is where he took classes."

Little enjoyed her company as they worked on the swans, and as she told him the rich history of Hampton Institute. "The campus choir practices in Clark Hall, that's the building next to Armstrong-Slater. Nathaniel Dett, the director of the choir, is also a world-renowned composer. I sing soprano in the concert choir. This spring we're going to Europe, and we will be singing before the Queen of England. In fact, the dormitory Virginia-Cleveland Hall, was said to have been sung up by the choir. We sing every Sunday in the chapel. Do you sing, Little?"

"I know that once they were the Hampton Jubilee Singers."

His answer surprised her. "How did you know that? Have you been here before?"

"No, my uncle Canada and my high school guidance counselor attended Hampton." Looking up at the chapel, he thought it was an amazing building, especially the bell tower. "That sounds great. I'm not a great singer, but I play the piano. My mother made my brother and I take lessons since we were three years old. I played for the church choir back home."

"I play the piano too. Did you have a piano at home?"

"Yep. My grandma Edna gave me hers. She was the one that insisted my mother get me lessons. For ten years, she gave my brother and me lessons. Every day she made us practice and I hated it. But my brother Swoosh, he loves to play to this day. He's a natural."

"Is she still alive?"

"No, she died when I was thirteen; she was ninety-eight years old. I believed she and Mimi Rhoda, her sister, lived that long just to give me piano lessons along with tutoring in Math, English, and other things. They both were schoolteachers."

"They sound like wonderful people."

"They were amazing. My mother said they were almost bedridden until I was born. Then they got a new lease on life. They started moving around doing things, going shopping, cooking, and whatever they wanted to do. They'd take Swoosh and I to the museum, the parks, Broadway shows, and all the sightseeing places in New York. Momma said I was just what they needed. I could always talk to them. I sometimes miss Grandma Edna and Mimi Rhoda."

"I love to hear you talk. I could listen to you talk for hours."

Little looked at Grace—she reminded him of an angel. "I got an idea. Let's make snow angels."

"Snow angels?" she replied inquisitively. "What are snow angels?"

"You don't know how to make snow angels? Okay, over there," he said pointing to the area in front of the chapel. "That looks like a good spot."

Together, they walked in the deep snow to the lawn in front of the chapel.

"Okay, hold my hand. Next, we're going to fall on our back in the snow. Then we move our arms and legs like this." Standing on one leg, Little demonstrated. "And when you get up you have a snow angel."

Grace was more than happy to hold Little's hand. Together, they fell back into the snow and began moving their arms and legs. While moving, they laughed wildly like two little children. Standing up, they walked over to the freshly shoveled sidewalk.

"What are those buildings over there, and where is the greenhouse?"

"That one is Stone Building. The bookstore, post office, alumni office, and men's dormitory are in there, and the other building is Wigwam Hall. Wigwam is a male dormitory. It was originally built to house the Indian students around the end of the century. I'm getting cold. Let's see if the chapel is open. It usually is."

As she continued to talk, they walked to the chapel. The door to the chapel was unlocked; inside, it was nice and warm. "After the snow melts, I'll show you the graveyard by James Hall where a lot of the Indian students were buried. The graves are old, most of them are of babies and children. They were moved here from Iowa by the government. Most of them died because of the change of climate and smallpox."

Looking around the inside of the chapel, Little was inspired. "It's beautiful in here, and the acoustics are great. This is really nice." For the next half hour, they sat and talked as she continued to give him a history lecture on the campus. "How come you know so much about the campus?"

"Tradition. As freshmen, we have to learn the history of the school. That's why we love Hampton, it's so full of tradition. It has a rich history. We have a great love for our home by the sea." Slowly, Grace rose to her feet and began putting her coat and gloves on. Shyly, she spoke, "We better get back to Holly Tree Inn. Everyone is going to wonder where we are."

"What about my tour?"

"How about we wait until the spring. Right now, it is too cold to walk around the campus. I promise, as soon as the spring comes, I'll give you a private tour."

"You promise?"

"I promise."

"Okay, during the spring, we'll finish the tour. I'm going to hold you to it. Let's go back by the front of the president's mansion. I want to see the house."

"We can't."

"Why not?"

"The president's mansion is the only original building on campus from when it was a plantation. It was built around seventeen eighty-five.

Students are not allowed to walk in front of the president's house, especially on the lawn in front of the mansion house. This school is full of tradition and rules."

"Okay, then let's run back. It's getting cold too." Laughing as they ran back. Back at Holly Tree Inn, Little helped her get her gloves, coat, hat, and boots off. It was the first time he noticed she had an oval-shaped face and almond-shaped eyes. Also, her hair and long slender fingers were like his mother's. Grace got Little and herself a cup of hot chocolate. Together, they joined the other students by the warm fireplace.

That Friday, three days after his arrival in Hampton, Virginia snow still covered the ground. Dr. Haden made it over to meet him and took him to the shipyard to report for his first day of work. Wearing the white shirt and tie the Griffins had given him, he was prepared to go into his office.

In anticipation of his arrival, everything had been taken care of. To his surprise and delight, Dr. Waldstriecher had made arrangements with the shipyard for his employment back in November, when he first approached Little about the prospect of working there. A small reception was planned in his honor. To everyone's surprise, the brilliant young male student from the University of New England, who was to head the engineering department on the project was a Negro.

After surviving his first day, he found the weekend a peaceful and welcome reprieve from the shipyard. On Sunday, Dr. Haden invited him to Queen Street Baptist Church and to dinner at his house. It was in church when he first saw her. Their eyes kept meeting during the sermon. After church they finally met Mrs. Haden made sure of that. Seeing the two of them looking at each other, she made it a point to introduce them. The brown-skinned female appeared poised and graceful. When she walked, it was like she floated. Every strand of her hair was in place. The little make-up she wore enhanced her attractive appearance. To Little, she was the most beautiful sight in the church.

Cassandra Ellen Martin was her name. He learned she was a twenty-year-old college sophomore attending William and Mary College in Williamsburg, Virginia. Ambitious, her intent was to attend law school after graduation. She was a local debutante, Miss Hampton High, and an honor roll student in both high school and college. She is the pride and joy of her father, a very prominent businessman in the area. First checking with her parents, Mrs. Haden invited Cassandra to dinner. Little's reputation as a top student at the University of New England had preceded him in the Negro community. Her parents were extremely pleased to have their daughter in the company of such an outstanding and promising young man.

The following Sunday, the Martins invited Little to their house for dinner, along with the Hadens. Mr. Martin was a self-made man. He attended Hampton Institute in the days when it was known as Hampton Agricultural and Technological College. His trade was plumbing, and he later graduated with a degree in business. Getting a small loan from the savings and loan, he opened his own plumbing business. After several years he took a gamble and opened his own plumbing supply warehouse. It became the largest in the area; the shipyard, naval yard, and federal government were among his top contracts. Self-important, during the dinner he conversed about himself and his business while he puffed on a cigar. Mrs. Martin, also a Hampton graduate, was a principal at a local elementary school. She received her PhD in Elementary Education. She was a very intelligent woman and a good homemaker. Somehow, Little saw Cassandra as a combination of them both, but definitely a daddy's girl. They were fascinated with Little's manners, temperament, and his credentials as a presidential scholar. They recognized he had the character of an outstanding and respectable citizen. He was a young man of good character, reputation, and an excellent prospect for their daughter. They decided to encourage the relationship.

It took only a few days for Little to adjust to his work schedule. His days started early. He was up at six o'clock in the morning to get breakfast before catching the six forty-five bus for work. The bus trip to work took an hour and ten minutes. Due to the bus schedule, he always arrived early. If he missed the first bus, he would be an hour late for work. Unbeknownst to him, the person, who had agreed to pick him up in the morning and bring him back home in the evening, their work schedule suddenly changed.

Knowing he had to walk one mile to catch the bus in downtown Hampton, Mrs. White made sure his plate was always ready and on time. Special arrangements were made for him to leave work early on Tuesdays and Thursdays to take classes in the afternoon at the college. Other than that, he normally got off work at four o'clock and arrived home at six-fifteen, exhausted.

The one thing he could count on was his nightly phone call at seven-thirty from Cassandra. He looked forward to her calls. They were the highlight of his evenings. They'd talk on the phone for an hour. Her parents were strict about that. Although she was in college, she still lived at home with her parents. Sometimes in the evening on Wednesdays, she drove to the campus to visit him. The first Saturday, they went to the movies at the Wythe Theater on Kecoughtan Road, it was a special day for him. In the movies, he stole his first kiss from her; initially they both blushed. Later that evening when she dropped him home at the Holly Tree Inn, they kissed passionately in the car.

Something burst inside of him, a feeling he had never experienced before swept over him. For Little, it was love as never felt before. When they looked up, the windows of the car were fogged. Together, they laughed. This day he would always treasure in his heart. It was his first real kiss. He kissed the woman he loved. She was his first real love.

In the next few weeks, their relationship soared. The times they spent together and on the phone with each other were very precious to them. He looked forward to seeing her in church each Sunday. During the day, he dreamed about her. At night, he longed to be by her side. Thinking of her helped him make it through some of the trying times at the shipyard where things were not so great. Little knew he wanted to share his life with her; one day, tell her all about himself.

Conflict and tension seem to always be part of the job. Not knowing whether it was his age or race, Little had no clue as to what to do. Many of the older white men in the engineering department openly resented his being there. Other than two or three of the men, he found himself excluded from lunch and coffee breaks with the boys. Although many times they had to go back and implement his recommendations they were not open to his suggestions. The men constantly questioned his authority and credentials. They would cite how they had degrees in engineering and had been employed in the profession for ten, fifteen, twenty, thirty, and forty years. To them, he was just a student. The truth was he was more knowledgeable of the field and project than all of them.

Two or three times a week he spoke to his uncle Canada. It was at his uncle Canada's urging that he finally called Dr. Waldstriecher for back up. After the department supervisor got off the phone, his face was red. He could not apologize enough to Little. Dr. Waldstriecher established Little's credibility and position along with a Naval Commander in the Pentagon. The isolation and rejection at work made his relationship with Cassandra stronger, and Cassandra's calls in the evening became that much more important to him. He was able to confide in her. He thought she understood.

"Hey Little," said Marcus. "There was a message for you earlier to expect a phone call at seven tonight."

"Thanks Marcus. It's probably Cassandra. She said she was going to call me earlier than usual." When the hall phone rang, he answered, "Hello Cassandra, love of my life."

"Hello Thomas."

Pause.

"No, you tell me. Who is Cassandra? This is your uncle."

Pause.

"How many uncles do you have? I'll give you a hint, I'm your father's brother, and I live in Washington, DC."

Pause.

"That's right, it's your uncle Junebug," he said laughing. "I'd still like to know who Cassandra is."

Pause.

"Some girl you're seeing! You've only been there for a little over a month. Seems to me that you're working mighty fast nephew."

Pause.

"Hey, what happened to hello Uncle Junebug? How are you and Aunt Madie?"

Pause.

"Now, that's better."

Pause.

"No. Jerald told me you were there."

Pause.

"Your aunt Madie, uncle Canada, and I spoke with him last week. Kansas was playing Georgetown here in DC. Your aunt, uncle, and I were at the game and we saw him. He told us you were working in Virginia at the Newport News Drydock and Shipbuilding Company. That's really great. He said you're working on the nuclear project that you were working on at school.

Pause.

"I think it's a great opportunity for you. I can't tell you how proud your Aunt Madie and I are of you. I know Elijah and Ruth are also.

Pause.

Junebug sound surprised at the question Little asked. "My nephew, yours and Jerald's godfather, Canada. No, I didn't get your number from him. Does he know you're living and working in Virginia?"

Pause.

"Well, he never told me or Madie he called you or knew you were in Virginia. You know what. He probably got your number from Jerald when we saw him at the game, just like I did."

Pause.

"That's right; Jerald gave us your number. Is there a problem with his giving us your number? Thomas, maybe it's me, but you're sounding a bit hostile. Is there something wrong?"

Pause.

"No, I understand your being tired from work. I guess you're more used to studying than going to work every day. How come you didn't let us know earlier that you were in Virginia? You know we're only three hours from you."

Pause.

"It was a last-minute decision. I can understand that. So how is everything working out for you?"

Pause.

"Sound very good. Thomas, I'm afraid I have some bad news for you. I don't want to tell you this over the phone son. So, you're going to have to come here to DC."

Pause.

"I know. I really wish I could tell you. But it is urgent. If it wasn't, I wouldn't be calling you insisting that you to come to DC right away."

Pause.

"I don't mean for it to sound mysterious, but, due to the nature of the situation, I can't say right now. I promised."

Pause.

Irritated, Junebug responded, "Thomas, what is with you boy? Please don't argue with me."

Pause.

Junebug began getting upset with Little's attitude. "Just one-minute young man, I understand that you're tired. But you seem to have an attitude, and I don't like it."

Pause.

"Thomas, just who do you think you're talking to? I realize I'm calling you, and I'm not making any sense."

Pause.

"Okay, okay, Thomas. You win. I really don't feel like arguing with you. I promised your aunt Sarah I wouldn't say anything to you over the phone. But since you insist, your uncle Canada is in the hospital. He was in an automobile accident a couple of days ago."

Pause.

"He went to the store to get some ice cream a drunk driver ran a red light and ran into his car."

Pause.

"It's very bad Thomas. He wants to see you."

Pause.

"No, your aunt Sarah is alright. She wasn't in the car at the time."

Pause.

"No, your parents were called a few days ago. They said they would contact you, but Sarah said she was concerned about upsetting you unnecessarily."

Pause.

"Your aunt Sarah, she's taking it hard. My sister is also taking it very hard. She loves her son, and he has always been very good to his mother."

Pause.

"She's doing a lot better now."

Pause.

"Listen, if you take a bus up Friday after work, I'll see that you get a ride back down on Sunday. What time do you get off work?"

Pause.

"Okay, we'll pick you up at the bus station Friday night around seven. We should be able to make it to the hospital before visiting hours are over. Hold on one minute." Long pause. "Your aunt Madie said to tell you hello, and she'll have dinner ready for you when you arrive."

Pause.

"Okay, then we'll see you on Friday."

Distressed over his uncle's call, Little sought out his friend Marcus.

"Hey Marcus. It's me Little."

"What's up dude?"

"Are you still going to DC this weekend?"

"Sure thing. You don't have to stand in the doorway; you can come in the room."

"I'm listening out for the phone. I'm expecting another phone call."

"Yea cat," Marcus interrupted. "Sorry, I didn't tell you earlier—the voice on the phone was a man's voice. I forgot to tell you, it sort of slipped my mind."

"No problem Marcus. It was my uncle. He wants me to come up to DC this weekend. Mind if I ride the bus with you?"

"More than one seat on the bus. You pay to ride like everyone else. I can't stop you."

"I'll take that as a yes."

"You got it cat. Cecil is riding up too."

"Like you said, more than one seat on the bus. My uncle said that he'll pick me up from the bus station."

"Sounds good to me cat. I didn't know you had family in DC. Is everything alright?"

"My uncle, he's really a cousin was in an automobile accident."

"Bummer. How is he?"

"It's nothing serious. He'll be alright. Sometimes my family tends to overreact. I think they just want to get me up there to iron out some family problems."

Standing partially in the hall, Little heard the phone rang. "Seven-thirty sharp, right on time" he shouted. "That's my sweetheart; got to run cat." Picking up the phone he pleasantly greeted with, "Hello sweetheart."

Pause.

"How did I know it was you? I'll give you one guess."

Pause.

"No, sorry I can't this Saturday."

Pause.

"I'm going to be out of town. I have to go to DC on some business."

Pause.

"I'm leaving as soon as I get out of the office Friday with Marcus and Cecil. I'll be back sometime Sunday evening."

Pause.

"I'm not sure what time I'll get back on Sunday. It really depends on my ride. But I'll call you first thing when I get back."

Pause.

"I wish I could see you tomorrow night, but I have class. Then you know I have to get up early to go to work."

Pause.

"Ah Cassandra, I wish you wouldn't say that. You know I love you, but you know I can't skip class."

Pause.

No, I have to go Friday. I can't get out of it."

Pause.

"I'll try and get back early enough Sunday. If not, then I guess we won't be able to see each other until next Wednesday."

Pause.

Speaking in a soft tone, Little turned to face the wall. "No, I really do have to go. It's a family matter."

Pause.

"It's really personal. I can't tell you about it right now."

Pause.

Signs of stress could be heard in his voice. "Oh god. Cassandra you know that's not true. You know I don't have someone else in Washington. I'm being completely honest with you. I am not seeing anybody else."

Pause.

"Marcus and Cecil. They're going home for the weekend; their going has nothing to do with me. I told you before that I have family in Washington. Remember, I was supposed to go see my uncle Canada last week. You asked me not to go. I've been putting this trip off too long."

Pause.

"Don't do this to me, Cassandra. Look, my uncle Junebug called and said my Uncle Canada is in the hospital."

Pause.

"He was in an automobile accident."

"Cassandra I am not lying. My uncle Junebug called me this evening and said he was. Why would I lie just to go to DC?"

Pause.

"I know I've been saying I need to go to DC these last few weeks. But I wouldn't lie about my uncle being in the hospital."

Pause.

"Okay, look, I'll take a later bus to DC so we can spend some time together Friday. Okay? And I promise, I'll get back as soon as I can, and I'll call you first thing when I get back."

Pause.

"Okay sweetheart, I promise. I have to study too for my class tomorrow. I love you."

TOO LITTLE TOO LATE

Junebug sat next to Little on the couch in the den. "I hoped you would have arrived earlier so we could have gone to the hospital before visiting hours were over." Little shuffled in his seat and moved away from his uncle. "You know Thomas, ever since you arrived you seem so distant. You haven't said much at all this evening. What's wrong?"

"If I was able to, I would have come earlier. Like I said, I couldn't help it." Little turned his head and looked in the opposite direction from his uncle. *I don't know why you're even bothering to ask the question. You know good and well what's wrong.* "And I told you, nothing was wrong. How many times do I have to repeat myself?"

Junebug was getting disturbed with Little's attitude. "Thomas, look at me."

Little faced his uncle.

Perturbed, Junebug spoke in a softer tone. "I can tell something is bothering you and it's not about your uncle Canada. You can talk to me. Now, what is it son?"

You're not my aunt and uncle; Elijah's not my father and you know it. Irritated with his uncle Junebug's persistence, he responded in a negative tone. "I said its nothing. Like I told you, just work and all. Things at the shipyard aren't as I expected. I still have to get accustomed to working and not studying. There's a lot of pressure on the job. Besides, I had a pretty rough week on the job. This is the first weekend I've had off since I arrived. I guess I'm just not use to the routine yet, and then traveling up here on the bus. I guess I'm just a little extra tired and a little bummed out. That's all."

Junebug realized that he was getting nowhere and was becoming very annoyed with Little's negative attitude. He decided to back off and leave it alone. "Well, you won't have to get up too early tomorrow. Visiting hours began at eleven o'clock. Like I said, I had hoped to go tonight, but your bus arrived later than you said. Visiting hours are over at nine."

Using a very sarcastic tone, he looked dead into his uncle's face. "Like I said Uncle Junebug, I couldn't help it. I missed the first bus." *Visiting hours my eye. Is that where Ruth and Elijah are waiting for me at the hospital? This is a trick to get me up here so we can talk. You may have me here and get me there tomorrow. But I don't have to talk, and I am not going to talk to them. Your plan is just not going to work out.* Little began standing up. "It's late. If it's alright with you, I think I'll go to bed now."

"Sure. Good night Thomas." Junebug could not help himself to his last comment. "I sure hope you have a better attitude in the morning."

"Yea right, good night."

Grudgingly, Little got out of bed that morning as Junebug called out to him. He could smell the bacon and hear the eggs frying in the kitchen. All night, he tossed and turned in bed agonizing over meeting with his parents.

He wondered why he'd bothered to come. No sooner had he fallen asleep; he'd wake up. His mind was preoccupied all night with meeting his parents.

The thought of the meeting haunted and hindered his sleep. He also dreamed about his uncle Canada. His uncle stood at the foot of his bed and told him to be patient. Everything was going to be all right. They had a long conversation. It was a good, but a strange conversation. After showering, he made his way to the kitchen table, "Good morning, everybody."

Madie looked at him oddly because of his cold and impersonal greeting.

"Thomas, did you sleep alright last night? You don't look like you did."

Is it that obvious? "No, I didn't sleep too well."

"Here, sit down and have some breakfast." Immediately, she pulled out a chair at the table and indicated for him to sit. "Your uncle had to go to the store this morning. He should be back in a half-hour."

"Are Ruth…" Suddenly, the words of Mrs. Griffin echoed in his ears. "I mean my parents, are they here?"

"You mean here in Washington?"

"Yes."

"No. Why? Are they supposed to be?"

"No. I was just wondering. I mean, with all the secrecy about uncle Canada. I just thought."

"Boy, in all these years you haven't changed one bit. You're just like your daddy, always thinking. You just gotta know everything. You and Elijah are so much alike. I think I hear your uncle coming in the house now," she said as she placed a plate of food in front of him.

Sure! You can win an award for this outstanding performance, but I know you'll say anything to get me somewhere to meet with them. But it makes no difference to me. I just won't say anything.

Sitting at the breakfast table, Junebug looked at Little. "Thomas?" he said questioningly. "That scar on your neck. It looks like you had a tracheotomy?" Junebug leaned forward to exam the scar. With his finger, he pressed against it. Junebug's examination evoked a response that Little himself did not expect. A cold chill went up and down Little's spine as his uncle's finger touched his neck. "When did this happen?"

Immediately, he jumped back breaking the physical examination and visual inspection. In a hostile voice, he shouted, "Get your hand off me. You know what happened!"

Junebug shouted, "Young man, don't you use that tone of voice with me. Just who do you think you're talking to?"

Aunt Madie shouted, "Thomas, what's gotten into you?"

"Why didn't you tell me Elijah wasn't my father?"

"What?"

"You knew Elijah wasn't my father and you never told me. That's what! Brought me down to Canaan pretending it was my inheritance. Talked like those people were my ancestors while knowing good and well his heir was in the grave by that burned down house."

"Thomas!" Madie shouted in surprise. "Stop that right now. I will not have you disrespecting your father or my husband in my house. What's gotten into you boy? Have you taken leave of your senses? You're talking nonsense. Elijah is your daddy."

"Please Aunt Madie, I'm not a child! No, he's not my father. You know he adopted me!"

"That's a lie straight from the pit of hell! Where did you get this nonsense from? Boy, what in God's name is wrong with you this morning?"

"You don't have to pretend or play games with me Aunt Madie, I know the truth. And Uncle Junebug, I know Uncle Canada has been talking to you!"

Madie turned to face her husband. Junebug threw up his hand as a gesture to stop his wife from talking. She looked at him puzzled. "Harold, what is Thomas talking about?"

Junebug took a deep breath. After a long sigh, he looked at Little and his wife. "Sit down Madie. It's true, Thomas is telling the truth. Elijah adopted him right after he and Ruth got married, when he was about two months old."

She gasped. "Harold, you never told me that." She turned toward Little. "Thomas baby, I'm sorry. I never knew that."

"I promised Elijah and Ruth that I would never tell a soul. Not even you Madie. I'm sorry son; please try and understand, but it wasn't my place to tell you. I was respecting the wishes of your parents. I don't know how you found out. But whatever happened, one thing I do know Thomas, Elijah loves you very much. He loves you and cares for you like you're his natural born child. He has never treated you any different from Elisha and Esther. He loves all three of you the same. Is that what all this has been about?"

Little looked at his aunt. "I'm sorry Aunt Madie, for talking to you the way I did. I think I'd better leave."

"Calm down Thomas. Let's talk."

Little stood up, speaking harshly he shouted, "I really don't feel like talking about it right now. Call your brother. Ask him if you haven't already. I'm surprised he hasn't already told you."

Junebug stood up. In a very clear, raised, authoritarian voice he shouted, "Thomas Isaiah Thomas sit your ass back down in that chair right now! You're not going anywhere! Now, I don't know everything that went on or what's going on in your head right now, but whatever it is, we're going to get down to the bottom of it right now."

Looking defiantly at his uncle, Little stood his ground. Madie slowly walked over to Little and gently placed her hand on his shoulder nudging him to sit down. Slowly, he sat back down. Gently, she massaged his back as she spoke. "What's this about Canada? What does Canada have to do with it?"

Reluctantly, Little began telling them the situation involving the trip to Chicago. He explained to them how the situation with Bigger Thomas, Bessie, and his mother's mother caused him to leave. "I spoke to Uncle Canada when I was in Kansas at the Griffins. I didn't know what to do, so I called and talked to him. I told him what happened, how I felt, and that I didn't want to go back to UNE. He went over my options with me. We discussed the pros and cons. Finally, he said to take the job at the shipyard, because professionally it would be to my advantage and give me the break I needed. Uncle Canada always treated me like a grown-up, not like a kid or child or teenager. Since he graduated from Hampton, he contacted Dr. Hamilton and helped get me into the school and a place to stay on campus."

"Thomas, you could have come to us."

"I didn't feel I could talk to you. When Swoosh suggested Uncle Canada, I knew he wouldn't tell me what to do, and he would help me do what I wanted to do. During his business trips to Connecticut, he'd stop at the university to see me. He'd always take my friends and me out to dinner. He'd call regularly. I know he also visited Swoosh a few times. He and Aunt Sarah were always sending us money and care packages."

Junebug placed his hands on Little's. "Canada was closer to you because he lived up in New York with you while he was in college. I have no problem with that son. Now, you're telling me that Canada knew all the time that you were in Virginia, and he helped you get there?"

"Yes. He paid for my plane ticket. My plane was supposed to stop in Washington, and he was going to meet me at the airport. Because of the snowstorm the plane landed in Newport News instead. I was supposed to come to Washington a few weekends ago. We were supposed to talk about things, but I couldn't make it at the time. He never put pressure on me to talk to my folks about my plans, and he said he wouldn't tell them or anyone else. Except Aunt Sarah, he said he couldn't live in the house if he didn't tell her. But he promised she wouldn't tell anyone either."

"So young man, that is what the attitude on the phone that night, last night and this morning was all about?"

"Yes sir."

Junebug looked him in his eyes. "Well, then, you should know what it is like to ask someone to keep a promise. Then you, if anyone, should understand keeping a promise to someone—you would not reveal what they've asked you to keep. Just as Canada promised he would not tell anyone about your whereabouts, I promised your father I would not tell anyone he adopted you. I kept my word. Just like your uncle Canada kept his."

"Yes sir. I'm sorry. I thought you were just trying to get me up here to meet with my parents. I'm sorry."

Annoyed, Junebug pushed away from Little. "Thomas, I am surprised at you. First, young man, my nephew, who loves you very much is in the hospital dying. We would have never made up such a story just to get you up here. You, of all people should know us better than that. What would make you think such a thing? You know I understand why you're so upset, but to think you would think that we would do such a thing." Junebug began raising his voice. "You're right about one thing. Had I known what was going on, I would have driven down to Hampton and dragged your butt back to New York." While he was talking, the doorbell rang.

"I'll get it, Junebug."

"No Madie. Let me get it. Because if I don't leave this room right now, I might do or say something that I know I'll regret." He threw up his hands as he left the kitchen. "Right now, I just can't deal with this boy. You talk to him."

Moments later, he could be heard opening the front door. "Sarah. Come on in. We were just getting ready to go to the hospital. Thomas is here. He's in the kitchen with Madie."

"Hello Uncle Junebug." They hugged and kissed at the door.

Junebug followed behind Sarah into the kitchen. Madie stood up and hugged her as she came into the kitchen. "Hello Sarah."

"Hello Aunt Madie."

Little hugged and kissed her, "Hi Aunt Sarah. How are you?"

"How are you Little?" Sarah sat down at the table. "Aunt Madie, may I have a cup of coffee please?"

"Sure baby." Madie got up to fix the coffee. "How is Canada this morning? We'll be going over to the hospital shortly."

Sarah took a sip of the coffee. Her eyes began filling up with tears.

"Aunt Madie, Uncle Junebug it's been so hard. I really don't know what I would have done without the two of you." Sarah gripped Little's hand. "He was hoping to see you last night, Little. He didn't want me to leave. We talked until about three o'clock this morning. He knew he was dying, so he wanted to make sure I had everything in order. He said he didn't want a funeral. He just wanted to be cremated. He's always said that. Ever since I met him, he said he wanted to be cremated. He said to just have a simple memorial service after Sunday church service for him. Said he didn't want all that crying and carrying on or relatives traveling long distances. He said to have people send money to Hampton as a memorial scholarship instead of flowers and things. You know how that man was. Always thinking of others and Hampton. Then he told me who should get what, and he made me promise to get married again. He said I was young and beautiful and could still have a family. You know all arrangements have been made. There's nothing left to do but carry out his wishes. Canada always had his house in order. His life was so well organized."

She began fighting back the tears as she looked at Little. "Little, I told him that you were coming. I told him to hang on until you got here, but he said he had already seen you. That you visited him in the hospital earlier in the day while I was gone." Puzzled, Madie and Junebug looked at Little. "I thought Uncle Junebug said you weren't arriving until seven. I'm so glad you came early so he got to see you. He couldn't hold on any longer. Seeing you made all the difference in the world to him Little. He just couldn't hold on any longer. I'm glad he got to tell you good-bye. I knew he was tired after all that talking, so I was holding him in my arms when he closed his eyes to go to sleep. He looked so peaceful. Oh God." Tears started rolling down her weary-looking face. "Canada died. He died around three o'clock this morning in my arms." She could no longer contain herself as a flood of tears burst forth.

"Oh no Sarah," Madie cried out. Without hesitation, Madie, and Junebug hurried to her side. Putting their arms around her, they tried to console her while they themselves cried.

"I knew he was dying Aunt Madie. I was expecting it. I thought I was prepared for his death. Oh, Aunt Madie it still hurts. Oh God, it hurts so bad inside and out. What am I going to do? What am I going to do?"

Stymied, Little sat in his seat as the tears streamed down his face. He had delayed his trip because of Cassandra. She did not want him to go. If it had not been for the disturbing dream he had about his uncle Canada and his parents he might not have come. *If I didn't have that dream, I wouldn't be here now. I never went to the hospital. I didn't see Uncle Canada.* Little slowly began weeping. *Died, he died. No, Uncle*

Canada can't be dead; I never got to see him. I never got to see him. He died, he died and it's my fault. It's my fault that he never saw me, he never said good-bye to me. I didn't get to say good-bye to him. It's all my fault.

The quiet memorial service after church was simple like Canada requested.

Filled with guilt, Little called the shipyard for the time off. Then, a grief-stricken Little called Cassandra.

"But you said you were coming back early Sunday, and here it is Monday morning. You're just now calling me."

Pause.

"Well, I don't understand it Little. Why do you have to stay until Wednesday?"

Pause.

"Your aunt! What about me? Is everyone else going to be more important than me? I don't hear you saying anything about considering my feelings."

Little turned his back as he talked into the phone.

"I know you told me your uncle died. What do you want me to do? From what you told me, he's not really your uncle. He's not really in your family. I think you're just making up something to stay in DC longer."

Pause.

"I'll tell you what Little. This is getting us nowhere. If you're not here by tomorrow, then you can forget about us."

Pause.

"Yes I do mean it. If you loved me, you wouldn't have gone to DC in the first place."

Pause.

"Don't give me that family business. I'm supposed to be your girlfriend."

Pause.

"Look, like I said earlier, if you're not here tomorrow, then it's over. Good-bye and have a nice life."

Shocked and stunned by the death of his uncle, Cassandra's attitude added to his confusion. Inwardly, he had mixed feelings. He was torn between his family and his girlfriend.

"Aunt Madie."

"Yes Little."

"I want to go back to Hampton tonight."

"I understand Little. I know how close you and Canada were. We're all feeling his lost. I really wish you wouldn't go so soon."

"After we go over to Aunt Sarah's house this morning, you can drop me off at the bus station. I did promise her I would have lunch with her today. You won't need to drive me back down to Virginia."

"Okay. Let me go talk to your uncle Junebug and see what he says. I'm sure it would be okay with him."

Little was preoccupied during the drive to Sarah's house and during lunch. He knew he had not seen his uncle Canada as his aunt believed.

"Little," inquired Sarah. "You seem to be a million miles away."

"I'm sorry Aunt Sarah. I don't mean to be rude."

"Don't worry about it. I believe I know how you're feeling. Now that we're finished lunch, I want to give you what your uncle Canada left for you. When you told him you were going to be at Hampton, he was so happy. Little, he was so excited that you were at his alma mater, it was all he could talk about." Quickly, she put her hands to her mouth.

"Oh Little, I'm sorry."

"It's alright Aunt Sarah, I told them about Chicago and Uncle Canada helping me get to Hampton. They know that I made you and Uncle Canada promised not to tell anybody."

She walked over to Little and took him into her arms. "I'm so glad that you told them sweetheart. I felt so bad keeping it from Uncle Junebug and Aunt Madie. I know they love you just as much as Canada and I." Gently, she stroked Little's arm. "After you arrived in Hampton, yelling and screaming at Canada was all I could do to stop him from jumping in the car and driving down there to see you. Looking back, now, I wish I had of let him go. But, aside from yelling and screaming to stop him, we went shopping for you. He said his godson had to have a brand new wardrobe. You know Canada, I couldn't stop him even if I wanted to, so I joined him and loved every minute of it. Loving Canada meant loving you and Swoosh. You guys were a package deal. Come on." Taking him by the hand, she led him into the guest bedroom. "Aunt Madie, you and Uncle Junebug come on too." Opening the closet door, she showed him the clothes. "We brought you five suits, twelve shirts, three belts, and two pairs of shoes to match. Canada was a dresser, and he and I wanted you to be just as dapper as him. He was trying to get you up here to surprise you with them."

"Aunt Sarah, you shouldn't have."

"I know you can also wear his clothes. So, I want you to go into the room and pick yourself out some things. Also, pick out some things for Swoosh. Your uncle would have wanted you two to have first selection."

"But Aunt Sarah."

"No buts Little." Embracing her abdomen, she continued, "You know Canada and I thought we couldn't have children. When he was a teenager, he had the mumps. Ever since I've known him, he always thought of you and Swoosh. Both of you are our godsons. He always wished that he could have spent more time with you boys. But because of his job, he was away from home. Canada made a lot of money as an international negotiator. He was the best in his field. I remember he got his start with Congressman Adam Clayton Powell. He first worked for Representative Powell when he graduated from Yale's law school. Like Adam said at the memorial service, 'He was bright, young, extremely articulate, and the best-dressed man in all of Washington, DC.' Make sure you get some of Canada's cuff links, rings, and gold chains. He explicitly said that you and Swoosh are to have the first selection before anyone else. There are a few pieces that he especially wanted you to have. I put them in the chest over there with the rest of the things he said to give to you. Be sure you put some jewelry away for Swoosh. If you want, you and Swoosh can have all of it. Between you and Swoosh, I can't think of anyone else I'd rather see have Canada's belongings."

Little began to weep as he slumped on the bed. "I can't take everything Aunt Sarah. I really don't deserve any of Uncle Canada's possessions."

Sarah moved next to him and began gently massaging his back. "It's alright Little. He wanted you and Swoosh to have his things. Everybody knew you boys were his favorite. These things are yours because Canada wanted you to have them. I want you to have them. Now..." she said nudging him to get up, "The last thing Canada left for you is in the garage. It's large, so I put it in the garage. Uncle Junebug, would you get it out of the garage for me please?"

"Sarah, you sure I won't need help carrying it?"

"I guess you will need help."

Little lowered his head in shame. "But Aunt Sarah, you don't understand."

"What's wrong Little?"

"I never spoke to Uncle Canada before he died. I wasn't at the hospital like he told you. I didn't get here until after ten o'clock Friday evening."

Little sat back down on the bed and cried. "I feel so bad, so bad. I didn't come when Uncle Canada told me because I thought he was going to have my parents here. You know, to try and patch things up between us. Then, when Uncle Junebug called, I thought it was a trick to get me up here. Uncle Canada knew I'd never stay mad at him and he did say he wanted to help me work things out between us. I didn't trust him. I feel so bad, because he died, and I wasn't here for him."

Sarah put her arm around Little. "Don't fret over it, Little. Somehow, Canada saw you. What's important is Canada saw you, and he died in peace. You know the one thing your uncle was good at was forgiving. I know he forgives you, but whatever else you're feeling inside, you're going to have to work that out with God. You've got to learn to forgive others and yourself."

Junebug interrupted, "Why don't we all go into the garage. This way we can put it into my car; we won't have to bring it back into the house."

"That's what Canada would say. It makes no sense in moving things twice. Make one trip do for all. Better grab your coats."

The group entered the garage through the kitchen. Pressing a button, the garage door opened providing more light from the noonday sun. The three-car garage was well kept. An arsenal of mechanical and gardening tools hung neatly on the pegboard on one side. Canada's workbench was well organized and clean. Two cars, a brand-new black Lincoln Continental, and a white- and aqua-colored 1956 Buick Roadmaster were parked in the garage.

"Canada always loved to work out here and in the garden. That man was always calling himself fixing something. Thomas," she turned around facing him. Reaching into her purse she took out a key and dropped it into Little's hand. "This is for you. It's to the Buick. I told Canada you would need something to get back and forth to work. Since he did most of the shopping for your clothes, I said I was going to pick out the car."

"Aunt Sarah, this is his favorite car. He wouldn't even let you drive it."

"When I said this car, that man grabbed me and kissed me like crazy. Told me I couldn't have made a better choice. That's just how much he loved you Little."

"A car! Aunt Sarah, I don't know what to say." Something desperately was eating him up inside. *This Buick is his most prized possession. Swoosh and I joked about which one he loved more, this car or Aunt Sarah. I don't deserve it.* "I'm sorry Aunt Sarah, I can't take this," he cried with tears rolling down his cheeks.

"Oh yes you can son, and you are. I told you, Canada knows how much you liked the Buick when you were here on vacation with your parents. He wanted to give it to you himself. He said you needed something to get back and forth to work, especially after the guy who was supposed to give you a ride backed out. Unfortunately, he died before he could give it to you. God rest his soul, before he had a chance to give it to you himself. He was looking forward to giving it to you himself. He was so excited. Just like a little child. So, now it's yours. Go ahead, get in it and start it up."

Reluctantly, Little sat in the car. Starting it, the engine purred like a kitten just as he had remembered. "The registration is in the glove compartment. Canada had me register it a week ago in your name, so the paperwork and everything is straight. He looked at the odometer; it has only ten thousand miles on it. Canada mostly liked to sport around town in it when he wasn't off on a business trip."

Little got out of the car and hugged his aunt Sarah. "I don't really know what to say."

"Don't say anything. Just remember Canada always loved you and he expected you to always do the right thing. I know Canada is gone, but I'm still here. Like always, if you need anything, I'll always be here for you. Okay?"

"Yes Aunt Sarah."

"Now, let's go back into the house, so you can pick out some clothes for you and for Swoosh. Then we can put your things into the car, so you can get back to Hampton."

AFFAIRS OF THE HEART

I'm so glad I get off early today. These guys are about to drive me crazy. I'd rather be in class taking a test with crazy old Kravitz than be with this bunch of rednecks. Walking to the drafting table of one of his co-workers, Little stood at the table momentarily before addressing him. *God, I hate to, but I have to.* "George, why did you make those changes without checking the calibrations to see if the changes would work? You know these changes will not allow the capacitor to operate at maximum capacity. If I hadn't caught it, it would have caused another delay in the entire project."

"Check with Jim. He told me to make the changes."

"George don't just push it off on Jim. You're equally aware that all changes must be approved, and calibrations must be completed. Then any changes must be approved by me before you submit them."

"Hey Thomas, like I said, check with Jim."

"No George, you're just as responsible. You're…never mind," Little crossed over the room to the hallway. *If anything, I detest it's having to confront Jim Bestler. He has given me a hassle ever since I came to work here. Every time we talk, it becomes a major confrontation. I hate having to deal with that racist redneck. Now here we go again. Why does he think he can just walk over me and get away with it? What does he hope to gain, or prove?*

Little took a deep breath before entering Jim's workspace. "Jim, I just spoke with George. He said you told him to make these changes." Little rolled the plan out on Jim's desk. "Why would you approve changes when the calibrations were never completed? I specifically told you before you change anything, you are to check the calibrations and to check with me before sending them forward."

"Hey boy, just who do you think you are? I don't take my orders from you. I've been an engineer for over thirty-two years, way before you were born, and probably long before your mammy knew your pappy. And I definitely was working here long before you were out of diapers. Don't think you're going to come around here Mr. UNE and tell me what to do! I don't have to take orders from a kid, especially from your kind."

Little knew the real issue. However, he also knew what Jim was trying to do. "Look Jim, as long as I'm heading this project, and you're assigned to work on it, you'll take your orders from me."

"Who says?"

"So says the United States Navy, that's who placed me in this position. Now, if you don't like it, you can transfer to another department."

"Boy, I'm not going anywhere. I was here before you arrived on the scene, and I'll be here long after you're gone. So, you people had better get used to me being around and in charge."

"Well, as it stands right now, I am here. I am in charge, and I'll be here until after this project is completed. So, you had better get used to that. Until I'm told otherwise, I want those calibrations and specification completed according to the specifications that I gave you. Then after you've made the appropriate changes, send them to me for my final approval." *I'm so glad today is a short day for me. If I have to spend another minute with this clown, I'm gonna kill him.* "I want those calibrations and specifications on my desk first thing in the morning."

Raising his voice for everyone in the area to hear, Jim shouted, "And if they're not, what are you going to do boy? If you want them that bad you better do them yourself!"

Everyone looked up from their desks at Little as he passed by. Little knew there wasn't much he could do. Jim's defiant behavior, which began the moment they met had gone unchecked for the past few months. It was his insolent behavior that encouraged the other members of his team to also challenge his authority. Little knew his options, he could keep trading insults with Jim, or walk away as he had done many times before, but, this time, he could not resist. As he walked out of the office, he answered loud enough for everyone to hear. "The real problem is Jim, you wanted to head this project so bad. You feel because you've worked here for over thirty years you deserved to be named project head. But you're not project head. I am. If you were as good of an engineer as you think you are, they would have made you project head, not a college student, and a black one at that. Now, if they're not completed by tomorrow, then I guarantee the front office will be answering to the United States Navy for your insolence."

Little had scored a big one. Jim's face turned red with embarrassment as his long-time colleagues turned to face him. He was fuming. "What are you all looking at?" he shouted. "Get back to work."

An angry Little gathered his books and paperwork together. Getting into his car, he remembered the last time he talked to his uncle Canada about Jim. He said, "I know, Uncle Canada. God does not give us any more than we could bear."

Canada responded. "Little, the trials we go through come from three sources, God, Satan and self. Now, God did not bring this upon you. Neither did the devil. You chose to leave home the way you did. God would have you honor your parents."

In it, Little knew there was some truth. However, in this particular instance it was one of those remarks he was not too fond of and resented his uncle saying.

"What are you saying Uncle Canada?"

"I'm simply saying, be careful what you ask God for. But most of all, be careful what you blame on God."

Little remembered that he had to stop to the jewelry store on Mercury Boulevard before going to class. *I got to get out of here. I can't let these continual confrontations with Jim mess up my days and my weekends.* Getting out of building A and into the warm spring weather made him feel better. After leaving the jewelry store, he drove directly to Armstrong-Slater Hall for class. To his delight, class was canceled. *Good, I can go to my room and get some rest before I go out tonight with Cassandra.*

As he approached the steps of Holly Tree Inn, he saw Grace sitting on the porch. "Hey Grace."

"What's up Little? Shouldn't you be in class now?"

"Class was canceled. Dr. Segal's out sick again; it's that flu bug going around. How's everything going for you?"

"Are you kidding, between working here for Miss White and classes, things aren't so good, but then they could be worse," she laughed. "How are things on your job?"

"How much time do you have?"

"It's that bad?"

"Yea, I'm convinced the day after my last day will be my best day. Things haven't changed since we spoke yesterday, but then things could be worse."

"Yea, you could be working for Mrs. White," laughed Grace. "No, just joking. What happened?"

"I'm almost at my breaking point with that Jim Bestler, the guy I told you about who's been giving me a hard time since the day I arrived. The man still openly challenges me, and then he twists things around as if he is in control. Truth is, the way everybody in the department follow after Jim, he is in control. I've tried everything, working with him, through him, and around him, all your suggestions, my uncle Canada's and even Mrs. Picott's. I can't seem to win. Everyday, it's a fight with the guy. I think he goes home at night and dreams of what new stunts he can pull on me the next day. I believe the man thinks his life's mission is to make me miserable. Today, like always, he said, 'you people' and said, 'I don't have to take orders from your kind.'"

"Your kind!"

"Yeah, my kind. And I thought I had it bad with the white students at UNE. But those old white men at the shipyard are worse than the students. Now I know where their children learn their racist terms and behavior. They learn it at home, and it's reinforced in school. You know, being here at Hampton, it's been so nice for me. When I'm on campus, I don't have to worry about being judged based on the color of my skin; my black skin is not the problem. At UNE, I felt like I was under a microscope all the time, like my every move was being watched. I always felt like there was someone breathing down my back, just waiting for me to slip up. At the shipyard, I always got to be on my guard. I feel so much more comfortable and relaxed here on campus. But, when I go outside those gates, it's a whole 'nother ballpark."

"That's another story Little. I'm almost sorry I asked you about the job. It's too nice of a day to talk about troubles. Let's change the topic. How's the new car?"

"Besides Cassandra, the car is the best thing that happened to me in a long time. It's a lifesaver. Having that car these past few weeks has made my life so much easier and better for me. First, I get to work on time. I can go in early and stay late if I want to. Then, I can get to class and not have to rush in all upset and no more of that running for the bus while eating my bacon."

Noticing Mrs. White standing in the doorway Little raised his voice, "I can enjoy Mrs. White's wonderful breakfast and dinners, savoring each and every delicious morsel. I can savor the flavors in my mouth."

"I know you can," she bellowed.

Little and Grace played as if they were startled by her voice, "Oh, Mrs. White, how are you?"

"The more you enjoy it, the more you eat. I don't mind you eatin' more because I'm determined to put some meat on your skinny bones, Mr. Thomas. I don't want your mother accusin' me of starvin' her baby. Now, y'all stop talkin' about Mrs. White. You never know when I might show up. I know you knew I was standin' in the doorway. Y'all just tryin' to butter Mrs. White up. Keep up the good job, it's workin'." Laughing at them, she turned and walked away.

Little continued, "Having the car, you and I can go places, sightseeing—and do all the different things that I've wanted to do for a long time. The best part is that I can get to see Cassandra more, and she and I can go places too. I can't wait for it to get warmer so I can take you to Virginia Beach. The car is a blessing and a relief, especially in getting away from that shipyard."

"I'm sure it is. Now that you mentioned it, I can use one myself. How are things going with you and Cassandra? The last time we talked, the two of you were going to go to the movies; I believe you were in the middle of a big argument."

"You know how Cassandra is. Cassandra is Cassandra. She's nothing like you. She gets upset easy and for no reason at all, especially since I returned from DC. But then again, the most important part is we're still together."

"Amazing."

"Well, we resolved that old problem, then we went to the movies, but somehow, we got into another big argument all over again."

"Again."

"It was really stupid; sometimes, I don't understand her. She can be so spoiled, selfish, and judgmental at times. I really hate it when she's closed-minded. Sometimes, I don't know which is worse, her foul language, her smoking cigarettes, her jealously, or closed-mindedness."

"Try all of the above. But then Little, we've been over this before. I don't understand why you put up with her. I told you she doesn't feel the same way about you, as you feel about her. You two don't even share common interests. She smokes, and you don't. You don't like her smoking. She cusses. I've never heard not even one foul word come out of your mouth—she drinks, and you don't drink. She loves wild parties and now has you going to them. Exactly what do you see in her? She has you acting like someone you're not. Believe me, you really need to slow down and assess the relationship."

"Thank you Doctor Spock. No Grace, it's not all that bad. So she has a few bad habits. Couples have arguments all the time."

"Have you ever heard your parents argue? I've never heard mine say a cross word to each other."

"No Grace, it's not like that."

"Then tell me, what is it like?"

"I mean, not that we have arguments. We have disagreements. But that doesn't mean we don't love each other. And just because we don't share all common interests, doesn't mean we don't enjoy each other's company. Besides, you don't know anything about my past. I could be a murderer. Despite what you think or feel, I'm not Mr. Perfect."

"You got that right. They say love covers a multitude of sins. Come on my friend. Today's a nice spring day. No offense, but I don't feel like spoiling it by talking about Cassandra. I got an idea, let's get outdoors and go for a walk around the campus. The azaleas are gorgeous right now. Besides, I promised to give you a personal tour."

"Good idea. I need to go by the greenhouse. I want to get some flowers for Cassandra."

Holding hands, Little and Grace walked around the campus to the greenhouse. Entering the building, they did not see Mrs. Picott.

"Hello Mrs. Picott. Where are you?"

"Who's that calling me?"

"It's your favorite genius and his favorite sidekick."

"Oh God, not you two again? Come on back here. I'm in the second bay watering the plants." Little and Grace walked into the back where Mrs. Picott was watering plants. "What do you want now? You two were just in here yesterday and the day before that and the day before that. Don't you two have someone else to bug? Lord knows you ain't gonna give me a moments peace."

"So that's how you're going to treat your favorite and best customer."

"Best customer! Best customer my eye. Boy you haven't spent over five dollars in here since the day I met you. If I depended on your business, I would have been out of business long time ago. Besides all the free advice I give you. I should start charging you admission." Mrs. Picott looked at Grace. "I see you're in good company today. How are you Grace?"

"I'm fine Mrs. Picott."

"Now, what can I do for you, Mr. Big Spender?"

"I want to get some roses for Cassandra. We're going out tonight. We're celebrating our fourth month together."

"Oh no, here we go again. Little, I'll sell you the roses, but my heart goes out to where they're going. I've told you about that girl. You're going way too fast. You need to slow down."

"I told him the same thing, Mrs. Picott."

"Little, I like you and I like Cassandra. What bothers me and what I don't like is the two of you together. I've told you, she's not the right girl for you. She's way too fast for you. You're a very nice fella, and she a not so nice of a girl."

The trio walked to the front of the greenhouse. "Well, if she's not the right woman for me, then who is?"

"Grace for starters."

Grace blushed. "Mrs. Picott."

"He asked me Grace. I think the two of you would make a very nice couple. I've known Cassandra all her life. I've known her from the day she was born, and I've known her parents for a long, long time. The girl is spoiled rotten. She's a big daddy's girl. A snob, and very conniving just like her daddy. Cassandra cares for nobody but Cassandra. She's got a drinking and drug problem. She and her parents are more concerned about their social status than anything else. Now, her mother and brother are a little more down to earth. There's still hope for them."

Mrs. Picott continued to talk as she prepared the box of flowers for Little. "Now, I don't talk behind people's backs. I'm not saying anything that I haven't already told them to their face. The girl has had sex with practically all of her boyfriends. And believe me she's had several. Either you're a dog like those other guys and just want to get into her panties too, which I don't believe you are, or you're a fool in love with the wrong person. And if you're in love with her, you just better be careful because that girl will hurt you and think nothing of it. She's done it before; she'll do it again. You're no different from the others."

Little protested, "People do change Mrs. Picott,"

"A leopard doesn't change its spots. Here are your roses. Now, pay me. I put some extra Baby's Breath in them. I know how she likes her roses. So where are you two going tonight?"

"We're going over to Norfolk for dinner."

"Well, have a nice time. Grace, sorry we didn't have time to talk."

"He's a fool in love. Next time Mrs. Picott. Bye-bye."

"Grace, how about we take the long way back? We'll walk along the waterfront. There's something I want to tell you." Passing behind James Hall, Grace and Little walked along the water edge. *I don't know why I continue to visit Mrs. Picott. She's always putting down Cassandra. She doesn't know Cassandra the way I do. She's changed.* "Grace, what do you think about what Mrs. Picott said?"

"Why are you asking me?"

"I don't know. It's just that you've been a real friend to me. I value your opinion and our friendship. When I'm with you, I can talk and be myself. You've always been honest with me. I respect what you have to say." Walking by the point across from where Black Beard the pirate head was hung, Little stopped.

"What I say, Little, would it make any difference?"

Little paid her no attention. "Grace, I want to show you something."

Eagerly, Little removed a small package from his pocket. Opening it, he revealed a diamond engagement ring. "I'm going to ask Cassandra to marry me tonight."

Grace was stunned by his announcement. "Little, isn't it a little too soon? You've only known each other for four months. You really don't know her that well."

"I know all about her that I need to know. It doesn't take years to know a person or to know you're in love. Cassandra and I, we love each other. We fell in love with each other the first time we met."

"Little, after all the trouble she has put you through. How can you say you love her or that she loves you?"

"Sure, as a couple, we have our problems. But what couple doesn't? It doesn't mean we don't love each other. And we've always managed to work out our problems."

"No Little. You've always managed to give in to her. Didn't you hear a thing Mrs. Picott said?"

"Sure I did. I respect Mrs. Picott and what she has to say, but she's not always right. Besides, I just wanted to know your opinion about what she said."

"Little, what I say, would it make a difference?" Grace waited for him to give her a response. "I didn't think so. If you have to ask me about what Mrs. Picott said, then you're not sure about Cassandra yourself."

"That's hitting below the belt Grace. Besides, why are you getting so worked up?"

"You asked the question, not me. I've always been honest with you. I'm not going to start lying to you now. I think we have a great friendship and I value it. I hate to see you make a mistake. And believe me, you're about to make a big mistake." Grace turned, facing the Old Soldiers Home. "A really big mistake, and I believe you know it. You just don't want to face the truth."

"I didn't ask for you approval Grace."

Grace sharply turned and faced Little with tears in her eyes. Angrily she shouted, "Well, what do you expect me to say Little? I think it's terrific that you're about to ask a girl to marry you who's not right for you. A girl that has caused you nothing but trouble since the day you met her. She burned a hole in your suit. She cussed you out because you wanted to go to a game with some of your fraternity brothers. She can't stand your being friends with me. Wake up Little, and smell the coffee. What do you want me to say? I'm thrilled that you're about to throw your entire life away?"

"It's my life. I don't get it, what's it to you anyway? I don't know why you're so hostile. I just asked you one simple question."

"But you don't mind it if she gets hostile and throws stuff at you. You're so blind. I don't know what it is about you. With all your intelligence you refuse to see. The truth is, you don't want to see or hear the truth. You can't deal with the truth. You wouldn't know the truth if it were staring you right in the face. And you're right. It is your life. Why should I care? But I do, and you're too blind to see that!"

"Where do you get off calling me blind? You don't know me!"

"I know you better than you think. Ever since I met you that first day in January you've had something eating away at you on the inside. I don't know what it is, but I know it's there and if you don't get over it, it's going to destroy you. Whatever it is, it's made you blind to the real world. You're so blind to the truth until you can't stand hearing the truth. The real problem is Little, you don't know yourself."

Little was perturbed by her words. *She's just like Mrs. Griffin, thinks she knows me and can see right through me. I got news for you, no you can't and I'm going to stay away from you; I'm going to stay as far away as possible.* To avoid detection, he became defensive. "Oh yeah! Like you really know me! I come to you for some support, but what do I get. You know Grace, you're starting to get on my nerves. I got enough problems at work. I don't need any more from you or from Mrs. Picott."

"Support?" She?S sarcastically laughed. "Support for what? Why don't you see your girlfriend, Cassandra, for support? I thought that was what a relationship was all about. Hey, why don't I just give you a gun for you to blow your head off! That way you'll get it over quickly. One thing I agree with you on Little. You've got Cassandra, so you've got enough problems. You don't need me or Mrs. Picott helping you to ruin your life. And if that's the way you feel about it, the next time you have a problem with Jim, see your girlfriend Cassandra for support. The next time you and Cassandra have an argument, no, I mean a disagreement, don't come crying on my shoulder. Every other day you've been crying on my shoulders about how stubborn she's being or how selfish or jealous she is. I showed you support when I told you to go see your uncle. No, you chose to stay and please Cassandra. She's the reason why you never saw your uncle before he died. I tell you to leave Thursday night so you could see your uncle in the hospital, but no, Cassandra wanted you to stay with her. So, your uncle Canada died without seeing you. After you got back, on whose shoulder did you grieve? It certainly was not hers. She didn't want to hear it. She didn't want to hear that you didn't have a chance to say good-bye to your uncle. Her rag tag butt sure doesn't mind riding in the car or seeing you in the fancy suits and jewelry he left you. Then, there's all the other stuff. It's always what Cassandra wants. She stomps, you come running. Where was she when you were grieving? Did she show you support? No! She wanted you to take her to a party so she could show off your car. Remember, I'm not the one who isn't sure of what I'm doing. Believe me, she's going to break your heart, rip it out of your chest and stomp on it. And when that happens, don't come crying to me, Mr. Thomas!"

"Oh, don't you worry about that happening Miss Perfect. First of all, that's not going to happen and if it did, you'll be the last person I'd go to."

"That's fine with me Mr. Thomas Thomas."

"Me too, Miss Grace Johnson."

"Get out my way," she shouted brushing pass him. "I'm going back to Kennedy Hall. I hope you enjoy your date from hell and have a good life."

"Don't you worry about my life! You're just jealous."

Little's words struck a nerve with her. Grace turned around and stomped her foot. "Awww, jealous. Jealous! You, you!" Rushing back to Little, she grabbed the box of roses out of his hand and threw them into the river. Turning around she ran off crying, leaving Little standing on the river edge watching the roses float down the river into the Hampton Roads Bay.

"Grace, what did you do that for? Come back here. Grace, I said come back here."

"Go to hell, Little!"

Laying down on the bed, Little laid on his back with his hands tucked under his pillow behind his head. Looking back on this evening he thought about how good it was. *No, it was great. The best time we've had yet, and the best is yet to come. If this is what being engaged is like, I can't wait until we get married.* Smiling, he relaxed upon the bed. His day started out perfect—Jim Bestler, his archrival called in sick. The entire day was without incident. The other engineers without Jim around to instigate or provoke him worked as a team. Everything went smoothly and his evening turned out to be even better. After work, he met Cassandra for dinner. She was full of life, laughing, and talking like never before. Today, she was unlike herself in every way.

For the first time in a long time, Little enjoyed his dinner and his walk in the park by the James River Bridge with Cassandra. Tonight, he felt he was with a woman he had never known before. She was carefree and very loving toward him. Together, they laid in the grass on a blanket, holding each other. They were cozy and began passionately kissing. They both were swept away with a strong desire to become closer to know each other more intimately.

Night had fallen as they arose to go to the car. Arriving at her house they found no one was home. She invited him in. Seated on the couch in the living room they shared a coke and some small talk. Disappearing upstairs, five minutes later she returned in a euphoric state. The smell of her intoxicating perfume overshadowed the another slightly powerful odor he detected that contributed to her blissfulness. Sitting on the couch they held each other. Slowly, she unbuttoned his shirt and began kissing him on his bare chest. He could feel his heart pounding fast as she caressed his midsection. Sensitive to her sensuous touch, his body responded as she began stroking his rigid penis. He placed his hand upon her breast. She gasped in ecstasy as he kissed her erect nipple. Together, they laid down on the couch. He slipped his hand up her dress; she was not wearing panties. Overtaken by passion and by the power of the flesh, he slipped his fingers inside her moist vagina. She moaned sighs of rapturous delight and began loosening his belt.

Are you going to take her just like your father took your mother?? the voice asked.

His fleshly desire overpowered the voice he heard inside. Simultaneously, they jumped up as they heard a car engine driving into the driveway. It was her parents returning home from their evening out. Moving quickly, they ran into the family room and turned on the television as he put on his shirt and buttoned it. Tucking his shirt into his pants, he fastened his belt while she straightened her clothes. Seated on the couch, they laughed as her parents came into the house.

"Hello Mother, Father. How was dinner?"

"Good evening Mr. and Mrs. Martin."

"Hello sweetheart. We had a very nice time," her father replied as he leaned over and kissed Cassandra on the forehead. Patting Little on the shoulder he responded, "Hello son. Did you kids have a nice evening?"

"Yes, we did, Father. We went to dinner and then to a movie. We just got in a few minutes ago."

Mrs. Martin looked at Little, "What movie did you go see Thomas?"

"Oh, we…"

"Mother! Who really looks at the picture? We really just wanted to be together."

"What were you two laughing about when we came in?"

"Gosh Mother. Do we have to get the third degree every time we go out? Father, please. Would you say something to her?"

"It's late," Little said, standing up. "I'd better be going. Good night Mr. and Mrs. Martin."

"Son, you might as well call me father. Now that you two are engaged to be married, you're practically in the family."

"Good night Thomas. I'll see you to the door," Mrs. Martin firmly stated.

"Mother, he's my finance. I can see him to the door."

Little gave Cassandra a kiss on the cheek. "I can see myself out. Good night Cassandra; good night everybody."

As he lay reminiscing, he remembered how all week Cassandra had been talking about setting a date for their wedding. They had decided not to tell her parents right away. It was a promise she did not keep.

He thought about twice before when he and Cassandra had been intimate. They had agreed they did not want a sexual relationship, and although they were committed to each other they would wait until they were married. A few other times they had laid together on the bed, but they were fully clothed. Although she desired to have sex those times, he let her know that he wasn't ready. He told her he was raised and taught that premarital sex was a sin. And from what he had seen, sex could do more harm in a relationship than good.

Etched in his mind was the fear of creating a child who would be like himself, a bastard. But for some reason unknown to him, this time it was different. Had her parents not come home, he knew they would have fulfilled the lustful desire burning inside. This time, he would have done it knowing neither of them was in full control nor thinking as they should have. Nor were they prepared for any potentially ensuing consequences.

As Little lay with his hands behind his head his thoughts wondered back to the night he proposed to Cassandra, and to his argument with Grace earlier that day. His relationship with Grace reminded him a lot of his relationship with Swoosh. *Funny, I can talk to Grace about Cassandra and Swoosh. But I can't talk to Cassandra about Grace or Swoosh. Cassandra can get so jealous when I talk about them or spend time with some of my friends on campus. She talks all the time about her former fiancé, Paul. It never bothers me, but I can't say one word about Grace, my friends, or my Alpha brothers.* Deep in his mind, he knew there was an element of truth in what Grace and Mrs. Picott said about Cassandra.

It scared him more now than ever before. *The truth. The truth is hidden deep within me and that's where it's going to stay. Nobody has to know it. She's got some nerve saying something is eating me up inside.*

Unconsciously, he touched the scar on his neck. Instantly, he felt a strong presence of his mother's mother's hands tightening around his throat. Sometimes, when he was with Cassandra, he had the same feeling, a feeling of being choked. He felt angry when he felt her fingers touching his neck. His anger, once again, began burning inside.

That's nonsense. I love her. Shrugging off the feeling, he again thought about what happened earlier tonight. Hearing the knock on the door, his attention was distracted. Frowning, he glanced at his clock radio on the nightstand and thought, *Who in the world would be coming to my room at twelve thirty in the morning?* "Come in. It's open."

The light from the hallway mingled with the dim light from the lamp in his room casting a glaze like halo around the image standing in the doorway. Little thought he recognized the person he was looking at. *It can't be.* "Cassandra?"

Softly, she spoke. "I want you to make love to me Little," she said as she closed the door behind her, locking it. "I want you to make love to me now. Here." She moved closer to him as she stepped to the bed where he was laying. Standing in front of him, she let her dress slipped down to her ankles revealing her naked body underneath. Kneeling beside him, she began kissing his bare chest. Shifting around, she straddled him and repeatedly kissed and sucked on the nipples of his chest. Sliding her body downward, using long strokes of her tongue she licked his abdomen and moved closer and closer to his navel. Slipping her fingers under the waistband of his underwear, she slid his underwear off. Holding his testicles gently between her fingers, she began kissing them and then licking and kissing the inside of his groin. Finally, she began stroking and kissing his penis.

Little panted and cried out in ecstasy as his heart raced and his body trembled with uncontrollable excitement. Never before had he ever felt such desire, passion, and pleasure. He did not want her to stop.

Sliding her body on top of his, she wrapped her fingers around his neck. Her thumbs pressed wildly against his larynx as her tongue slid deeply into his throat. He tasted the liquor. He felt her hands tighten around his neck and her thumbs pressing into the scar. Suddenly, he began choking. A feeling, violently stronger than the sexual desire he was experiencing was evoked inside of him. "No, Cassandra. No," he said pushing her off him. "I can't, not now. I don't want you this way. We promised to wait until we're married. Besides, you've been drinking. You don't want to do this. You don't know what you're doing."

"It's alright Little. I only had a rum and coke; just a little to relax me. I'm not drunk."

"That smell; it smells like marijuana. You're high!"

"I smoked a joint on the way over, but I'm alright. It helps me to enjoy sex a lot more. I have some more in my pocket. Would you like some? We could smoke it together. Then you'll see how good sex can be. When I was engaged to Paul, we'd do it together all the time. I told you that. I know it's your first time, and I want it to be very special for you. I want you to enjoy it too. I want you to make love to me Little. I want you to make love to me more than anything. Honest, honest I do. I want my first time with you to be very special."

"No Cassandra." Little got off the bed and began putting on his pants. "No Cassandra, not like this; this is not right. I don't want to. No, it's not that I don't want to with you, because I do. I really, really want to make love to you with all my heart, but I just can't. I also want my first time to be very special, and I want it to be with you. But not with you like this. Not with you being high, and not until were married.

"But why Little? Why? We love each other; we're engaged to be married. That's why I feel it's alright for us to do it now."

"I can't bring myself to do it now. What happens if you get pregnant?"

Zipping up his pants, Little knelt down beside her. Taking her hands into his, he began kissing them. "Cassandra, you felt the same way about Paul, and the two of you broke up. I can't see us bringing a child into this world that may end up hating us because of this one night."

"We're not going to break up Little. I don't understand what you're talking about. We're going to be married in a few months. I want to have your baby. If I get pregnant, we'll just get married sooner, but don't worry, I'm not going to get pregnant. You can take it out before you come. I'll understand. I've done it that way before."

"It's not that simple Cassandra. First, before we go any further there's something I need to tell you. You need to know why I feel the way I do."

"All I need to know is that you love me."

"I do love you Cassandra. I love you more than you'll ever know."

Holding his face in between her hands she pressed her lips against his. Panting wildly, she begged him. "Then make love to me right now Little. Make love to me now. Please, I want you, I want you now." Again, Little pushed her away as he stood up. She quickly unbuckled his belt and pulled down his pants. Holding him, she began kissing his groin.

"I love you Little, I love you. I can make you happy. I'll show you; I can make you happy."

The temptation was great and more than he felt he could bear. His fleshly desired the pleasure of her touch, and to be one with her. Initially, he offered her no resistance. The pleasure he derived from her kissing his groin and stroking his penis and the fear of offending her had him transfixed in one spot. He felt he was about to climax. "Cassandra, no," he pleaded as he pushed her away and pulled up his pants. Grabbing his bathrobe, he placed it around her. Holding her in his arms he kissed her on the forehead. "Cassandra, this is not easy for me to do or say, and you're not making it any easier."

"I just want you to love me Little. We love each other, there's nothing wrong with that," she whined as she laid in his arms. "I just want you to make love with you, to give myself totally over to you."

Holding her, he gently stroked her hair. "Cassandra, I know the effects of alcohol. My mother was raped by my father after she had a drink. Four days later my father killed a wealthy white woman and his girlfriend, my mother's sister. He died in the electric chair before I was even born. He died even before my mother knew she was pregnant with me. You asked about the scar on my neck? I got it because my mother's mother hated my father for killing her daughter. She tried to kill me. You see, I can't risk our child ending up like me. Growing up like me, a bastard. I've got to know you love me for me, and it's not the alcohol or drugs talking."

Instantly Cassandra's mood changed. "Oh, I see," she replied breaking the embrace. She gathered up her clothes and started getting dressed. "Why didn't you tell me about your family earlier?"

"I love you, Cassandra. I wanted to tell you before. I really did."

Angrily she looked at him, "When? After we were married? Or were you going to wait until after the honeymoon?"

"No Cassandra. It's not like that. I just found out about it myself in December. That's when she, my mother's mother tried to kill me. You're the only person outside of my family I've told about it. You know, you just don't meet a person and tell them your whole life story right away. But it's different with you, with us. We love each other. We can share these things. Just like you shared your relationship with Paul with me, I want to share my relationship with my family with you."

"Oh, I see. Look, Little, it's late. My parents might wake up and find me missing. I'd better go."

"Cassandra?"

"Yes."

"Do you still love me? I still love you."

"I got to be going Little."

"Cassandra," Little called out to her and grabbed her arm as she walked pass. "I love you Cassandra. Please don't walk away from me." Holding her, he tried to kiss her.

Cassandra tried pulling away from him, but he was holding her tightly.

"No, Little, don't do that. Please let me go."

Little continued to hold her, "What's wrong Cassandra? I love you. Don't you still love me? Okay, okay baby, I'll make love to you. He gently pushed her toward the bed. We can make love right now Cassandra. Please, please, I'm ready,"

She struggled to get away from him. "Let me go Little. Please Little, please don't rape me," she cried.

Stunned by her pleading remark not to rape her, Little released her immediately. "What? Cassandra, you know I'd never hurt you. I love you."

Rushing to the door, she looked back and shouted, "You're an animal just like your father."

Little stood watching as the door closed behind her. *What did I do? Oh my god what did I do?*

A week passed. Cassandra had not called or returned his calls.

"Hey dude," it was Marcus. "You're normally on the phone at this time. What are you doing here in the library? In fact, I haven't seen your old lady all week."

"I've got to start studying for finals, and I have a report due at work." That Sunday, Little hurried to church hoping to see her. In church she dared not look at him and left directly after service, never saying a word or looking in his direction. Mr. Martin looked at him with disdain and turned him away, saying his daughter did not want to see him anymore. Furthermore, he and Mrs. Martin preferred that he not come around the house or call any more. Little could not believe what he was hearing. He was the same man that just days ago welcomed him into the family. The same man, who was pleased about their engagement now turned him away with disdain. Two days later in his mail, Little received a large envelope. Inside was a small package. Without opening it, he knew it could be only one thing.

"Little, the banana tree in the back needs some of the leaves taken off," shouted Mrs. Picott.

"Mrs. Picott, the one day I take off of work you have me here in the greenhouse working harder than I do on my paying job."

"Well, I didn't tell you to come down here. You and Grace volunteered of your own freewill."

"I don't know about Grace, but I was drafted and as you can see, she left an hour ago and hasn't come back. Speaking of Grace, where did she go? I thought she was supposed to come back."

"I did too. The two of you hardly spoke to one another. What's going on?"

"I have no idea Mrs. Picott. I think it's a female thing."

"Is that right?"

Little stopped and rested.

Mrs. Picott looked stood up and looked at him. "Boy, if you want that slung dug you better work a little faster. It's Friday, I want to go home sometime this evening."

"Okay, okay. You drive a real hard bargain."

"Little?"

"Yes Mrs. Picott."

"It's been almost two weeks and you haven't said a word about what happened between you and Cassandra."

"I'd rather not say right now. So, you and Grace need to stop asking me. When I'm ready to talk, I'll let you know."

"You still think you love her?"

"I'm not going to lie to you Mrs. Picott. Yes, I do, and I miss her. Maybe, if I knew why she doesn't want to see me, it wouldn't hurt so bad. But it does."

"I tried to warn you. Believe me Little. You should be glad you're rid of that one."

"That's easy for you to say Mrs. Picott. I love her. We were going to get married."

"Little, you're a very nice young man, you deserve better. I told you that you were moving too fast. But you'll find someone who will appreciate you."

Together, they continued to cut the branches off the banana tree. "Sound like someone just came in the front door. I wonder who that could be now."

Little sarcastically replied, "Mrs. Picott, the only way you're going to know who it is, is by going up front to see."

"You know, you're such a smart boy. How did I ever survive all these forty something years without you? Now Mr. Smart One, finish pruning those branches, and I'll be back as soon as I take care of the customer."

"Thanks for the warning."

"Hello, Mrs. Picott, are you here?" a voice shouted out for her. Little recognized the voice. It was Mr. Martin, Cassandra's father.

"Hold your horses, I'm coming." Entering the front part of the greenhouse, Mrs. Picott greeted Mr. Martin. "Hello Sam, what rock did you crawl out from under?"

"I'm glad to see you too Jean. I'm fine."

"That's good. Now, what can I do for you?"

"I need to order some floral arrangements for next week's banquet. The one I called you about last week."

"Hello Mrs. Picott."

"Well hello Cassandra. How are you Sweetheart? You're looking lovely today."

Little heard Cassandra's voice. *Cassandra, she's here. I've got to see her. If her father wasn't here, maybe I could talk to her. Maybe, he'll leave and I'll have a chance to talk to her.* Little wormed his way to the first bay adjoined to the front of the greenhouse. Hiding behind a tall plant he could see Cassandra and her father. Seeing Cassandra made his heart pound. *Mrs. Picott is right. She's so good-looking. Oh baby, if I could only talk to you. Whatever the problem is, I know we can work through it.*

Almost two weeks had passed since they last saw each other. He remembered the last time they held each other in their arms and kissed. He still had no clear idea or understanding as to why they were no longer together. Seeing her reminded him of how much he loved and missed her. *If I only let myself make love to you that night, we would still be together. If you would only give me another chance, I'll make love to you like you've never known, even if it means I have to smoke a joint or have a drink. Oh Cassandra, just give me another chance. I'll do anything to get and keep you, my love.*

After completing his business, Mr. Martin walked out of the greenhouse. "I'll be right there Daddy, I want to ask Mrs. Picott something."

"Okay, but hurry up Sweetheart. I have a few more stops before I'm finished."

Cassandra walked behind the counter and stood next to Mrs. Picott. "Mrs. Picott, have you seen Little?"

"Yes, I have. Why?"

"Did he tell you about our breaking up?"

"The two of you broke up? When did that happen?"

"He's probably too ashamed to tell you."

"Tell me what?"

"You know. Why we broke up."

"No, he hasn't told me. Why did you break up?"

Now I'll know what I did wrong. Why she broke off the engagement and returned the ring. Whatever it was baby, I'm going to fix it.

"He tried to rape me."

Little was stunned. *No, no I didn't. Why would she say that?*

"Cassandra, I don't believe that. I know Little. He's always been a perfect gentleman."

"Believe me, because he did. He has everybody fooled with that innocent act of his. You know, it's in his blood. Did you know his father was a rapist and mass murderer? His father raped his mother and was sent to the electric chair for murdering his aunt and a white woman. Little was the result of that rape. He told me that himself. Now, can you see me marrying an animal like that! When I told Daddy about his background, he went berserk. This past December, Little's own grandmother tried to kill him. That's how he got that scar on his neck. He's definitely a lowlife. I don't care how smart he is. I could never humiliate myself by marrying a lowlife like that. That has got to be one screwed up family. What a combination—he has a father that's a rapist, a murderer, and a convict." Cassandra placed her hands on her hip as she shifted her position to a more aggressive stance. "I'm going to tell everybody in the church, everybody in the shipyard, and everybody on campus about his family and how he tried to rape me. By the time I finish with that lying rapist, there won't be a rock left for him to crawl under. And to think, I let him kiss me."

Mrs. Picott, not acting surprised began laughing. "He told you that old story and you believed him?"

"What do you mean? I believed him. It's true."

"Girl, Little pulled a fast one on you this time. But I'm so glad he found you out before it was too late."

"What do you mean he pulled a fast one on me? He's in love with me and he wants to marry me."

"Just what I said, he pulled a fast one on you. Little's family is very wealthy. Two of his uncles and an aunt are doctors. His aunt and uncle are professors at the University of Illinois and another one of his uncles owns the top accounting firm in Chicago. It's the biggest in the state." Mrs. Picott began acting very crafty. "You know his uncle that just died, Canada? He was a bigwig in DC, for the government. His name was James Canegata."

"You mean the famous negotiator for the state department everyone's talking about?"

"That's right. Little inherited more than just a car, some jewelry, and a few suits. The man and his wife had no children. Little is getting a whole lot more than you can imagine or you'll ever have. Little told me he was going to tell you that story because he wanted to make sure you weren't a gold digger like I said you were."

Cassandra walked to the other side of the counter. "I don't believe you."

"You don't have to. But I do know he was testing you to see if you really loved him. He needed to know it wasn't just his money you were after. And if I were you, I'd be careful whom I tell that story to. From what I understand, you two did more than just kiss. I know you've been to his room in Holly Tree Inn more than once, and your drinking and smoking habits is no real secret. I heard you can be a real animal and you're hot in the panties when you've had some liquor and been smoking that dope."

Extremely agitated, she began shouting, "That's not true. That's a lie and he know it. Little is lying. He's such a liar. It's all a lie. I never visited him in his room during the night. He's a liar. He's lying. I only kissed him. He knows I only kissed him, honest. He better be careful who he talks to, spreading vicious lies about me. When you see him, be sure to tell him that for me. He's no gentleman if he kisses and tells." Hearing the car horn blow, she left shouting, "He's no gentleman."

"Okay honey, I'll see you later."

SHIPYARD SHIPWRECK LOVE AFFAIR

Little watched as Cassandra left the greenhouse. His shame and anger grew inside of him as he listened to Cassandra reveal his dark past with Mrs. Picott.

As Mrs. Picott walked into the first bay she laughed. "Hey Little," she shouted, "I don't know what kind of lie you told that girl to get rid of her, but I'm sure glad you did." She was stunned to see him standing in front of the plant where he was hiding. She stopped, his face was turned pale. *Oh my god, what Cassandra said. Could it be true?*

He looked away in shame and began gasping for air.

"Little, are you alright?" Looking at him, she knew something was not right. "Little, here, sit down," she said directing him to sit on the edge of the flowerbed. "Try taking slow deep breaths. I'm going to get you some water." Mrs. Picott left the room and quickly returned with a glass of water. "Here, drink this." After he calmed down, she asked, "How long have you been hiding there."

"When I heard Cassandra's voice. I just wanted to see her, so I hid behind the plants."

"Little, you didn't try to rape her, did you?"

"No Mrs. Picott. Honest, I didn't try to rape her. That night she came to my room in Holly Tree Inn, she'd been drinking and smoking pot. She wanted to have sex, and I told her no. I wasn't ready." Again, he began hyperventilating.

"Take your time and breathe slowly."

Slowly, he regained his breathing. "When she came over to my room that night she had been drinking and smoking. I told her no."

"What was all that stuff she said about your father?"

Little looked down at the floor in shame. "That was true. My father raped my mother and killed her sister and a wealthy white woman in Chicago. He died in the electric chair before I was born. I didn't find out until last December. My mother's mother vowed to kill me. She tried to this past December. That's why I came to Hampton. I just couldn't bear going back to New York. Not right now or ever again. I needed a break." He felt more like running and hiding than facing Mrs. Picott. How could he ever face her again knowing what she now knew about him? *What is she thinking about me, the boy genius from UNE? Son of a murdering rapist, whose father died in the electric chair for killing two women.* His dignity, pride and respect were taken away in just minutes. "Now everyone is going to know."

"No, they won't Little."

"Thank you for covering for me. Please, Mrs. Picott, I gotta go now."

Quickly he stood up to walk pass her.

"Little," she called out to stop him.

"No Mrs. Picott, please," he said shielding his face and his tears from her. "Right now, I want to be by myself and please, please don't tell anybody about, you know, about my father. I feel bad enough and so ashamed, dirty, so ashamed." Again, he could feel the hands of his mother's mother tightening around his neck as he gasped for air. *Now I know. Now I know why she left me. It's all her fault. She left me because of her, Ruth. It's all Ruth and Elijah's fault. Everything I loved, anything that's meaningful in my life, they've managed to destroy. Her mother from the grave is still killing me. Why, why didn't they let her finish me off then? No, they just want me to have a slow and painful death. How much more of this hell do I have to take? I hate them. I hate them all. They had better not speak to me ever again.*

Mrs. Picott reached out and grabbed his arm, stopping him. "I'm not going to let you go out there like this Little. Wait, have some more water. Just wait until you catch your breath. Sit down for a few minutes."

Little began crying. "There, there, just let it all out. You'll be alright; you're going to be just fine." She held him in her arms and comforted him as he wept. After a few minutes she handed him some tissue to wipe his face. "Listen Little..." she said looking him in the eyes. "First, you don't have to worry about me telling anyone. Okay?"

"Thank you, Mrs. Picott."

"And I want you to know, you have nothing to be ashamed of or feel dirty about. You're a good person, a very good person. You have a heart of gold. I don't think I know a kinder, gentler person. You're not responsible for your father's actions."

"Thank you, Mrs. Picott, but I want to go," he said wiping his face.

"Little, I don't want you to go. There's a lot of water around here. Promise me you won't do anything foolish."

"I won't give her mother that satisfaction. I promise."

"Okay. If you need to talk, I'm here okay?"

"Thank you."

"Grace, have you talked to Little this weekend?"

"No Mrs. Picott. I haven't seen him all weekend. He usually eats in the student cafeteria on weekends. His car was parked in the same spot all weekend. I don't know where he is. I checked with Mrs. White this morning before I went to class. She said he ate breakfast earlier than usual and left for work. I was worried about him all weekend. I stopped by his room on Saturday and Sunday morning. He hasn't been to his room since Friday morning. He hasn't been there since we came here to the greenhouse Friday morning. I stopped back by on Friday, but you had already left. What time did he leave?"

"We left around four-thirty."

"It's not like him. Did something happen when he was here?"

"Well Grace, if Mrs. White saw him this morning, at least we know he's still alive."

"I thought I saw Cassandra and her father coming from this direction on Friday. Did something happen?"

"You know Cassandra. She didn't know Little was here. She started telling lies about him. She said he tried to rape her."

Grace appeared upset. "That's a lie. I know Little, and he wouldn't ever try to do anything like that to her."

"I know, but Little he heard the whole thing. He was really hurt. He loved that girl. I don't know what he saw in her. I told him she was going to break his heart."

"I know. We tried to warn him. He just had to learn it for himself."

"What are we going to do Mrs. Picott? The time when we were here when he brought her the roses—the same night he proposed to her—Little and I had a big fight after we left the greenhouse."

"Is that why you two haven't been speaking?"

"Sort of. We walked on the waterfront. He showed me the ring and said he was going to ask her to marry him. I don't know what got into me. I don't know what I said or did. I just remember throwing the roses in the river and telling him that when she broke his heart don't come crying on my shoulders. I was so mean to him."

"Don't worry, he'll come around. He just needs a little space to breathe. Grace, you love him. Don't you?"

"I don't know what you mean, Mrs. Picott."

"Yes you do, you don't have to pretend with me Grace. I can see it in your eyes every time his name is mentioned. Your eyes light up. The two of you spend a lot of time together."

"No Mrs. Picott, you're wrong."

"Stop denying it Grace."

Slowly, she lowered her head. "Is it that obvious?"

"To everybody on campus."

"I do love Little Mrs. Picott. Everybody on campus but Little knows it, and he's too blind to see it."

"He loves you too."

"No he doesn't Mrs. Picott. I don't think so. Even if he does, he doesn't act like it."

"Yes he does. He just doesn't know it."

Grace leaned against the counter. "You really think he does?"

"I know he does. He just has some things to work out inside of himself."

"But Mrs. Picott, loving him hurts so badly. Right now, I just want to get him out of my system. It's just been too painful. I can't carry on like this." She began to softly sniffle. "What am I going to do Mrs. Picott? What am I going to do?"

Mrs. Picott opened her arms. Grace ran to her for comfort. "Just give him a little more time; just a little more time."

It was late Monday afternoon, Little sat at his drafting table. Glancing at his watch, he noted he would be getting off work in an hour. He spent the entire weekend in the one place on campus where he could go to be alone to think. No matter what time of day or night, the pottery shop was opened. *Mr. Gillard should be pleasantly surprised when he walks in this morning. I scrubbed the place down really good.* So far, to everyone's advantage the day was without incident.

"Here, nigger boy, you wanted to check this blueprint?"

Little could not hold it back. "You know Jim, I'm just a little sick and tired of your racist remarks." Loud enough for everyone to hear, Little attracted the attention of everyone in the area. "I've been putting up with your bull for the last five months. You know racism is an attitude, and you got it bad. It's your problem not mine, so get off my back. What are you going to do next? Come in wearing your white sheet and hood to try and scare me? Maybe, if you and your boys burn a cross on my lawn, you'll feel better. Well, I'm not scared, and I don't scare easy, so back off!"

Embarrassed because Little attracted all the attention, Jim softly said, "I'm gonna git you for that one, nigger."

Little was still loud, talking to him. "So, you're going to get me. Well come on, you coward. Under your breath and behind my back you make all kinds of remarks. You really feel like a big man, don't you? Yea, go ahead and run, you coward."

Seeing everyone gathered around, he shouted, "What are all of you looking at? Go back to work."

Moments later, Mr. Casey, the vice president, came to Little's office. "Mr. Thomas."

Still angry, Little turned, "What now." Seeing it was Mr. Casey, he stopped.

"Is something wrong, Mr. Thomas?"

"No sir. I'm sorry, I have a headache."

"I just came down to remind you that we have a meeting with Admiral Massenberg tomorrow morning at nine o'clock. It was changed from two o'clock."

"The meeting is tomorrow? No, no one told me. I just received your memo this morning about it being next week."

"Mr. Thomas, I sent your entire department a memo regarding this meeting three weeks ago. I sent out memos regarding the time change last week. I expect you to have that report ready."

"I never received the memo."

Jim came into the office. "Mr. Thomas, I personally gave the memo to you last week." Walking over to Little's desk he began moving papers around. Picking up a pink envelope, he handed it to Little. "Here it is, under the blueprints I gave you last week. The envelope is still unopened."

"Jim, you're trying to pull another fast one. You never gave me this memo," Little shouted in protest.

"Mr. Casey, his attitude has been a problem since he came here. I'm glad you're here to witness it yourself."

"You planned this whole thing Jim. You know…No…No, I'm just not going to get into it with you right now Jim. You won't trap me like this again."

"Mr. Thomas, if there is a problem, I want to know about it."

"You want to know about it? I told you what the problem was four months ago, and you still haven't done anything about it."

"Have the information for the meeting with Admiral Massenberg ready for tomorrow. I don't want any excuses Mr. Thomas. Dr. Waldstriecher assured me you could handle it. If you can't, let me know now so we can let Mr. Bestler take over the project before its way too late." Mr. Casey walked away.

Jim turned to face Little. Pointing his finger at him, "I told you. You'll pay for it. This is only the beginning, and I make good on my promises nigger boy."

The morning meeting with Admiral Massenberg began in the large boardroom of the main building. After taking several facts and figures the meeting was moved to Building A in Little's work area with his team. Gathered around the table was his engineering team, Mr. Casey, Admiral Massenberg, and two vice presidents from the shipyard. Admiral Massenberg stood up. "I won't pull any punches. I am extremely displeased with the pending delays and potential cost overruns of this project." All fingers seem to point at Little. Having produced a report, Jim Bestler led the troops in the charge as he put on an excellent presentation.

Little stood up to address the group, "Admiral Massenberg, the project has not progressed forward at the appropriate rate, and it will be going into a significant cost overrun laden with many more delays. The main reason is I do not believe the Newport News Drydock and Shipbuilding Company is capable of handling such a massive undertaking the magnitude of this project. I recommend that the Navy move the project to its shipbuilding facility in San Diego, California."

Mr. Casey jumped up out of his seat. "Mr. Thomas, you're out of line."

The admiral looked with amazement at Little. "Is this the young man from the University of New England who's supposed to be heading the project?"

"Yes sir."

"He started the project. Let him speak. I want to hear what he has to say for himself. Son, I hope to hell you have documentation to back up what you just said."

"Yes sir, I do." In his possession, Little had several drawings. "First, I'd like to explain this meeting was scheduled three weeks ago. Even though my signature is on this document, I was not informed of it until this past Monday. I was informed that I had to have a full report prepared today for your visit. Someone intentionally did not inform me of this meeting."

Picking up the blueprints, Little opened them up. "Admiral Massenberg, I direct your attention to these blueprints. Please notice, the changes were made without any of the calibrations being adjusted accordingly. All these schematics are off by varying degrees. The changes were approved without being sent through the appropriate channels. If you notice, the signature on the bottom approving them is my name but not my signature. Here are several blueprints and schematics done the same way. I have here memos complaining to the management of these irregularities, yet management has done nothing to correct the problem. All this talk about teamwork is not true. There is no teamwork here. What you see here amounts to incompetence, insubordination, sabotage, and possibly treason. And the shipyard's management failure to act appropriately and expeditiously."

Well Little, you've blown it now. You might as well go all the way. You ain't got nothing else to lose. "Admiral Massenberg, I'd like to direct your attention to that man over there, Mr. James Bestler. He has caused numerous problems on this project. As I said earlier, the project has not progressed forward at the appropriate rate and will be going into a significant cost overrun and delays because of Mr. Bestler. It was Mr. Bestler, who knowing the calibrations were not completed, and who fraudulently signed my name to the changes. Either, after thirty-two years on the job Mr. Bestler is incompetent or, as an engineer, is outdated. In either case, he should be fired or at least removed from this project to something more suitable for a man of his limited capabilities and knowledge."

Skillfully, Little worked his way around the table and stood behind Jim. "Perhaps, he thinks it's a joke to waste the taxpayers money and the United States Navy's time. If that is the case, then he should be held personally responsible for the millions of dollars in cost overrun." Next, he moved behind Mr. Casey and the vice president of governmental projects. "Management has consistently ignored my numerous complaints to this very day. Considering the nature of this technology, could it be Mr. Bestler is a spy, planted here to sabotage the project? If that is the case, it's a cover-up, including top management of the shipyard. If that is the case, then Bestler and management should be arrested as spies and charged with treason. Somehow, I don't think he's intelligent enough to pull that one off. But then, who knows."

Gesturing, Little shrugged his shoulders. "I don't know. Maybe, he felt it was more important to have something on paper to show you, even if it isn't correct." Ending up at his original position at the table, Little concluded his summary. "Then again, maybe he's just another dumb Joe Smo trying to ensure himself a job until he's old enough to retire at the expense of the United States Navy, and your reputation Admiral Massenberg."

Picking up a packet of material Little handed it to the admiral. "Admiral Massenberg, here is my full report and account of the project. I've also included projections of how the project will end up on its present course should it remain here at Newport News. I've included projections of how it will look if my recommendations are followed. Now, if you will excuse me, I have a headache. I'm going home. I have two finals to take tomorrow." With that, Little walked out of the room.

"Little, it's only eleven-thirty. What are you doing home from work?"

"Well Mrs. White, I just got myself fired."

"What? What do you mean you got fired? What happened?"

"Jim Bestler won. I just made a complete idiot of myself in front of Rear Admiral Massenberg. Give me a double coke on the rocks please."

"Tell me what happened Thomas?"

"I don't know. All I know is this has got to be the worst time of my life. Tomorrow, I'll probably fail my two finals."

REDEEMED

Disheartened, Little sat with his head hanging low, pulling the petals off of the yellow rose Mrs. Picott had discarded. Walking over to the opposite side of the table, she stood in front of him, placed her hands on the table and leaned forward. "Boy, what are you doing? What is the matter with you this morning?"

Unmoved by her, Little continued to dismember the rose of its petals.

"Little!" she shouted. "Boy, I'm talking to you."

Little momentarily paused from plucking the petals off of the rose. Slowly, he looked up at Mrs. Picott. "Uh?"

"Boy, you look like something the cat dragged in."

"Told you, I have a headache."

"That's no reason for you not going to work today."

Without looking at her, he responded. "I told you Mrs. Picott, I got fired."

"Little, now we went through this yesterday," she scuffed shaking her finger at him. "What makes you think you got fired? You weren't there Wednesday because you took off for your finals. So, tell me, how do you know you were fired? Did you call in this morning to ask?"

Continuing to pluck the petals off of the rose, he nonchalantly he replied, "No."

Perturbed by his attitude, she placed her hands on her hips; in a commanding tone she shouted angrily, "Then how do you know you were fired if you didn't call?" Grabbing a stool, she stood at the table across from him and stared directly into his face. In a laughing manner, she said, "Boy, you've got to explain this on to me."

Annoyed and irritated by her persistence, Little threw the flower on the table in defeat. "Mrs. Picott, why do you have to scrutinize everything I say or do? I told you what happened Tuesday. It doesn't take a rocket scientist to figure it out. It's all part of life. Besides, you know how they are at the shipyard." Quickly, he glanced up at her. "You told me that yourself." Again, he picked up the rose and began to pluck off the petals. "I know what I'm doing. You're talking as if I don't know how to conduct my own affairs. Can't a man get a little understanding around here?"

"You're right Little. It doesn't take a rocket scientist to figure it out. What it takes is a phone call. When I told you about how they were at the shipyard, you didn't listen to me then. And you're not listening to me now. If this is what you call conducting your own affairs, then you certainly don't know what you're doing. Let me tell you something boy. I've lived a lot longer than you have, and you haven't begun to live. You may be smart book-wise, but you don't know a thing about life or living. Now, if you came here for sympathy, you came to the wrong place." She paused briefly. "Little, do you know what your problem is?"

"No, I don't, but I'm sure whether I want to know or not you're going to tell me." In frustration, she slammed her fist on the table. "Your darn tootin' I'm going to tell you. I'm about to give you a real dose of reality. Now, put that flower down and listen to me. I don't want you fiddling with that rose while I'm talking to you. I want your undivided attention." She waited for him to put the rose down. In defiance, instead of putting the rose on the table, Little stopped and looked directly at her with a cold, hard stare.

Not moved by his defiance, Mrs. Picott pressed on, "You and those eyes. But your looks don't scare me."

Little turned his eyes upward.

"You can roll your eyes all you want to. It doesn't bother me."

"So, what is my problem Mrs. Picott?"

"Your problem is you're naive, spoiled and you don't want to listen to anybody. And then to top it off, you're mad at everybody in the world for everything that's happened to you." Again, she paused and waited for his reaction. Little rolled his eyes and sucked his teeth as he looked away from her. "Who you should be mad at is yourself," she continued. "You got a big chip on your shoulder and you need to start facing reality."

"What are you talking about Mrs. Picott? I'm not spoiled or mad at anybody, and I don't have a big chip on my shoulder." Again, he turned to the flower.

Suddenly, she leaned over and shouted as she snatched the flower from his hand, startling Little. "You don't! Huh, with that attitude you could've fooled me." She sat on the stool across from him. "If you're not mad, then tell me why you're not talking to your parents?"

"What?"

"You heard me! You're blaming your parents for Cassandra breaking up with you. You act as if it was their fault."

Little turned away from her. "I never said that."

"You didn't have to. Look at me Little."

Defiantly, he turned to look her directly in her eyes. Aware of his posture, she entrenched herself more. In a voice of authority, she spoke to him as if he were her own child. "I'm going to tell you the truth whether you like it or not. You're mad at your mother and father for not telling you the truth about being adopted. You're mad at your dead grandmother for trying to kill you. You're mad at your little sister and brother because they were born Thomases. Swoosh, Michael, and the Griffins—you're mad at them for getting after you about not talking to your parents. You're mad at Grace because she's honest with you and she's going home for the summer. Boy, you're so mad 'til you're mixed up and don't know what to do. You loved your Uncle Canada so much, but you're mad at him for dying. Need I say more? Oh yea, and now you're mad at me for telling you these things."

Feeling uneasy, nervously he let out a fake laugh. "Wrong, wrong, wrong, Mrs. Picott. You're so wrong."

"Am I Little? I forgot, you're also mad at Grace."

"Grace," he shouted interrupting Mrs. Picott.

"Yes Grace."

"Now tell me, why am I mad at Grace? I've got to hear the answer to this one. Please, make it good. Mrs. Picott."

"Because you love her, and you don't know how to tell her. And you know you've hurt her."

Little's mouth dropped open in disbelief as he looked at her shaking his head from side to side. "Oh God, Mrs. Picott, I don't believe you! What do you do at night? Go home and dream up these things? No, I know, the plants. The plants tell you these things. No, I know what it is. You've been inhaling to much fertilizer."

"Believe me Little, you don't fool me one bit. You're only fooling yourself. You can fool yourself, but you can't fool me. And the day you stop lying to yourself about it; you'll feel a whole lot better. When you finally stop denying and fighting it, you'll be a lot happier."

Pretending to consult the spirit world, Little rotated his hands around and around the half-plucked rose lying on the table. "And what else does your crystal ball tell you now, Swami Picott?"

"You know, I can't wait to meet your parents."

"That will be the day."

"You know I'm gonna meet them one day. I can't wait to see these people that spoiled you so rotten."

"Who are you calling spoiled. I am far from spoiled."

"That's what you think. Of all the students I've known, I can't say any of them have ever been as spoiled rotten the way you are."

"I thought you said Cassandra was spoiled worse than anyone you've ever known."

Laughingly, she exclaimed, "I said spoiled the way you're spoiled. She's rotten spoiled; you're spoiled rotten. Your parents gave you all the love and protection and proper guidance. They spoil you by doing it. You're used to getting all the attention."

Knowing in the art of negotiations, the first one that speaks loses, the two sat across from each other, not uttering a word. The telephone rang breaking the silence and the air of contention. "Who's that calling me now?"

Little responded sarcastically. "I don't know. Oh Great Swami. Please tell us."

Mrs. Picott laughed. "Oh boy, shut up and pass me the phone. Hello, Greenhouse."

Pause.

"Yes, you got the right place. He's here. Little," passing the telephone receiver to him, "The call is for you."

Little looked puzzled as he reached for the receiver. "Who knows to call me here?"

Stretching her eyes wide, she smiled and said, "Oh Great Swami Little, I don't know. Please tell us."

Little laughed as he took the receiver from her. "You got me Mrs. Picott. Hello, this is Thomas Thomas." Little's back straightened as he listened to the voice on the other end. "Yes, I'll hold." His facial expression went from inquisitiveness to anxious surprise. "Hello sir."

Pause.

"Yes sir, five o'clock. I'll be ready." Hanging up the phone, Little jumped up from the stool screaming. "Yes, yes, yes."

"Well," Mrs. Picott responded. "Well, what was that all about? From the look on your face, I can tell it wasn't bad news."

Joyously, Little shouted as he grabbed and hugged Mrs. Picott. "Oh God, believe it or not, that was Admiral Massenberg himself. He's sending a car for me at five o'clock. We're having dinner at Fort Monroe's Officers Club tonight."

The dry summer night air was exhaustingly hot. A steady breeze blowing from the bay across the campus made it a pleasantly bearable evening. Little sat on the swing in the inn's screened-in porch, swinging. His thoughts were fixed on Grace and when they first met. Somehow, from the day they made the angels in the snow, he knew their relationship was destined to be a very special one. He chuckled to himself as he remembered her promise to give him a personal tour of Hampton's campus. She made that promise in January. It was now seven months later, and she still hadn't given him the tour.

Together, like he and Swoosh, he and Grace had been through a lot, and they share many things in common. He thought about how she was normally so sensible, except for the time she threw the box of roses he bought for Cassandra in the river. Other than that, she was always so prudent. He knew what he loved most about her—she was always cognizant of his feelings, and perceptive of his needs, as well as the needs of others. There was something else to it. Around her, he felt relaxed. He didn't feel pressured, tensed, as if something or someone had a noose around his neck. Most of all, around her he could be himself. He recalled the time they went to the drive-in theatre in Portsmouth to see *The Imitation of Life*. He cried for the longest time, together they cried. His was the last car to leave the drive-in. He didn't feel ashamed crying in front of her. She didn't find his sensitivity unmanly. She told him, for her, it showed how strong of a man he really was.

Like him, she enjoyed the simpler yet meaningful things in life, like holding hands and walking along the waterfront. They enjoyed watching the ducks swimming, the seagulls flying and playing on the water's edge. Seeing minnows swimming along the riverbank, they'd pretend he was Poseidon, the Greek god of the sea, and Grace was his wife, Amphitrite, a sea goddess. They named the minnows—Antaeus, Arion, Merman and Polyphemus. They'd make up adventures for them as they watched the minnows swim along the rivers' edge.

For hours, they'd talk about sailing away for parts unknown on one of the yachts moored at the dock. Some days after class, they found just a drive in the countryside along the York River exhilarating and rejuvenating from the day's activities.

As part of the student activities, each semester Hampton brought in world-renowned performing artists and shows. Duke Ellington and the Chinese Ballet Dancers appeared that spring semester. In March, two weeks before the performance of the Chinese Ballet Dancers, Little surprised Cassandra with tickets to the performance. He was looking forward to it. The day of the performance, Cassandra was in one of her moods. She didn't want to go and insisted that he himself not attend. The same thing occurred with the Duke Ellington concert. Because of the money he had invested he attended both performances with Grace. It was one of those rare times he disobeyed Cassandra. The consequence was that he never heard the end of it from Cassandra. Looking back, he was glad he attended the performances with Grace. Together, he and Grace were moved by the performances and found them cultural, exciting and refreshing. He was impressed with her knowledge of the Chinese ballet dancers, and she rocked with him to the sounds of Duke Ellington.

The May moon was shining bright in the sky, the stars were twinkling, and the night air was warm. The music of Duke Ellington and the voice of Lena Horne rang fresh in their minds and alive in their souls. The concert had a spell binding effect on them. After the concert they, like they did so many times, took a walk along the waterfront. The night was lit by the bright moon in the sky. As they walked, they held hands. Standing under the tree close to the Katherine House, Little placed a magnolia blossom in her hair. Her long, thick, black hair gleamed in the moon light. Their eyes met. That was when it happened, on the waterfront, under the tree close to the Katherine House. They looked at each other differently and saw each other as they never had before. Neither of them had expected it, nor were they prepared for what happened next. For the first time they saw each other as they had felt. Feelings emerged that they both tried desperately to deny and kept hidden from the other. Afterwards, they both agreed it was a mistake. It should have never happened, and it should never ever happen again. In shame, they felt if they had not been caught up in the mood of the moment and under the spell of the moon, it would have never happened. It was the music, the night air. There, they placed the blame. Little knew that something inside of him burst. He enjoyed it more than he had imagined or wanted to admit. It was, for the both of them, their first time. That night with her, not only did he feel alive, but he felt complete. Despite their true feelings, they agreed that it was not right and should never happen again. For the next few days out of fear and shame, they avoided each other.

Little continued swinging back and forth. A big smile appeared on his face as he reminisced about Grace and himself. Looking up at the July evening starlit sky, a feeling of sadness came over him. Instantaneously, he knew what it was. He was missing her. Without her, he felt lonely, abandoned, and incomplete. He missed having someone to share the experiences of his workday, someone, like Grace who was understanding and helpful. When he felt depressed or even excited, unlike Cassandra, he could always count on Grace to be there for him. When his uncle Canada died, it was Grace he sought out for comfort. He remembered how hurt and broken up he was inside. Most of all, it was in her arms he laid and cry. It was her words that consoled him in his time of grief, giving him the strength needed to forgive himself for not being there. It was in her arms he found comfort.

If anyone, he longed to share his past, the secrets of his heart, and his future with, it was Grace, but he knew he couldn't risk it. He missed her and wished she had stayed for summer school. *If she had only stayed for summer school, maybe I wouldn't be so lonely.*

The porch door slowly creaked open. "Hello Little. It was so nice out tonight, I thought I'd come over to spend it with you."

After almost losing her, it was her voice he had relentlessly craved to hear for many days and night. He laid awake on his bed many nights longing for her. Finally, she called him. He was glad she was there. Despite all that was said and done, he was glad to have her back in his life. Their dates after getting back together were good and getting better. "Hi sweetheart, I'm glad you came over. Come on over and sit down here next to me," he said, patting the seat of the swing.

Leaning over kissing him, Cassandra hurriedly sat down and snuggled under his arm. Quietly, they sat together swinging on the swing. Little was enjoying the quiet moment. She broke the peacefulness of the evening to talk about her wedding dress. "Mother and I went shopping today. I finally selected my wedding dress. It's the perfect dress."

Little did not respond. "Little, why are you so quiet?" she asked as she poked him in his side. "I know, let's go for a walk along the waterfront so I can tell you all about my day and the dress." Insistently, she stood up and began tugging on his arm.

Little slowly rose off of the swing. Immediately, Cassandra locked her arm in his. Arm-in-arm, they walked down to the waterfront. Cassandra continued to talk about shopping for the dress. Little's mind was a million miles away. "You're awfully quite Little. Little…" she said slightly nudging him. "What are you thinking about?"

"Uh, oh, I'm sorry. Yes."

Pouting, she politely scolded him. "Here I am all excited about my wedding dress, and you haven't paid any attention to a thing I've said."

"I'm sorry, I had a tough day at work. Go on, what were you saying?"

"I know what's wrong with you Mr. Thomas," she scoffed. For a moment, Little felt she had invaded his private thoughts and discovered whom he was thinking about. "I know what my baby needs. You need some fun to brighten up your life. Tomorrow night the Alphas are having a picnic at Old Buckroe Beach. After the fireworks show they're throwing a party at Bay Shore Pavilion. Why don't we go? It should be fun."

Without realizing it, they had stopped under the tree near the Katherine House. He looked at Cassandra. Gently taking her into his arms, he pulled her body next to his. "Nothing," he responded. "I'm not thinking about anything. I just want to enjoy being with you. I want to savor this moment alone with you on the waterfront." He backed her body against the tree. Leaning forward, he pressed his body against hers and passionately kissed her.

Cassandra became like putty in his arms. She passionately yearned for more. The more they kissed, something inside of her burned hotter, but what was inside of him dwindled until it was no more. He smiled at her. He knew then what it was and that it was dead forevermore. Joyfully, he kissed her on the lips.

I can see it all so clearly now. It's as plain as the nose on my face. Nothing can and nothing is going to go wrong now. I am free. Free from the misery I put myself through, and from what I let others put me through. Just think, a few weeks ago my whole world seemed to be falling apart. Cassandra, my job, and my relationship with Grace, it's all changed. After dinner with Admiral Massenberg, things changed. Everything has changed. My job—Admiral Massenberg was impressed with my recommendations. Now, Cassandra is back in my life. This kiss told it all. Nothing and no one is going to stop me from doing what I have to do.

That previous week during dinner with Admiral Massenberg at Fort Monroe Officer's Club things had changed. Admiral Massenberg informed Little that he consulted with the engineers at the Pentagon. Needless to say, they were impressed with Little's findings and his proposed plans. Admiral Massenberg placed Little in complete charge of the project and stated he would report directly to his office in the Pentagon. He even offered Little a job with the Navy upon completion of the project. The next day when Little went into the office Jim Bestler and Mr. Casey were gone from the department. No explanation was given. And now, Cassandra was back in his life. Now, he was free, free at last and released from that which eluded him for so long. *From here out, nothing can go wrong for me.*

Exceptionally excited, gently he whispered in her ear. "Let's go back to Holly Tree." Anxiously, Cassandra agreed as she latched onto his arm. Once again, she was ready to give herself to him. Within, she knew this time, it was his time. He was ready to be one with her. For him, at last the time had come. He was ready for his destiny. That which lay beyond this night. No longer could or would he fight the feeling he had burning inside. He no longer wanted to fight it.

Cassandra knew, without a doubt, she was finally going to have her way with him by letting him have his way with her. She desired to please him as never before and feel him explode within her. Tonight, their fate would be sealed forever. Tomorrow was the fourth of July, but for her, the sparkle and fireworks would be tonight as they exploded together.

No matter what it took, Little was at last determined to claim the woman he desperately loved and desired to have in his life. No one and nothing is going to stop him from seeing her and sealing their fate forever. He was determined not to lose her again. It all was unfolded in a single kiss, the kiss under the tree near the Katherine House. Last night, when he kissed Cassandra, something died inside, freeing him. He continued to think about her as the 1956 Buick Roadmaster sped along Route 258, headed toward Roanoke, Virginia. The feelings and emotions he had felt so strongly and passionately inside for Grace, he would no longer bridle.

Last night, when he and Cassandra arrived at Holly Tree Inn, as usual, they were not on the same wavelength. He walked her to her car, said good night and went to his room leaving her by her car on the curb. In the kiss, it became clear to him that the feelings and emotions he felt so strongly and passionately were for Grace, not Cassandra. What had died inside of him was the love he thought he had for Cassandra. The flame that burned brightly inside was for Grace. That night, in the kiss, he realized that he never really loved Cassandra—he told her so at the curb.

Now, he found himself, at six o'clock in the morning, driving to Roanoke to declare to Grace his love for her. His mind had been clouded all this time by his own self-pity. His own self-pity had blinded him to the fact he was in love with Grace. He loved Grace. She knew it. Mrs. Picott knew it. Marcus said it. Swoosh had said it, and Cassandra accused him of it.

The first time that he realized he loved her and that she loved him was the night after the Duke Ellington concert when they passionately kissed under the tree near the Katherine House. It was the first time they had kissed. The kiss said it all. His love for her had come alive. It wasn't a mistake. Within himself, he knew he was not only the last one to know it, but he was also the last one to admit it. Now, he had to tell her. Pressing the gas pedal to the floor he sped along thinking how much he really cared for and loved Grace.

You're a bastard. Your father raped your mother. He killed your mother's sister. He killed a white woman and he died in the electric chair.

The thought began to invade his mind. Slowly, he eased back off the gas pedal. The car began to slow.

She won't want you. She's a nice girl, from a good family, a pastor's daughter. You got to tell her, when you do, they won't want you. They don't want the son of a murdering criminal in their family. No one will want any part of you, and no one wants anything to do with you. No, Little, you don't deserve a decent girl like her. You and Cassandra are two of a kind. The two of you belong together.

Little stopped the car by the side of the road and turned off the engine.

Forget it. Little, you can't have her because you can't risk telling her. Be happy with just her friendship.

With his opened fist, he began pounding the steering wheel. "If I tell her, I'll lose her for good. I know. I'll lose her for sure. I can't risk it. I can't risk losing her friendship. Who am I fooling?"

Tears began to roll down his cheeks as he started the car. Turning the car around, Little headed back down the highway toward Hampton. Seeing a country store gas station ahead, he decided to stop. "Excuse me sir, do you have a pay phone?"

"Um uh, over in the corner yonder," the old man replied pointing in the direction of the phone. Sitting in the phone booth, Little placed a long distance collect call.

Unsure of himself, for the next twenty minutes a confused and bewildered Little poured out his heart and soul over the phone. To his own amazement, he revealed things he had not mentioned before. He expressed feelings that he himself was unaware of. After explaining his dilemma, he listened to every word the voice on the other end told him. He emerged from the phone booth with an answer.

As he drove up the long dusty driveway to the house it reminded him of the house in Canaan. A well-groomed gentleman dressed in black wearing a minister's collar emerged from the house. He stood on the porch watching the approaching vehicle. Removing his white summer straw hat with a black band, the light skinned gentleman pulled out a handkerchief from his pants pocket to wipe his brow. His wavy thick hair was matched by his thick black mustache.

"Hello Reverend Johnson," Little greeted him as he stopped the car. "How are you sir?"

Moving swiftly, Reverend Johnson walked off the front porch. "Well, bless my soul, if it ain't Thomas. Good to see you son," he exclaimed, approaching the car. "I'm just fine son. What about yourself?"

Little exited the car and extended his hand toward Reverend Johnson's hand. "I'll be. The wife and Grace will be glad to see you. Grace said you probably weren't coming. I know she'll be surprised and mighty glad to see you."

"Where is everybody?"

"Church is having its annual Fourth of July picnic on the river out by Hollow Cove. You almost missed me. The wife forgot her favorite apron, bless her heart. I just came back to get it," he said smiling. "I'm headed back there now. You're welcomed to leave your car here and ride with me, or you can follow me. It's about fifteen minutes from here."

Little bit his lip tightly. "Reverend Johnson, may I speak to you for a few minutes."

"Sure son. Let's get down to the river with the family. We can talk there," he said placing his hand on Little's shoulder.

"No sir," Little spoke up. "Excuse me but," again he hesitated. "I mean, I need to speak to you privately Reverend Johnson. Please, it's very important." Reverend Johnson detected the seriousness and urgency in Little's voice. "Why sure son," he stammered. With his hand he gestured toward the house. "Why don't we get out of the sun. We'll go inside the house where we can sit down and talk."

Thirty minutes later, an anxious Little found himself following Reverend Johnson to the river. Driving up to Hollow Cove, his heart pounded when his eyes fell upon Grace. The sun was shining brightly around her, casting a glow. She appeared as a celestial being. Her shoulder length hair gleamed and sparkled from under the summer hat adorning her head. Unaware of his presence, Little walked up behind her. "Grace."

The sound of his voice caught her off guard. Her heart fluttered when she heard him. Silently, she prayed. *Oh dear God, please let it be him.*

Taking a deep breath, slowly she turned around. With mixed emotions she responded, "Little. What are you doing here?"

"I had to see you Grace."

Hesitantly, Grace turned her back to him. "Little, please go." He moved closer to her. "No," she put her hand up to stop him from touching her. "Please, don't touch me. Just get back in your car and go back to Hampton."

"Grace, I love you."

"No, don't say that." Tears filled her eyes. "Stop playing with me, Little. You and Cassandra are getting married. I'm sure she won't be happy if she knew you were here seeing me and telling me you love me."

Little took out his handkerchief and handed it to her. "Listen to me Grace. I love you. You were right all along. I was so blind. I don't love Cassandra, it's you I love. It's you I want to be with."

Burying her eyes in the handkerchief she softly sobbed. She had longed to hear those words from his lips. But for her, it was too late. "No, please don't do this to me Little," she cried as she moved away from him.

"Grace, I love you, and I know you love me."

"What makes you think I love you?"

A small girl ran up to Grace and started pulling her by the arm. "Miss Grace, will you come play jump rope with me?"

"Not now Roberta. I'm talking."

"Do you like him? Are you going to kiss him?"

"Roberta," she shouted, "That's not nice of you."

"Are you going to marry her Mister?"

"Roberta, you're not being very nice. He is not my boyfriend and I'm not going to marry him. Now go play with the other children, or I won't play jump rope with you later."

Roberta started skipping off shouting, "Miss Grace has a boyfriend!" As they watched the little girl skip off, Little took Grace by the hand. Let's go for a walk."

Instinctively, she withdrew her hand. "I'll go only if you promise to leave afterwards."

"Okay Grace, I promise. After I've said what I've come to tell you, if you still want me to, I'll leave." Standing apart they began walking away from where the group was picnicking. "Grace," he began, "do you remember the night we kissed under the tree near the Katherine House? I know now it wasn't a mistake. I felt it, and I know you felt it too. We both felt it, and I've been an idiot denying it and pretending it never happened. I knew then that I loved you. I realized I loved you from the first time I saw you on the stairs in Holly Tree Inn. After we made the angels in the snow, I felt it then. I know you felt something too. I've never been in love before. It was so new to me. I didn't know what to do. Like a dummy, I've been fooling myself. I was blinded by selfishness, pain, and stupidity. I didn't think you cared about me or could have loved someone like me. I should have known something the day you threw the roses in the river. I saw it burning in your eyes. I know it now. I love you and you love me."

Biting her lip, Grace slipped her hand into Little's. "I fell in love with you from the first time I set eyes on you that day in January. I wanted to say something to you, but I didn't know what to say. I didn't want to make a fool out of myself. Me, I'm just a country preacher's daughter, and you are a handsome man from the big city. I was happy just being your friend." Grace wiped her eyes and removed her hat. "I didn't realize how much I cared for you until you showed me the ring you bought for Cassandra." She let out a small laugh. "You don't know how much I wanted to throw that into the river. Maybe our kissing that night wasn't a mistake, but it was wrong. You belonged to another, even as we speak Little. You're engaged to Cassandra."

"No, no Grace. That's over. I can't marry Cassandra. I already told her. First, I don't love Cassandra. I realize now that I never loved Cassandra. You were right about me, there is something I've been holding on to that's been eating me up inside. There is something I got to tell you before our relationship can go any further. You were right, there's been something eating inside of me. It's what's been eating at me since last year." Little became silent and looked at himself somewhat shamefully. "It's about my parents and my birth. After I say what I have to say, as I promised, I'll leave. But Grace, I'll never stop loving you."

"Shhh," she said, pressing her finger against his lips. "You don't have to say anything."

"No Grace, I have to tell you. I need to tell you, so please hear me out. I'm not who you think I am."

This time she pressed her lips against his lips, kissing him. "No Little, you're the sum total of all you are and all you will become. I know all about what happened in Chicago. Your father raping your mother and about your being adopted and your grandmother trying to kill you."

Little was shocked. "You knew. But how? How did you know?"

"That day in the greenhouse when you were talking to Mrs. Picott after Cassandra left. I was in the greenhouse hiding. When I saw you crying, I knew inside you were hurting really bad. You can't imagine how badly I was hurting for you. I was scared. I didn't know what to say to you. I was scared that if I showed myself to you, you'd run away from me and I'd lose you for good."

"So," inquisitively he looked at her. "You knew all this time and never said anything? Here I was thinking you wouldn't want to be with me if you knew. I should have known that you're not a shallow person. You're kind, loving, and decent. The kind of person I want to love and be loved by."

"Little, who your father is and what he did has nothing to do with who you are and how I feel about you. I love you Little. I love you very much, probably more than you'll ever know."

"That's funny. It's just what my aunt Sarah said."

"Your aunt Sarah?" she responded inquisitively.

"All last night and on my way here, all I could think of was you. I didn't want to lose you or your love. This morning on my way here, I began thinking about my past. So, I started to go back to Hampton. I didn't know who to talk to. I needed someone to talk to. Before, I could always talk to you. When I saw the store, I stopped and called my aunt Sarah. It was so funny—she said she was waiting for my call. First, she read Matthew 7: 24–27. She said, 'God's word is love and everyone who hears and does his word is like a wise man who built his house on the rock; when the rain fell and the floods came and the winds blew and beat upon the house it did not fall, because it was founded upon a rock. Those that hear and do not do his word are like a foolish man who built his house on the sand; when the rain fell and the floods came and the winds blew and beat upon the house it fell, and great was its fall. My house should be built on God's love; God is the sure foundation, the rock.' Then she read me 1 Corinthians 13, the love chapter. Then she said my answer was in a special compartment concealed in the glove compartment of the car."

Wrinkling her brow, she exclaimed, "The glove compartment of the car! What kind of answer is in the glove compartment of a car?"

"That's what I thought. Somehow, she and my uncle knew. I was always talking about you. They knew you were the one. I talked with your father when I stopped by your house." Little reached into his pocket, "Grace, I know there is no other woman for me. There's no other woman. I want you to be my wife."

Not realizing they had returned to the area where everyone was, Little got down on a bended knee and took Grace by the hand. The eyes of the picnickers turned. The entire congregation was staring at the couple. As he placed the ring on her finger, Little asked, "Grace, will you marry me?"

Grace, totally unprepared and completely surprised covered her mouth as she laughed and cried simultaneously. Looking up, she saw the river in which she was baptized. Then she saw her father and mother. Reverend Johnson nodded his head in approval. Hugging her husband, her mother displayed a broad smile on her face. Grace looked at Little on bended knee. Only minutes ago, she begged him to leave her alone. She was afraid of being hurt and needed time away to rid her heart of him and the love for him that burned deeply inside of her. He promised that after saying what he had to say, he would leave. Tears of joy filled her eyes.

"Little, yes, I will, I will," she happily replied, falling into his arms.

JUBILATION

To Little's delight, the summer could not be over soon enough. His remaining summer weekends were spent in Roanoke with Grace and her family. On Friday morning, he packed his car, directly after work and not a minute later, he found himself driving down Route 258 across the Canada River Bridge to 58 and onto Highway 220 headed for Roanoke. Sometimes, Chester, Bertha, and Preston, students attending summer school, hitched a ride with him to South Boston and Danville. He welcomed the company, but his main objective was getting to Roanoke. On Thursday nights, Mrs. White prepared her famous peach cobbler for Little to take to Grace on Friday.

Reverend and Mrs. Johnson treated Little like a son and looked forward to his visits. Their two younger sons and two younger daughters looked forward to his arrival as well. He was always a welcomed guest in their home.

Little was especially looking forward to this weekend. It was homecoming at Bent Road Mountain Baptist Church where Reverend Hughes was the pastor. For months Grace told him about the church on the top of the mountain and the one lane road that led to it. He had a good time last Saturday at Bent Road and Holy Tabernacle Baptist Church gathering. The church Grace's father pastored hosted an annual baseball game at the park. The food, the fun, the games and the fellowship were more fun than he could ever remember.

One night at a special Saturday evening service honoring Mother Battle, the oldest member of the congregation, Little decided to honor her by playing the piano and singing her favorite hymn, "Only What You Do For Christ Will Last." His melodious baritone voice filled the sanctuary as the sound of angels ushered them into the very presence of God. The sound of the piano flowed, filling the air with the sweet fragrance of the Holy Spirit. No one, not even Grace, knew he could sing or play as he did.

Afterwards, he was the talk of the congregation and Roanoke community. The members continued to talk about how they loved to hear him sing and play. Mother Thompson each Sunday told him, "Boy, it uplifts my heart and blesses my soul when I hear you sing and play the piano. The Lord has blessed you with a gift. It brings joy to my soul when you and Grace sing together."

After that, it seemed as if every mother of the church had a favorite song—they all wanted him to play the piano and sing their favorite song.

After church he and Grace would laugh and poke fun at the elderly ladies swooning over him. Mother Battle remained Little's favorite. The spry eighty year old was the first one he sang and played the piano for. Smiling and showing all of her pearly white false teeth, she would walk up to he and Grace with her cane; she'd poke Grace and flirt with Little. She would laugh and say, "Grace, don't let um outta yo sight. If 'n I wer' a few yars younga, I's gibe ya a run fo' yor monay. I wasn't always old. In my younga days, I was a knockout."

Teasing her, Little would respond, "And you're still a good-looking woman Mother Battle."

"I know better than to leave you alone with my man," Grace would say, gently tapping Little on the arm.

Mother Battle would laugh and reply, "I know I am n you better not. I still got it you know."

Each week some mother of the church would bring Little something to eat or give him something as a small token of their appreciation. Grace would look at him and jokingly say, "Little, I've got to put a stop to this. You know they're spoiling you rotten."

OLD SHIP OF ZION

The last holiday marking the end of summer was rapidly approaching. Little had only to fulfill the one request his aunt Sarah made of him that day on the road to Roanoke. The request she asked was that he attend the family's Labor Day picnic in Washington, DC, with Grace. Labor Day and the picnic were a week away. For Little, it meant in three weeks, Grace would be back in Hampton for the fall semester. Even though he did not mind the drive and would miss everyone, it also meant he would not have to travel every weekend to Roanoke. He and Grace could see each other seven days a week instead of only on weekends. Now, they could spend more time together. In his mind, he had it all planned. They would have dinner together in the little cafeteria, enjoy a hamburger and soda at the Snack Bar, or sit quietly together under the Emancipation Oak. They would take long walks along the waterfront and enjoy a good movie in Odgen Hall or at the Wythe Theatre. Together they would enjoy the upcoming concerts and plays on campus. Most of all, they would go for relaxing rides along the York River. The best part of it all was this time it would be different. Having declared their love for one another they would enjoy being together as a couple, engaged to become husband and wife.

Little was overjoyed with the opportunity to present his fiancée and show her off before his family. He knew Aunt Sarah, Auntie Madie, and Uncle Junebug would instantly love her like he himself loved her. Most importantly, they would approve of Grace and give their blessing. Just as her mother and father had approved of him—had they not,

Reverend Johnson would have never agreed to the engagement—his family would approve of Grace. Like him, they, too, would see her as a precious jewel, his jewel to love and cherish. How could they not?

The previous weekend when they were together in Roanoke, Grace also expressed her joy regarding the upcoming Labor Day event. Having heard so much about his family and relatives, she was anxiously looking forward to finally meeting them, especially his mother and father. Despite the darkness, as he told her stories, she could hear in his voice how much he loved and missed them. Grace persuaded her parents to also attend the picnic. To her and Little's surprise and delight, her father decided it would be a great time to formally announce their engagement. Although excited, she admitted to Little she was a bit nervous.

In the midst of his experiencing joy over the upcoming event, Little was also experiencing strong feelings of apprehension. Torn apart on the inside, he felt reluctance about attending. The celebration meant seeing his parents whom he had not seen in almost ten months. For the first time in a while, he realized he had not seen them since December of the previous year. It would be the first time he would see them since the tragic events in Chicago. His mother's mother trying to kill him, learning his mother was raped—learning he was the result of that rape. The last time he saw them he learned his father murdered his mother's sister and a rich white girl. The last time he saw them he learned about his father dying in the electric chair. It was at that time he also learned his mother's mother never wanted him to see the light of day and the man Elijah Thomas who raised him he believed was his father.

That was the time he ran away, left home and began to systematically eliminate them from his life. Everything and everybody he wanted to forget—he would have to see them again. He would be forced to see them face-to-face. He did not relish the thought of seeing his parents. Nor was he looking forward to introducing Grace and her parents to them.

The very thought of his parents meeting Grace besieged him with anger. He expressed his reservations to Grace. He remembered her words so clearly, "Little, you're afraid to see them because you've been so consumed by your anger for so long. You're afraid to let your anger go. You're afraid that when you see them your heart will melt. You know you love them, just like you love me. But you need to let your anger go before it destroys you and our relationship."

He tried his best to put her response out of his mind, but he could not. Little made all the sleeping arrangements. Grace and her family would stay with Aunt Sarah in her home and he would stay at Uncle Junebug's and Aunt Madie's. All plans had been confirmed. The die had been cast. There was now no turning back. The first Monday in September was Labor Day. Everyone was expected to arrive at Aunt Sarah's on Friday night. Saturday was reserved for cooking. On Sunday, they would attend church. Being an out-of-town guest, Reverend Johnson would deliver the sermon. Monday was the picnic.

As planned, everybody arrived at Aunt Sarah's by Friday evening on time. However, Reverend Johnson, his wife, and Grace were staying with his brother and family not too far away in Alexandria, Virginia. Upon arriving at his Aunt Sarah's, his Uncle Canada's Alpha brothers' valet parked cars while Sarah's Alpha Kappa Alpha sorority sisters served the guest. When Little entered the house, to his surprise, Mrs. Picott and Mrs. White we're sitting in the living room. Mrs. Picott laughed and said as they hugged, "Boy, we wouldn't have missed this for the world."

Answering the door, to Little's amazement, on the other side were his aunts Lanet and Shera, his uncles Jerome and Kenneth from Chicago. Swoosh and his parents arrived shortly before Dr. Griffin, Mrs. Griffin, and Michael. Stephanie, Alejandro, and Bobby entered the house along with Aunt Madie, Uncle Junebug, and his parents. They all were there to celebrate the occasion. Shocked, Little was overwhelmed by the love, support, and friendship of all those with whom he shared a special and close relationship and bond.

Friday night seem to never end with people dropping by until late in the evening. Everyone had stopped at his Aunt Sarah's house to meet and greet one another, most of all to meet Grace. There was no shortage of music, dancing, talking, laughter, food, and storytelling. It came as no surprise, but still Little was amazed and marveled at how everybody instantly fell in love with Grace. Little marveled how with great ease, she moved around the room meeting and greeting everyone. Her soft laugh, the warm touch of her hand and her warm embracing hug; everyone instantly fell in love with Grace.

Saturday morning breakfast was at Aunt Madie's and Uncle Junebug's house. Little awakened to find Stephanie, Grace, and her mother in the kitchen along with his aunts cooking breakfast. For the entire day, the kitchen was abuzz with the women joyfully preparing the weekend meals and the older women teaching the younger women the art of soul food cooking. The men gathered in the den to tell their tall tales. Alejandro added to the family's story with how Little became known as king of the clambake.

With food prepared and a caravan of cars, early afternoon everyone left to gather in the backyard of Reverend Johnson brother's house in Alexandria, Virginia. White, pink and red azaleas bloomed along various pathways around the yard. The expansive yard was surrounded on each side by eight feet high hedges. In the middle of the yard was a gazebo decorated with flowers and several long tables covered with red and white checkerboard tablecloths. Dishes of corn on the cob, potato salad, bake beans, fried chicken, collard greens, and an assortment of pies and cakes were on top. Closer to the house was a brick grill. The smell of chicken, ribs, hot dogs, and hamburgers cooking filled the air. This promised to be another fun-filled afternoon and evening with greeting more family members and friends as they arrived.

After a while, standing in the gazebo, the Reverend Johnson called everyone together to ask the Lord's blessing upon the meal. "Now, before I bless the food so we may commence to partaking of food, my wife and I have an announcement to make. Come on over here, honey," motioning to his wife. "It is good when family and friends gather together for a day of celebration. The Lord has richly blessed us, and we have much to be joyful about. The Bible says, 'He who finds a wife, finds a good thing.' When I found my wife here, I was truly blessed. The next big blessing in our life was the birth of our first born, Grace. God has blessed her to grow up to be a beautiful, loving, and precious woman. When she was born, we began praying the Lord will prepare the right man to be her husband. We prayed for a God fearing righteous young man. Grace and Little, please come here and join us. You too, Mr. and Mrs. Thomas, please join us."

Little and Grace stood by her parents' side. Elijah and Ruth also joined them, standing by Little. "This afternoon, it is with great honor that my wife and I announce the engagement of our daughter Grace Lynn Johnson to the son of Elijah and Ruth Thomas, Thomas Isaiah Thomas, better known as Little. Now, if you see me cry, choke back tears, it's not because I am sad. It's because I am happy. I am happy that God has answered his humble servant's prayer. Please join me as I pray a prayer of thanksgiving and a prayer for them."

Reverend Johnson positioned Little and Grace in front of him. Taking their hands, he began praying.

"Heavenly Father, our most gracious God. To the God of Abraham, Isaac and Jacob, we come before your throne of grace today to ask your blessing upon these, our children. Father as they stand here before you, we ask that your Holy Spirit lead and guide them in all of their ways. When the temptations and cares of this world rise up and try to overtake them, we pray your Holy Spirit will lead and guide them in your will. For we know it was you, Lord, that ordained this union. While yet in the womb of his beloved mother, you called Thomas forth, you blessed, kept, and preserved this young man. You preserved him that one day he would meet Grace while she too was still in the womb. We pray your will be done in their lives."

He placed his hand on the head of Little. "Lord, strengthen Thomas to fight off the fiery darts of the adversary. Whatever stumbling blocks the devil puts in his path, Lord, we pray you will stay with him and guide him safe upon the shores, from all hurt, harm, and danger. Lord, we know you are a healer. We ask that you heal the pains of the past."

Touching his father and mother, Reverend Johnson continued. "We thank you for his parents. We thank you for their obedience to your voice in raising Thomas in your presence, and the love they have for each other and their children. Touch them Lord, and continue to bless them. Now, be with my child Grace. We thank you for her, Lord. Give her the strength to stand with Thomas. To wait upon you, Lord. May she seek you with all her heart and in all her ways. May they pray and serve you together as one and continue to seek your face.

"And now Lord, bless all those gathered here today. Father God, because of you we were able to raise up this morning clothed in our right mind. We want to thank you for having the activity of our limbs and that our bed was not our cooling board and our sheets were not our winding sheets. We thank you Lord for bring us here safely over the highways and byways without hurt harm or danger. Now Father, we ask that you look down from your heavenly habitation and bless us again this day. We thank you for the land and for the harvest that the land has brought forth for the nourishment of our bodies, for your namesake. To him that is able to keep us from falling, these things we ask in your son's name. We ask in the name of Jesus Christ, our Lord and Savior. Now everyone please repeat after me. Amen."

The family and guest echoed, "Amen."

"Now then, we can commence to eating," Reverend Johnson announced. Guests began congratulating the couple on their engagement. For the remainder of the evening there was more talking, more stories of the kids, pictures, and plenty of laughter and eating.

Sunday morning started out early. As usual, Aunt Madie woke everyone up with her shouting, "Time to get up. Don't want to be late for church this morning. Reverend Johnson is preaching this morning." She and Stephanie had prepared breakfast for everyone. Little could see a close and tight relationship growing.

Junebug could see his wife was in seventh heaven. "She always loved a house full of people." He laughed as he declared they had more beds in the house than most folks have dishes.

It was a beautiful September, Sunday morning. The sun was shining high in the sky. The church seating capacity was filled. Reverend Johnson stood behind the pulpit to deliver his sermon. Looking over the congregation, he acknowledged the pastor and the other ministers. "Brothers and sisters," he said, addressing the congregation. "It is the honor for me to bring you a message from our Lord and Savior Jesus Christ this morning. But it is not for me to break the bread of Life with you this day."

He turned to the pastor, then back to the congregation as he continued. "For you see, there is one here today who's shoes I am not worthy enough to unlatch. He is a graduate from Morehouse College in Atlanta, Georgia. He earned his PhD in Theology from Boston University. He comes to us by way of Montgomery, Alabama, where he is the pastor of Dexter Avenue Baptist Church. Most of all, I am proud to say I am his friend and brother in Christ. He's a minister of the Gospel who needs no introduction. Brothers and sisters, I give you the Reverend Dr. Martin Luther King." The congregation anxiously looked around to see Dr. King. No one had seen him enter the church. Reverend Johnson beckoned him. "Dr. King, please come and deliver to us a word from the Lord this morning."

Expressions of amen and jubilation arose from the congregation as Dr. King came from among them and ascended into the pulpit. It was both a momentous occasion and life-changing experience in the life of all under the sound of his voice.

Dr. King began to speak. "To Pastor Charles, my brother and dear friend, Reverend Johnson, members of Mount Moriah Baptist Church, and honored guests. I came today not to feed, but to be fed. But I recognize the journey that God has sent me on. Like what the apostle Paul said, 'I must be prepared in season and out of season.' Please turn with me in your bibles to Luke 18: 1–8. And it reads, 'And he told them a parable, to the effect that they ought always to pray and not lose heart. He said, In a certain city there was a judge who neither feared God nor regarded man; and there was a widow in that city who kept coming to him and saying, "Vindicate me against my adversary." For a while he refused. But afterward, he said to himself, "Though I neither fear God, nor regard man, yet because this widow bothers me, I will vindicate her, or she will wear me out by her continual coming."

And the Lord said, Hear what the unrighteous judge says. And will not God vindicate his elect, who cry out day and night to Him. Will He delay long over them? I tell you; I will vindicate and protect them speedily. Nevertheless, when the Son of man comes, will He find faith on the earth?'"

Dr. King continued, "The Constitution of the United States says every person born in these United States or naturalized is a citizen. Each citizen has a right to vote. Today, I tell you that we all, having been born on these shores are American citizens and we have a share in the American dream. That dream includes living in peace and harmony with our neighbors and all mankind. It means sharing in the American pie. There are those who say that if the pie is divided up anymore, then it means they would have less. That is not what we are saying today. We are saying that we want our equal share of the pie. It will not mean less pie by giving the right to vote to those who have been denied that right. It means the pie will be more bountiful. Again, I tell you the Lord shall vindicate, and we shall be vindicated.

"Together, if we work in the fields harvesting potatoes, we receive wages of ten cents per pound harvested. Every person working should receive their wages based on that amount they gathered, not on the color of their skin, or their social or financial class. Again, I tell you the Lord shall vindicate, and we will be vindicated. We are saying public education should be available to all citizens of these United States, not only to the privileged. The Lord will vindicate, and we will be vindicated.

"We are living in a time and in the richest nation God has on this planet. People often ask me, 'Dr. King why do you teach and preach what you do?' They say, 'To break the yoke of our oppressor, we must arm ourselves. Why do you say we must pray?' The apostle Paul said in Ephesians 6:12, 'For we fight not against flesh and blood, but against the principalities, against the powers, against the world rulers of this present darkness, against the spiritual hosts of wickedness in the heavenly places.' The color of a man's skin does not make him your enemy. White men are not our enemy. But it is the spirit of ignorance that we fight against, it is the spirit of hatred that we fight against, it is the spirit of fear that we fight against. Against these things, I tell you, there are no cardinal weapons.

"It is only through the power of prayer and supplications and having on the whole armor of God that we are able to stand. Though they may turn the dogs lose on us, they may turn the fire hoses on us, they my shoot us and hang us from the highest tree. I tell you my brothers and my sisters, we will be vindicated. Others say, 'Come let us burn the city to the ground.' As the children of Israel marched around the City of Jericho and the walls came tumbling down; we, too, must march around our cities. I say to you, we must shout to the hallow halls of Congress. We too must blow the trumpet in Zion and shout out until the walls of hatred, until the walls of segregation; until the walls of injustice, until the walls of bigotry, and all that exhaust itself against the power of God comes tumbling down. I tell you, we will be heard, we will be vindicated.

"My brothers and my sisters, shall not our God avenge us as he did the children of Israel? There are those who ask, why does the Negro want to vote? I submit to you, not only does the Negro want to vote; it is our right and our duty to vote. Two great wars, World War I and World War II, were fought to preserve the right to vote. The Negro soldiers fought side-by-side with white soldiers and died like any other soldier to preserve the right to vote. But unlike the white soldier, the Negro soldier returned to America to be denied the right to vote. Yes, I tell you today, our God will vindicate us.

Immigrants from France, Germany, England, Russia and other European and Eastern European countries left the place of their birth. They came to the shores of America to gain this right to vote. Yet, the Negro, born here in these United States of America, continues to be denied his birthright, given to him by the United States Constitution. The right to vote is the Negroes constitutional-given right. And the European immigrants continue to come and are granted the right to vote. I tell you, we will and shall be vindicated.

"We Negroes joined, joined arm-in-arm with our white brothers and sisters, we are going to march on every state capital. From the pecan trees of Tallahassee, to the Missouri River in Jefferson City, to the gardens of Sacramento, together, we shall march to the county seat, together we will march on the hallow halls of the United States Congress. Together, we shall march to the White House and declare to this nation, it is our right, and we will perform our patriotic duty and vote. We shall have our voice in the governance of the land of our birth. Our God shall vindicate us.

"Not all of us came over on the Mayflower. Many a passenger rushed to the port side of the ship and rejoiced as they viewed the Statue of Liberty standing in the New York Harbor. Many white Americans have checked the manifest of the passenger ships to find the names of their ancestors listed. If you check the manifest of the passenger ships that stopped at Ellis Island, you may not find your family name listed. Our ancestors may not have come by way of the Mayflower. They may not have passed through the halls of Ellis Island. They may not have rushed port side of the passenger ship to see the Statute of Liberty holding up her torch welcoming them to the shores of this country. They may not have read the inscription, 'Give me your tired, your poor, your huddle massive yearning to breathe free.' But if you check the manifest of the many slave ships landing on the shores of Maryland, Virginia, or the slave ships landing in North Carolina, South Carolina, Georgia, and Florida; ships that arrived on these shores long before the Statute of Liberty stood in the harbor, you may find your ancestors listed. Both our ancestors came by ship; one passenger and the other slave, but they both arrived on these shores by ship. Their names are listed on the ship's manifest. My brothers and sisters, we shall, and will, vote. I tell you, we shall be vindicated.

"But I tell you today, it's not the ship by which we arrived on these shores, but it's the ship that we chose to be on when we leave this side of the Old Chilly Jordan. As for me, I will be leaving one day on the ship found in the words of that Old Negro spiritual, that Old Ship of Zion."

The choir began singing, the congregation in thunderous applauds stood to their feet, and joined in singing the Old Ship of Zion.

After church everyone gathered at Sarah's for the meal and a memorial service for Canada. Guest mingled and engaged in polite conversation until ushered into the living room for the memorial. Part of the furnishing for the large room was a white Steinway grand piano. Next to the piano was a three-foot portrait of Dr. James Lionel Canegata.

"First, I want to thank everyone for coming to celebrate the life of my husband. I know many if not all of you, whether his fraternity brothers, fellow church members, or work and business associates would love to say something about Canada. He touched so many lives in so many ways. For this celebration, I chose not to have speeches, Canada would not have wanted that. Canada loved music. A big part of Canada is our godsons, Thomas Thomas and Jerald Jefferson."

Looking at him, she held her hand out motioning. "Jerald, please come up."

Swoosh walked over, held her hand as he stood next to her. "Most people know the infamous Swoosh as a star basketball player. While he is best known for his skills on the basketball court, Jerald's first love is the piano, and he is an accomplished concert pianist. What is not widely known about my godson is the many concerts he's performed. There were times when Canada's negotiations were extremely intense, Canada would fly Jerald to where he was for a private performance. Jerald will be playing Canada's favorite, Beethoven's "9th Symphony in D minor."

After hugging and kissing her on the cheek, Swoosh pulled out the piano seat. Sitting on the seat his entire demeanor transformed to formal concert attire. A spotlight focused on Swoosh seated at the piano. The living room became his concert hall as his music held his audience captive. An arousing sound of applause rang out as he played the final note. After a brief pause, Swoosh stood, the audience continued to applaud as Swoosh bowed. Standing upright, he was back in Sarah's home. Another bow, looking up, on the right standing next to Sarah was Dr. King. Again, taking a bow as he stood up to the right of Sarah was Canada, smiling at him, applauding.

Before the memorial ended in a final tribute Swoosh and Little sang Canada's favorite spirituals, "Blessed Assurance" and "Only What You Do For Christ Will Last."

PAINFUL MEMORIES

Aloof and lost in her thoughts, Ruth stood at the kitchen sink preparing to wash the evening meal dishes. Once again, her mind was preoccupied with thoughts of her firstborn child. What had happened in Chicago kept turning over and over again in her mind. Scenarios of what ifs continued to cloud her judgment and vision. *What if I saw Miss Sophie? What if I had raised him knowing Elijah was not his father? What if Elijah had not adopted him? What if Elijah and I never married? What if I had stayed and raised him in Chicago? Oh God, what if my mother had succeeded in killing him?*

She stood gazing out of the window with a blank expression on her face. She was in pain. The pain was more than she wanted to bear. Her mind continued to wander as it churned over and over the past few months. The events weighed heavy on her heart. Last summer—it was the end of his first year in college. She missed his coming home. He stayed at the university to work on the project. She missed him then and she longed for him even more so now. It was a distant and long ten months ago when she last looked forward to his being home for Christmas.

Traditionally, the weeks leading up to Christmas were always the most exciting in the Thomas household. That year it was going to be even more special. Little would have been coming home from college. In her mind, it had all been planned. First, there was the family tradition. They would go to Long Island to the tree farm to pick out a tree. Then the five of them would trim the tree, decorate the apartment, and she and Esther would bake homemade cookies. Later that evening, they would drink hot chocolate, eat cookies and sing carols. The next day, Little would take Elisha and Esther downtown Christmas shopping. Again, that evening they would drink hot chocolate and sing carols as Little played the piano. The neighbors would stop by to join the festivities. Every year, it was the same.

However, things were now different. Little would not be there. Instead of receiving her son into her bosom, she lost him. *Forever*, she thought. Painfully, she remembered the day the neatly bundled world she had created began unraveling. It all began with a telegram from Chicago. She knew it was going to be nothing, but bad news. *Nothing good comes in a telegram.*

Her past, her shameful past, had finally caught up with her. For Ruth, the drive to the university was the longest and toughest part of the entire journey. Although Little had made a feeble attempt to conceal it over the phone, in his voice she detected the confusion; his feelings of betrayal and distrust were revealed in his voice. She knew her son. Etched in her memory forevermore was the expression on Little's face when he looked at her as he approached the car. Looking at the back of his head from the backseat of the car made the journey to Chicago, at minimum, bearable.

In her mind, the worst of this situation was yet to come. It was not about to end. Seeing her long-lost brothers Jerome and then Kenneth was a measure of sweetness. It had been years since she had last seen them. In fact, although not by choice, she had long since resigned to the idea of never seeing them ever again. At least, she didn't think on this side of the Old Chilly Jordan.

Along with her pain there was a joyful place also in her heart: Grace. Sarah told her about Little and Grace's relationship and engagement. Then one day in early August, Grace called her. It brightened her heart easing away much of her pain and worry. After that, they talked on the phone every week. Ruth was so happy to talk to Grace. Through Grace, she learned how her son was doing. Ruth was happy; Little had Grace in his life. Finally, meeting Grace face-to-face in Washington was a big blessing for her. Seeing Grace for the first time, she hugged her tightly and held on. She pretended for part of the hug that it was her son whom she longed to hold. Grace had reassured her, "Just give him some time. He'll come around. It won't be long. I'm helping him work through his pain."

Little did not want to and was warned by Grace not to cast a dark shadow on the occasion. Briefly, he hugged his mother's neck and shook his fathers' hand. He would not risk becoming emotionally overcome; therefore, he would not allow his eyes to meet theirs. He did and said all the right things, smiling in all the pictures and showing affection toward his mother when people were around by kissing her on the cheek. In public, he was being the perfect son. But at the house, when no one was around, he was cold, distant, and insensitive. He didn't talk and he avoided her and his father as much as possible. It hurt her. It hurt Elijah, but they said nothing. By the end of the engagement dinner and Labor Day weekend, she was relieved to get away from the flesh of her flesh and bone of her bone. It hurt too much. But, in her heart, she held sacred the prayer Reverend Johnson had prayed.

HEALING PAIN

It was a wonderful time of the year around the campus. The campus was in its glory and full bloom with students, faculty, and administrators greeting each other. Most of the activity was taking place in front of Odgen Hall. Each night after dinner the incoming freshmen students lined up on the steps wearing beanie caps. The upper classmen gathered to teach them the school's "Alma Mata." The cheerleaders would lead them in several cheers and introduce the football team. It was full of fun and excitement as the various activities took place. They called it orientation, their way of introducing and welcoming the new freshmen students to the Hampton Family. Little was very happy with Grace back on the campus. They vowed to go to Roanoke at least once a month.

Time was passing quickly; Thanksgiving was just a few days away. All things pertaining to his being at Hampton were rapidly approaching an end. His portion of the Naval project at the shipyard, his employment at the shipyard and Hampton's Fall semester was ending in a few weeks. Then Christmas and the beginning of a New Year would be upon him. He would have to return to UNE in January for his senior year.

The prospects of the ending project frighten him, but the offers of a permanent position with the Navy or the shipyard were promising. Both the shipyard and the Navy wanted him to stay; he desired to stay as much as they wanted him. They were definite prospects. Just to be near his Grace, he was strongly considering staying.

He had no plans of ever returning to New York, but Grace was working hard at changing his mind. She knew in his heart that he really loved his mother and father. He just needed time to recognize it himself. He wanted to go to Roanoke for Thanksgiving with her. But she insisted that he spend the time with his family in New York. He loved her very much and with her he was very happy. They were very happy together. His love for her was so strong that he would do anything to please her.

He waited until the Tuesday evening before Thanksgiving to call his parents, letting them know he would be there for Thanksgiving. Right away Ruth got busy planning to make everything just right for her beloved son, whom she so dearly missed. She was overjoyed to have her son home, so she prepared all of his favorite foods as part of the Thanksgiving dinner.

Elijah was very reluctant. In his heart, he feared for her. He cautioned her, "Now, baby, don't get your hopes up so high. I don't want you getting hurt any more than you already have been." Elijah begged her. She ignored him and continued to gather together her pots and pans. "Honey, don't get too wrapped up in this visit, he's still not over everything. He's still carrying a lot of anger and unforgiveness in his heart toward us."

As painful as it was for him, he distressfully reminded her about the Labor Day weekend and how he practically ignored them at Junebug's house. "You remember how the entire family was gathered for the Labor Day picnic. Grace's parents, the Reverend and Mrs. Johnson, were there to formally announce the engagement of their daughter to Little, and all of his school friends from Hampton and UNE were there. It was a really joyous occasion. Everybody was so happy; Little was on his best behavior. He was cordial and polite to us because he had to in front of all those folks. He made small chit chat with us and was in all the pictures physically, but his heart wasn't for us. We both know if the Johnson's hadn't been there, Little would have avoided us totally." Elijah continued to plead with his wife.

Ruth, not wanting to heed the words and warning of her husband, carried on as usual. But, deep inside, she knew Elijah was right. "Elijah, our son is returning home," she pleaded. It's all I have to hold on to. Seeing him is all I have to look forward to. Just seeing him will be enough for me Elijah. Please don't take that away from me honey, please. It will be all right, you'll see. It will be alright."

"I know it'll be all right honey. But will you be Ruth? I'm so scared for you."

"You don't have to worry about me. I'll be all right. Honest, I'll be all right," she softly whispered.

Withdrawing his pleas, Elijah admitted to himself that he was not going to win this battle. As he took her into his arms and gently kissed her, he concluded the conversation by saying, "Woman, that boy gets his stubbornness from you. He gets it honest." Holding her in his arms he wanted to believe that everything would be alright; he truly wanted too. Most of all he wanted to protect her. Protect her from being hurt by the one she loved so much. Inside himself, he also missed his son and desired to see him as well.

Little decided to work the full day and leave for New York after work. It was very late, just as he had planned when he arrived in New York at his parent's place Wednesday evening after the long seven-hour drive. Elisha and Esther were in bed. Using the excuse of being tired, he avoided the eyes of his parents and any extended conversation with them. The next morning, he stayed in bed until late morning. The aroma of the turkey, collard greens, candied yams, baked macaroni and cheese, chitterlings, and his favorite cake filling, the apartment did not move him. It was only when Swoosh came to the apartment that he decided it was time to get out of bed and shower. Then, he went out to visit neighbors and friends.

As they prepared to go out, kissing Mrs. Thomas, Swoosh smiled and whispered in her ear. "At least he's here Madear; that should count for something. At least he's here."

"Thank you Jerald," she responded tightly clutching his hand.

During dinner as usual, Swoosh carried the entire conversation and how he was doing at the university. Fully aware of Little's distant behavior, he felt he had to carry the conversation. Had it not been for him, it would have been a very bland occasion. Early Friday morning, Little left for the seven-hour drive back to Hampton. Again, he left without saying good-bye.

Finally, the long-awaited moment arrived. It was Little's last week at the shipyard. While sitting at his desk the telephone rang. It was Swoosh on the other end, yelling and screaming at him. Like the previous days before, he paid very little to no attention to Swoosh. Ever since Thanksgiving, for Little, Swoosh's yelling and screaming had become a routine. It was like a broken record, he had heard it all before, a thousand times over and over again. His having left early the next morning after Thanksgiving the way he did; not being sociable and hurting Madear and Pop with his distant bad, ungrateful, unsociable attitude and behavior.

He knew from Swoosh he would never hear the end of it. Tired of the same old rhetoric, to end it he decided he would have to stop talking to Swoosh. So, he did just that; he no longer accepted any of Swoosh's phone calls, nor did he return his calls. To further punish Swoosh, he stopped returning his mother's calls. Now, Swoosh was calling him at his office. Little was outraged. *Calling me here on my job, the boy has finally flipped out and has lost his mind.*

Yelling into the receiver, he shouted at Swoosh, "You've got some nerves calling me on my job. Don't ever call me here ever again. No, just don't ever call me anymore. Do you understand? I mean it, Swoosh. Don't ever call me again." Little slammed down the receiver.

After work, Little was still fuming with Swoosh as he arrived at Holly Tree Inn. Going to his room, he found Grace had left him a message taped to his door. She wanted him to meet her at the greenhouse. Just seeing her message brought about a change in his attitude as a broad smile lit up his face. His shoulders dropped as the tension was released; he instantly became relaxed. Quickly changing his clothes to something more casual, he eagerly dashed off to be with the love of his life. *It's getting late, maybe we'll go off-campus, eat dinner in a nice place tonight. Yea, nice candlelit dinner at a nice restaurant. Maybe we'll go to that little place on Mercury Boulevard. Somewhere private where we could hold hands, stare into each other's eyes, and I can steal a kiss or two.* As Little approached the greenhouse, Grace, seeing him walking down the road met him just inside the doorway. Their eyes met; tears filled her eyes.

"Baby, you're crying. What's wrong?" he asked as he tried to take her into his arms.

"You have to call Swoosh," she softly replied, pushing him away from her. Instantly, Little became angry as a wave of tension flushed over him. In a strong accusatory and angry voice, he retorted, "I don't believe it. Did Swoosh call and say something to upset you? I don't believe him; he's gone too far! Grace, he has no right getting you mixed up in this. It's between Swoosh and me. Swoosh shouldn't be calling you because he's got a problem with me. Now he's gone just too far."

"No Little," she pleaded pressing her fingers against his lips. "You've got to call him. It's your father. He's been calling you about your father."

"This had better not be one of his sick tricks," Little retorted.

"Are you that consumed with anger? How can you be so blind Little?"

"Okay, Baby. I'm sorry. What's wrong with Pop that Swoosh has got to call you?"

"He's in the hospital."

"What! Pop? Swoosh said Pop is in the hospital?"

"That's why he's been calling you. Swoosh said the doctors, they don't think he's going to live," she said, fighting back her tears.

As if a dagger had just been plunged into his heart, hearing her words, Little fell back against the doorframe of the greenhouse. "Oh my God, no."

"Swoosh said he's been trying to call you all week. He called me to tell you because he said you weren't listening to him and not returning his or Madear's calls." Grace wiped the tears from her cheeks as she continued. "Call him now. He's at Madear's. Miss Picott said it's all right for you to use her phone." Lightly, she pressed her hand against his chest. "I'll be in back with Mrs. Picott so you can have some privacy."

Little rushed inside the greenhouse and stood against the counter in disbelief, gasping for air. "Oh God, oh my God." Picking up the phone, his heart pound and his pulse raced as he tried dialing. *What is the number? What is the number?* he mused, hitting himself in the head. "Swoosh, Swoosh," he frantically called. "Swoosh, Pop, what's wrong with Pop? Grace told me you said he was in the hospital."

While listening to Swoosh, Little looked upward. His eyes began filling with tears. Little cried out into the receiver, "Oh God, oh dear God. Nobody told me Swoosh. Honest, nobody told me. I didn't know about Pop." His voice cracked as he fought back tears. "I didn't know Pop was in the hospital." Again, he was silent as he listened to Swoosh's response. Nervously, he began hitting himself in the head.

Little began begging Swoosh as he fought back the tears, burying his face in his arm on the counter. "Oh please don't do this to me Swoosh. Please don't do this to me. Oh God, I didn't mean to hurt them. You know I really didn't mean to hurt them."

Pause.

"No, I'm not happy he's in the hospital. I don't want him to die." Unconsciously, he started pulling his hair as he cried into the phone.

Swoosh continued to speak sternly. What he was saying caused streams of tears to flow down Little's face.

"That's not true Swoosh. I do love him, I do. I know I haven't acted like it. I know you never disrespected or hated your father, even after all the things he did to your mother."

Little softly sobbed as he listened.

"Yes, I know I was wrong for the way I acted during Thanksgiving. Again, he began hitting his head with his hand. "I've been a complete fool. Oh God, I'm sorry, I'm so sorry. Oh God, Swoosh, what am I gonna do? Tell me, what am I gonna do?"

Pausing momentarily, he closed his eyes. "Momma, Swoosh, how's Momma?"

As Swoosh responded, Little lowered his head on the counter and began whimpering as he listened.

"Swoosh, what happened? Why is my father in the hospital? What happened?"

Pause.

Little reacted to Swoosh's sharp response with a sharp cry, "Oh Swoosh, I don't want this. I do care Swoosh," he cried out. "I really do care about Pop and Momma. Please Swoosh, don't do this to me Swoosh. Please don't make me suffer. If he dies, I'll never forgive myself. I wouldn't blame Momma if she never speaks to me again."

As Swoosh spoke, Little wrapped his arm around his stomach and held on to it as his gut ached with great pain.

"Oh God no, no, no. Please God no."

Pause

"No, no Swoosh, that doesn't make me happy. I know I said that, but I didn't mean it when I said it. I didn't know what I was saying. Honest, I didn't. I'm so sorry I said it."

Pause.

"I know it's too late to take it back now. I'm so sorry I said it."

Little sobbed into the receiver and rocked back and forth as he held his stomach.

"I remember, Swoosh. I remember what I promised that day we were in Canaan."

Pause.

"Oh God no, Swoosh. I didn't mean to break my promise to him. Please, Swoosh. Please don't do this to me. Please, please, please."

After a few seconds, he gathered himself together. "I'm coming home. I'll be on the next flight out of here tonight."

Pause.

"No, I will. I'll be on the next plane. I promise Swoosh. I want to come home. I'll call for a flight as soon as I hang up with you."

Little softly sob as he listened.

Hurt by Swoosh's reply, he softly asked, "Momma said that? Not to call me anymore? She doesn't want me to come home?" Hearing those words scared him. He did not like how it felt. "What do you mean she doesn't want me to come?"

Pause.

"Swoosh, you have to believe me. Nobody's called me in the past three days but you. I never got a message from Momma."

Swoosh's voice could be heard as he shouted.

"No. Please Swoosh. You got it all wrong. I'm not calling Momma a liar." Little banged his head on the counter as he shamefully slowly said, "It's my fault, she did call. I didn't return her call. I didn't know why she was calling. Oh God, oh dear God. What have I done? What have I done? I'm so sorry, so sorry. Oh God, what have I done?"

Pause.

"Oh God, Swoosh, what do I have to do to make things right? Tell me, Swoosh, what do I have to do?"

Pause.

"Oh God, oh God," Little cried out loud. Mrs. Picott and Grace rushed into the room just in time to catch him from falling to the floor.

Holding him, they let him cry.

"Grace, take Little back to his room so he can pack. Little, I'll call the airline."

Grace sat on the bed silently watching him pack. She felt awkward seeing him in so much pain and not knowing what to say or do. It was difficult for her. She wanted to cry, but she fought back her tears. Many times before she was able to comfort him; now she felt at a time when he really needed her she was at a lost. She didn't know what to do. Hearing the phone ring, Little jumped. Freezing, he stared in the direction of the phone. Grace quickly rose from the bed. "I'll get that." After a few minutes she spoke. "That was Mrs. Picott. She said the next scheduled flight to New York is leaving in two hours from Norfolk. She booked your reservation."

Hastily, Little packed his clothes in his suitcase. Reaching into the closet, he momentarily hesitated as his eyes fell upon the black suit hanging in the closet. Relieved about the phone call, he looked at the suit. "No, no. I got no use for you. Not now, not now."

Her heart ached for him and was heavily burdened. Aware of his emotional state she could only offer to drive him to the airport.

Except for the occasional weeping, they rode in silence. For most of the trip Little held his head between his hands. His head pound with enormous physical pain. Pain from the shame and guilt he now felt; guilt and shame because he broke his promise and rejected Elijah as his father. Guilt and shame because in his anger he said things he did not mean. He was filled with guilt, because he allowed his anger to overcome the truth. Shame because he had allowed his anger to drive a wedge between him, his father, mother, and Swoosh. He felt shame because he knew, despite everything he had said and done, his father and mother still loved him dearly. A love he refused to return. Ashamed and guilty, because in his heart he knew his father only wanted to protect him. Guilty because, he got what he thought he wanted.

Grace felt Little's distance from her. She recognized that he was in an awful lot of pain, but she respected his need for privacy and to be alone with his thoughts. She knew given time he would share with her what he was feeling inside. Knowing all that he had been through with his parents, she knew he really loved them and never meant the foolish things he said. He just needed time to work things out. He just needed some time to work out his pain; and time to discover his love for them and for himself. She had prayed time would not run out. She was now praying that time had not run out.

When she met them at the Labor Day picnic, just like when she first met Little that winter day in Holly Tree Inn, she instantly fell in love with them. She saw Little in both of his parents, the loving spirit and kindness of his mother and the strength of his father. His behavior mirrored his fathers' behavior. For his pain could heal and he could forgive them and himself, she was determined to do all she could to encourage him to change his attitude. Without the healing, she knew their love would never be complete.

As they arrived at the airport, Little spoke his first words since the phone call. "Swoosh said he was electrocuted."

She was glad that he was beginning to release what he was holding inside. However, she wasn't prepared for what he said. "Oh no," she gasped as she clung to the steering wheel tightly. "Did he say how it happened?"

"On the job five days ago," Little wiped the tears from his cheeks. "He was helping the repair crew. The power was supposed to be off because of the ice storm. A tree limb broke from the weight of the ice. It fell, hitting the power line. It was raining very hard. The wire landed in the puddle next to him. Said the shock knocked him thirty feet from where he was standing. He's been in a coma since. Said the doctors are surprised he's still alive, but they don't expect him to live much longer."

Little leaned forward as he buried his face in his hands and wept; Grace gently held him and rubbed his back as he cried. "Said that if the power hadn't killed him the fall alone should have." Little stared into his hands and wept. "It's all my fault Grace," he blurted out. "He was electrocuted and in a coma. It's all my fault."

"Little, Swoosh didn't say it was your fault, did he?"

"Swoosh didn't have to say it. I know it is."

"Oh no Little, that's not true. It's not your fault. Why would you even think it was your fault?"

"Don't you see? I wished it. When I learned about my real father, Bigger, I was so angry at Pop. I wished it was him instead of my real daddy."

"Little, you shouldn't think like that. Back then you were shocked and hurt. You yourself told me how you felt. It's times like those we say a lot of things we don't really mean. It's not your fault. Please don't even think that Little. It's not your fault."

"I wish I could believe that Grace. I really wish I could believe that it's not my fault, but I can't. Pop always said be careful of what you wish for. It might come true. Don't you see Grace? I wish for it... and, now, it's come true." As he stared into his hands, Little paused for a moment. Leaning over, Grace touched him and placed her hand in his. Feeling unworthy, he moved away, "I got to go inside. I still have to check in and purchase my ticket."

It was the first time he had ever rejected her touch. It made her shutter. Pushing her away the way he did, she knew he was hurting badly inside. "Little, if you would like me to, I'll wait with you in the terminal."

"No, please Grace, I want to be alone. I don't know but I have too much on my mind right now. I'll be all right. Please, go back to Hampton. I'll call you. I promise. I'll call you."

"Little, I'm praying for Pop and for you," she softly called out to him as he removed his suitcase from the back seat of the car. "I love you."

"Thank you, I know you do. And I love you too." Grace watched as Little turned to walk to the terminal. Suddenly, he stopped. "Grace," he shouted, dropping his suitcase as he raced toward the car. "Grace, I need you. I don't want to be alone. Please, come and wait with me."

Together, in silence they sat at the terminal holding hands. The section where they sat was nearly empty. Little leaned his head on Grace's shoulder until it was time for him to board the plane.

The airplane was sparsely occupied. Looking around, he quickly found his seat closer to the rear of the plane. He was alone with his painful thoughts. He sat gazing out of the window into the darkness of the night. So transfixed, disturbed, and emotionally distraught, Little barely heard the voice of the passenger addressing him as the passenger sat down next to him.

"Excuse me," The young man spoke a little louder. "Excuse me, but I believe my seat is here next to yours."

Little looked at the person addressing him—it was a young man close to his age. His smooth skin was jet black. He had high cheekbones and flashed a set of bold pearly white teeth. Little wished he would go away.

"Oh, hello. I'm sorry I didn't hear you." *Of all the empty seats on the plane, they had to assign someone a seat next to mine. Why can't he find another?*

"That's alright, you seemed to be preoccupied." The stranger smiled, "Of all the empty seats on the plane, they assigned our seats together."

"I'm sorry, but I have a lot on my mind."

"I'm not disturbing you, am I?"

A strange feeling came over Little as he looked perplexed. "No, it's alright."

"Are you headed for New York?"

"Yes."

"So am I." The plane started taxing down the runway. They both sat quietly as the stewardess gave the normal safety speech. "So, what's your name?"

"Thomas, but my family and friends call me Little."

"Well, I'm pleased to meet you Thomas, or may I call you Little?"

Little looked at the stranger. For some strange reason his voice sounded familiar, but he could not remember where he had heard it before. In the stranger's presence, he was feeling relaxed and comfortable. For some strange reason unbeknownst to him he did not mind sharing his space with the stranger. "It's alright, you can call me Little."

"I saw you sitting in the terminal. The young lady you were sitting with is she your girlfriend?"

"She's my fiancée. Her name is Grace."

"She's very attractive. She seemed very nice."

"She is."

"Are you from Norfolk?"

"No, I'm from New York, but right now I'm doing some work for the Newport News Drydock and Shipbuilding Company. I was also taking classes at Hampton Institute. That's where I met Grace, but I'm really a student at the University of New England."

"The University of New England, that's great. But then, how did you get from UNE to Hampton Institute and the shipyard?"

"It's quite a long story. My major is nuclear engineering. I've been working on a special project regarding nuclear subs."

"Wow, that's great! You must be a very intelligent person!"

"Not really."

"Believe me, you're extremely intelligent, gifted and talented. To be attending UNE. It's the number one Ivy League university in the world—and working on a nuclear submarine at the shipyard. No ordinary person can do that!"

Little chuckled. "Well, when you put it like that, I guess I am." For the first time since he received the news about Elijah he smiled. He felt relaxed; he found the young man a pleasure to talk to.

"But the semester is not over yet. Why are you going to New York?"

"To see Elijah, he's in the hospital."

"Oh, I'm sorry to hear that; I hope it's nothing serious. Is Elijah your brother?"

"Well, he is my father. No, he's not really my father. He's my father by adoption. I never met my real father."

"Why not?"

"They, my mother and father never married. He died before I was born. My mother married Elijah when I was two months old. Elijah adopted me. That's why my first name is Thomas. Thomas, that was my father's first name, and my last name is Thomas because Elijah's last name is Thomas. That's how you get Thomas Thomas."

"So Elijah is really the only father you've ever known."

"I guess you can say that. He's the one that started calling me Little."

Little started recalling the pleasant memories. "My mother said when I was a baby, he would hold me in his hands and say I was so Little until he just started calling me Little. The name stuck."

"Sounds like you really love him. What happened to him?"

"What happened to him?"

"Elijah, your father. You said he was in the hospital."

"Oh, he works for Con Edison, the electric company in New York. During last week's ice storm, a power line broke; he was electrocuted."

Little began to reflect on his growing up and shared with the young man his relationship with Elijah. The more he talked the easier he found talking. Little began to open up more as he spoke. To his own amazement as he reminisced, he began to laugh about some of the things he did with Elijah.

"I envy you Little. My father was killed when I was young. My mother never remarried. You were blessed to have a man like Elijah in your life to raise you as his son. What about your real father? Have you ever asked your mother about him?"

"No. I didn't find out about being adopted until December last year when my mother's mother died." Before he realized it, the words came out of his mouth. "Apparently, he raped my mother. I was the result of the rape. He died in the electric chair for killing a rich white woman and my mother's oldest sister Bessie. She was his girlfriend. When my mother's mother found out that my mother was pregnant with Bigger's baby, that's his name, she vowed to kill me. When she met me last year, she was on her deathbed and she almost succeeded."

"Trying to kill you?"

Little opened the collar of his shirt showing the stranger the scar. "She choked me, crushed my windpipe. I remember choking and losing consciousness. I remembered watching her from the corner of the room as she held on to me breaking my neck. Then she had a heart attack and died. I watched my aunt Lanet who's a doctor tried to revive me."

After saying what he did, Little felt relieved. He said it. He told a complete stranger, someone who had no vested interest in him, someone his own age. Immediately, he began telling the stranger what he remembered about that night. "I remember seeing this bright light. I started moving toward the light. A voice on the other side pleaded for

God not to take me. I remember the voice distinctly said, 'Father, not now, please don't let it end like this.'"

Little paused. "You know that's strange. That was the second time I heard the voice say those exact same words. I wanted to go to the light, but God answered the prayers of the voice."

Little began talking about growing up in New York, learning his mother was from Chicago, that she had two brothers, a deceased sister, and that her mother was still alive after all these years. He talked about his feelings as he had never talked before. He talked of his hurt, his pain, feelings of betrayal and abandonment. Most of all he talked about feeling so dirty, unclean and unworthy to be looked upon. He talked about his running away to Kansas because he was so mixed up inside and feeling unloved. He told the stranger things that he had not shared with Grace. He shared feelings that he did not know had grown inside of him over the past year.

As he talked, he had no feelings of shame or condemnation from the stranger. He shared with the stranger his relationship with Cassandra and discovering his true love for Grace. As he talked, he felt as if a big burden was being lifted off of his chest. He expressed feelings that he was not aware of—feelings of anger, love, hate, confusion, deception, and unworthiness. He found it easy talking to the stranger. He found it a release and a relief. As he talked his feelings continued to pour out of him. His burden became lighter and lighter as he talked.

The plane landed; Little continued to talk as they entered the terminal and waited for their luggage. The stranger continued to listen. Together, they sat down as Little continued to unload his burden.

"When Swoosh called me and told me about my father being in the hospital I cried, but I didn't know why I was crying. I know I felt guilty, ashamed, and scared. But I didn't know why."

Finally, the stranger spoke. "Little, earlier you said you heard the voice inside your head say those words before. I believe you said, 'Father, not now. Don't let it end this way.'"

"That's funny. In hearing you say those words, you sound just like the voice I've always heard speaking to me inside my head."

"I do? Tell me, when was the first time you heard the voice say those words?"

"You know, I've never told anyone this, not my mother, father, Swoosh, not even Grace. I was so ashamed of what I tried to do. But for some reason, I don't mind telling you. I told you about my first day in the resident hall at UNE and about Bobby's parents. After his mother said what she did I went back to my room. I remember looking out of the window and seeing my face in the glass. I was so mad; mad at what I saw in the window. I hated what I saw in the window. I climbed up on the desk and threw my body against the window. I tried to kill myself. I was trying to break the window so I could jump out. I remember the voice pleading with me to stop. The window cracked—that's when I heard the voice say, 'Father, not now, don't let it end this way.' That's when I fell off of the desk. If I hadn't slipped, I would have gone through the window. I wanted to kill myself. If it had not been for the voice, I would have."

"Little, in your heart you know you love Elijah, and he is your true father. That's why you cried when you learned he was in the hospital. Elijah is a good man, a good husband to your mother, and a good father to you and your brother and sister. He has and will always be there to love, protect, and guide you. You're scared he will die and no longer be here for you. You were afraid of losing him and all that he means to you. Deep in your heart you know that's why."

The stranger continued, "To truly free yourself, you must sometimes ask the most difficult questions, despite being afraid of the answers. Sometimes, we get sidetracked. Things happen in our lives that knock us off course or we sometimes stray from our path. It sounds like you got knocked off of your course. But you're getting back on track and you don't understand why because you feel you don't deserve it."

The young man touched Little's heart, sending a sensation throughout his body that caused him to shiver. "Most of all, you're afraid of what may be inside of you. You're afraid of what's inside of you. But the rage you've experienced, there's not a black man living today or that has ever lived, that hasn't experienced that rage and the self-hatred. I know because I've experienced it myself. It consumed me and cost me my life. But I got a second chance. I wish my mother remarried and I had a strong hand of a man like Elijah to guide me. Hear me. Being a father is more than just the man from whose loins you sprung—more than the man that planted the seed in your mother. You may be the bone of bone and flesh of flesh of another man, but Elijah is your father."

Little looked perplexed. "You felt that rage? I don't understand. What do you mean a second chance?"

"Little, to understand you should, no, you need to ask your mother about Bigger. Don't be afraid of the part of him that is in you. Don't be afraid to embrace those parts of him or those parts of yourself."

Little felt the stranger had read his heart. For the first time since Chicago, he felt free. "But I'm afraid to ask the questions. I don't know if I can. How will I know when to ask?"

"Trust the feeling you have inside your heart. Don't close out the world. Don't close out your mother. Don't close out your father."

"But what if I fail?"

"You'll never know until you try. It's better to have tried and failed, than to have failed to try."

"Talking to you, I feel so much better, I feel so relieved." As they shook hands Little embraced the young man and held him tightly. "Thank you for listening to me. Thank you," he softly whispered in the stranger's ear. "You know, all this time, I never asked you your name. I don't know who you are."

The young man held Little and whispered in his ear, "All you need to believe right now is that I'm that voice inside of your head. I've always been here for you and I will always be here for you. I am everything that is good, kind, and decent inside of you. That's who I am. And remember, through God, there is forgiveness and redemption."

Together, they walked out of the terminal, Little turned around to hail the cab.

"Remember this one thing, Little, if every Bigger had an Elijah in their life, there would be more Littles in this world."

As the cab stopped Little pondered momentarily over what the stranger said before he responded. His voice sounded like the voice that stopped him from hitting Mrs. McGinnis and stopped him from smashing through the window that day in the resident hall, hurling himself below to his death. The voice he had heard in his head so many times talking to him. As he turned, he spoke, "I still don't know your name." As he turned to face the stranger, looking up, the strange young man was gone.

The December night air was frigid. Although it was nearing the end of the year, it had not snowed. Remembering his Uncle Canada caused him to change his mind. Instead of going home from the airport, he decided to take the cab to the hospital.

Walking into Elijah's hospital room he felt a strange and cold sensation. A cold shiver went up his spine. The room was filled with flowers and cards. Knowing how everyone loved his father, it did not surprise him. Slowly, his eyes fell upon Elijah's massive body lying on the hospital bed. His head, arms, and hands were wrapped in white bandages. Only his fingers from the knuckles were exposed.

Lying there, to Little he appeared weak, frail, and so helpless. Never before had he seen his father so thin and pale. Initially, he hesitated. He was afraid to move close to him. Gathering courage, he moved closer touching him lightly on the shoulder. Little's lips trembled with pain, grief, and fear. He started to cry.

Slowly, he picked up Elijah's hand and held onto it. He recalled the many days when he was a little boy holding his father's hand. His hands were always so big and strong. They felt so powerful. He remembered how he always felt secure and safe whenever he held those hands. Now, his father's hand felt cold, lifeless. Grasping his father's hand between his he began to pray. "Oh Lord, please, please don't let him die. You know I love him. He's a good man and he's always put you first in his life. He raised me loving you. Please, don't let him die, Lord. Please don't let him die."

Little kissed him on the forehead. "Daddy I'm sorry, I'm so sorry. I didn't mean to hurt you. I broke my promise, my word. I'm so sorry. You're all the father I know and the only one I want to know. I'm so sorry I acted the way I did, running away that night in Chicago, not speaking to you or Momma. I know everything you did was because you loved me. I know now you did it because you love Momma and me. I can't say I understand it, because I don't. But I know you did it out of love. I'm so sorry. Please forgive me. Please forgive me. Don't die daddy. Please don't die. I still need you. I love you and I want to let you know it." An exhausted Little pulled up a chair and sat at his side

"I'm not going to leave you daddy. I'm not going to leave you. I'm going to stay right here by your side until you're all right. I promise." Softly, he laid his head on his father's bed next to his hand. Shortly thereafter, he drifted off to sleep, exhausted.

The next morning Little was awakened by a hand on his shoulder. Sleepily, he looked up. It was his mother. Guarding herself, cautiously she kept her distance. Little could hear the distance in her voice. "Swoosh said you told him you were coming sometime yesterday. We didn't know you were here."

Finally, she had built the wall protecting her heart. The distance between them scared him. "Oh Momma," he cried as he stood up, "Momma, please forgive me. I'm so sorry for the way I've been acting. Will you forgive me, Momma? I love you, and I'm so sorry," he sobbed softly as he moved toward her.

Just a few short weeks ago, she had longed to hear those very words from her son. She could see by the redness in his eyes, he had been crying, but now, now things had changed. Ruth stood unmoved by Little's plea of forgiveness. "I'm sorry, son, being here for my husband is all the load I can carry in my heart right now. I am glad you're here." As she spoke, her words were stoic and unmovable.

"Momma?"

Ruth held her hand up to silence him. "I told Jerald to tell you that you didn't have to come."

For the first time in his life, Little felt his mother's coldness. It was a side of her he never knew. He understood. It was the side that allowed her to survive having to give up her family. He felt the distance between the two of them. He had finally got what he for the past several months sought. He finally got what he thought he wanted. Only now, after having experienced what he sought, he realized that it wasn't what he expected or wanted, and it didn't feel good. He felt alone, isolated from her, and in a different world. He felt in a cold cruel world, a world void of his mother's love, where he was unprotected and vulnerable. It terrified him. He felt as if someone reached up and ripped the breath of life out of him. The pain was too great and extremely unbearable. His knees began to buckle.

Unable to control himself, fearfully he fell at her feet and began weeping. "Oh God, what have I done? What have I done? Please, please, Momma. Don't turn me out of your heart. Please don't turn me out of your heart. I love you, Momma, and I love Pop too. I know you and Pop were trying to protect me. I know you didn't want or mean to hurt me. I just want to tell him I love him; I love both of you. I'm so scared. I know it's all my fault Pop's dying, and I feel it's all my fault. Please, please, Momma, don't push me away. I'm so scared. I couldn't go on living without you or Pop."

Ruth's heart began melting as a mother's love began to replace the coldness. "Hush that nonsense," Ruth softly spoke as she knelt down to embrace her son. "It's not your fault. Don't go blaming yourself." She placed her hands around his ears, gently pulling upward lifting Little to his feet. She held onto him, pressing him close to her bosom as he wept. "Hush that nonsense. Don't go blaming yourself. It's not your fault baby; it's not your fault." The tears rolled down her oval-shaped face as she embraced her beloved son. "It's not your fault."

Little had longed to be held in the comfort of his mother's arms. "Oh Momma, Momma, I've been such a fool carrying on the way I have. Not speaking to you or Pop and running away in Chicago the way I did. I'm so sorry. I'm so ashamed of myself for acting the way I did. If I were a better son, Pop, he wouldn't be there in that bed right now. I'm so scared of losing him forever. I'm scared of losing you." Little buried his head in his mother's chest and cried.

Ruth steadily rocked him as a babe in her arms. "No baby, no. We can talk about that later; right now, we have to be strong for your father." Ruth could feel her son's exhaustion, but most of all his pain. Her mothers' intuition told her Little had been crying all night at his father's bedside. She eased him into the chair. "Here, sit down, Little." Getting another chair, she sat down beside him. They both held on to Elijah's hand.

"He's got such big strong hands, Momma. When I was small, I always liked for him to pick me up with those big hands. I always wanted to be big just like Pop. I remember how he would hold my hands between his and we played that game. In the winter, sometimes, I would pretend my hands were cold just so he would sandwich my hands between his. His hands would guide me across the street and around the playground. His hands were my world. I love him Momma, just like I know you love him, and he loves you and me. I would watch how he would hold you in his arms, so secure and with confidence. I always believed there wasn't a thing those hands couldn't take care of or heal. I wanted them to take away Chicago. I was hurting so badly inside. I wanted those hands to take away the pain, but they didn't. And when they didn't, I got scared, and then angry. I got so angry and confused when they didn't Momma. I don't know why, but I did because those hands didn't."

"I know Little. I always felt so safe and secure in his arms too. There's not a thing Elijah wouldn't do for us. When you were born, Elijah was there. When I first saw him pick you up with those big hands and hold you in his arms, my heart pound with excitement. When you were a baby and you were sick, he'd pick you up; you would always calm down and stopped crying. You'll fall asleep in those arms. In his arms, you were so tiny, so little."

A broad smile came across her face as she spoke. "He fell in love with you the moment he saw you. He's a good man. Before we married, when he'd come home from work, the first thing he wanted to see was his Little. He was the first to call you Little. Two months after you were born, we got married. He told me we should tell you the truth. He wanted you to know the truth. He wanted to raise you knowing he adopted you. He chose you to be his son. He never even asked about your real daddy. It didn't matter to him, because he loved us both. It's my fault that you didn't know. So much time passed. After a while, I just couldn't bring myself to tell you."

Ruth sighed. "You don't know how much I regretted not telling you. Every year, those bad dreams you had. I knew what they were all about. I knew I had the answer to stop them, but I was scared. I was scared to tell the truth. Scared of losing you; scared of losing Elijah. I never told Elijah, and I had no idea he knew until that night in Jerome's house. I'm glad you know now. I only wish I had told you instead of your finding out the way you did in my brother's house. But I was scared, so scared. Scared that I would lose you, scared I would lose Elijah. I felt so dirty and ashamed. I didn't want you to feel dirty or ashamed like I felt."

Ruth looked at her husband. "Then my mother was no help. When you started having the reoccurring nightmares around the same time of year, I knew what was happening. I felt dirty and shameful all over again. But I was too scared and ashamed to say anything to your father. I thought if I told you the truth, I'd lose you. I never told Elijah neither because I was scared. Scared I'd lose him too. I never hated you for what Bigger did to me. I always looked at you with love. I never blamed you for being here. You were innocent and pure. To me, it was Elijah's love for you that kept you that way. I didn't want to spoil it by telling him or you. When I was feeling dirty and ashamed, all I had to do was see him holding you and I felt redeemed. Somehow, he always seemed to know, and he'd hold me too. When he'd hold us, all was right with the world. I felt cleansed. I wasn't ready to lose you Little, and I'm not ready to lose your father. I was so scared I had lost you. I was hurting so bad inside, so bad." Affectionately, she kissed Elijah and Little's hands.

Gently, Little caressed his father's hand. "Momma, you don't know what it meant being the son of Mr. Elijah Isaiah Thomas. I was so proud of being his son. Every kid in the neighborhood loved him. Walking down the street holding his hand, I felt so proud. I knew I was special because he was my daddy. Being with him he made me feel that way and then the other kids would all say I was the luckiest kid in the whole world, and I knew it. Everybody that knows Pop loves him. I didn't mind sharing him with Swoosh, or any of the other kids because I knew he was my father, not theirs.

"If anything I knew, it was, he was my father and nobody, not anybody could ever take that away from me. Not anybody. But that day in Chicago it was taken away. I was so scared. I felt as if I had been left out in the cold with no protection. I felt I was no different from the other kids in the neighborhood. I got so mad at him. How could he have done that to me! For the first time in my life, I felt that those hands couldn't help me. They weren't there to protect me. As much as I wanted him to, he couldn't protect me from the truth. I wanted him to grab me and hold me. Tell me it wasn't true; that you were mistaken. Lying. But he didn't Momma. He didn't." Tears rolled down his cheeks as he reminisced of that horrid day. "I was so hurt, so angry. I was lost and so scared. I was so mixed up inside my head. I didn't know what to do, so I ran. I wanted to keep on running until the pain stopped, until there was nowhere else to run."

"I know son. I don't blame you because I wanted to run myself, but your daddy was there for me. You didn't stay long enough to give him a chance. If you had waited a little while longer, he would have held on to you. He tried. I remember he kept telling me to give you time, give you time. He said there's a big open wound in you. I had to give it time to heal. I knew there was going to be a scar for a long time to come. I didn't expect it to last this long. But one thing I do know is there's a whole lot of healing in those hands. Believe me when I tell you Thomas, I never wanted to hurt you, and I never wanted to hurt your father. If I could have, I would have taken the secret to the grave with me. But I'm glad it's out. It's over with. Now we can start healing. I know those hands will help your wound heal and the scar to go away if you let them. I know they will, because they did for me. Every time he was there for me, waiting. He's there for you, waiting. Just give him a chance. He knew you would be back; just give him a chance."

Little stood up and walked over to the window. He stared at his reflection in the glass. He pressed his hand on it as if to touch the person in the glass. He thought about what the stranger had said. "Momma?"

She detected the change in his tone and sensed there was something deeper troubling him. "What is it, son?"

Little stared at the reflection in the window. "What was he like?"

"What was who like?"

"Him." Little pointed at the image in the window. "Him. Bigger Thomas. What was he like?" He turned to face his mother. "I read the newspaper clippings and what they had to say about him."

"Oh no, son, he was nothing like what they had to say in those newspapers. The Bigger Thomas I knew was nothing like what they wrote about in the newspaper."

"Then what was he like?"

Ruth stood up and walked to the other side of the bed. Gently, she sat down and held Elijah's hand in her lap. "The Bigger I knew was a kind person. He had been dating my sister Bessie for about two years, so he was over at our apartment a lot. Sometimes, he would bring my mother flowers and candy. That's why she liked him so much. He paid a lot of attention to her; she loved it. He was always a perfect gentleman around Momma and me. I got to know him because sometimes when he would come over and Bessie wouldn't be home; he and I would sit down and talk. He enjoyed talking to me. He told me things that he didn't tell my sister or anybody else. He was a dreamer. He had dreams, big dreams. He would share them with me. He was originally from Jackson, Mississippi, and moved with his family to Chicago when he was in grade school. He quit school in the eighth grade because of finances; he wanted to be a medical doctor. Even though he quit school in the eighth grade, he was really smart. He used to read a lot, and he was good in math and in science. People, not even Bessie or Momma didn't get to know him like I did. He was sensitive, warm and he had a hardy laugh." Ruth paused as she reflected. "He loved living in the city, but he hated the rats, the cramped space, and the conditions his family was forced to live in. Even though he teased them a lot he was really good to his mother, sister, and brother. He used to talk about making it big one day and moving them into a house of their own. He talked to me about them all the time. He was always so kind to me. That's why I never thought he would have…" She hesitated. "He would have done what he did."

"It's alright Momma, you can say it. You never thought he would have raped you."

She let out a long sigh. "Yes, I never thought he would have raped me." Having said it to her son, Ruth felt relieved. "But it seemed like every time he'd make one giant step forward; he'd go back three. In those days it was hard for Negroes, especially for the men. We didn't mix with white people like you do today. The more he tried, the worse things got for him and lots of colored folks. He always told my brother and I to stay in school no matter what. He'd say education was the key to getting out of poverty."

But the anger just built up inside of him. The rage was there, he was a time bomb waiting to explode, an accident waiting to happen."

"But what about all the fighting, stealing, drinking…didn't he go to reform school, Momma?"

"That was another side of him. It was like he was made up of several different people. There were his friends, Gus and Jack, that were up to no good. He'd get around them and do just what they would do. Go out and rob someone for some money, break in and rob houses, robbing Negroes. Then whenever he'd get with that sister of mine, he'd go wild, and it would all come out. Oh, now he loved having his fun just like the next man. He'd joke and laugh and talk, but when he'd go out with that wild sister of mine, or get with his gang of friends, he was totally wild. But I guess he needed that too or else he would have exploded long before he did."

Ruth continued, "With Bessie, he was able to release some of the pressure built up inside of him. The anger and frustration of not working, living on relief in a rat and roach infested building. Feeling trapped in a situation, not knowing how to get out. I remember him telling me a story about how he woke up one morning, there was a big rat on his bed. His mother and sister were screaming. He killed it with a pot. The landlord didn't care. All he cared about was collecting his rent money."

"Momma, sometimes I feel the same way. I have the same rage inside of me that Bigger had inside of him. I told you about what happened that first morning at school with Bobby and his parents. I wanted to kill somebody. I remember seeing myself in the window and hating myself for being black. I don't know, at times, I still feel that way. Am I like Bigger? I'm scared that one day I might do the same things he did."

Ruth shook her head from side to side as she walked over to Little and embraced him. "Oh, son, there's not a black man alive that hasn't felt that rage on the inside. Not just Bigger, but your daddy and my brothers. Two weeks ago, a young black man dressed in the finest Brooks Brothers suit was in the hospital's employment office. The secretary told him that they weren't hiring janitors right now. He looked at her and politely said, 'That's fine because I'm not looking for a janitor position. I'm the new neurosurgeon, Dr. Crawford.' I could see the rage in his face. I know he felt bad, and I felt bad for him. All Negro men have that rage inside of them. There's not a Negro mother alive that isn't scared for her son. Scared that there will come a day when he won't be able to control that black rage inside; scared he'll end up hurting himself or someone else. Scared he'd end up in jail or somewhere lying in the street dead from being stabbed or shot. Scared that he might be hunted down like a dog and lynched from a tree by a white mob. Every time they hear a gunshot or hear about a shooting, they pray their son is all right. They pray that the police haven't beat him up or shot him. You're scared to pick up the phone late at night when it rings, because it might be someone telling you your child is dead. There's not a Negro mother alive that isn't afraid for her son."

Little paused and walked away from her and stood by the window. "Momma."

She sensed his changing persona. "What is it son?"

"I told you about the incident with Mrs. Henderson, Bobby's mother. But I never told you, Pop, or Grace this because I was too ashamed, too scared. I'm almost too ashamed to tell it to you about it now. The man I met on the plane today was the first person I ever told."

"Son, never feel too ashamed to tell me anything. I'll always try to understand."

Little looked at the floor. "That day I hated myself so bad, I tried to kill myself by smashing the window with my body. There was this voice inside my head trying to stop me. I felt something holding me back. If I hadn't slipped off of the desk, I would have been dead today."

"Oh my poor child, my poor child," she said as she took him into her arms. "I'm so glad you slipped off of that desk. Telling me this makes me glad you ran away to the Griffins. I rather you had run away, me never seeing you again and have you alive, than for you to hurt yourself."

"But what do I do Momma? What am I supposed to do with the anger inside of me?"

"I don't rightly know what to tell you son. It's all according to how you deal with the anger inside. You can live and die like Bigger or you can turn to alcohol and drugs like others. You can marry and take it out on your wife and children by beating them. Or you can do like your daddy, and just what you've been doing, hold your head up high and keep on going. It's not easy. Sometimes, I wonder just how Elijah does it. I know it hurts him. Lord knows, I wonder just how he does it. For you, just keep listening to that voice inside of your head. That voice is everything good, decent, and kind that's inside of you."

"The guy on the plane said the same thing. He said he was the voice inside me."

"Maybe he is, maybe he is. But I'm glad you talked to him. Sounds like you met your guardian angel."

"Momma, am I like Bigger?"

"You are in one sense. All the good things about you remind me of Bigger." She turned and looked at Elijah. "He nurtured all those good qualities in you, making you the man you are today. That's why you're like your father lying there in that bed, strong and determined to make it against all odds. You're more Elijah than Bigger. If Elijah was Bigger's father, he would be that medical doctor today."

Little pushed away from her. "But Momma, when you see me don't you see him? I'm the result of his raping you. What happened to you over twenty years ago, aren't I a constant reminder of that? How can you love me? How can you stand the sight of me? How do you do it?"

Ruth took him in her arms and pressed his head against her bosom. "Oh my precious child, my precious child. When I see you, I see a strong young Negro man, whose gifted, brilliant, and talented. I see everything good in Elijah and Bigger. I see my son, the child I gave birth to. Sure, the way you were conceived wasn't the right way; it's not the way I would have chosen. But what you are and what you're becoming is far greater than what all the Biggers of this world could do to me. Of all the mothers in this world, I am blessed. God blessed me with you and through you."

"The paper didn't have a picture. Do I look anything like him? Am I anything like him Momma?"

She paused and looked at his reflection in the mirror. "It's strange what the years do to your memory. I can remember his smile, his laugh, but I can't recall his face. But, I guess, physically, you're a little taller, but not quite as dark. It's strange what the years can do to your memory. You're handsome just like Bigger was, and he was a very good-looking man. You have that same beautiful pearly white teeth and smile. But in statute, you're taller than Bigger will ever be. You will be all that he couldn't be but wanted to be. If he were alive today, he would be so proud of you."

"But seeing me day after day Momma, how could you love me knowing what he did to you? I'm the result of his raping you. You lost contact with your family. You might not have ever seen them again."

"Thomas, I am so proud of you. You brought a whole lot of joy into my life. If someone had told me that I was going to have a wonderful son like you, I would have willing given myself to Bigger that night. I never regretted a day in my life–giving birth to you. I regret not having told you the truth. But I've never regretted or resented having given birth to you. Maybe you don't understand it now, but you will someday. Someday you will. My brothers and I are back together again. That's all that matters."

"But am I like him?"

"You have his eyes, his face, beautiful smooth flawless black skin and his smile. But inside, you're more like Elijah than Bigger. Elijah is your father. He instilled in you and gave you the things Bigger only dreamed of. You patterned yourself after Elijah. His ways have become your ways." She walked over to the bed and again sat in the chair. Taking Elijah's hand in hers she held it to her cheek. "All the goodness, the strength, love, and compassion of this man is in you. He poured himself into you and you filled yourself up with him. He is your father, and you are his son, in all your ways. You are just like him. You walk like him. Talk and think just like him. He is your father nothing will ever change that. Nothing can or will ever change that."

"Maybe,… Maybe I'm not saying it right." Little bit his lip and looked upward as if he was searching for the words on the ceiling. He turned and looked at his reflection in the window. With his finger he pressed against the reflection, he asked, looking at himself, "Momma, is Bigger a part of me?"

"You're bone of his bone and flesh of his flesh, Thomas. He'll always be a part of you."

"But he was an animal Momma; a vile, despicable, savage animal."

"No son! He was not an animal. He's the man from whose loins you sprung forth."

"That's what scares me Momma."

"Oh Little, don't be afraid of that part in you. There was an awful lot of good in Bigger Thomas. It was life circumstances that frightened him. In a weak moment, he succumbed to life's circumstances. He was a decent person."

"But, Momma, I don't understand. How can you say that about the man that killed your sister and raped you?"

"I remember that night looking at him afterwards. He felt so bad for what he had done to me. I remember him picking the sheet up off the floor and covering me. He couldn't look me in my eyes. But I looked into his, and I could see the hurt. Mr. Max, the lawyer that defended Bigger and helped me move to New York said Bigger told him that he did a real bad thing to the one good person in his life, and that's what he should be punished for. He told him that he knew he had hurt the only true friend he had very badly. He told him that I was the one good, decent person who understood him, and he really loved and treasured our friendship. But he felt he was not good enough to have me. He knew he hurt me very badly. He was ashamed of what he did to me. Mr. Max said first he thought Bigger was talking about his having killed Bessie. He didn't understand what Bigger was talking about until he met me. Somehow, the good that was in Bigger got lost along the way. He got sidetracked. Killing that woman and Bessie was an accident. Mr. Max believed Bigger was telling him the truth. All the good that was in Bigger is in you. That's why I gave you his name, Thomas. I knew that good part of him was in you."

"What if you're wrong Momma?"

"But I'm not son. Elijah was there to nurture and cultivate that part in you. He helped that part develop and grow. To help you become the person you are today. That's why I married him."

"You said Mr. Max said his killing that girl and your sister was an accident?"

"Yes, he said Bigger told him the whole story. He hit Bessie with a brick—"

Little interrupted. "He hit her with a brick in an old, abandoned tenement building. Every year in my dream I saw it. The white girl, she was in bed. The pillow…I was scared. I could smell the liquor when I smothered the white girl in my dream. I only did it to keep her from making noises. It happened…"

Ruth completed the sentence, "When her mother came into the room." Ruth looked at her son with surprise. *He knows the story.* "Bigger was telling the truth."

"I never told you, but I saw it all happening in the dream. Momma, Bigger wasn't an animal or the monster they said he was! He was scared; it was an accident. He never meant to kill that girl or your sister."

"If only Bigger had an Elijah in his life." Slowly, Ruth raised her hand and held it out too Little. With pride and confidence, he walked over and took his mother's hand as he sat in the chair next to her. He held on to Elijah's hand and slipped his arm around his mother.

"That's just what the man on the plane said. He said Elijah is my father and I am his son. I believe, no, I know that now. Now, I just want to tell him that Momma. Now, I just want to let him know that he is my father and that I know it. If he dies, I'll never forgive myself."

"No, son, we can't think like that. Your daddy is strong. He's going to live. We've just got to believe and have faith in God."

Elijah's fingers moved to tighten around Ruth and Little's hand. They both felt the weak clasp of the hand around theirs. Tears of joy began to flow as they looked at him. Elijah's eyes opened, and a faint smile daunted his lips as he moved them faintly saying, "You're my son, and I love you."

In two weeks, Little and Elijah were both home for Christmas. This year, it was special for Ruth Thomas. Both, her husband and her son were home. The long-awaited healing process had begun. It all had gone as tradition dictated. This time with Little leading the charge. First, he drove Swoosh, Esther, and Elisha to Long Island to the tree farm to pick out a tree. The six of them trimmed the tree. This year it was Little's strong arms that lifted Esther up to put the angel on top of the tree. They decorated the apartment while Ruth and Esther baked cookies. Later that evening, they drank hot chocolate, ate cookies, and sung Christmas carols. The next day, Little and Swoosh took Elisha and Esther downtown Christmas shopping. Again, that evening they drank hot chocolate and sang Christmas carols as Swoosh let Little play the piano. The family ended the evening watching *It's a Wonderful Life*.

"Every time a bell rings, an angel gets his wings."

TIME

The middle of January had passed. Little thought about the project at the shipyard as he drove; it had come to an end. It was time for him to return to the university for the final semester of his senior year. Leaving Hampton was hard. Leaving Grace was even harder. After saying good-bye to his family, he started on his drive from New York to the University of New England in Connecticut early that afternoon. It was a short three-hour drive. Due to the weather, the drive to the university was taking longer than usual. As Little neared the Groton exit snow began falling harder as the Nor Easter gathered strength. Directly before him, covered in snow, he could barely see the sign marking his exit off the highway. He recalled the last time he saw snow close to this was last year in January when he flew from St. Louis airport to Patrick Henry Airport in Newport News, Virginia. But that time he had company. Mrs. Picott, he recalled, it was his first time meeting her. "Boy, at least that time we had one another to talk to; distracting our minds from the hazard of the road the winter storm created. This time is altogether different. Mrs. Picott isn't driving, I am. I've never driven in blizzard weather conditions before."

Along the route, he could make out where other drivers had slid off the highway into the median or into the guardrail. Several times he himself had almost lost control of the Buick, nearly colliding with another vehicle or off of the highway. As he slowly itched down the exit, he scarcely made out the slow moving, odd looking snow-covered figure along the roadside. "What in the world is that?" As he got closer to the figure, it appeared to be a woman, steadfastly trudging through the blistering wind and snow.

Suddenly, without provocation her feet swung above her head. Her snow-covered head met the snow-covered earth where her feet had once threaded. The bags she was carrying flew into the air and landed softly in the fresh falling snow. Seeing it, the Charlie Chaplin style fall was comical. Reacting quickly, without thinking, Little immediately slammed on the brakes, sending the car skidding across the road toward the snowbank where the woman had fallen. He heard the thud as the car came to an abrupt stop in the snowbank. His racing heart pounded as he got out and rushed to the front of the car where the woman lay. The car had stop only inches from her body. "Are you alright," he asked as he took her by the arm to help her to her feet.

"Um fine, jist a lil' shaken from da fall I guess," she replied as she leaned on one knee, struggling to get up with Little's assistance.

He was especially relieved to find that she was not injured from his car. Close up viewing her face, he determined she had to be around fifty years old. "Are you sure you're alright?" he questioned, as he began brushing the snow off of her.

The woman was wobbly as she rose to her feet. "Um okay, jist a lil' dizzy from da fall."

"Here, come with me to my car. It's warm inside and you can sit down," he said, guiding her to his car.

Her speech was slow and slurred. "Thank ya young man," she said as he sat her down in the car. "I best be on my way." Struggling to get out of the car she experienced a dizzy spell. Wobbling, she fell back on the seat. "Oh Lawd," she gasped, um jist a lil' dizzy."

"No, you stay right here in the car." Little cautioned her as he lifted her legs into the vehicle. Swiftly, he gathered up her bags of food and placed them in the rear seat. "My name is Thomas Thomas. Wherever you've got to go, I'll be more than happy to take you. You shouldn't be out in this weather. Besides, it's way too dangerous in this storm for you to be walking home."

"Please ta meet ya Mr. Thomas. I'm Nettie Mae Johnson. Folks call me Miss Nettie. Nice of yo' ta offa me a ride. Wen' I left da house dis morin' it wern't snowin'. I don't want ta take you outta yo' way. I don't mean ta be a burden."

"You're no burden Miss Nettie, and you're not taking me out of my way. It's not a problem. Besides, you shouldn't be out in this weather. It is far too dangerous for any of us to be out here."

"I knows it is."

"Well Miss Nettie, you tell me where you have to go, and I'll take you there."

"You will?" she feebly smiled. "God bless ya son. Dat's so nice of ya. May da Lawd bless you fo' being so kind. Wen I lefts da sto' back dere, it weren't snowin' dis bad."

In a very short time and without warning, Little and Miss Nettie found themselves in the mist of the New England blizzard as the snow started falling heavier. As the winter storm continued to rage, Little drove deep into the woods to a part of the area he had never been or knew existed.

Had it not been for the trees lining the roadside, the road would have disappeared completely and would have been totally impassable. The wood framed shotgun houses they passed resembled those he passed this summer along route fifty-eight in Virginia. Old, gray, and weather worn wood-framed shot-gun houses.

Had he not seen it for himself, if someone had told him such shanties existed in Connecticut, he would have never believed them. Unlike Virginia, there were no cotton fields, cornfields, or tobacco fields to be worked. There were orchards of apple trees and open fields.

Beyond the small neighborhood of old houses, Miss Nettie pointed him to the road leading to where she was staying. Little could see the big snow-covered farmhouse sitting on the hill just above the neighborhood of shot-gun houses, over-looking the fields.

When they got out the earth was cold and hard beneath their feet. The snow was coming down harder and the wind was stronger, forcing them to abandon the car at the foot of the small hill. He thought to himself, *there was no way Miss Nettie could have made it back here from the store. She would have frozen to death in this blizzard.*

Inside the house, Miss Nettie quickly took off her hat, coat and boots and disappeared upstairs. Little looked around the house; he could feel it was growing colder inside. The fire inside the wood-burning stove heating the house was dying out. Acting quickly, he stoked the fire with the poker and added a few pieces of wood. Seeing the radiator, he instinctively knew the house had a furnace. Descending into the basement he found what he was looking for. Chuckling to himself for being such a sleuth he knew exactly what to do. He recalled the many times at home back in New York he helped his father light the furnace for the apartment building they lived in. Before long, he had the furnace lit and stoked with coal.

Miss Nettie emerged from the back room. "Lawd, if I knowed it wer' gonna be dis cold. I'd of never come up norf. I'd of wait fo' da summer." Picking up the coffeepot, she proceeded to make coffee and placed it on the stove with a kettle of water. "Lawd, is dat heat I feels comin' up from da radiator?"

"Yes ma'am, I lit the furnace. Miss Nettie, you said something about coming up north. Where are you from?"

"Me? I come har' from West Palm Beach, Florida, but I wer' born in Georgia."

"Florida! Then what are you doing here in all this cold weather?"

"Lawd, I ask myself da same thang. I come up hare ta visit wid my chirens fo' Thanksgivings. Dey lives in New Haven. While I wer here, I promise my friend Rubie I' check on her daughter Anna Mae. She ain't hear from her in a while."

"Are you here with your husband or somebody?"

"Husban!" she laughed. Baby, my husban died in 1935 when he wer' eighty-five years old. Buried him in Cat Creek Primitive Baptist Church Cemetery. Dats in Valdosta, Georgia, Lowndes County."

"Miss Nettie, that was almost twenty-five years ago. Are you sure?"

"Now, I mights be old, but I gots a good mem'ry. I knows names, places n' streets. I married James Johnson when I wer thirteen years old."

"Thirteen?"

"Yes, baby. In dose days we married young. Thangs ain't da same now. My folks dey die wen I wer' round ten." She walked over to the chair and sat down. "My Momma, she wer' Cherokee Indian n' my daddy, he from da Islands. Wen dey die, my two younga brothas wer' sent to da Islands ta live wid my father's people n' I stay wid my mother's people in Georgia. I hatta take care of my aunt's chirens, clean da house, feed da animals n' werk in da cornfield. Her chirens dey ain't gotta do a thang. Dey wer' clean, fed, has good clothes n' dey go ta school ev'bry day. Dey got deys own beds, I sleeps on a pallet on da flo'in da corner likes a dog. Dey gives me two dresses, so I wash one whiles I wears da other. My aunt, wer' mean ta me. Treat me real bad cause I brown skin n' not light like da utter Indian chirens. I wer' darka dan dem cause my daddy wer' a dark man. At night, I go in da cornfield n' cry. I wer' treated so bad, I pray n' ask da Lawd ta takes my life. I wer born Nettie Smith, n' has two brothas. Ain't see em since dey went wid my daddy's people. Never hear from dem agin ta dis day. Dat's bin ova fifty years."

Suddenly, she was silent. Little could see the tears in her eyes as she recounted her childhood. Struggling, she slowly got out of the chair to get some coffee. "Would ya like some coffee ta warm ya up? I got some milk if ya want ta make hot chocolate if ya prefers. Dis heat sho' do feel good." She chuckled. "Da heat from da house fo' da outside of da body. Coffee warms up da insides of ya. I kin make you da hot chocolate." Feeling a dizzy spell, Miss Nettie leaned against the wall.

Little rushed over to help her. "Here, you sit down, Miss Nettie. I'll make you a cup of coffee."

"I musta bump my head harder dan I thinks wen I fell in da snow." Somewhat saddened, she tried to make light of the dizzy spell and chuckled. "Lawdie be, I gots a big knot on da back of my head," she nervously chuckled as she felt the back of her head.

Seated again, she rested while Little made her a cup of coffee and himself some hot chocolate. Taking a sip of her coffee she continued, "Ooh, das jest how I likes it, strong, black n' sweet. Now where wer' I? Oh yes, now Mr. James Johnson lived on da farm a few miles from my aunt's. He hears 'bout me from da neighbors. His wife died and he got fifteen youngens."

"Fifteen!" Little blurted out in surprise.

"Dat's what I say, fifteen," she replied with a big smile on her face. "His first wife, she giveum five chirens, den she dies. His second wife, her name were Beulah, she has ten chirens by him and she dies. He wer' a bridge builder so he wer' away from da house most of da time. He needed someone ta tend ta his chiren whiles he off buildin' bridges. Dat's wen he hears bout me n' asks me if I kin take care of his youngens wiles hes away. James a respectable God fear'n man n' not wantin' folks talkin', he marries me to keep it respecable. Consider'n how I wer' slav'n fo' my aunt n' her kids, I figa if I gotta take care of a house n' kids, I rata be takin' care of my own house, so I marries him. Me n' Jay, dat's what I calls him, we has ten chirens, cept only seven live. He wer' a good man, husban n' father till da day he dies." She continued to talk and sip on her coffee. "I wer' visitin' my oldest daughter Vera n' my baby girl Beulah in New Haven. I wer' twenty wen I has my first chile. Now um gonna tells ya bout my chirens; all of ems born in Valdosta, Georgia. First my daughter Vera, she marries a Miller n' dey got two boys, Henry n' Junior. Vera's son Henry is six monts oler den my baby girl Beulah. Let's see, Vera lives on West Street in New Haven. Den dere's Mozella, she a Wilson. She da only one of my chirens still livin' in Valdosta. She got a son J.W., den her girls Brownie Mae, Baby-Sis n' her boy Junebug. I bin callin' dem by dose names since dey wer' lil' thangs. I k'ant member deys real names. K'ant forget my daughter Annie. Now, she marries John Singleton from Detroit. Deys da reason I move from Valdosta ta Florida. Den nexs my son Charles, we callum Bush. He live in New Haven married ta Stella n' dey son is Butch. He really named afta his daddy n' dey lives on Newhall Street. Den dere's my son James, he marry ta Ruth n' dey live on Atline Street in

New Haven. My son Richit, he fight in da war ova in Coraya, he live in Jupiter, Florida. N' den my baby girl Beulah Mae. She a beautiful girl. She married a boy name Wallace Dozier from West Palm Beach. He a real good look'n fella, bout yo' height, no I thanks Wallace is talla. But he light skin n' dey got six good-lookin' chirens. James, she had him before we moved from Valdosta to West Palm Beach n before she marry Wallace, so I raise him, he in da army. But now Beulah n' Wallace deys chiren's is Edwhat, Wallace, Beatrice, she name afta his mother, Miss Beatty. She live ova on 8th Street in West Palm Beach. N' den days Deatrice. Den deys my fravrit Richit. Dat boy real smart n' best lookin' of da bunch. He named afta his Uncle Richit, my son. His first name is Harold afta his daddy's brotha, Harold. N' deys da last one Steve. They spell his name S-T-E-P-H-A-N. Now, dey all lives in New Haven in a nice place call Brookside. My grandson Henry, Vera's chile, he da one six monts oler den my baby girl Beulah. Now, deys growed up togeter like brotha n' sista. James, my husband, he was seventy-five years old wen Beulah was born on March 15."

Little interjected, "the Ives of March."

"Whats da eyes of March?"

"March 15. It's the day Julius Caesar was killed."

"I'm sorry ta hear that. He was a friend of yos?"

"Oh no," Little chuckled. "Julius Caesar was the emperor of Rome."

"I didn't knows dat. Well dey does say wen somebody dies a baby is born ta take dey place. Now, Henry, we call'um H. B., he got a fine wife, Rosalie. Dey chirens is Carl, Alfred, Donnie n' Ronnie, deys twins n' I knows she just had a lil' girl. Annie, she never has no chirens. Her birthday on da thirteenth of March, Beulahs on is da fifteenth n' Beulahs daughter Beatrice birthday on da eighteenth. My Jay loved himself some Beulah. He born in 1850 a slave. I wer' born afta slave'y in 1880. Dat man use ta sit round n' tell da chiren story afta story bout slav'y, da Civil War n' Mr. Lincoln, he werr' da president of America at da time. I tell my granbabies; deys da granchirens of a forma slave."

"Miss Nettie, tell me. How did you get from Valdosta, Georgia, to Florida?"

Miss Nettie took another sip of her coffee and sat back in the chair. "Let me see. I bin widowed fo' bout eight years, raisin' Beulah, HB n' Beulah's son James by myself. Annie, she n' her husban John Singleton dey moves to West Palm Beach from Detroit. Dey has lots of money. Dat John a smart man. Said he wer'nt gonna werk fo' no white man all his life. He bought lots of land n houses in West Palm Beach. Den deys sends fo' me, HB, Beulah n' James ta come lives wid dem in Florida. We lives on 13th street in one of deys houses. I bin hare since."

"Why did your children move up north?"

"My son Charles, we calls him Bush, he da first ta come up norf, den Vera n' her husban lookin' fo' jobs. Beulah n' Wallace come up on vacation ta visit Bush n' his wife Stella. Bush ask Wallace if he could borrow some money. It his brotha-in-law n' deys stayin in his house, so Wallace loans him dere train fare back ta West Palm Beach. Bush ain't paid him back ta dis day. My boy James found out. Went ova dere n took Beulah n Wallace out of Bush house. Took dem to live wid he n his wife on Atline Street. Wallace gits a job wid Seamless Rubber Company on Hallock Avenue in New Haven n' dey bin dere since. Wallace a smart fella, he goin' ta school, da Culinary Instatute on Whitney Avenue in New Haven, ta be a chef."

Miss Nettie took a long sigh. "But alls my chirens done well, n' I's so proud of ev'ry last one of em."

INNOCENTS

"Oh Gawd, it hurts, it hurts," a voice from the upstairs room ranged out. "Miss Nettie, Miss Nettie," the voice screamed. "Where are you Miss Nettie?"

Reacting to the cry, Miss Nettie quickly rose to her feet and started up the stairs. Still not fully recovered she lost her balance and fell back into the chair. Little jumped up to steady her.

"Dat's Anna Mae, I needs ta go ta her." Holding on to him she made her way up the stairs to the bedroom. Seeing the young girl lying on the bed tossing from side to side crying, Little began looking around for what was scaring her.

"It's comin', Miss Nettie, it's comin'," the girl screamed.

"Okay Anna Mae, it's okay baby. Now, lay on yo' back likes I tells ya n' takes deep breaths."

Turning on the light, Miss Nettie moved over to the bed. Little continued looking around the room to see what she was talking about. "Okay, Anna Mae, de baby is ready to come," she said examining her.

Little eyes widened. "Baby," he shouted. "What baby?"

"Little, put a pot of water on da stove. Wen its hot po' it in dat basin over dere. Den git da scissors n' po' some hot water over um and brang da clean towels n' da blanket I sets out on da table downstairs. We gonna be deliva'n dis baby tonite."

Nervously, Little responded, "Delivering a baby? I don't know nothing about delivering a baby Miss Nettie. Have you done this before, Miss Nettie?"

"Boy, dis ain't no time fo' you to be askin' fo' my kredintial. I delivas many a babies in my time n' I has sevin of ma own. Now hurry up n' put dat water on da stove. Dis baby ain't wait'n fo' you ta ask no mo' questions."

Nervously, Little paced the kitchen floor as he waited for the water to get hot. From the upstairs he could hear Anna Mae crying out in pain; each time she cried out his pace quickened. He could hear Miss Nettie reminding her to take deep breaths and try to relax between the contractions. "Mamma said a watched pot never boils, a watched pot never boils," immediately, he turned away from the stove.

After a few minutes, the water started to boil. He began to remove the pot from the stove when Miss Nettie shouted, "Little, come on wid dat water, dem towels, n' dat blanket. I needs yo' help wid deliva'n dis baby."

Little rushed up the stairs to the room and filled the basin with hot water. "I'll be right back, I forgot the blanket and towels." Returning to the room, he reentered just in time to catch Miss Nettie from falling on the floor as she suffered another dizzy spell. "Helps me ta da chair, kan't stand on my feet no longa, um dizzy," she said in a faint voice. "Little, you gonna have ta take ova en'delivas dat baby yo'self."

"But Miss Nettie, I told you I don't know anything about delivering a baby!"

"Uma tells ya how, jist follow my direction n' you do jist fine. Now, go ova dere n' stands at da foot of da bed by her legs. Anna Mae, I wants you ta keep takin deep breaths jist likes I tells ya. Little, now spread her legs open wide." An embarrassed Little hesitated. "Dis ain't no time to act shy boy," Miss Nettie clamored weakly. Immediately, he moved Anna Mae's legs apart. "Dats right, likes dat. Anna Mae, wid da next pain push."

Anna Mae cried out with the contraction. "I can't Miss Nettie, I can't."

"Yes you kin. Takes a deep breath n' push wid da pain."

Little, thrust into an uncomfortable position, was still feeling embarrassed and stood looking away from her.

Anna Mae took a deep breath and began to push.

"Little, dis ain't no time fo' you ta be lookin' at da wallpaper," shouted Miss Nettie. "Looks at her private, n' tells me what does ya see?"

Hesitantly, Little responded instantly in a weak commanding voice. "I don't see anything. Water is coming out."

"Water spose ta come out, don't want no dry birth. Jist put some mor' towels unda her. Den feel inside her private, see if you kin feel da baby's head."

Embarrassed at her direction, Little shouted. "Miss Nettie, I can't do that!"

"Yes ya kin, ya got ta Little. Dis baby gonna come n' youse da only one who kin do it."

Little looked at her then at Anna's face and then again at Miss Nettie.

"Why do I have to feel inside of her? What am I feeling for?"

"Ya gotta make sho' da baby ain't comin' feet first; what deys call breach. Baby's head should be first, not da feet or behind. Now, go head, reach inside her private."

"What do I do if it is breach? What am I supposed to do if it is breach? Miss Nettie, I don't know what I'm doing!"

"Den you gotta push da baby back inside her stomach n' turn da baby round."

"Oh God, please don't let the baby be breach. Please let the baby be head first." As he placed his hand at the opening of Anna's vagina Little prayed. Hesitantly he touched her and slowly slipped his hand inside her vagina. Relieved, Little sighed. "I think I feel the top of the baby's head."

"Don't feels likes a foot or behind does it?"

"No ma'am," Little replied.

"Dat's good."

"Thank God." Feeling slightly relieved, Little looked at Anna Mae for the first time. Beyond the swelling and the sweat rolling down her face from childbirth, he could tell she was a young girl, not many years younger than himself. He thought perhaps she may be around sixteen or seventeen years old, but definitely no older than nineteen. Darker than himself, her pretty cocoa colored skin was flawless and smooth. "Okay Anna," he said in a reassuring voice, "Take a deep breath, then give a big push with the next contraction. I know you can do it."

His confident strong voice gave her a feeling of reassurance. "Okay," she softly replied. For the first time she looked at Little, smiled, and began to push.

"I see the head, I see the baby's head Miss Nettie," an excited Little exclaimed. "What do I do next?"

"Git da towels n' waits fo' da baby ta come out."

Little eyes widened as he continued to watch the head crowning.

Taking another deep breath, Anna grunted with pain as she pushed again.

"The head is out; it's all the way out. Something is wrong Miss Nettie. The baby's' facing down."

"No, dat's fine, all babies come in da world facing down. Make sho' da cord ain't wrapped round da baby's neck."

"How do I do that?"

"Use yo' finger ta feel round da baby's neck."

"The head—it's starting to turn."

"Dat's good, da baby's movin down da birth canal. You doin' good; both ya doin' real fine. Git da towels Little, cause da babies gonna come out quick."

Before he could turn to get a towel off the dresser, the baby slid out onto the bed.

"It's a boy! It's a boy," he shouted! "Anna, it's a boy; you have a son! God, look at him, he's beautiful," Little exclaimed joyfully. Gently picking up the baby, he held him in his arms. "Oh, Miss Nettie, the baby, he's not breathing."

"Dat's nat'ral. First, stick yo finger in da baby's mouth ta clean it out. Den, holds him by his feet upside down n' tap him on his behind."

Little looked puzzled. "What? Turn him upside down?"

"Turn him upside down n tap him on his behind."

"They really do that?" Little did exactly what he was told. Immediately, the baby started crying. A sudden exuberance rushed through Little as he marveled at the miracle of life in his hands. He was breathless, holding the newborn baby in his arms. He stood motionless, adorning the new life, which he helped bring into the world. *One day, it will be Grace and my child I'll be?*

"You gotta cut da birth cord."

Little's mind was still far away as he marveled at the life he held in his arms. Dreaming of the day he and Grace would raise their own family.

"Little," Miss Nettie again tried to get his attention.

"Yes Miss Nettie. What am I supposed to do?"

"First, lay da baby on Anna Mae's belly. Git da strang outta da water. Tie it one inch from da baby. Next strang tie bout three inches from da first. Den cuts da cord in da middle of da two strangs."

Little followed Miss Nettie instructions.

"Dat's good, now git da towels n' clean da baby up n' wrap him in da blanket. Den gives him to his mamma."

Little began wiping the white slippery substance off the baby. "Wow, Miss Nettie, I never knew bringing a baby in this world could be so wonderful. It's a miracle, Miss Nettie. Look at him. Just look at him, he's so precious, so tiny, so innocent."

The blizzard was nearing an end as the snow continued to fall faintly to the earth. All was quiet inside and outside the country house. A tired Anna Mae, after nursing the baby, fell fast asleep. It took much convincing, but somehow Little managed to get Miss Nettie to lay down. He could hear Miss Nettie snoring in the room across the hall from Anna.

Little looked at his watch, it was after ten thirty. The electricity had gone out about forty-five minutes after the baby was born. Using the kerosene lamps, he discovered in the basement he slowly descended the stairs to the basement to put more coal in the furnace. Going back upstairs to the living room an extremely exhausted Little sat on the couch. Anxious, he was too excited to sleep. His day had begun very early.

To be on time for his Monday morning eleven o'clock class, he woke up at six o'clock in the morning. He was on the road by seven o'clock and should have arrived at the University of New England two and half hours later. The snow started coming down around eight-thirty when he was only about an hour away. About nine o'clock is when the storm began. It took him another hour to get to the exit. That's when he saw Miss Nettie on the road.

While driving in the storm, time seemed to have ticked away very slowly. After arriving at the house, Little knew the roads would be impassable and decided to wait for the storm to end before completing his journey to the university. Anna's labor lasted over four hours. For Little, time passed very quickly when he was delivering the baby. Never did he think his day would have ended like this.

Wiping the frost off of the window, Little peered out. The light of the bright moon revealed that the surrounding area was covered deep in snow. Instantly, he knew he was not leaving anytime too soon. The road was completely covered with snow. He could barely see the top of his car where they had abandoned it at the foot of the hill. He didn't know how long he had been staring out of the window. Looking again at his watch, it was after one o'clock. He noted that before long the sun would be rising in the sky to usher in a new day.

Tired from all the activity of the day but fully awake, he trotted over to the stove to make a cup of hot chocolate. Again, with cup in hand he sat down on the couch to rest. Looking at his hands, they were big, and his fingers were long and slender. His hands, like his father's hands, were big and strong. He could only think about the life he held in them earlier. *In these hands I held a new life. I brought a new life into this world with these hands, a new life. It's unbelievable; I held a new life in these hands. He, the baby, was so tiny, so fragile and so new to this world.*

It was a time, a special time in his life. For him, a part of this puzzle called life was finally beginning to come together. He knew that after today, he would not be the same person. After today, he could not be the same person he was just a few hours ago. His life was changed forever.

RETURN TO INNOCENCE

It seemed only a brief time after he drifted off to sleep, in his dream he heard the sound of bacon frying and smelled its aroma filling the air. His sense of smell told him that he was back at home in New York and it was his mother in the kitchen. Slowly, he could feel hunger pains in his stomach arousing him. As he slept, he felt a sudden blast of cold air and snow rushed into the house.

"Little close dat dor'. Don't want da baby to catch his def of cold n' Anna Mae is open," Miss Nettie shouted. "I though you wer' still sleep. U'm cookin' breakfast fo' ya now. By da time ya washes up, it'll be ready."

Little, still lying on the couch, did not see the shivering figure wearing a worn coat step into the house and catch a quick glimpse of him as he swiftly passed.

"Is that you, Miss Nettie?" the deep voice shouted as the figure move toward the kitchen. "Oh, Miss Nettie, I'm so glad to know you're here. I was so scared that you were caught out in the snowstorm and lying frozen in the snow." The figure rushed into the kitchen. Grabbing Miss Nettie, he hugged her tightly. "Oh, I am so glad to see you. I'm so glad you're alright." Breaking the embraced he asked, "Anna, where is Anna? Is she alright, Miss Nettie?"

"She doin good. Now, where ya bin? We wer' worried bout you, boy."

The man continued to talk as he removed his hat, coat, and boots. "Shortly after you left for the store, Anna Mae started having labor pains. I went to get the doctor and to find you. I called the doctor, he said he was going to come and then I called the store. They said they would keep you there until the storm was over. By that time, it was snowing so bad the people whose phone I used wouldn't let me out of their house. They wouldn't let me leave their house. They say it was too dangerous outside. Since the doctor promised that he would come to the house they said that she would be safe."

"Sit down while I pours ya a cup of hot coffee," she ordered him pulling out a chair.

"How is Anna? Is she alright? I saw the doctor's car outside buried in the snow. Is he with her now? I was so worried about you and Anna that I didn't sleep at all last night. I got up the first thing this morning and came as quickly as I could."

"You show does ask a lot of questions. Anna Mae fine, n' you gota boy."

"What you say Miss Nettie, I gota a what?" the man asked excitedly.

"I say you gota son. Anna Mae give birth last night ta a big healthy baby boy."

Surprised and excited by the good news the man jumped out of the chair and hugged Miss Nettie. "Oh, Miss Nettie, I have a son, a son! Can I go up and see them?"

"Now, don't you go dere wakin' up Anna Mae n' dat baby. You kin go up n' peep at da baby n' Anna Mae. But you got ta be quiet. Anna Mae and da baby needs dey rest."

By the sound of the voice the young man spoke with a southern drawl. Little suspected the man was from the south. Hearing the voices, Little got up to go into the kitchen. At the same time, the man started out of the kitchen to go upstairs, Little walked into the kitchen and they bumped into each other.

Startled upon seeing Little, he asked, "Are you the doctor? Anna is okay isn't she doctor? Anna and the baby, they are all right, aren't they doctor? I thought that was your car outside." The young man grabbed Little's hand and began shaking it. "I'm so glad you made it here in time in all this bad weather. I was so worried; I didn't get to sleep at all last night."

"No, I'm not the doctor," Little replied. "I'm Thomas, I brought Miss Nettie home in the storm."

"It wer' Thomas hare dat deliva da baby. If it wer'nt fer him I be dead in the snow somewhere n' Anna Mae would have had dat baby on her own wid no help. She might o' died if it wer'nt fo' him."

"Boy, am I please to meet you Dr. Thomas; I'm Johnathan Ballard, Anna's husband. I was the one who called you from the house down the road. Then I was out looking for Miss Nettie. I'm so glad you were here."

Miss Nettie laughed as she entered the living room. "Little here ain't no docta yet. But he did a real good job delivain' yo son. Afta ya peeps at da baby come down fo' breakfast. I made plenty to eat. Little, go wash up, da food gonna be on da table."

After a few minutes, Johnathan returned beaming. "Oh, Miss Nettie, he's so beautiful. He's got all ten fingers and ten toes. I can't wait to hold him."

Little and Johnathan sat down to eat breakfast. Miss Nettie had prepared bacon, sausages, grits, scramble eggs, and a pot of coffee. "You men folk git aquainted n' eat up. I gotta take care of Anna Mae n' da baby. U'm gunna fix a plate of food for her. She needs nourishment to gain her strength to feed dat baby."

"Thomas, are you from New Haven?"

"Johnathan, please call me Little. I'm not used to being called Thomas, except by teachers. No, I'm from New York City."

"New York City. That has to be an exciting place. What you doing up here?"

"I attend the University of New England."

"I didn't know any Negroes student attended there. You must be real smart to go there. Before I married Anna, I was going to college in Florida. What are you majoring in?"

Little studied Johnathan's face as they talked. He perceived they were about the same age. Johnathan, a brown-skinned twenty-year old was about five ten and weighed around one hundred seventy-five pounds. His light brown eyes matched his sandy brown hair.

"I'm majoring in Nuclear Engineering. What did you major in Johnathan?"

"That's interesting. I was majoring in Agricultural Engineering. I plan to return to college when Anna and I get on our feet."

"How long have you been married? I mean, why didn't you wait until after you finished school before you got married?"

"We were so much in love that we just decided not to wait. I can still go back to school. I have a year left. I'll just transfer to a college up here. New London College it's not far from here. I have a lot of credits in math, so I'll switch my major to Math. I'll become a teacher. Then after I finish, Anna can go back. She was majoring in Nursing."

"Being married and having a child is going to be difficult."

Johnathan was offended by Little's concern. "Don't worry about it. We'll make it," he snapped.

"I'm sorry. I didn't mean to offend you Johnathan."

"No, I should be the one apologizing to you Little. It's just that it's a sore spot with me. I know you meant well. It's just that everyone was against our getting married, including her mother, my mother, and my roommate. They said I was throwing away my education and my life."

"Johnathan, no doubt they were all concerned. How long have you been married?"

"We got married this past August."

"Hare's he is, yo' son Johnathan," Miss Nettie announced as she entered the kitchen passing the infant into his father's arms.

Johnathan's brown eyes lit up as Miss Nettie placed the tiny baby in his arms. In total awe, he looked tenderly at the infant lying in his arms for the first time. Little perceived it as a look of love and adoration. Slowly, Johnathan passed his son to Little. "Little, Anne Mae and I are indebted to you. I want you to do us the honor of naming our son."

Beaming with great pride and joy, Little looked upon the tiny bundle resting in his arms. There was no doubt in his mind as he called out the baby's name. Immediately, Johnathan agreed as he added the middle name.

Later that afternoon with shovel in hand, Little and Johnathan began digging through the knee-deep snow. Eagerly, like two little boys they began the task of shoveling a path from the house to the road where Little's car was buried. Off to the left of the house in the distance near the edge of the woods they could see a small herd of deer forging for something to eat. Their brown coats blended in with the bare trees. In the field on the opposite side, they saw a rabbit scampering as it was pursued by a quick red fox.

Their attention was drawn to the sound of children's laughter. Carefully, they made their way down the road to where a small cluster of adults had gathered. Proudly, Johnathan announced to his neighbors the birth of his son, Canegata Thomas Ballard. Shouts of joy and praises ranged out as they patted Johnathan on his back and congratulated him on his new arrival. Stepping aside, he introduced his neighbors to his son's godfather, the man who delivered his son during the snowstorm, Thomas Thomas.

The women flocked around Little wanting to hear every little detail of the birth. Each chimed in from time to time, adding her own comments and experiences. Proudly, Little gladly obliged the women, making sure not to leave out the slightest detail.

Shortly afterwards, the oldest member of the community slowly strolled over to where the group had gathered. "Is you da ones stayin' in the old Lathrop place?" the old man asked pointing to the house.

"Yes sir, my name is Johnathan Ballard."

"Who's da new owna, the person you werkin fo'?"

"I'm the new owner."

"Well I'll be. If dat don't beat all." The old man laughed. "A colored man ownin the Lathrop place."

"I bought it from a Mrs. King. She lives in Florida."

"Yea, dats her name now. Miss Imogene Kang. But when she live here, she was Miss Imogene Lathrop. She called me a spell back n' asks me ta clean da place up fer youse. Told me she was sellin da place. Befo' she were a Kang she was married to Mr. Lathrop. Mr. Jessup Lathrop. See, I knows dis as the old Winchester farm befo' Mr. Lathrop bought it. Back in dose day it was da the best apple orchard and dairy farm in all of Konnectecut. I rememburrs when he bought it, Mr. Lathrop bought it just for her. They were married for two years and never had no cherins. Mr. Jessup's daddy was a hat maker in Danbury, Konnectecut. I use to werk fo' him up dey. Jessup inherited the business, but he sold it to buy this farm for his wife. She was from New York side, from a fine family. His parents were growing old so dey come to live with dem on da farm. The father, he lost his mind. Got dat mad hattars dayease. Poor old man went crazy from it. Sometimes, we had to tie him down in a chair to keep him from hurtin' his wife n himself. He pulled knives and guns n' run around naked. It wer breakin' por' old Lady Lathrop's heart. Yea, I rememburrs it, likes it wer' yesterdy. Mrs. Lathrop was given him his medicine. I says, ta his wife, Miss Sonia, Miss Sonia you givin' him too much ain't ya. She say, it was a different medicine from da docta. Den she take some n' took him in da house upstairs to dey bedroom. I thought it was strange. She wer' all dressed up and him too, likes day wer' going to a fancy party. It wer' Miss Imogene dats come home n' finds dem both in da bed dead. Po' Miss Imogene, almost killed her findin dem like dat. Folks round here that rememburs him say he was a real mad man, but he wen't always like that. Then about six months later Mr. Lathrop was cleanin' his gun when it axdently went off killing him. Miss Imogene wer outside havin' a tea party wid her lady friends when it happin. When she came in the house she found him layin in the parlor in a pool of his own blood, dead. Lawd, po' thang almost lost her mind afta' dat. Da week afta da funeral, she left da house n' never been back since. She paid me to keep up da property. I recon dats been omost twenty yer' ago. Every now an den, I gits some money in da mail to take car' of da house. She said youse was comin'. I waitin' fo' n lookin' fo' some white folks. Didn't thank it was gonna be no colored folks buyin' da place. You got all three hundred acres? I guess she wer' gonna git rid of da place, wern't nothin' but missery fo' her." The elderly Mr. Petersen started walking away from the gathering. "Yes Lawd. Dat Mr. Lathrop was one mad hattar."

After his departure, the conversation turned to the latest weather update and what was happening in the community. But the main topic centered on the birth of the newest member of their community, Canegata Thomas Ballard. "Canegata," one of the men shouted. "Wer'nt dat da name of the Negro man workin fo' da govberment?"

"Yes," Johnathan replied. "He was Little's uncle."

The crowd was impressed to have the relative of a celebrity in their mists.

"Every Negro in dis country were proud of Mr. Canegata. He made all us Negroes feel proud. Give us respectability. Yo's son got a proud name."

Johnathan smiled and placed his hand on Little's shoulder. "I know he does, and I have a very good friend."

Several of the men began discussing hunting the deer to keep them from dying a horrible death of starvation. As the group talked about the coming Spring, the wind began blowing. Once again, snow began falling rapidly. The group quickly dispersed going to their own houses for shelter.

As the pair made their way back to the house, standing far off in the distance they could see the smoke rising out of the chimney. The moment was picture perfect. Sitting high upon the hill was the large white farmhouse with its wrap around porch. It was picturesque with its snow-covered roof, and smoke rising up from the chimney. After a brief snowball fight, the snow covered half-frozen pair entered the house.

"Brrr," Johnathan groaned as he shook the snow off his coat. They both raced toward to the stove knocking each other over to warm their hands joyfully laughing. "It sure is nice and warm in here. I'm so glad you knew how to turn on the furnace. I don't know a thing about heating systems. Where I'm from in Florida we don't worry about heating the house and nobody gave me instructions about this place."

Miss Nettie stood at the stove cooking. "Now y'all stop all dat noise befor' ya wakes da baby n' Anna Mae," she scoffed. "I done made some lunch fer ya. I see'd y'all done lots of werk shovelin' da snow. Go wash up n' I'll has da food on da table wen you finish cleaning up." Miss Nettie spied the water dripping from their wet trousers. "Lawd, look at da mess y'all done made. I declare y'all men folks ain't nothing but a heap of trouble. Now, git befor' I tans both yo hide wid dis hare mop." Before long, Miss Nettie placed a hot ham sandwich and a bowl of soup before each of them. They wasted no time in devouring the meal before them.

Johnathan carefully came down the stairs carrying Baby Canegata in his arms. "Isn't he beautiful, Little? I've never seen anything so wonderful. See your goddaddy, Canegata," Johnathan said, pointing toward Little. The baby's eyes followed his pointing finger. "Look at how tiny his hand is, Little. It's so small," he commented, as he played with the baby's hand. The baby wrapped his fingers around his father's finger. "Look at that. He's got a strong grip. Boy, you're a strong little fellow, yes, you are. When you grow up, you're going to be whatever you want to be; a doctor, lawyer, senator, or a nuclear physicist, like your uncle Little here. You're going to be whatever your heart desires," he exclaimed as he pulled Canegata closer to his chest. "I'm going to give you all the love and I'm going to protect you, kiss your boo boos and make the pain go away. No matter what, I'll going to always be here for you."

Watching Johnathan with his son, Little could see how much he loved his child. It was like he had heard this conversation and experienced the feeling of protection before. Baby Canegata's eyes wide open seemed to pay attention to every word coming out of his father's mouth.

Johnathan gestured to Little. Smiling, Little opened his arms to receive his godson. He brushed his fingers against the baby's head stroking the thick black hair on its head. Baby Canegata cooed and smacked his lips. Little looked adoringly at the bundle in his arms as the small blue eyes stared intensively back at him.

Miss Nettie stepped into the kitchen. "Boy, why you brang dat baby down hare?"

"He was crying Miss Nettie. When he cries and I pick him up he always stops. Then he falls asleep in my arms. Anna can never get him to fall asleep, but he always falls asleep in my arms."

Little chimed in, "You know I noticed that. You seem to be the only one that can stop him from crying, and he always falls asleep in your arms. He never falls asleep with me. He stops crying, and he's always quiet when I hold him. But he doesn't fall asleep. Why is that, Miss Nettie?"

Dats cause he feels safe in yo' arms, Little. But when he in his daddy' arms, he feels safe and saycure."

INNOCENT LOVE REVEALED

The snow continued to fall throughout the night into the next day, burying the paths they had previously shoveled earlier that day. Off in the distance, they heard the sound of gunfire. It was the men out hunting the deer. For the next three days, the storm continued to rage forcing everyone to stay inside. Johnathan and Little passed the time playing chest and exchanging college experiences late into the night in front of the fireplace.

During one of their many discussions, they were pleasantly surprised to find out they had pledged Alpha Phi Alpha Fraternity. Each noted in detail their pledge period and did a few steps. Their conversation dwindled, as each game became more challenging and required greater concentration and strategy. Periodically, they would take turns braving the bitter cold to gather firewood from the woodpile behind the house for the fireplace and made sure the furnace was stoked with coal.

It was the twilight hour of the night when Little walked across the yard to the woodpile. He could hear the frozen snow crunching beneath his feet with each of his steps. Instinctively, he knew he had heard that sound before. Momentarily, he hesitated; the air was quiet and still. With the exception of the light coming from the shotgun houses in the distant, pitch-blackness surrounded him. He was alone in the bitter, cold, darkness. Spontaneously, he raised his half-frozen fingers to his mouth to warm them with his breath. His hot breath mingled with the bitter cold air creating a stream of mist flowing though his fingers. Watching the stream of mist emerging through his fingers, he suddenly realized this was a scene similar to a scene from his past. It haunted him. He dwelled on the mist and then looked around. There were no rows of boarded up vacant tenant housing. This wasn't Chicago. He was not being pursued by an angry mob. There was peace; a serene peace. For the first time, he recalled he was not being haunted by the dream that had become very much a part of his life. He realized that after his trip to Chicago the nightmare had ceased. He stood in the darkness and in the cold dwelling on the nightmare and what had happened in Chicago. A cold chill, like the cold water that knocked him off of the roof went through his body causing him to shiver. Shuttering, he quickly grabbed some wood from the pile and returned into the warmth of the house.

His mind was off in the distance when he sat down after placing the logs in the fireplace. Johnathan thought he was contemplating his next strategic move. But Little's mind was elsewhere, in the distant past. He remembered the look in Johnathan's eyes when he was holding Canegata. It was a look he himself had known. He had felt those warm eyes before. Strangely, he recalled it was the look his father had when he first looked upon him. Somehow, he could remember those eyes, but he was just a newborn infant. How could he?

It was late. Johnathan and Little just finished their tenth game of chess of the day. Johnathan stood up and walked over to the fireplace. Picking up the poker he began adjusting the burning logs. Popping sparks rose up the chimney. The intense games had left him deep in thought.

"Little."

Questioning his voice, Little could hear he was lost deep in his thoughts. "What is it Johnathan?"

"It's amazing how quickly time goes by. We've gotten pretty close this past week. I've really come to like you and I have a great respect for you. I just want you to know that I'm really glad you were here these past few days. I don't think Anna and I know anybody who we would have let name our son or name him after. We're proud that you're his godfather." Johnathan began stuttering as he continued, "Now, that the weather has cleared up, I just want to say I'm sad you'll be leaving tomorrow. I'm really going to miss your company."

"Hey man," Little replied, "I know how you feel. I wish it was still snowing too. I'm sorry that I have to be going. But you know, I'm going to come by every chance I get to see you, Anna, and Canegata. And I got to introduce my fiancée, Grace, to you. I know she's going to love meeting all of you."

"I'm looking forward to meeting her. She's really got to be someone special."

"She is. You'll get to meet her this Easter when we have Canegata baptized at my church in New York. I know she'll be coming up for Easter. I can't wait to call and tell her about you, Anna, Canegata, and Miss Nettie."

"I just wanted to thank you for being here."

"You don't have to Johnathan. I know that, and I'm glad I'm here."

"I know, I know. I just had to say it."

"Listen, we're still going to New Haven in two weeks to take Miss Nettie to her children, right? That should be a nice outing."

"Yea, we are. Right now, I'm tired. I'm going to go to bed. Good night Little."

"Good night Johnathan." Little could tell his friend was still troubled by something. "Are you alright Johnathan? Is something troubling you?"

"No. I'm alright; just tired. Thanks for asking."

"Listen, before you go up to bed, let's sing the hymn."

Linking arms, they softly sang their fraternity hymn and prayed their fraternity prayer.

The weather had changed to unseasonable warmth for March. All, but a few traces of snow were left on the ground as a remnant of the recent storms. As he had promised, Little returned to take Miss Nettie to New Haven. A tired Anna decided not to make the trip in hopes of getting some extra rest and peace.

Johnathan proudly showed off Canegata to Miss Nettie's family and boasted of Little's heroics in the delivery. It was a wonderful afternoon in Brookside where they had lunch and met her children and grandchildren.

It was early evening when the trio, Little, Johnathan, and Canegata began their journey back home. Johnathan, holding the infant in his arms, looked at him lovingly as he lay peacefully asleep. The sun appeared as a red ball of fire in the western sky. A troubled Johnathan began speaking from his heart. "Little I need to talk to someone. I need some advice. But I don't know how to say it or where to start."

Little focused on the road ahead of him sensed he was deeply troubled within. Little spoke quietly, "Just take your time my friend; take your time."

Johnathan took a deep breath. "Well, I told you my family was against my leaving school to marry Anna. My mother had lots of high hopes and dreams for me. I'm the first person in my family to finish high school and to go to college. Anna's family tried to discourage us from getting married. She's the oldest child and she was the first one in her family to go to college too. Well, her mother spent one semester in school, but she had to leave because she was pregnant with Anna. And Anna's father, he quit college to marry her mother. We both understood. They wanted more for us than what they have, and they wanted us to have a better life. Both our mothers worked for the white people. My mother is a maid. She cleans houses all day, and then she comes home and cleans up after us kids. Anna's mother has a catering business. She caters all the rich white people's parties and she basically cooks for the same family."

Johnathan took another deep breath before continuing, "Anna and I have known each other since kindergarten. We grew up in the same neighborhood and attended the same church and went to the same schools. Everybody always said we were going to get married one day. After I graduated from high school, I went to Florida A&M in Tallahassee. She graduated a year later. She enrolled in Florida A&M too. I planned to be an agricultural engineer. I was planning to get my master's degree. Anna, she was a nursing major. She's a real smart girl. Well, she was in her second year and I was in my third year when we got married. I love her Little, and I would do anything for her. If I had to, I'd die for her."

Looking down at the baby resting peacefully in his arms he pulled him closer to his chest as if to protect him. "And now with Canegata here, I love him too and I'd die for the both of them. During the summers and school breaks, Anna and I worked for a wealthy white family—the Kings. It's the same family my mother and Anna's mother works for in Palm Beach. We started working for them since, before we were in high school. Mr. and Mrs. King really liked us. Without their help, we couldn't have gone to college. The Kings were paying for our college education. We owed them a lot."

Suddenly Johnathan became very quiet. Instinctively, Little knew not to break the silence. Whatever it was, he knew it was eating away at Johnathan deeply inside.

"I didn't know it," Johnathan continued. "Nobody knew it. Anna was scared to tell anybody, especially Mrs. King. You see, Mr. King was approaching her. Little, I love her. I wasn't going to let her go through this by herself. She'd been through enough with Mr. King forcing himself on her and her being scared to tell anybody. She kept it to herself for a whole year. She said she felt trapped. He told her if she said anything to anyone then they would fire our mothers, and her mother would never get another catering deal, and he'd stop paying our college tuition. She said it happened about three times. She would cry when he was on top of her. The last time it happened, Mrs. King returned home and heard her crying. She came into the room and found him on her—she was furious. Mrs. King was mad. Anna said she told Mrs. King everything. We were at school when Anna found out she was pregnant. When she told Mrs. King that she was pregnant, Mrs. King said she wasn't going to let her children grow up around his bastard child, and it would never share in her children's inheritance. She told Anna to trust her; she'd take care of everything. That's when

Mrs. King called me. She said if I married Anna, she would give us her farm up north and see that both of us finished college."

"She gave you the entire farm."

"All three hundred acres; every piece of furniture, the pots, pans, all the pictures, and everything in and outside of the house, she gave to us. When she signed the deed over to us, she had only one condition. That was, we had to leave Florida and promise not to tell anyone. We were especially not to tell Mr. King that the baby was his." Johnathan drew a deep breath, "I know I'm breaking my word by telling you. But I had to tell somebody. It's been a tremendous burden on my heart. I know I can trust you Little. I know you'll keep it to yourself. I told Anna that I was going to tell you—she understood and agreed. She said it was alright to tell you. I would have married Anna even if Mrs. King didn't give us this place. That's one of the reasons why I couldn't name him after me. But it's Anna I love and care about. I love her, and I love Canegata. They're all I have and nothing else really matters. I just want to know Little, what do I tell him? Regardless of who planted the seed, he's my son, and I love him. But he is also the son of a multimillionaire. He does have some rights. What do I tell him? Should he know the truth? I know I did the right thing, marrying Anna. I love her and nothing will ever change that. And giving him my name was the right thing to do. I was here with them all of these months watching him grow inside of her; I'd die for both of them."

"Are you afraid someone is going try and take him?"

"Mr. King has three girls—twelve, ten, and eight. He doesn't have any sons. I'm scared one day, should he find out he may want to claim his only son."

"Did he know that Anna was pregnant?"

"Mrs. King said she wasn't going to tell him. She told him she was going to send her away and make it so he couldn't touch her anymore. She arranged the entire wedding. He was there. She told me she knew it wasn't Anna's fault. She had wondered why Anna would almost beg her to let her go with her whenever she was leaving the house. So, she knew what happened wasn't Anna's fault. I don't know Little. What do I do?"

Staring at the road ahead of him, Little replied, "Johnathan, I believe you're going to be a very good husband to Anna, a good father to Canegata and to any other children the two of you may have in the future, just like my father Elijah has been to me. But most of all, I do know in your heart you're going to do whatever is right by Canegata and Anna. Whatever you do, it will be the right thing. Most importantly, a father is more than the man whose loins you sprung from or the man that planted the seed. If every Bigger had an Elijah in their life, there would be more Littles. You're Canegata's Elijah."

Johnathan looked perplexed at his friend. "I don't understand."

Softly, he replied, "You will, Johnathan, you will. After I finish, you will."

BOOK SIX

FINAL DAYS

The Thomas household was alive and filled with laughter. It had been a long time since there was an infant in the Thomas household. The big Easter celebration and baptismal of Baby Canegata would provide just the opportunity. After hearing so much about them—Johnathan's, Anna's, and Baby Canegata's arrival was eagerly awaited. They were welcomed with open arms and as members of the Thomas family.

Excited with anticipation, Ruth answered the door. "Anna and Johnathan," she reached out to hug them. "Come on in. It's so good to finally me you. We've heard so much about the three of you from Little. We feel as if we already know you."

"We feel the same way, Mrs. Thomas."

"Anna let me help you with the baby." Anna happily passed her bundle of pride and joy to the woman. "Oh look at him; he's so precious."

"Let me see the baby Momma; let me see the baby," Esther said excitedly. "Can I hold him?"

"Esther, where are your manners?"

"I'm sorry. Hello Mr. and Mrs. Ballard. Can I hold him now, please?"

"Is it all right Anna? She's held babies before. In fact, my big girl babysits now."

"What's all the fuss about?" Elijah echoed, as he wheeled himself into the living room.

"Elijah honey, Johnathan, Anna, and Canegata are here. This is my husband, Elijah."

Johnathan shook his hand and Anna hugged and kissed him on the cheek. "Mr. Thomas, we've heard a lot about you from Little. It's a pleasure to finally meet you."

"I hope it was all good," he laughed. "As many times I had to whip that Little, I don't know what tall tales that boy is liable to say."

"Oh Elijah, you shouldn't tell such a tale. Johnathan and Anna, don't you listen to him. I did all the whipping around here. If I remember right, you might have whipped him twice. You probably beat more of the boys in this entire neighborhood more times than you did to your own two sons."

"That's all it took, just two good whippings; never had another minute of trouble out of Little, Swoosh, or Coconut. You're probably right about the other boys. Now, let me see this precious little one you got here," he said, motioning to Esther to give him the baby.

Carefully, Esther laid Canegata in her father's arms. "He is a pretty boy. I just want you two to know I'm honored that you named him after my nephew and son."

"Believe me Mr. Thomas, meeting you, the honor is all ours," Anna replied. "Johnathan and I were so grateful Little was there. He was a godsend. He's really been a good friend."

Elijah laughed as the baby grabbed his finger. "He's a strong baby too. You should have named him Sherman."

"Sherman," everyone shouted in surprise.

"Do y'all have a hearing problem or what? That's what I said, Sherman."

"Oh Lord, here he goes again. Now, honey, tell us, why should they have named the baby Sherman?"

"Look how strong he is," he replied displaying the baby's grip on his finger. "And his little body reminds me of a Sherman tank. Like the ones they used in World War II and Korea." Elijah sat and thought as everyone looked on. "I got it."

"Got what?"

"A name for the baby."

"He's got a name. Its Canegata Daddy," Elisha responded.

"Tank."

"What?"

"Tank. That's what I'm going to call him, Tank."

Anna laughed. "Believe it or not, I was telling Johnathan the other day that he's strong and built like a tank."

"Then that settles it" Elijah replied. "We'll call him Tank."

Elisha looked a Canegata. "Believe me, it's better than what he calls me."

"Why? What's your nickname?"

"I call him Coconut," Elijah responded.

"Coconut," Anna laughed. "Why?"

"Because when he was born the fuzz on his head reminded me of a coconut, and his head was shaped like a coconut."

"Please Pop, just don't call me that in public!"

Ruth shook her head. "Lawd, I don't know what I'm going to do with this man and his giving out nicknames. Some of the names he's come up with for these kids around here. Swoosh, Turk, Bebop, and Chop. He's given almost every child in this neighborhood a nickname. They call him the godfather of nicknames."

"Now, I have to defend my title. All of the names I gave them were for a reason and they stuck. Turk and Chop got their names because of their birthmark. Turk has a turkey shape on his left forearm, and Chop has a birthmark shaped like a pork chop on his upper right thigh. Now, it was a whole year before I named Bebop. When he walks, he has a bebop in his step, and the same thing with Strut. Swoosh likes to tell everybody it is because of his jump shot. But I named him that because he was always swooshing around everybody's feet. Look at him today, you could say it was prophetic."

"I'm your Baby Doll, right Daddy?" Esther said leaning over hugging her father's neck.

"That's right, you're my little Baby Doll, because you looked just like a baby doll when you were born. And your mother is my Sweet

Angel. Ain't that right honey? First time I saw her, she looked just like an angel, and she made me the sweetest buttermilk biscuits. They still melt in my mouth like butter to this day. Ain't that right, baby?"

"All these years, and I'm still sweet."

Elisha shook his head. "Would you believe people actually bring their baby here for him to give it a nickname. It's so embarrassing."

Ruth laughed as she rubbed Elisha's head. "He gave all your friends a nickname and half of your brother's friends too. There's not a child born in this neighborhood that he or Mr. Johnson haven't given a nickname. Okay, now that Tank has a name let's sit down so we can get acquainted."

"Where's Little?" Johnathan asked.

Elijah quickly responded, "Grace is flying in today. Boy was so anxious to see her; he left for the airport two hours early."

They had not seen each other since he left Hampton in December of the previous year, when he rushed to his father's hospital bedside. As Easter Sunday approached, he was excited about the baptism. However, even more exciting for him was seeing Grace. The best part was that he knew it would be her first time in New York City, so he wanted to make it special, very special. He was anxiously looking forward to spending time alone with her. The drive back to the house together was going to be just the beginning of a wonderful Easter weekend together.

As he waited in the terminal a big commotion took place at the gate next to where he was sitting. He could see the horde of reporters and photographers rushing to the gate as the stewardess opened the door for the deplaning passengers. Little watched as the passengers getting off the flight passed him and found their family members waiting for them in the terminal. Curious, Little waited to see what celebrity was attracting so much attention.

Finally, the last passenger came through the door. The cameras started flashing as the photographers snapped pictures, and the reporters gathered close to get an interview. Inquisitively, Little walked over to the gate. To his surprise, Swoosh came bouncing down the terminal pursued by the crowd of reporters. Once again, for the third year in a row, Kansas had captured the national title, and Swoosh was the team's star player. "Swoosh. Hey Swoosh. Over here."

Recognizing the voice and then seeing Little, Swoosh quickly brushed passed the reporters, rushed over and embraced him. "Little. Man I'm so glad to see you. You're a lifesaver."

"I wasn't expecting to see you at the airport."

"It's good seeing you too," Swoosh sarcastically responded.

"No man," Little laughed. "I mean I thought you would be off playing in some big tournament game somewhere. You know I'm always glad to see you."

"School is out for the week, so I decided to take a few days off and get away. I don't have a game until Thursday. So, I said let me go home and check out Madear, Pop, and my folks. Besides, I want to see your godson; be there for the baptism. You know I can't miss that and besides, this makes me his uncle."

"Man, I'm so glad you're here. I was really praying you would make it."

The horde of reporters continued to gather around the pair shouting questions to Swoosh about his game, his plans for completing school, playing pro ball and being drafted.

"Excuse me one minute Little." Swoosh turned to face the press.

"Come on guys. I already told you I'm not making any decisions until after the season is over. As soon as I make a decision, I promise you'll be the first to know. So, for now please go away and let me have some private time with my family."

Acting as if they did not hear him the reporters continued to shout out questions. They continued to press toward the two and take pictures.

"Look, I'm trying to be nice. You might as well leave because I'm not making any statements today. Thank you. Besides, if you don't leave, you'll read about it in an exclusive in my high school newspaper."

It was to be the sports story of the year. The university was ranked number one again, and Swoosh was its star player. Upon hearing the threat, afraid of losing a big scoop to a high school newspaper, the reporters turned to walk away.

"God, I can't go anywhere without the press hounding me." Pointing to a lounge area in the opposite direction of the reporters, Swoosh said, "Come on Little, let's go over there away from the press."

"Hey Swoosh, what did the reporters mean about you being drafted?" He shouted in surprise at Little, "Not you too!"

"What do you mean not me too, what?" Little looked puzzled. "What do you mean?"

"Nothing." Swoosh paused momentarily. "No, it's just that everybody wants to know if I'm being drafted. They want to know if it will be the Nicks or the Lakers or if I'll wait until I finish college before going to the pros. You know, the usual. What are my plans after graduation? That's all. I thought you were trying to get the inside scope to place your bet like everybody else. People have big money riding on my decision. I've just been under a lot of pressure from this whole thing. It's starting to get to me." Swoosh's tone changed to his old usual self as he laughed and slapped Little on the back. "Hey, I should be asking you the questions. If you're not here to pick me up, what are you doing at the airport?"

"Waiting for Grace; her plane should be arriving in about twenty-five minutes. I thought I'd get here early."

"You haven't seen her in a while. So, your kind of anxious to see your lady?"

"Yea, I am. We haven't seen each other since December. By the time I got back down to Hampton to get my clothes and my car, school was on winter break. There wasn't enough time for me to go over to Roanoke."

"You really miss her."

"I do, but we call each other twice a week and we write three times a week."

"Well, I'll wait with you. That way I can ride home with the two of you."

Swoosh looked around, "Let's go sit down in the VIP lounge; hopefully, no more of those reporters will see me and start asking more questions."

"The VIP lounge," Little shouted, surprised.

"Being a big college basketball star, it's part of the deal. I get cars, money, and plane tickets. I never have to pay for anything. We players get first-class treatment wherever we go. The alumni can't give you enough.

You wouldn't believe some of the offers I've been made. If Madear knew, she would have slapped me upside my head for taking too long to say no to some of the things; especially to the women."

Little laughed. "Are you sure you said no?"

"Hey, you know me better than that. But then, I'm not going to kiss and tell."

The pair sat in silence for a few minutes. Little's tone of voice changed from fun-filled teasing to serious. "Hey Swoosh."

Having heard that tone before, Swoosh perceived Little's mood. He turned to face him. "Now what is it? Don't go getting all mushy on me Little, especially the way you did when I was getting on the train to leave for college."

"No Swoosh, all joking aside. I just want to thank you for being there for me. You know, for not giving up on me and for forgiving me for the way I was acting. You know; especially that first night at the Griffins when I couldn't breathe."

"Hey man, you know you don't have to say anything. You would have done the same for me. If it weren't for you, I wouldn't have made it this far. It should be me thanking you. But I know what you're saying. Times were really tough for you for a while, but I knew you'd pull through it. Man, I won't ever forget that night. I really thought you were dying. I was scared out of my mind. I'm just glad you're alive and here today."

"You know, when I first learned that Pop wasn't my real father, I was so hurt. No, I was more scared than hurt and so confused. His being my father was so important to me. When I thought that was taken away from me, I just didn't know how to handle it. I'm glad you were tough on me and didn't give up. You made me realize how important Pop and Momma are in my life, and that being a father is more than having a kid."

"You know, Madear and Pop are important in both our lives. I know I don't have to tell you this, but you know with Grace you have a real good thing too. I'm really happy for you. I only hope that one day I'm blessed to find a real good woman like you got. You have great parents and a good woman that loves you. Whatever you do, don't let her get away."

"I don't plan to do that."

"You know, it's strange how things worked out. Remember the night you said you were lonely? You wanted someone to love and to love you? All because you decided not to go back to UNE, you found that special someone."

"God does work in mysterious ways." Little laughed. "But I also remember that was the same night you tried to kill me."

"I know. Wasn't that a funny fight? I didn't want you to die, but, three weeks later, I was sure going to kill your ugly behind."

"Life is strange and filled with all kinds of funny twist and turns. You know, you're going to be the best man at my wedding."

"I'd better be. Who else could fill the position; growing up with a little knucklehead like you?"

"Now, don't let your head get too big. Hey, they just announced Grace's flight is arriving. You want to?"

"Yeah, let's go land her plane."

Together, like two little boys, as they watched Grace's flight land on the runway. Like old times they pretended to be the pilots onboard. Together, they landed her plane safely. Little rushed to the gate; his heart pounded with joy when he saw her. Racing to the doorway he grabbed her as they embraced.

When the merry trio arrived at the apartment, Little was amazed to see that his aunts, uncles, and cousins had also arrived from Chicago and Washington. Everyone was there to share in on this blessed event.

"Oh my God. All of you didn't have to come for the baptism," he exclaimed.

Aunt Shera responded, "That's what family is all about Little. We may have missed yours, but we weren't going to miss your godson's. Like I said, that's what being family is all about."

On Saturday Little, Grace, Anna, Johnathan, and Swoosh went sightseeing—the Statute of Liberty, the Empire State Building, Times Square, and the United Nations. They rode the subway, the ferry to Staten Island and ate lunch in Battery Park. They stopped by the Apollo for the afternoon matinee show and shopped for Tank's baptismal outfit at Saks Fifth Avenue.

Later that evening as a special treat, Little took Grace to dinner and to Carnegie Hall for a performance of Eubie Blake and Marion Anderson. It was a perfect evening; the two of them were alone together at last.

Despite his wheelchair, Elijah was determined to not let it change his life. As customary for him and Ruth on Easter Sunday morning, he arose early to attend sunrise service. Upon returning home, she joyfully went about her task of preparing breakfast for the family and guests. Then they were all off to church. As they drove through the streets of New York, the streets were crowded with people walking up and down the sidewalks, sporting their new spring outfits. They could see that in the traditional fashion of Harlem, the Easter parade had begun.

True Light Baptist Church was thick with so many people, extra chairs had to be set out in the isles. Reverend Harrison delivered his traditional Easter Sunday morning sermon. As usual, he did not forget to acknowledge those who faithfully attended church only three times a year; Christmas, Easter and Mother's Day, provided Christmas was not on a Sunday. Without exception, the baptism of Canegata Thomas Ballard was a highlighted moment. Anna and Johnathan, the proud parents, Little and Grace, the very proud godparents. Both their parents and Swoosh, the very proud uncle.

After church, the family gathered back home to rejoice. Looking around at all of the people, Johnathan folded his arms and said, "Little, you are well loved and very blessed. You are a blessed man to have all your family and friends around you like this."

"You know Johnathan, I never thought of it that way. You're right. I am well loved by all the people in this room and that makes me a very blessed person. Thanks for reminding me. You, Anna, and Canegata are also part of my family."

"And we're very proud to be Little," Johnathan responded.

Parting always seemed to have become a factor in their lives. Along with arriving comes departing. Early Wednesday morning at six o'clock, Little drove Swoosh to the airport to fly to his final season game against Kentucky. Swoosh was pursued by a lone reporter at the terminal.

Stopping Swoosh at the terminal, he shouted, "Jerald Jefferson. Swoosh, is it true you received your draft notice from the United States Army like your fellow teammate and childhood friend Clarence Jenkins, better known as Smoothie?"

Little was stunned by the question. Swoosh became extremely angry. "No man, it's not true. Get out of my face. I'm sick of you reporters sticking your noses in my business. Just leave me alone."

Quickly Swoosh pushed Little. "Let's get out of here." The two left the area and found a private spot to sit down.

"Swoosh, what that reporter said about being drafted into the army, is it true? Were you drafted?"

"No man, I wasn't."

"What about, Smoothie? Was he drafted?"

"Oh God, you didn't know he was drafted?"

"Drafted? But he's in college."

Swoosh was perturbed with Little's lack of awareness. "That doesn't matter anymore. Because of the war in Korea, the government is drafting guys like us right out of college and things are getting worse. The government is committing troops in Southeast Asia and all over the world."

"But the Korea conflict is over."

"That's what the government wants us to believe. Soldiers are still fighting, dying in the demilitarized zone and their getting ready to go fight somewhere else. The word on the street is that brothers are returning home in body bags. Two weeks ago, Cornell Jackson's brother came home in a body bag."

"Body bag? What's that?"

"Man, where have you been? A body bag! That's what the army ships your dead black ass back home in when you get killed." Swoosh lowered his head into the palms of his hands. He turned and looked at Little. His eyes were filled with sadness. "I'm sorry Little, I didn't mean to yell at you. It's just that it's all starting to get to me."

"It's alright."

"Man, I haven't got a draft notice, but I know plenty of guys that have. Most of the guys on the team got one. It's only a matter of time before I get mine. I don't have a problem serving in the army, but there are all kinds of wars going on around the world, and the US government wants to get involved. They don't care whose life it costs."

"That's not true Swoosh."

"It's not? Look at what happened to Uncle Canada."

"Uncle Canada? What does he have to do with this? He was killed by a drunk driver."

"That's what they want you to believe Little. That's what I thought at first."

"What are you saying Swoosh? What happened to Uncle Canada?"

"He was working for the State Department. He was involved in the peace talks, involving Berlin. He was leading the delegation and he was involved in this thing with Nikta Kheushchev, the leader of Russia and the leader of Cuba. Uncle Canada dies and the other guy, not a scratch on him. He may have had liquor on his breath, but he wasn't drunk. Uncle Canada's death was no accident."

"How do you know that?"

"One of the professors at UK is an expert on communism and its threat to the world's stability. The US views communism as a threat. It's spreading to Southeast Asia to an unheard-of country called Vietnam. Uncle Canada was at UK a lot conferring with him. He'd take me out to dinner; we'd talk." Swoosh looked up in the air to avoid the tears as he struggled to talk. "Two weeks before he died, he told me if anything should happen to him that Aunt Sarah, you, and I would be well taken care. He made me promise to see that Aunt Sarah marries again; for us not to make her feel guilty if she did."

"How come he never said anything to me?"

"He wanted to talk to you. But he felt you were going through enough problems of your own at the time. He made me promise to stand by you no matter what happened and to be there for you if he wasn't around. He said it was all up to me." Swoosh buried his face in his hands. "That's partly the reason why I wasn't at the first memorial service. We had said our good-byes."

Little held him as he comforted him. "What are you going to do?" he quietly asked.

Swoosh wiped his eyes. "I don't know man. I honestly don't know. I've heard some of the white boys at school talking about dodging the draft; leaving the country."

"Hey man, no. You don't mean that!"

"I'm seriously thinking about it Little."

"What about your family and your friends? What about all your plans?"

"Wise up Little," he snapped. "What good are your family, friends, and plans if you're dead!"

"But what about your country? Would you really desert your country like that?"

"My country? Where were you Little? I mean, weren't we both sitting in the same church and on the same pew next to each other that Sunday when Dr. King spoke! God, man, don't you get it? Brothers are being drafted left and right. They're being sent to the front line, and they're dying. They're being killed. Killed for what? More blacks are being drafted than white boys. More black men are being killed than white boys and for what!? Look what happened to Pop and his friends. He fought in World War II, just to come home to have his wife, his kid, his parents, and her parents killed by white folks. Just to have his house and businesses burned down to the ground. Do you think any white man spent one night in jail for the burnings and killings?"

"Look at Rosa Parks! Black folks pay the same fare as whites and they have to ride in the back of the bus. They can't even sit where they want to on the bus. Black folks can't eat at the same lunch counter with whites. Now they want me to die for somebody else's freedom, when I don't have the same freedoms here in America. It's a lot of bull Little. It's bull."

Swoosh got up and paced the floor. "Sure, they just love to see me shoot the hoop, run up and down the court. My playing ball brings that school in millions of dollars a year. The alumni even invite me to their house for fancy parties and dinners. Make me all kinds of offers of money. But let me try to talk to their daughter. Sure, I'm good enough and they're happy for me to shoot a little hoop with their sons, but I'll never be good enough to date, let alone marry their daughters. I won't forget—one guy invited us to his house for dinner. I noticed a mark on the plate, the saucer, the cup, glass, and silverware that I used. After dinner, I saw his wife throwing everything I ate off in the trash. I let her know I saw her throwing them away. When we were leaving, I made sure that I held both her hands, and I kissed that white bitch good-bye on both of her cheeks. Let her throw her cheeks and hands away. I bet she's still scrubbing her face and hands to this day." He sat down in the chair across from Little. "It hurts… Little, it hurts really bad, and I'm scared. Like it or not, I'm not going off to no war for their benefit. Not to protect their rights, only to be denied my own. I'm just not."

Swoosh got up and moved toward the window. "Tuesday, I was down by Lenox Avenue, and I heard this brother named Malcolm X preaching. He said revolution by any means necessary. He said that Christianity was the white man's religion. He said the white man was the devil. I thought about that woman, and how she just threw away her good china because I ate off it. At first, I was going to follow the brother because a lot of the stuff he said, I could identify with. But then I had to think of all the good white folks, and all the bad black folks I know. Ephesians came back to me: 'We wrestle not against flesh and blood, but against principalities of darkness.' Calling the white man a devil is too easy. It's the easy way out. I had to ask myself, why are we in Korea? Who would I be fighting for? What would I be fighting against? What would I be fighting for?

"My fight is not against the North Korean people. They've done nothing to me. Little, I can't begin to tell you one thing about those Korean people, North Korea or South Korea, East or West Berlin. But what I can tell you about is my people, our people, and white people. I can tell you because of white people my father couldn't attend his own father or mother's funeral. I can tell you why Pop has lived in pain for many years and why your daddy died in the electric chair. It was because of the ways of white folk."

Little sat in his seat; his head was spinning. In all the years Little knew Swoosh, they had grown up together, they had shared the same playpen, sandbox, crib, the same bed and ate at the same table. They grew up as brothers. It was years before they knew or understood the difference. They attended the same schools and were in the same classes. In all the years he had known Swoosh, he never knew his brother had so much rage inside tearing him apart. Oddly enough, Little knew it was the same rage he felt inside too. For years it was tearing him apart inside, yet he never knew Swoosh felt it also.

Swoosh always appeared to be so carefree—for some reason he believed Swoosh was immune to it all. Little was amazed at Swoosh's ability to camouflage his feelings, even from him.

Swoosh continued, "If I couldn't play basketball, do you think I would have been accepted in their school? Look what happened to you when you first arrived at UNE. Look what's happening out in California with the group called the Black Panthers. How many black people died at the hands of whites and the whites never served a day in jail! Blacks have died because a white woman yells rape, and he wasn't even on the same side of the street. Emmitt Till, he was only fourteen years old. How many of our people ended up being strange fruit hanging from Southern trees? How many whites do you think paid for those crimes?"

"None."

"That's right Thomas. To date, not one white person stood trial for the crime of murdering a black person. If they did stand trial, they weren't convicted for hanging a black man, woman, or child. Not with an all-white jury. Look at the peaceful demonstrations Dr. King's lead in Selma. They were far from non-violent. It was the white folks that are violent. Bull O'Connor was the sheriff. He was the most violent of them all. Have you read about Brown vs. the Board of Education of Topeka, Kansas? From 1865 to 1900, we've had three black politicians serve in the United States Senate. George Wallace, the governor of Alabama, defied the president of the United States and he's still in office. One day, he'll probably run for President of the United States and win. You got Strom Thurmond, James Eastland, Herman Talmadge serving in the United States Senate calling themselves segregationist. How many other racists are serving in Congress? In high school or in college, we never had one course teaching us about black people in America. The only thing we learned was that black people came from Africa, were slaves, and picked cotton."

Little could sense the frustration and anger in Swoosh as he continued talking. "They didn't teach us that a black man invented the red light, the gas mask, the light bulb, or the Charleston. Thomas, who was it that told us that their forefathers arrived in America long before the Mayflower?"

Little answered, "Pop did when we went to his home in North Carolina."

"That's right Little, Pop did. They didn't tell us about free blacks living in America who were here before the Pilgrims. Lies, lies, and more lies. They made us all believe we came over on slave ships. They've been teaching us nothing but a bunch of lies. Columbus never discovered America. He never set a foot on these shores to begin with and he was lost. To add insult to injury, what do they do? They made a big holiday of it. The white man slaughtered the Indians, killed the men and children, raped their women, and convinced the world the Indians were the savages. It was the French that first introduced scalping. The white man paid top dollar for the scalps of Indians. They don't teach us that in their history books."

Jerald began pacing back and forth. "No Thomas—Korea, Vietnam and Russia, those are the white man's wars, not mine, not yours, or black Americans. Let the white man fight it if he wants to, but I'm not. You can if you want to, but I'm not going to be a part of it. The white man's own kids don't want to fight it, so why should we?"

For the next few minutes, both men sat in silence until they heard the announcement of the boarding of Swoosh's flight. "Thomas, please I don't want us to part like this. I'm not going to lie to you or try to pretend, but I'm scared. I don't know what the future holds for either one of us. I don't want to get on that flight alone." Jerald made no efforts to hold back his tears. "I don't know when, or if we'll see each other again. It might be never." The tears steadily rolled down his cheeks as they embraced. He looked him directly into his eyes. "Right now, I can't bear to be on that plane by myself Thomas. Promise me you'll be flying the plane with me Thomas."

Thomas could no longer fight back his tears. "I promise Jerald. I'll be in the cockpit piloting the plane right beside you; just like always. I promise."

They both wiped their eyes and faces as they left the lounge area. Thomas stood at the window, watching his friend and brother reached the top step. Jerald turned to Thomas, pretended to shoot the ball at the hoop. Together, they uttered to each other, "Swoosh."

Uncertain, and filled with grief, Jerald unsnapped the sleeve of his university basketball jacket, folded back the cuff of his shirt to expose the scar on his wrist. Holding up his arm, he faced it toward the terminal. "Brothers."

Thomas not knowing when or if he would ever see his brother and trusted friend ever again, rolled back the cuff of his shirt sleeve and pressed it against the glass window. "Until death us do part."

They knew. Jerald quickly disappeared into the plane. As he promised, Thomas sat in the pilot seat and taxied the plane down the runway. He piloted the plane as it took off into the air, tearfully watching until the plane faded into the clouds.

REDEEMED

Little entered the quadrangle and looked around. The grass was a deep dark green. The budding foliage was opening up with the dawning of the spring of the year. The daffodils, tulips, and other perennials were in full blossom. The building and ground maintenance workers were working hard at planting new shrubs, bushes, and other flowering plants. Everything looked different, yet they were the same—still unchanged.

For a long time, he stood in the same place reflecting on his life. Almost four years ago, he stood in almost the exact same spot thinking that one day he, too would ascend those steps and make his declaration. He thought about how later that evening he was being hailed as king of the clambake. Now, four years later, he was looked upon as magna cum laude of his graduating class. Was this the Camelot years as the press proclaimed, or was it the prelude to something beyond every one's comprehension and imagination?

In a few weeks, he would be graduating, yet he still had many decisions to make. The one thing he recognized that the most important in his life was his relationship with God. His faith in God was strong and would be everlasting. He knew it was God who carried him through the terrible dark days and who was still protecting him. Also important was his relationship with his parents.

Time had healed the wound between him, his mother, and father. A result of all of the pain was that the bond between them had become stronger. Another relationship he recognized and cherished was his with Grace and his relationship with his family and friends. Each had contributed important redeeming qualities to the development of his character and influenced the choices he made and those that he would be making in the future.

Slowly, he ascended the steps of Massachusetts Hall. Those that preceded him made their declaration of their engagement, setting a wedding date, going to Europe, passing a course, admittance to graduate school and getting a job. Standing at the podium, Thomas looked over the menagerie of students that had collected on the quadrangle.

Everyone and everything are changing. The group that once dressed in all black, reciting meaningless poems and snapping their fingers as a sign of approval was fading off the scene like Dobbie Gillis to what they now deemed as psychedelic colors. The preppie look was slowly becoming a pair of faded old jeans, once called dungarees and worn by poor farm boys and tee shirts. Beads hung around their neck; headband kerchiefs were tied around their forehead. The once ruling clean crew cut look was losing ground to the long free flowing, unwashed hair. The words cool, dig, and daddio were replaced with the word peace, love, and flower power. The status quo conservative student body was now noisy and beginning to defy authority. Camelot. Change was on the horizon. Rock n' roll was here to stay.

Was this Camelot or the dawning of the Age of Aquarius? It was a revolution, a cultural, social, economic, and sexual revolution. An explosion of unknown magnitude was about to occur. The country was on the verge of losing its innocence. Rebellion against the status quo was swiftly becoming the norm. No longer would patriotism go unquestioned. Mistrust of the United States government, and a growing mistrust of anyone over thirty was the call of the day. Revolution was inevitable.

The country was on the verge of losing its youth. The college students would become the new Indians and the new niggers for soldiers to fire upon. It was in the air. This is Camelot. Their own children, they shall turn against them. After all, cowboys need Indians. The innocent shall be slaughtered. Babies, just babies; in the name of patriotism, their own parents shall despise them because they choose not to go off and fight in a war. They chose not to die in a war that was not their own. This is Camelot.

They shall be labeled as Hippies, love children, and flower children. These terms they shall use to describe themselves. White women liberating themselves from the status quo that harnessed their breast; they were opting to go natural and watch them burn.

His father was born colored, became a Negro, now was Black; Afro-American, soon to be African-American. Equal rights amendment and women's liberation were being ushered onto the stage. Sisters refused to join the women's liberation movement and rightly so. They declared, "How can we be free when our Black men are still in chains." Black, white, his dark skin shall be preferred and favored over his own brother's tan complexion. Tan, light-skinned, or high yellow-skinned Negroes were being rejected. Equal Employment Opportunity Commission, Affirmative Action, and the Great Society was all part of the bulging landscape. This is Camelot.

Burning incense, they no longer disguised the odor. Openly, they smoked pot while their sons, fathers, and brothers died in an undeclared war. Heroin would be king in Camelot.

Little opened his mouth and shouted at them. "In the name of God, wake up! Look at what you're doing to yourselves. You've made the uncorrupted appear corrupted. In rejecting everything good, you've thrown out the baby with the bath water."

REUNION

Thomas looked over at the bed across from him as the alarm clock rang loudly. Reaching over, he turned off the sounding alarm. His eyes fell upon the five small black and white snapshot photos of he and Elisha. Slowly, he picked them up and thought about how young they both looked. His skin was smooth, and he had no facial hair.

Momentarily, he stood up and glanced out of the window. He could see his reflection in the glass. The sun was shining bright promising to be another beautiful June day in New England. It was a perfect day for a graduation. Getting himself together, he headed off to the bathroom to shave and shower.

As he emerged from the bathroom, he shouted to the figure lying in the bed next to his. "Coconut," he got no response. Again, he shouted. "Hey, Coconut, come on sleepyhead. It's time to get up."

Elisha peeked out from under the covers. Little laughed, "Boy, in all these years you haven't changed at all. Still sleeping with your head under the covers."

Elisha's deep voice rang out, "What time is it?"

"It's seven-thirty."

"It's still too early, just a few more minutes."

"Not if you want to get something to eat for breakfast. Come on, get up and take your shower. Today is going to be a long day."

"Do I have to?"

"I'm afraid so." Little watched as Elisha sat up in the bed and stood up next to him. He was only a few inches shorter than himself.

Playfully Elisha punched Little in the shoulder. "That's right; you're graduating from college today."

"Yea, and don't forget, when you see Momma and Esther today don't forget to compliment them on how good they look."

"Why?"

"Remember Aunt Shera had them fly to Chicago to have her dress designer, Madame LaSalle or something like that make them their outfits."

"Boy, I wish I had a little brother."

"Why?"

"Then I'll have somebody to boss around and tell what to do and say."

"Okay, Coconut, I got the message. It's just that I can't get over how tall you've grown. You're only fifteen and you're already six feet tall. It seems like just yesterday when I was changing your diapers."

"Well, it's been a long time since I was in diapers, and, this time next year, I'll be taller than both you and Pop. Then I'll be the big brother," Elisha responded as he disappeared in the bathroom.

"But, you still got a head shaped like a coconut, Coconut."

Again, he picked up the five black and white snapshots of him and Elisha. Sitting down on the bed, he noted the changes. "God, where has the time gone? I had to wait until I was twenty before I had a beard or a mustache. He already has fuzz growing on his face. He'll be shaving everyday by the time he's sixteen."

Little's reminiscing was interrupted by a knock on the door. Slowly, he made his way to the door. "Alejandro and Stephanie," he shouted as they hugged each other.

"Little, I can't believe it. It was four years ago when I showed you this room, and now you're graduating."

"I can hardly believe it myself. Look at you, Ale. You've gotten so big!"

"All that soul food cooking Aunt Madie been teaching Steff and having us over for meals all the time," he exclaimed as he rubbed his slightly protruding stomach.

"What's all the noise?" Elisha shouted as he exited from the bathroom with only a towel wrapped around his waist.

"Elisha is that you? Ale, look at how tall and skinny he is. Oh my god, I can't believe it," she exclaimed as she ran over and kissed him. "Now I can see why they call you Coconut. Look at all that peach fuzz on his face and chest. You look like a coconut."

Embarrassed, Elisha ran back into the bathroom and slammed the door. "Little, get me my clothes," he shouted.

"Did you hear that voice Ale? It's deeper than yours. I can't get over how tall he's grown. We just saw him last year." Stephanie walked over and stood next to Ale. "Hey Little, we have a surprise for you."

"What? You didn't have to buy me a graduation gift."

"We wanted you to be the first to know. Well, actually, my parents and Ale were the first to know. But we're going to have a baby."

"That's great! Congratulations! I'm psyched. I'm happy for the two of you. When?"

"It's not due until November."

As they talked there was another knock on the door. "Come in, it's open." The door opened slowly; a head appeared inside. "Michael, I wasn't expecting to see you," Little shouted as he walked over to greet his friend.

"Did you really think I was going to miss your graduation? My parents are here too. Hey Steff and Ale." Michael stood in awe as he looked past Stephanie and Ale. "I know that's not Elisha."

"Hi Michael."

"Listen to how deep his voice is. You sound just like your daddy."

The slightly ajar door pushed open wider as three tall males entered the room. "Hey, hey, hey, someone said the party is in this room."

"Oh my god; it's Smoothie, Bebop, and Turk. Where did you guys come from?"

"My main man Little." They slapped each other five and hugged.

Grace maneuvered her way into the room, shouting, "Okay, all you tall men get out of the way and let a lady through."

"Grace. Hi, Honey," Little said as he grabbed her and kissed her. "Grace, these are the guys you heard me talk so much about; Clarence, better known as Smoothie, Howard, better known as Bebop, and Turk, whose name is William."

"So, this is the fine lady Swoosh has never stopped raving about."

"Yep, this is my fiancée, Grace Johnson. Boy, I'm so glad to see you guys. Hey, Smoothie, Bebop, and Turk, I really missed being with you guys."

"Well, we didn't miss you."

Little laughed. "Okay Smoothie, so be like that."

"Naw Little, it ain't like that at all. Man, it was just like you were in college with us. Swoosh started tutoring us like you tutored him when he was in high school. He'd say, 'Little said this. This is the way Little taught me to do it. Little said try and do it another way. If it doesn't work for you this way, try another way.' Every time we turned around, the brother was quoting you."

"Hey Smoothie, don't forget the Christmas break he spent in Kansas with Doc Lance."

"We don't know what happened to him, but the guy was unreal. He came back more charged up than ever. It was like he was mad and determined to make all of us succeed whether we wanted to or not. He was hard on us about our studies and everything you could imagine." Laughing, he added. "He even had scheduled times for us to go to the bathroom."

"Yea man, but he got us through UK. I even got an A in Calculus. And Bebop and I graduated with honors."

"Bebop? Honors? Man, you barely got out of grammar school."

"You can say that again." He laughed as he slapped Smoothie and Little five.

"Check this out Little. I'm going to work on my master's degree at NYU. I got a job in our old high school as a Math teacher."

"Yeah, he plans to be another Mr. Reid."

Ale chimed in, "You heard that Coconut? Smoothie just might be your Math teacher next year. Then you'll have to call him Mr. Jenkins."

"Not me, I'm moving."

Smoothie looked at Elisha. "I know that ain't Coconut."

"Can't be Coconut. He's still a small kid," Bebop replied.

"I don't know who he is, but I know his voice is deeper than mine."

"Moving? And just where are you going to go little brother?"

Little spoke up. "My folks are moving to Canaan, North Carolina, where my father grew up."

"You're kidding! When did all of this happen?"

"Swoosh told you guys about Pop's accident and that he was in a wheelchair. Well, a few months ago some junkie tried to mug him."

"I didn't hear about that. What happened?"

"You know Pop. He beat the man half to death."

"Now that sounds just like Pop."

Elisha chimed in, "The worst part was Aunt Mattie came running down the hall screaming. 'Ruthieee, come quick.' Scared Momma to death. That old lady ran outside and started beating the man with her cane."

"You're kidding! Aunt Mattie did that?"

"The police had to pull her and Pop off of the dude."

"Sounds serious!"

"Pop had always talked about one day going back home. So, Momma thought this was the best time. With all the street crime and drugs, they say Harlem ain't what it used to be. They sold the building, and they're packed and ready to go next month."

"Neighborhood won't be the same without them. What about Uncle Clarence and Aunt Mattie?"

"Apparently, they're moving south also, and so are Swoosh's parents."

Smoothie put his arm around Coconut. "Well, I feel sorry for that junkie after Pop and Aunt Mattie got through with him. You know that old lady can be mean when she wants to. I know because she tore my hide up many times and then called my folks from that window."

Turk laughed. "That old lady saw everything from that window. I used to wonder if she had legs. All you could see was her head and chest." Everybody laughed in agreement. "Things won't be the same without Pop. He kept all of us kids in the neighborhood in check. I just assumed he'd always be around for my kids. You know, to give them a nickname and keep an eye on them like he did for us."

Smoothie laughed. "I know what you mean. I thought the same way myself. I loved him to death, but I was scared of him too. I won't forget the time my older brother Jimmy skipped school and went to Mount Vernon with his friends and took me along. The guys were in the alley shooting dice. I had to go pee when all of a sudden Pop appeared out of nowhere. He grabbed Jimmy by the collar of his shirt, told Sam and Cornell to freeze. You know that slow deep voice of his. He said, 'You boys are supposed to be in school. I know your parents don't know you're up here cussing and gambling.' The other two guys said, 'Shut up old man.' Before anybody knew anything, Pop had pulled his belt off and hit the two of them. Then he picked Jimmy up with one arm, told Sam and Cornell to drop their pants and bend down. 'You know I don't whoop no clothes.' He beat the three of them right there in the alley."

The others agreed and nodded their heads. "Sounds just like Pop."

"I was so scared. I peed all over myself. Those guys were seventeen. Pop told them to get home and had them on punishment for a month. I never skipped school again and they didn't either. You never knew where that big yellow Con Edison truck was going to be in New York State and maybe New Jersey. Man, to this day I cringe each time I see one of those yellow trucks. You just never knew when Pop might jump out. Everybody knew and respected Pop."

"I still have to live with the man. Now you guys know what I have to go through."

"Coconut, Pop is a real good man with a real big heart. I remember the time my folks were out of work for a while. I found out Pop paid their rent and bought us food. Every kid in the neighborhood always had a nice Christmas. Pop saw to that. He's a good man. A real good man. Did your mother find out how he was getting down the steps in the wheelchair?"

"That was so funny. You know how stubborn Pop is. He never lied to Momma. She'd ask how he got the groceries he'd play it off. 'Sweet Angel, with all these kids around here, you know I could always ask any one of them.' One day I forgot my medicine at home, so the school called Momma at work. Dr. Isenberg gave us a ride to the house. When we got there, we saw Pop come out on the stoop looking like he was getting ready to go down the steps. So, we sat in the car and watched him. He got out of his wheelchair, sat on the stoop and lowered the chair to the ground with a rope. He has that strong upper half of his body. He leaned against the banister and came down the steps."

"Sounds just like Pop."

"The three of us sat in the car and watched him. Dr. Isenberg told Momma Pop was determined to walk again, and said he believe Pop was going to walk again. Pop went to the store; we waited inside the hallway for him. When he came back, we watched him carry the bag of food up the steps. Then he went back down and dragged his wheelchair up. He rolled himself into the foyer. Momma stood there. He was shocked. It was so funny. I think for the first time I saw Pop scared of Momma. She wanted to kill him, but she just gave him his hat and said, 'Next time you go out, put on your hat and scarf.'"

"I would have loved to see the look on his face."

"It was funny. But I know Momma's right. That junkie had a gun, he could have killed Pop. When I heard that gun go off and Aunt Mattie screaming, I won't forget that look on Momma's face. She was so scared. But you know Pop. There's no stopping my father."

"That's so true. He's one determined man."

"Hey Smoothie, I thought Uncle Sam drafted you."

"Me and all starting five and three other members of the team were drafted. Coach thought something was strange. He and the president took us to the governor's office in Topeka. Governor called the president of the United States. It seemed fishy because no one from the other top teams were drafted. Next thing we knew, we were back in school."

Ale asked, "But didn't you get drafted by the pros? You were picked in the first round with Swoosh, and you too Bebop."

"After what you did for us Little, being picked was the honor. Just knowing I was good enough to get in the NBA was all I needed to know."

"What I did for you?"

"Yea, if you hadn't taught Swoosh—pushed him and encouraged him—none of us would have made it through college."

Turk chimed in, "Hey man, I was a year behind you guys. When I got on campus, I had all easy classes. I made straight A's my first semester. I never went to class. Then Swoosh got hold to me. He asked if I wanted to go to Egypt, France, Spain, and around the world. I said yea. He took me to the library. Said I could travel to all of those places without leaving the building. That's when the brother found out I couldn't read.

He personally tutored me. He hooked me up with all kinds of people at the university. After a while, I couldn't get enough of the library. I started attending class and I made my own grades, but I had to stop playing ball."

"How did you get by Coach Lamel without knowing how to read? You made good grades in high school."

"I faked it. I used to get the test from the guys ahead of me. Most of the teachers were ditto queens. They gave the same test every year. I kept a book in my pocket and pretended to read when I saw Coach. I usually got the book from someone who read it. We'd talk about it and the rest was history. I just wanted to play ball. I didn't know I was only cheating myself out of an education."

"What about your basketball scholarship?"

"Swoosh started this organization with the basketball players. The money and things the alumni gave us, and I mean they gave us tons of money; we started investing it instead of spending it. He said the first thing we had to do was invest in ourselves. So, the money from the investment paid my second semester, but now, brother, I got myself an academic scholarship."

With the revelation, everyone started giving each other five. "That's really great."

"It is. We owe it all to you Little."

"But why me?"

"If it had not been for you pushing Swoosh, he would not have been there to push us."

"I don't know what happened to him that Christmas at Dr. Lance's. But whatever it was, it made him work on us. That's the main reason why I decided to go into teaching instead of playing pro ball. What you did for us, I want to do for others. Help our people get out of the ghetto. I want young brothers to know that sports aren't the only way out of the ghetto. I want them to know that they got a brain and for them to learn how to use it. Show them that education is the key out of poverty. I want to let them know that in life, education is the real game."

Turk continued, "I loved the library so much that I volunteered to work in it three days a week. I started cataloguing stuff. I found stuff that they didn't know they had. So, they hired me."

"Yea, but then they fired his behind."

"Fired you. Why? I mean, how do you fire someone who's volunteering?"

"They said I spent too much time reading and not enough time working. A professor that I was helping with some research hired me. That's when Swoosh gave me the idea of hiring my services to graduate students and faculty. I'd do all kinds of the research, and they pay me. I charged by the hour. I knew the library like the back of my hand, depending on the amount of information, the nature, and complexity of the topic, I'd averaged around three searches in a few hours. Now, I plan to be a full-time researcher when I graduate from graduate school."

"Man, I can't believe it. All you guys talked about in high school was how much you hated school and wanted to play for the pros. Now that you have the opportunity, you're passing it up."

"Remember Rerun?

"Yea. He was a year behind us. He was always in trouble with the law."

"The brother got into UK. Swoosh turned him on to learning. Now, you never see him without a book in his hand. He's on the dean's list and now talking about going to law school."

Turk laughed. "Yea, the brother now plays chess. He's on the chess team and the debate team. I must say he's really good."

"You should. You haven't beat him at chess yet."

"Bebop, you play chess?"

"I try."

"Oh, shut up man. You know your number two on the chest team. He's mad because Rerun is number one."

"Hey, I was the one that taught the brother how to play."

"Yea, but Swoosh taught you."

"You guys have really done well."

"And we owe it to you and Swoosh."

"If anything, I owe it all to my father. Speaking of Swoosh, has anyone seen him?"

"Not since he was picked the number one draft choice. He'll be playing for the New York Nicks."

"You're kidding!"

"Nope."

"When?"

"Last night."

"Yes I was, and here I am," Swoosh shouted, running through the crowd. "Move aside and let me through."

"Oh my god, its Swoosh!" Immediately they hugged and gave each other five.

"Man, I'm so glad to see you. Wait, wait one minute. Remember what you told me that day at the train station?"

Puzzled, Swoosh looked at him. "Brother all I remember was you snotin' and cryin' real hard."

"Yea, right." Little went to his closet and took out the basketball. "First, you told me that whenever I needed you to just bounce it and you'll be there. Then you told me when you got drafted by the NBA to return it to you."

Swoosh held the ball tightly to his chest. "And all these years you kept it."

"And I bounced it many times. It never failed." Holding up his wrist, he said, "Brothers."

As they had done so many times. Swoosh placed his wrist against Little's. "Until death us do part."

"Aw, now, ain't that sweet. But I'm hungry, let's get breakfast," protested Elisha.

TRIUMPHANT GLORY

In the University of New England's traditional fashion since its founding the pageantry of the academic ceremony was about to begin. It was a yearly, coveted ritual by the university and its faculty Inside the huge auditorium, decorating the stage stood cascading floral arrangements resembling Indian headdresses and colorful flower beds. Plants and small trees decorated the stage; intentionally placed floral arrangements hailed throughout the building. Above the stage amidst the royal blue curtains, hung the university's emblem, a symbol of its outstanding education and prominence throughout the land. The university's 250-voice choir, along with the 250-voice guest choir from Hampton Institute stood on the stage prepared to sing. In front of the podium was a spray of gladiolas enshrouding the scarlet-colored pillow awaiting the arrival of the University's Mace. A soft bed of white, pink, and blue pansies accented the surroundings.

The University of New England was well known and was highly envied throughout the academic world for its academic pageantry. The history of the academic dress reached far back into the early days of the oldest universities. The statute of 1321 in England required that all "Doctors, Licentiates, and Bachelors" of the University of Coimbra wear gowns. In its time, the gowns may have been counted necessary for warmth in the unheated buildings frequented by medieval scholars. Hoods seem to have served to cover the tonsured head until superseded for that purpose by the skullcap. However, today's academic regalia reflected that which the representatives of various American colleges and universities adopted, following the conference at Columbia University in 1865.

As a time-honored tradition, the academic dress worn by those in the procession included the cap, gown, and hood. Some faculty wore a cap made of black serge, others of broadcloth and others of velvet. Many wore gowns of black, but what made this pageantry the most coveted was that the many-colored gowns were determined by the university from which the bearer's highest degree was awarded.

The doctorate gown round had bell sleeves; faced down the front was velvet and three chevrons on the sleeves were of the same color. Some of the facings and velvet chevrons were of the color distinctive of the subject. The full shaped hood was four-feet-long with five-inch silk, satin, or velvet border on the outside of the rounded base. The border of the hood represented the university from which the wearer received their degree.

The gown of the master's degree, as well as that of the bachelor's was black in color. Both were lacking the trimmings of the doctorate had oblong sleeves and were open at the wrist. The sleeve base hung down in the traditional manner. The rear part of its oblong shape was square cut, and the front part had an arc cut away. It was designed to be worn closed. The black bachelor's degree gown had pointed sleeves.

Throughout the United States, there had been no change in the standard colors that represented the various disciplines. The color facing the hood indicated the following:

Arts/Letters/Humanities	White Business
	Drab Education
	Light Blue
Engineering	Orange
Fine Arts/Architecture	Brown Music
	Pink Nursing
	Apricot
Philosophy	Dark Blue

Physical Education	Sage Green
Public Health	Salmon Pink
Science	Yellow
Social Work	Citron
Dentistry	Lilac
Law	Purple
Library Science	Lemon Yellow
Medicine	Green
Pharmacy	Olive
Theology	Scarlet

The 1000-piece orchestra continued to play the prelude "Afro-American Symphony" by William Grant Still, as locals, world dignitaries, family members, friends, alumni, and visitors continued to pour into the six thousand seat auditorium. As always, it promised to be a grand occasion.

Marking the beginning of the academic processional at the precise moment both, the orchestra outside and inside, simultaneously began playing the processional music "Symphony in G-Minor, subtitled "Song of a New Race" by William Grant Still. Finally, the long-waited monumental moment of academic procession composed of over three hundred twenty-five faculty, administrators, reunion classes, and honored guests; 631 undergraduate and 428 graduate and professional students had begun.

First to enter into the auditorium in the long line of the processional was the academic provost. Dawning his blue doctoral robe, facing down, dark blue, and three chevrons on the sleeves of the same, he was bearing the University's Mace. The mace was the grandest and only one known in existence.

The three-foot-long cone shaped mace was the original top of the giant petrified wooden totem pole that once stood on the sacred ground where the school was built. Totem poles were not indicative of the Northeastern Indians. It was rare, one of the few found in the east.

Legend speaks of its origin, and how it arrived from the Pacific to the Atlantic. It was specially handcrafted for a great and powerful wealthy Tsimshian Chieftain as a gift, symbolizing his wealth, greatness, and secret society. As a symbol of their friendship and peace among their people, it was passed to the Lakota, then to the Ojibwa for their greatness in the land. From the Iroquois of Ohio, it was presented to Uncas, chief of the Mohegan tribe to stand overseeing the ceremonial ground of the village. It was a journey that would span over a hundred years before it would arrive to represent the Algonquian nation in this sacred area of Algonquian Bay.

The mace crown was a bird of keen vision, long broad wings, and a strong soaring flight, the golden eagle. The eyes of the eagle, fashioned from topaz with onyx in the center symbolizing its sharpness of vision, stood out. In its powerful hooked bill, it carried a branch. At the upper most part of the branch was fire made from ruby. Strands of gold laced the head and neck of the majestic bird. From the eagle's breast rose a Nootka cypress. To the left, a large Kodiak bear stood, etched as part of the tree's trunk. The bear's huge arms extended upward, forming the canopy and branches of the tree and the eagle's outspread wings. The claws made from the tusk of a walrus spoke of the power and dominance of the bear. On the right side of the tree, wearing a majestic headdress stood an Indian chief. His arms were folded in the universal Indian language of hello. Its base, carved from the jawbone of a whale inlayed with beaver tooth, represented the river of life, the bountifulness of the waters, and the richness of the land. The eagle held a Chinook salmon in its powerful talons. Each piece of the spectacular formidable mace represented harmony with mother earth, the wind and fire. It was an exquisite piece of craftsmanship to behold.

Next was Dr. Garvey, president of the university. He was wearing a scarlet robe. Following in line was the commencement speaker, Dr. Ralph Bunch, the campus chaplain, and Magna Cum Laude Thomas Isaiah Thomas and the president of the student government. Four honorary degree recipients and the chairman of the board of trustees followed. Members of the faculty and of the five-year reunion classes followed. Each was fashionably dressed in their appropriate degree academic garb.

Lead by the dean of the respective college within the university carrying the banner, the baccalaureate students bearing their hood on their right forearm, followed in order. Candidates for the master's degree, wearing their hood were next in line. The doctoral degree recipients in their gowns of scarlet were adorned wearing their hoods as they entered into the auditorium. Finally, the professional school candidates, Law, Library Science, Medicine, Pharmacy, and Theology candidates entered. All wearing doctoral gowns of the university's color, scarlet red. The College of Law, gown faced down in purple velvet with three chevrons of the same color on the sleeves and purple hoods. The College of Library Science, gown faced down in lemon yellow velvet with three chevrons of the same color on the sleeves and lemon-yellow hoods. The College of Medicine, gown faced down in green velvet with three chevrons of the same color on the sleeves and green hoods. The College of Pharmacy faced down in olive velvet with three chevrons of the same color on the sleeves and olive hoods and the College of Theology, faced down in scarlet velvet with three chevrons of the same color on the sleeves and scarlet hoods.

The invocation was given by the University's chaplain. Both choirs and the orchestra followed with a performance of "Hallelujah" from *Messiah* by G. F. Handel. As Magna Cum Laude, Thomas was next on the program as the speaker. The five-foot-ten, slightly portly, sixty-year-old Dr. Garvey rose to introduce him. Well known in both the national and international communities as a syndicated columnist and humorist, he was presiding over his fifteenth commencement as the president of the university. As a philosopher, he stood tall in his field.

"To the faculty, staff, and students of the university, our next speaker is no stranger to us, and he needs no introduction. To the alumni, guest speaker, family members, visitors, and friends, he is a young man of unusual talents. No doubt you have heard of his works and accomplishments. To name a few of his credits; he is a member of Phi Beta Kappa, a presidential scholar, soon to be Rhodes scholar, and no doubt, one day, he will be a Nobel Prize recipient. One might look around and see today's program is different from the commencements we've had in the past. We are honored today with the Hampton Institute College Choir performing next to the University of New England's. You may ask why, and some may be offended. No doubt you have observed the recipients receiving honorary degrees are persons of color; therefore, you may question and object, and you may be offended. This morning's commencement speaker is a great man. He is a man of color. You may feel scorn, and you may be offended. Alas, some are here today in protest. What pity and what shame.

"Last August, Mr. Thomas, Phi Beta Kappa, magna cum laude, the class valedictorian, met with the faculty, the commencement committee and me regarding the university's past, and its respective place in today's changing society. In questioning its practices, he reminded us that the university was not a collection of books, buildings, and philosophies. But that it was comprised of people interacting, expressing ideologies, and attitudes. That among that attitude there would be no problem granting honorary degrees to five white males during commencement; in fact, it had become an expectation. Many of us were uncomfortable with what he expressed. I know I was. He came armed with a list of all the past honorary degree recipients from this institution since it granted the first one.

"Considering myself the most enlightened and the leader of this institution, I was very shocked, appalled, and ashamed. In his words and wisdom, he stated the faculty at UNE was considered an august body of intellectual intelligence of the academic and research community with a world-wide reputation. But the history records also proved them to be a bunch of retentive, aged, pontificating good-ole-boys." He paused and laughed. "I must say, Mr. Thomas has a way with words. Mr. Thomas pointedly reminded us that UNE was supposed to be the head and not the tail, leaders of the crusade, not just participants and explorers treading on uncharted territories, not spectators and homebodies playing it safe. As a bearer of truth, he has an artful way of handling this faculty, and a way with words that provokes one to examine self.

"I am told there is a statute in front of Tuskegee Institute, in Tuskegee, Alabama, of a male lifting the veil of ignorance off of a former slave's head. It serves as a statement that education opens one's eyes. He asked us, had education blinded ours? Being at this institution had we became puffed up with pride and self-serving in self-importance and indulgence. He did not cease there. He continued issuing a challenge for us to find one person of color to award an honorary degree, if not living then posthumously. Like God told Lot, if he could find ten men who would serve him, he would spare the city. Mr. Thomas said, 'To redeem your reputation, I'm only asking that you find one dead one.' When it comes to the question of race and race relations, I am ashamed of the university's record. For we have not done all that we are capable of doing and all we should be doing. Instead, we in all cases have turned a deaf ear to the problem plaguing our nation, our university, and the American society.

"He challenged our minds, our motive, and our way of conducting education here at UNE. We accepted the challenge. We were overwhelmed with our findings. We have fallen far short. I can no longer deny it. We have been the problem. More precisely, we have been at the forefront of the problem. I'll have you to know despite what you may think, or how you may feel, today marks the dawning of a new day and of a new way of the University of New England doing business and forming its place in our society." He turned and looked at Thomas. "Thank you, Mr. Thomas, for your patience with us and for educating us.

"History. American history is rich with the contributions of many a Negroes in all aspects of life. We thought we knew, but we are ignorant of them. No, the truth is to preserve our attitude of superiority we did not want to acknowledge the Negro for their contributions. In writing of the writings of our books, recording of our history and bringing about equality, we intentionally and systematically denied the

Negro their rightful place in history; an irrespective act based solely on the color of their skin. A sin for which I am greatly ashamed and standing before you I hereby repent. I am proud to announce this fall will mark the opening of a black studies program at UNE. A course shall be required irrespective of discipline, undergraduate, graduate, and professional for all students to take. I'm no fool. I know there will be much resistance, but either you join us or move aside. If you do not move aside be prepared to be trampled on because the University of New England is going forward with or without you."

Again, he looked at Thomas. "Mr. Thomas, I want to thank you for opening up our eyes, for waking us up, and for not giving up on us. Most of all, I here publicly seek your forgiveness." Dr. Garvey walked over to Thomas and extended his hand. Thomas stood to his feet and accepted the extended olive branch. In a very unprecedented move, Dr. Garvey embraced him. A thunder of applauses sounded throughout the auditorium.

Returning to the podium, he again addressed the audience. "Before Mr. Thomas speaks, will all of you please rise as both choirs sing the Negro National Anthem, "Lift Every Voice and Sing," by James Weldon Johnson, and arranged by Hampton's former choir director, the renowned composer and director Nathaniel Dett, and directed by Mr. Charles Flack. The words are found in your program."

The audience rose to its feet, some rejoicing in the new day, others moving aside for fear of being trampled. Regardless of their reason, the entire audience stood to their feet.

> Lift every voice and sing
> Till earth and heaven ring,
>
> Ring with the harmonies of liberty,
> Let our rejoicing rise,
> High as the list'ning skies,
> Let it resound loud as the rolling sea.

Sing a song full of the faith that the dark past has taught us:
Sing a song full of the faith that the present has brought us:
Facing the rising sun
Of our new day begun,
Let us march on till victory is won.

Stony the road we trod,
Bitter the chastening rod,
Felt in the day when hope unborn had died;
Yet with a steady beat,
Have not our weary feet,
Come to the place for which our Fathers sighed.

We have come, over a way that with tears has been watered;
We have come, treading our path through the blood of the slaughtered.
Out of the Gloomy past,
Till now we stand at last;
Where the white gleam, of a bright star is cast.

God of our weary years,
God of our silent tears,
Thou who hast brought us thus far on the way; Thou who hast by Thy might,
Led us into the light,
Keep us forever in the path, we pray.
Lest our feet stray from the places, our God, where we met Thee;
Lest our hearts, drunk with the wine of the world, we forget Thee;

Shadowed beneath Thy hand,
May we forever stand,
True to our God, true to our native land.

    Filled with life and beaming with pride, slowly and humbly, Thomas approached the podium to an astounding standing ovation from the floor. From the podium he could see his family seated in the front. Behind his mother sat the stranger he had met on the plane. He was smiling at him, beaming with pride. It pleased Thomas to see him there. Addressing the audience, he began his speech:

"First, I want to give honor to my God, the God of Abraham, Isaac, and Jacob, who is the head of my life. President Garvey and, our distinguished speaker, Dr. Ralph Bunche. My parents, platform guest, alumni, parents, friends, relatives, and my fellow graduates. I count it as both an honor and a privilege to stand before you today to address you on this commencement day. It is a proud moment for me and for all of us who will be receiving a degree today.

"Just a short time ago, we entered this world-renowned bastille of higher education bursting with high hopes, ideals, dreams, and expectations. Each of us was armed with intent to find our niche in this university where we could be nurtured, so we may grow to our full potential with the expectation that one day we would go forth to make our mark upon this world. Matriculating here, we looked at it as a beginning, a step in the right direction. The ensuing years taught us that this was just one small step down the long road that lay before us.

"True enough, there were many twists and turns along the road. Some bends were deeper than other bends; a few of us were lost along the way and dropped out. Some of the mountains were steeper than other mountains, and still a few more gave up on the climb. Not all of the road was lit. Therefore, some lost their way in the darkness. It was at those times we found there was a hand reaching back to guide us to a light. Some parts of the road were perceived as impassable, but it was only by the grace of God that the few of us who are here today persevered.

"While it has been a long journey, not all the times have been tough. We had a lot of fun along the way; we made many friends and made discoveries, both great and small. We had our triumphs, and we suffered many defeats, especially our football team." Laughter echoed from the crowd. "But overall, those of us who have made it to this day—we had good times along the way. We have many fond memories and great discoveries. Who would have ever thought a young, Black, seventeen-year-old freshmen from Harlem, New York, would be a presidential scholar and be crowned king of the Clambake?"

A round of applauds and many of his fellow graduates stood as they applauded. "Now, we are about to be unleashed upon a cold, cruel, and sometimes unforgiving and unsuspecting world. However, we are determined to make our mark. What will that mark be? Last week, I overheard a fellow classmate talking about the financial empire he will be inheriting. A legacy his grandparents left his father and now his father was leaving to him. It caused me to look around and I began to think. I looked at the world in which I live, work, and play. I asked myself, what am I inheriting? I was not referring to personal finances. I wanted to know what kind of world I will be inheriting. I ask you today, what kind of world will we be inheriting? I ask of the parents and grandparents, what kind of world are you leaving us?

"It was the generation before us that split the atom and a weapon of great destruction was created. Its destructive power unleashed upon the innocent citizens of Nagasaki and Hiroshima. There was once a country called Korea. Today, it's known as North and South Korea with a demilitarize zone in between. America and Russia are two great nations known as the two great superpowers. Between them, there is a nuclear arms race. It is a race to see who can build the most and biggest nuclear arsenal stockpile. They are building a nuclear weapons arsenal to display how many times they each can blow up this world. I tell you we are inheriting a world that is facing nuclear annihilation. We have only one world. There is only one planet earth.

"I submit to you we have inherited a world filled with pain and suffering. There once was a united country called Germany, and a city called Berlin. Now a wall stands in between, separating mothers and fathers, brothers and sisters, and sons and daughters. Then as always, there is the question of race and civil rights. It is an enigma of the American society. Segregation still rules in a society calling itself a democracy. People denied the right to a basic education and denied the right to employment to make an honest days' wage to feed their family. The American Revolution echoed the theme of no taxation without representation. Yet, Black Americans are expected to pay their fair-share of taxes and they are denied the right to vote. Why? It's all because of the color of their skin. Ignorance, prejudice, and racism are still the law of the land and continue to blind the eyes of America, home of the brave and the free. The land is bountiful my fellow graduates, we have a big job ahead of us. The time is now for us to take action to correct the ills plaguing our society and the errors created by the former generations and our forefathers.

"Several species in the animal kingdom are facing extinction. Nuclear waste, toxic chemical waste sites in the name of the almighty dollar exist throughout our land. Classmates, the task ahead of us is to turn things around for the good of all mankind and not to judge a man by the color of his skin, economic, or social status. Not only is it our task, but it is our obligation and responsibility. I ask you, what kind of world will we leave for the next generation? What kind of world will we leave for our children and our grandchildren to inherit?

"To this charge I plead guilty. I was a part of it. In the name of peace, I worked on a weapon that has great capability of nuclear destruction. I've had to ask myself, is that what I want to leave as my legacy to my children? Is it how I want to be remembered? I've chosen a path to use the knowledge I've gained to support life. I've chosen a path to aid in the relieving of pain and suffering. Using nuclear medicine to create a better society is more important than using it to destroy life. In the name of Almighty God, I ask you to join me in preserving life, preserving our world, preserving our planet, and leaving to our future generations a world and society of which they can be proud. Let us leave to them a world in which they can live, grow, prosper, and be happy. Thank you."

A thunderous round of applause and cheers echoed from the audience. Thomas bowed and waved his hands in acceptance of the crowd's applauses and standing ovation. Again, applause and cheers thundered throughout the auditorium, as the crowd stood to their feet in an arousing standing ovation. As he walked to his seat, he was enthusiastically congratulated by all on the platform.

Dr. Garvey entered the podium. "Mr. Thomas, you never cease to amaze us all. Yes, my generation has left your generation an overwhelming and almost insurmountable agenda. But the one thing I firmly believe, with you, and those like you at the helm, my grandchildren and great grandchildren will have a secure future. Because of you and persons such as yourself, the world will be a more promising place to live. And now it is time for the awarding of the honorary degree, the Doctorate of Letters. I want you to know, Mr. Thomas, the committee accepted your challenge. Not only did we find one, but we found so many men and women of color whose numerous contributions to society were so great, it was difficult for us to choose. After much debate, we narrowed the field to the following candidates: Dr. Ralph Johnson Bunche."

Dr. Bunche stood to his feet and came forward to the podium and stood alongside Dr. Garvey. "Dr. Bunch is accredited for bringing about the first truce, then an armistice, and in 1949, the end of the Arab-Israeli conflict. He was born on August 7, 1904, in Detroit, Michigan. He attended the University of California at Los Angeles, where his athletic abilities in high school earned him a four-year scholarship. In 1927, he graduated magna cum laude, class valedictorian, and a member of Phi Beta Kappa. This graduation brought five medals for excellence in various studies, plus a scholarship for further work at Harvard University, where in 1928 he received a Master of Arts degree. He taught at Howard University in Washington, DC. In 1931, a Rosenwald Fellowship enabled him to go to Europe and Africa to gather first-hand material on social problems for his doctorate. In 1934, he received his PhD in political science from Harvard. In 1936, Dr. Bunche was codirector of the Institute of Race Relations at Swarthmore College. In 1944, the State Department selected him for the Associate Chief of the Division of Dependent Territories. Upon confirmation, above the objection to a Negro having so important a job, Dr. Bunche became the first Negro in American history to be in full charge of an office in the State Department. When the first meetings to draft a charter for the formation of the United Nations were held at San Francisco, Dr. Bunche was there as advisor to Commander Harold Stassen. Many of Dr. Bunche's recommendations became a part of the Charter of the United Nations, and diplomats of all the governments of the world became aware of this brilliant young Negro in Washington. In rapid succession, various commissions and appointments followed: the United States delegate to the International Labor Conference at Paris in 1945 and presidential appointee to the Caribbean Commission in 1946. He was the US Commissioner to the West Indian Conference in the Virgin Islands, and attendance various United Nations sessions in London and Paris. In 1947, he was asked by Trygve Lie, then United Nations secretary general, to fly to Palestine to aid the United Nations Special Committee in negotiating peace between the Arabs and the Jews. When Count Bernadottee was assassinated, the United Nations appointed Dr. Bunche as acting mediator. After over forty-two days of negotiating, he secured a cease-fire a month later, after intense negotiating was the signing of a peace that was hailed around the world. Leaders of the Israeli delegation said that morning that Dr. Bunche earned the gratitude of all humanity and the sheik heading the Arab group called him one of the greatest men on earth. It was an honor, and in 1950, he was granted the Nobel Peace Prize. With great honor and pride, I present the Doctorate of Letters to Dr. Ralph Johnson Bunche." He placed the hood over the head of Dr. Bunche.

"Margaret Walker." Dr. Walker stood to her feet and came forward to the podium and stood alongside Dr. Garvey. "Margaret Walker, born July 7, 1915 in Birmingham, Alabama, grew up in Meridian, Mississippi, and Birmingham, Alabama. At the age of sixteen, she met the eminent Negro poet and writer, Langston Hughes. He suggested she send some of her work to the Negro magazines. In 1931, *The Crisis*, a national organization of the NAACP, accepted one of her writings entitled *I Want to Write, I Want to Write the Songs of My People*.

"After graduating from Gilbert Academy in New Orleans, Louisiana, in 1930, she attended Northwestern University, in Evanston,

Illinois, where she received her bachelor's degree in 1935. In 1940, she received her Master of Arts degree from the University of Iowa, where her collections of poems were so excellent that they were accepted in place of the usual dissertation. A Rosenwald Foundation Fellowship for Creative Writing in 1944, she has been the recipient of many awards and honors. She served as the Professor of English at Livingston College, in Salisbury, North Carolina, at West Virginia State College, and today is the Professor of English Literature at Jackson College in Jackson, Mississippi. It is with great pleasure that I bestow upon you, Dr. Margaret Walker the honorary degree of Doctorate of Letters."

Dr. Garvey placed the hood over her head and on her shoulders.

"Theodore K. Lawless, MD."

Dr. Lawless stood to his feet, came forward to the podium, and stood alongside Dr. Garvey.

"Dr. Lawless was born in Thibodeaux, Louisiana in 1892. Known wherever dermatologists gather, Dr. Lawless is one of the world's leading skin specialists. His career stretches back over a period of forty years. He achieved eminence in his chosen field by hard work, superb training, and outstanding intellect. Educated at Talladega College in Alabama, the University of Kansas, Columbia and Harvard; he received the MD degree from Northwestern University in Evanston, Illinois. He has worked in Vienna, Freiburg, and Paris. From 1924 to 1941, Dr. Lawless taught at the Northwestern University School of Medicine. For many years, he has been Senior Attending Physician at Provident Hospital in Chicago, Illinois. Once he declared, 'I am happiest when I work and so I work as much as I can.' A millionaire, the distinguished dermatologist is a prodigal with his earnings as he is with this skill. In 1956 through his efforts, Dillard University in New Orleans, Louisiana, secured a $700,000 apartment building. A chapel on the Dillard campus bears his name, and several other colleges attended by Negroes have benefited from his philanthropy. However, his generosity is not restricted to his race alone, or just in America. A $500,000 dermatology clinic stands erected in the state of Israel at the Beilinson Hospital Center, mainly through his efforts. The clinic bears his name. It is with great honor that I bestow the Doctorate of Letters upon Dr. Theodore K. Lawless."

Dr. Garvey placed the hood over his head and on his shoulders.

"Brigadier General Benjamin O. Davis, Jr."

General Davis stood to his feet and came forward to the podium and stood alongside Dr. Garvey. "Brigadier General Davis was born December 18, 1912 in Washington, DC. He graduated from West Point in 1936. After a year in the rank of first lieutenant, he was promoted to captain. In February of 1941, he was assigned as aide to his distinguished father, who was then stationed at Fort Riley, Kansas, as brigade commander of the Second Cavalry Division. In June 1941, Captain Davis was assigned to Tuskegee, where the first Air Corps training unit for Negro pilots had just been set up. In March 1942, he was successively promoted to major and lieutenant colonel on the same day, and later he was made commander of the Ninety-Ninth. In May 1942, he was ordered to the Mediterranean where he became the first Negro officer to command an Air Force combat unit. In 1944, he was made a full colonel. Colonel Davis won the Legion of Merit Medal, the Distinguished Flying Cross, the Air Medal with four oak leaf clusters, and the Silver Star. In 1954, he was promoted to the rank of general. General Davis was named vice-commander of the Thirteenth Air Force, based in the Philippines. It is with great honor that I bestow to General Benjamin O. Davis, Jr., the honorary degree of Doctorate of Letters."

Like the others that preceded him, Dr. Garvey placed the hood over his head and on his shoulders.

"The late Dr. James Lionel Canegata. Receiving the degree for Dr. Canegata is his widow, Dr. Sarah Powell Canegata."

Thomas was surprised and overwhelmed as he watched his aunt ascend the stage and walk to the podium. He had no idea. Embracing her, Dr. Bunche stood at her side. Dr. Garvey motioned for Thomas to come stand by her side.

Dr. Garvey continued. "Born September 4, 1924 in Canaan, North Carolina, Dr. James Lionel Canegata received his bachelor's degree in political science from Hampton Institute in 1944, and his Master of Arts from Columbia University in 1945. While a student studying at Columbia, he fell under the tutelage of Dr. Ralph Bunche, which continued as he studied for his law degree from Georgetown University in Washington, DC, and his PhD in international affairs. Dr. Canegata, having learned from the master, Dr. Bunche, worked for the United States Secretary of State and was well known throughout the international community as a great negotiator in commerce and trade. Two years ago, the world mourned his death. Accepting this honor today is his widow, Dr. Sarah Powell Canegata. It is with great honor that I bestow the degree of Doctorate of Letters posthumously upon you, James Lionel Canegata."

"Dr. Garvey, it is a great honor to accept this for my late husband. He would be honored if you placed the hood on his cousin and godson."

Dr. Garvey addressed the auditorium, "Mr. Thomas is the cousin and godson of the late Dr. Canegata. Greatness is upon this family bloodline." Dr. Garvey then placed the hood on Thomas. "It is my privilege and honor to bestow the Doctorate of Letters upon you. May God continue to bless you and your household."

Afterwards, Dr. Ralph Bunche spoke as the commencement speaker, "First, I want to acknowledge God, Dr. Gavery, platform guest, the graduating class, and the family and friends here today. I want to pay a special tribute to my good friend and colleague the late Dr. Canegata, better known to all as Canada. He was a very promising young man. In the few short years I knew him, he accomplished much in the state department and the United Nations. Governments around the world mourned his death, as did I and his family. He is sorely missed, but never forgotten. But I am proud to see in the wings there is another, his godson Thomas, affectionately known to many of us as Little. He always spoke of him with great pride and adoration. It was at the invitation of James, I first met Thomas when he was just an infant being christened. Watching his parents, Canada, and Sarah as the proud godparents along with their second godson, Jerald Jefferson, Jr., who last evening was drafted by the New York Nicks, I knew then he was a special child. They both are. Needless to say, throughout the years his uncle Canada, as he called him, taught him well and left a profound mark upon his life."

Dr. Bunche went on to deliver a very powerful and moving commencement address. The audience stood awarding him with a five-minute standing ovation.

The orchestra began playing the ceremonial recessional "Pomp and Circumstance (Military March No. 1 in D)" by Edward Elgar. As Thomas passed, Swoosh and Grace jumped in the recession line linking arms with him one on each side. They wrapped their arm around each other as they walked out of the auditorium.

Outside, Little saw him. "Hey, there he is."

"Who?"

"The guy I told you about on the plane."

Quickly, he approached the trio. Grabbing Little's hand he shook it vigorously. "Little, I can't begin to tell you how proud I am of you. I was so proud to see you standing up there at the podium giving that speech." Pulling out his handkerchief, he wiped his eyes. "Something must have blown in my eye," he said. He then embraced Little, squeezing him tightly. "What did I tell you? See what one man can do. It all goes back to your father Elijah. He deserves much of the credit."

"I was happy to see you. I'm honored that you made it to my graduation. Did you know you were sitting right behind my family?"

"Believe me, the honor is all mine. This must be Grace and Jerald. I mean Swoosh. Grace, you're as every bit as beautiful as he said you were."

Grace smiled and hugged him. "I want to thank you. He told me about your conversation on the plane, how you really helped him. I was really worried about him. I prayed that God would send someone to comfort him. I'm so glad you were there to keep him company and to help him through everything. God answered my prayer through you."

"Little has told me so much about the two of you. I'm just glad to have had the opportunity to meet you both. I feel as if I know you."

"Yea, man, I'm glad you were there for my brother," Swoosh said shaking his hand vigorously. "From what he told us, you were just the person he needed to talk to." Swoosh did not understand why he felt compelled to embrace the stranger. Without hesitation, he followed his feelings. Upon embracing him, Swoosh felt an assurance, a peace, and oneness with the stranger.

He gestured to Grace. "Hey, let me take a picture of the three of you before the crowd comes."

Grace handed him her camera. The three huddled together. Grace on Little's left, close to his heart, and Swoosh on his right, his right-hand man. As he snapped the first shot, the people began pouring out of the auditorium.

"Please, I want to get a picture of you and Thomas," Grace shouted.

"There are a lot of people who want to see you. You'll get one of me later."

"But I want you to meet my family, and I still don't know your name."

"I'll be here, I promise. Your family, friends and your public are waiting for you. Afterwards, just look for me over by the fountain."

"With all these people around, how am I supposed to find you?"

"Today is why it could not end before, Little; you'll understand all of it. Don't worry you'll be able to see me. I promise you'll see me later waiting for you by the fountain," the young man shouted as he disappeared among the crowd of people.

The stranger quickly slipped out of sight as a people gathered around to greet and congratulate Little. Everywhere people were hugging and kissing, and a lot of pictures were being taken. The crowd continued to press around Thomas, Grace, and Swoosh. His family gathered around him, all his aunts, uncles, and cousins, Mrs. Solomon, his friends, and many other well-wishers.

Standing next to his mother and father was an older woman and four adults. "Little," his mother said. "I have some special people that I want you to meet."

"Hey Little," someone shouted, "the Alphas are gathering near the fountain to sing the hymn."

"The Alphas are about to sing the hymn, Momma."

"Oh, go ahead. We'll be right here.

"I'll be right back Momma, I promise."

The fraternity gathered to sing the hymn and pray the Alpha prayer. Little, Swoosh, Michael, Turk, Bebop, and several of his Alpha brothers from Hampton, along with other young men joined the group.

Keeping his promise, after singing the hymn and praying the prayer, Little returned to where his mother and her friends were standing. "Grace and Jerald, I want you two to meet some friends of mine too. Little, this is Madame Vera T. LaSalle and her husband."

The eyes of the crowd had been watching the caramel skinned, slim, attractive well-dressed woman. Little had noticed that several people stopped to eagerly shake her hand. She moved forward to greet him. Gently, she kissed him on the cheek and hugged his neck tightly. "These past few weeks, I've heard so much about you from your mother and father. I'm really glad to finally meet you."

She stood about five feet ten inches. Little had gathered by the way the crowd kept watching her that she was someone of importance, but he could not grasp the strong hug and tears in her eyes. "Your being here at my graduation is special for me, the famous Madame LaSalle and her husband. It makes me feel really special. And the dress you designed for my mother and sister are beautiful." Little leaned over to kiss his mother and hugged Esther.

"Thank you, believe me the pleasure was all mine. Grace, you are as every bit as beautiful as Ruth said," she said as she hugged and kissed Grace.

"Thank you, Madame LaSalle. Meeting you for me is a dream come true."

"Then you must allow me to design your wedding dress."

Grace blushed with excitement. "Oh, Madame LaSalle, I could never afford…"

"My dear, don't worry. It will be my honor and privilege." Gently she hugged Grace. "And this gentleman is my husband Paul."

The dapper dressed gentleman stood taller than his wife. His silver hair glistened in the June sunlight, indicating that he was several years older than her. He extended his hand forward to shake Little's. "Thomas, I can't tell you how proud we are of you."

Little smiled politely. "Thank you, sir, and for coming to my graduation.

And these are my future in-laws, the Johnsons, and my friends Stephanie and Alejandro, Jerald, Leonard. I hope you come to the reception, then I'll introduce them all to you."

"Little," his mother interrupted, "This is Madame LaSalle's brother and his wife."

Little perceived from their looks they were around his mother's age.

Without speaking a word, the man grabbed him and held him tightly making Little slightly uncomfortable.

Elijah moved closer to Ruth and put his arm around her. "Little, this is their mother, Mrs. Thomas. Mrs. Thomas, Bigger Thomas's mother. She's your grandmother."

The three of them looked nothing like he had imagined. Since that day in Chicago, he had wondered what Bigger's mother looked like. He recalled his mother saying Bigger had a brother and a sister. He had wanted to ask his mother about them, but again it was another one of those unasked questions. Now, for himself, he could see. Their brown-skinned complexion was not as dark as his nor were they as tall. Little fought back his tears.

His grandmother reached up and stroked his face with her fingers. Her eyes filled with tears as she looked upon her grandson up close for the first time. Little could see the love in her eyes. "Lawd, you look so much like my Bigger and his daddy. Tall with high cheekbones—that pretty smooth, clear dark skin and the same pearly bold white teeth. My having to live through the pain of the trial and bowing my head in shame. Mr. Max having to move us from our home in Chicago to

Gary, Indiana, to save our lives. Seeing you standing up there, hearing you speak, and all the wonderful things people saying about you took away all the hurt and pain of all the years. Now, I feel. No, I know that my Bigger's death was not in vain. Through you, I believe God has forgiven and redeemed my child."

Little saw his grandmother for the first time. Slowly, the four embraced each other tightly and cried. As the four embraced for the first time a part of him that had been vacant for so long, the unexplained emptiness and void he had always felt inside was filled. Now, he felt and understood how his mother felt when she had found her long lost brothers. The completeness she felt inside, he too was now feeling.

Overwhelmed, he could not stop his tears. Little hugged his parents. "Oh, Mom and Pop, this is the best graduation gift you could have given me. Thank you. How? Where did you find them?"

"When I walked into Madame LaSalle's shop and saw Vera, I knew right away who she was."

The elder Mrs. Thomas tearfully said, "When Vera called me and said your mother was in her shop, I was so surprised. I never knew what happened to her. I never expected to see her again. Then she said Bigger had a son. I just couldn't believe it. I cried. Mr. Max never told us about you. And then today, your mother and father didn't tell us you would be speaking. Seeing you for the first time and up there speaking made me so proud." She placed her hand on his cheek. "I believe if my Bigger had a strong man's hand to guide him like your father Elijah, he might still be alive today."

As if in disbelief, again she began stroking his face. "You look so much like him and his daddy." Softly, she pressed her hand on his heart. "They had good hearts too. It's just that they let their fears, their anger, and the rage inside consume them. I believe all the good that was in them is in you. It just took a good man like your daddy to bring it all out." She looked over at Elijah and hugged him as she said, "Thank you."

Tearfully, Little responded, "Thank you, Grandma." He said it for the first time. Grandma. He called her Grandma. "Aunt Vera and

Uncle Buddy, thank you. You don't know how much this means to me; how much all of you mean to me."

"Baby, I have something for you. Here…" she said, handing the package to Little. Looking at him and clasping her hand together, she exclaimed, "Lawd, Bigger's son, my grandson." Little reached out to receive the gift and held it next to his chest. "I want you to open it now," she said reassuringly.

His hands trembling, Little slowly unwrapped the package. His eyes fell upon the content of the package. Its content momentarily caught him off guard. He stood frozen, staring at it. Grace and Swoosh's eyes widened as they too looked on in total awe.

"It's a picture of Bigger. He had it taken at a professional studio on his twentieth birthday. He gave it to me as a present the Christmas before he died. He had the most beautiful smile. I can still remember it to this day. High cheekbones, his thick, dark lips, those big, bold, pearly, white teeth. And when he smiled his mouth had a funny twist higher to the left and the biggest dimples just like yours. Your eyes sparkle just like his." Gently, she wiped the tears from her eyes. "Seeing you is like looking at him." Again, she gently touched his face. "At times, I'd get so mad at that Bigger of mine. That's when he'd flash that big bright smile of his and have that sparkle in his eyes. He'd say his smile was higher over the side of his heart, just to tell me how much he loved me. Both he and his daddy had the heartiest laugh. You could hear it above the crowd anywhere. That smile would melt away my anger in a flash. I couldn't stay mad at him long. He knew that."

The bells of the campus chapel began ringing aloud. Little stood gazing at the picture. Grace and Swoosh continued to stare on in amazement. Hearing a loud laughter, Little looked in the direction of the fountain. He could see the young man standing by the fountain as he had promised, laughing. With tears of joy in his eyes, he waved his hand at Little. Flashing a big bright smile, his thick dark lips framed his bold pearly white teeth. His smile twisted slightly higher to the left side. Little could hear him as he spoke. "This is why it wasn't supposed to happen that way. Thank you, son."

Slowly, Little lifted his hand and waved back. The young man turned and began walking away. Looking over his shoulder, he smiled and let out a hearty laugh. It was a laugh that Little, Grace, Swoosh, and Little Canegata heard above the noise of the crowd and the ringing bells. Again, waving his hand he laughed, turned and slowly faded into the air.

"I understand," whispered Little, "I know."

ABOUT THE AUTHOR

H. Richard Dozier, PhD, was born and raised in New Haven, Connecticut. Like many Black Americans, he has deep roots in the South. Unlike many Black Americans of today, he is the grandson of the former slave James Johnson of Valdosta, Georgia, born in 1850.

Richard, as he is known, has worked in higher education for over twenty years in various capacities. He began his career at Hampton Institute, (now Hampton University) in Hampton, Virginia, and has worked at the University of Missouri-Columbia, the University of New Haven, and Western Connecticut State University. He was the dean of Student Services at Palm Beach Community College in Palm Beach County, Florida. In 2007, he accepted the position as the vice president of Student Development at a college in Upstate New York.